MORE EMIGRANTS
IN BONDAGE

1614–1775

Engraved for the Newgate Calendar.

Representation of the Transports going from Newgate to take water at Blackfriars.

MORE EMIGRANTS IN BONDAGE

1614–1775

Peter Wilson Coldham

GENEALOGICAL PUBLISHING CO., INC.

Published by Genealogical Publishing Co., Inc.
1001 N. Calvert St., Baltimore, Md. 21202
Library of Congress Catalogue Card Number 2001099396
International Standard Book Number 0-8063-1694-2
Made in the United States of America

Contents

Memento Mori

Very soon after the dreadful events of 11 September 2001, I reached the stage in the editing of this book which required me to look again at the history of the plantation in Kent Co. named *Memento Mori* [Remember the Dead] bequeathed in the 1732 will of John Spencer to his son Thomas Spencer. This prompted me to reflect again how closely on both sides of the Atlantic we are bound together in our common history, faith, and destiny and to submit this work as a token of the sympathy and prayers we in the "Old Country" continue to offer for those who have died and have suffered loss.

Introduction

The original volume of *Emigrants in Bondage* published in 1988 acknowledged that there were some notable omissions from the list of transported convicts then printed which remained to be researched and remedied. These arose principally from the complete loss of the original documents of the Midland Circuit before 1800, several gaps in the surviving records of the Oxford Circuit, the lack of all Assize records for Suffolk between summer 1737 and summer 1742, and the inaccessibility of Quarter Sessions papers for many English counties. As an example of apparently irreparable losses, the Sheriffs' Cravings in the Public Record Office for the county of Suffolk contain two entries for the year 1734: the first records that James White "and two others" were sentenced to transportation, and the second that Samuel Sterling "and 10 others" were similarly sentenced, but these names do not appear in the surviving Assize or Quarter Sessions documents for this county.

During the many years that have intervened since publication of *The Complete Book of Emigrants in Bondage 1614–1775*[1] and its 1992 *Supplement*,[2] considerable efforts have been made to close the remaining gaps, and thus a very large number of additions and amendments to the original lists have been noted. These include abstracts of all the convict landings listed in the Maryland State Archives which have been carefully compared with the equivalent English records. Only additions and amendments of major significance, numbering some 9,000, have been included in this supplementary volume. A re-examination of original sources, to which summary references are made below, has yielded additional evidence for ships used in the convict trade and for the landing in Maryland and Virginia of 6,000 convicted felons. Some 45,000 transportees can now be accounted for and evidence of their places and dates of landing in America provided. A comprehensive and updated listing will, however, need to await the publication of a revised edition of the original volume for which the outlook is uncertain.

The material in the present volume has been arranged and annotated in an identical way to that in the parent volume of *The Complete Book of Emigrants in Bondage* to which reference should be made if an outline of the history and background of convict transportation to the Americas is required. Abbreviations used throughout are as follows:

AA Co.	= Anne Arundel Co.	Nl	= Northumberland
AHJ	= Alderman Hewitt's Journals	NM	= *Northampton Mercury*
		No	= Northamptonshire
als	= alias	Nt	= Nottinghamshire
AT	= Awaiting transportation	O	= Oxfordshire
Bal Co.	= Baltimore Co.	OJ	= *Oxford Journal*
Bd	= Bedfordshire	PC	= Privy Council Papers
Be	= Berkshire	PG Co.	= Prince George's Co.
BG	= *Birmingham Gazette*	PT	= Pleaded transportation
BJ	= *Bristol Journal*	QA Co.	= Queen Anne's Co.
Bu	= Buckinghamshire	R	= Reprieved for transportation
Ca	= Cambridgeshire		
Ch	= Chesire	RG	= *Reading Gazette*
City	= Sentenced by City Borough Court	RM	= *Reading Mercury*
		Ru	= Rutlandshire
Co	= Cornwall	S	= Sentenced to transportation
Cu	= Cumberland		
Db	= Derbyshire	s	= Stealing
De	= Devon	SC	= South Carolina
Do	= Dorset	Sco	= Scotland
Du	= Durham	SCr	= Sheriffs' Cravings (E389).
E	= Essex		
Fl	= Flint	SEK	= Sentenced at East Kent Sessions
G	= Gloucestershire		
GJ	= *Gloucester Journal*	SES	= Sentenced at East Sussex Sessions
Ha	= Hampshire		
He	= Herefordshire	Sh	= Shropshire
HJ	= *Hereford Journal*	SL	= Sentenced at Southwark
HO	= Home Office Papers	So	= Somerset
Ht	= Hertfordshire	SP	= State Papers
Hu	= Huntingdonshire	SQS	= Sentenced at Quarter Sessions
IJ	= *Ipswich Journal*		
Ir	= Ireland	ST	= Sentenced at Tower Liberty, London
K	= Kent		
Knt Co.	= Kent Co.	St	= Staffordshire
L	= London	Su	= Suffolk
La	= Lancashire	SW	= Sentenced at Westminster Sessions
LC	= Landing Certificate		
Le	= Leicestershire	SWK	= Sentenced at West Kent Sessions
Li	= Lincolnshire		
LM	= London or Middlesex	SWS	= Sentenced at West Sussex Sessions
M	= Middlesex		
Md	= Maryland	Sx	= Sussex
Mo	= Monmouthshire	Sy	= Surrey
NE	= New England	T	= Transported
Nf	= Norfolk	TB	= Transportation Bond

Va	= Virginia	WJ	= *Worcester Journal*
Wa	= Warwickshire	Wo	= Worcestershire
Wal	= Wales	X	= Stray records
We	= Westmorland	Y	= Yorkshire
Wi	= Wiltshire		

The principal additions and amendments obtained from English records and included in this volume have been secured from the following sources:

Central Criminal Records

Midland Circuit Criminal Process Book 1739–1742 (ASSI 12/2). Privileged access was granted to this very badly perished volume which has been inaccessible to readers for many years. Most, if not all, of the relevant written material has been retrieved.

Sheriffs' Cravings. These records (E 197, E 389, T64/262 and T90/146–160), which itemize expenses incurred by County Sheriffs for administering justice, including the cost of prisoners' food, hangings, whippings and transportation (though sometimes without including names), have been examined from 1718 to 1776. It should be noted, however, that the Palatinate counties of Cheshire, Durham and Lancashire, for whatever reason, did not claim against the Exchequer for costs incurred in transporting felons.

State Papers (Criminal). The collections of pardons on condition of transportation for 1718–1740 (SP 44/79–83) were re-examined as were the calendars of Home Office papers from 1768–1775. From the latter source some details of Scottish and Welsh transportees have been taken.

County Records

The County Record Offices whose holdings of transportation documents had not previously been examined were circulated to ascertain what additional resources might be newly accessible. Though a few gaps continue to exist, further record abstracts were obtained from the counties of Lincolnshire and Northamptonshire in the Midland Circuit. Local records and newspaper archives for Warwickshire, also in the Midland Circuit, have been abstracted and thanks are due to Mrs. Diane Fisher for permission to consult her indexes to court records from 1734. The most fruitful new source for this and other Circuits, however, has proved to be the meticulous records kept by Alderman John Hewitt Jr., three times Mayor of Coventry, of criminals sentenced throughout England during the period 1748–1763, including those transported and those who returned from transportation before serving their term. Hewitt had what amounted to an obsession to pursue all convicted criminals until they had fully atoned for their sins, even to the point of personally following one member of a gang to Ireland and from there back to London. In 1763 he wrote to the Clerks of the Peace of every English county requesting details of all convicts transported from within their jurisdiction since 1748. A large number responded giving the account required, but there were notable absentees including the City of London and the county of Middlesex which together provided well over half the national total of transportees. Many names of transported felons included in this volume have been culled from Hewitt's printed memoirs[3], but I am additionally indebted to John Russell of Coventry for permission to use his extensive abstracts based on Hewitt's notebooks.

The Quarter Sessions Order Books for Lancashire for the period 1718–1740, which were in very poor condition because of water damage and dryrot, have now been physically repaired but are still in a weak and discolored condition. Nevertheless privileged access has been afforded to the originals, and most, though by no means all, of the entries relating to transportation have been salvaged.

The local holdings of the City of York have also been compared against details obtained from central records of criminal proceedings, and the few additional details which resulted are now included in this volume by kind permission of Linda Haywood, who abstracted the York papers, and of the York City Archives.

Transportation records from the Sessions papers for Suffolk have now also been abstracted and are incorporated into this Supplement.

Printed Journals

Amongst the newspapers and journals examined for abstracts of Assize and Quarter Sessions trials, the following were studied for the periods shown:

Bristol Journal 1752–1765

Gloucester Journal 1737–1760

Hereford Journal 1770–1775

Ipswich Journal 1739–1742

Northampton Mercury 1720–1730

Oxford Journal 1753–1775, which includes in its issue of 5 December 1772 the text of a letter from David Benfield, who was transported from Oxford to Maryland in 1770, to his former jailer reporting his considerable success in the colony as a medical practitioner.[4]

Reading Gazette 1752–1769

Reading Mercury 1738–1754

Worcester Postman & Worcester Journal 1739–1775

Maryland Records

A thorough review of manuscript resources in the Maryland State Archives in Annapolis was undertaken in 1996 to identify in court and land records as many as possible of the documents related to the landing of convicts. The results have been checked and verified by my distinguished colleague Bob Barnes to whom I am further indebted for his contribution of additional notes on many felons named in this new work.

Peter Wilson Coldham
Purley, Surrey, England

Christmas 2001
AMDG

[1]Genealogical Publishing Co., Inc., Baltimore, 1988.

[2]Genealogical Publishing Co., Inc., Baltimore, 1992.

[3]*The Proceedings of J. Hewitt as Magistrate over Twenty Years in Cases of Riot, Coining, Murder, Burglary . . . Returned Transports etc.* London and Birmingham, 1756, 1779.

[4]*See* article in the *Genealogists' Magazine* (London), Vol. 26, No. 10 (June 2000).

MORE EMIGRANTS IN BONDAGE

1614–1775

MORE EMIGRANTS IN BONDAGE

Abbott, Ann. S Lent LC AA Co., Md., from *Hanover Planter* Jul 1773. M.

Abbott, George. S Sep 1753. Li.

Abbott, John. S Summer 1718 LC from *Sophia* QA Co., Md. Mar 1719. So.

Abbott, Mary wife of John. S Lent but pardoned in May 1773. M.

Abbott, Mary. S Oct 1773 T *Justitia* Jan 1774. M.

Abbott, Thomas. S Sep 1751. Li.

Abel, Thomas. S Lent LC AA Co., Md., from *Thornton* May 1771. M.

Abell, William. S Lent LC Bal Co., Md., Jul 1772. Do.

Abey, Thomas. S Jun-Dec 1745 T *Plain Dealer* Jan 1746. M.

Ablet, John of Holbrook, aged 23, full faced, light brown hair. S s horse at Sutton
  Summer 1740 R 14 yrs Lent 1741; escaped but recaptured and executed (IJ). Su.

Abraham, Moses. S Jan T *Tryal* Mar 1757. L.

Abrahams *als* Evans, Evan. S Montgomery s cow R Mar 1775. Wal.

Abrahams, Jacob. S Lent LC AA Co., Md., from *Thornton* May 1771. L.

Abrahams *als* Solomons, Joseph. S Lent T *Thornton* May LC AA Co., Md., May
  1774. L.

Abrahams, Levy. S May-Jul T *Tayloe* Jul 1773. M.

Abrahams, Moses. S Jul T *Tayloe* Jul 1774. L.

Abrahams, Sarah. S Oct 1773 T *Justitia* Jan 1774. L.

Abrey, Thomas. S Lent T Jun 1748 *Lichfield.* Sx.

Acland, George. T May 1751 *Tryal.* K.

Adam, Agnes. S Edinburgh for murder R Mar 1774. Sco.

Adams, Benjamin. T Oct 1750 *Rachael.* K.

Adams, Daniel. S Mar T Apr 1737. Wa.

Adams, John. S Lent 1732 LC Knt Co., Md., from *Falcon* Mar 1733. Do.

Adams, John. SQS Oct 1754 T *Greyhound* Feb 1755. M.

Adams, John. SQS Jan T *Thornton* May LC AA Co., Md., May 1774. Sy.

Adams, Mary. S Sep-Dec 1746 T Jan 1747 *George William.* M.

Adams, Mary. S Feb-Apr T May 1751 *Tryal.* M.

Adams, Philip. S Dec 1753 T *Thames* Mar 1754. M.

Adams, Thomas. S Dec-Jan T Mar 1750 *Tryal.* M.

Adams, Thomas. S 14 yrs for receiving Lent 1758 TB to Md. No.

Adamson, Margaret wife of Thomas. S Lent T *Thornton* May LC AA Co., Md., Jul
  1774. M.

Adamson, Susannah wife of George. S Summer 1772 LC Bal Co., Md., from
  Adventure Mar 1773. Du.

Adcock, Thomas. S s from manor house of John Allcock Summer R Nov 1736. Su.

Addicott, John. SQS Jan 1733 LC Knt Co., Md., from *Falcon* Apr 1734. So.

Addicott, William. SQS Jan 1733 LC Md. from *Falcon* Apr 1734. So.

Addison, Robert. S Apr T *Dolphin* May 1763. L.

Adkins, Sarah. S Dec T *Justitia* Dec 1774. L.

Adkins, Thomas. S for highway robbery Summer 1753 R 14 yrs Lent 1754 TB to
  Md. No.

Adkins, Thomas. S Lent T Apr 1765. Wa.

Adkins, William. S Summer T *Justitia* Sep 1767. Bu.

Adlington, George. S Lent T Apr 1758 *Lux* from London. Db.

Adrington, Richard. LC Md from *Isabella* Jul 1775 & sold to Samuel Dorsey Jr. X.

Adwell, John, *als* Jack Above Ground. S Jul T *Beverly* Aug 1763. M.

Agar, Daniel. S Lent 1735. Nt.

Agar, William. S Sep-Oct 1773 T *Justitia* Jan 1774. M.

Aglen, William. T Apr 1742 LC PG Co., Md. 1746. Do.

Agnis, John of St. Runwald, Colchester. SQS Apr T *Tryal* Jul 1754. E.

Aikland, Daniel. S for food riot in Abingdon & R 14 yrs Dec 1766 (OJ). Be.

Ainsworth, Mary. S Norwich Summer T Sep 1764. Nf.

Ainsworth, Michael. S Apr T May 1752 *Lichfield*. L.

Aistrop, Robert. R 14 yrs Oct 1772 T *Justitia* Jan 1773. M.

Akerman, Thomas. S Lent T Jun 1748 *Lichfield*. K.

Alam, John. S Summer 1745 T Jan 1746. Be.

Albey, Joseph. S Feb T *Thames* Mar 1752. L.

Alcock, Anthony. S Lent T Apr 1757 *Lux* . Db.

Alcock, George. S Summer 1732 LC Knt Co., Md., from *Falcon* Mar 1733. Co.

Alcocke, John of Willaston. R for Barbados Sep 1671 but LC Md from *William & Mary* Mar 1672. Ch.

Alcock, Thomas, aged 25. LC from *Gilbert* Md May 1721. X.

Alcon, Sarah. S Jan T Mar 1750 *Tryal*. L.

Alcraft, Francis of St. Saviour, Southwark. SQS Jun T Aug 1752 *Tryal*. Sy.

Alcroft, John. S Summer LC Bal Co., Md., Dec 1770 from *Trotman* & sold to Nicholas Norwood. Y.

Alder, John. S for house breaking Summer 1748 R 14 yrs Lent 1749 (GJ). Be.

Alder, John. S Mar 1752. So.

Alders, Anthony. T Jan 1736 *Dorsetshire* LC Va Sep 1736. Sy.

Aldridge, James. S for housebreaking at Earsham Lent 1761. Nf.

Aldridge, Mary. SQS Apr T *Thornton* May LC AA Co., Md., Jul 1774. M.

Aldridge, Robert. S Jan-Jun T Jul 1747 *Laura*. M.

Aldridge, Susanna. S Feb-Apr T May 1751 *Tryal*. M.

Aldridge, William. S Jul T *Tayloe* Jul 1774. L.

Aldwin, William. S s horse Summer 1724 R 14 yrs Lent 1725. Sh.

Alexander, George. S Lent T Jun 1739. Wa.

Alexander, James Jr. of Lambeth. SQS Apr T Sep 1751 *Greyhound*. Sy.

Alexander, William. S Apr-Jun 1739 T *Sea Nymph* to Md. M.

Alexander, William. S Apr T May 1750 *Lichfield*. M.

Alexander, William. SWK Apr T *Tayloe* Jul 1773. K.

Alford, John. S & TB to Md. 1753. No.

Alford, Nathaniel. SQS Jul LC Bal Co., Md., Dec 1772. Wi.

Algar, Arthur. S Lent 1731 LC Knt Co., Md., from *Falcon* Apr 1732. De.

Algate, Mary. S Lent T *Thornton* May LC AA Co., Md., Jul 1774. E.

Allam, Ann. S Sep-Oct 1773 T *Justitia* Jan 1774. M.

Allan, Thomas of Guisborough, weaver. SQS Guisborough Jul 1758. Y.

Allanson *als* Leacock, David of Carlton. S 14 yrs s horses Aug 1770. Y.

Allard, Paul. S Feb T *Tryal* Mar 1757. M.

Allard, William. S s chain at Upton upon Severn Lent 1761 & R for Army; found at large in Severnstoke & R 14 yrs Summer 1766. Wo.

Allcock *als* Hawkins, John. S s gelding Lent R Summer T *Justitia* Sep 1767. Bu.

Allday, Thomas. SQS Apr T *Thornton* May LC AA Co., Md., Jul 1774. M.

Allen, Ann. S Summer LC Bal Co., Md., Dec 1770 from *Trotman* & sold to William Barney. X.

Allen, Dorothy. S Jan-Apr T *Lichfield* May 1749. M.

Allen, Edward. S for life Feb T *Thames* Mar 1754. M.

Allen, Elizabeth. S Dec 1754 T *Greyhound* Feb 1755. L.

Allen, Elizabeth. S Lent LC AA Co., Md., from *Thornton* May 1771. K.

Allen, George. S Sep 1735 T Jan 1736 *Dorsetshire* LC Va Sep 1736. M.

Allen, George. S Summer 1746 T Jan 1747. De.

Allen, George. S Feb T Mar 1750 *Tryal*. M.

MORE EMIGRANTS IN BONDAGE

Allen, George. SQS May T Jul 1773 *Tayloe* to Va, taken from ship for review of case but law to take its course. M.

Allen, James. S Mar TB to Va Apr 1742 LC PG Co., Md. Wi.

Allen, John. S Lent T Apr 1737. No.

Allen, John. S s horse & R 14 yrs Jun 1741. Li.

Allen, John. S Jun-Dec 1745 T *Plain Dealer* Jan 1746. M.

Allen, John. R for firing an outhouse S Lent T Jul 1747. O.

Allen, John. S Dec 1750 T *Thames* Feb 1751. L.

Allen, John. S Dec 1754 T *Greyhound* Feb 1755. L.

Allen, John. S 14 yrs Lent LC AA Co., Md., from *Thornton* Jul 1773. E.

Allen, John. SQS May T Jul 1773 *Tayloe* to Va, removed from ship for review but law to take its course. M.

Allen, John. S Lent LC AA Co., Md., from *Thornton* Jul 1775. M.

Allen, Joseph. S Summer T from Bristol Sep 1754. St.

Allen, Joseph. SQS Aug 1736. Y.

Allen, Mary. S Summer LC Bal Co., Md., Dec 1770. Wa.

Allen, Phillipa. S May-Jun T Aug 1752 *Tryal*. M.

Allen, Robert. SQS Liskeard Jul 1733 LC Md. from *Falcon* Apr 1734. So.

Allen, Roger. S May T *Phoenix* Oct 1760. M.

Allen, Roger. S May T *Beverly* Aug 1763. M.

Allen, Samuel. R for pulling down mills Summer 1772 T *Justitia* Jan 1773. E.

Allen, Samuel. Jul 1783 LC Bal Co., Md., Dec 1783 from *Swift*. M.

Allen, Thomas. S Mar 1742 LC PG Co., Md. Do.

Allen, William. S Lent T Sep 1752. Li.

Allen, William. S Summer LC Bal Co., Md., Dec 1770 from *Trotman* & sold to Charles Howard. X.

Allen, William. S 14 yrs for highway robbery at Hutton Moor Mar 1774. Y.

Allerton, Robert. S Lent 1770 but escaped in London. Y.

Allies, John. S May-Jul T *Tayloe* Jul 1774. M.

Allin, Richard. S Aug 1752. Li.

Allison, Ann. S Bristol Sep 1757 (AHJ). G.

Allison, Robert. S Apr T May 1752 *Lichfield*. L.

Alliston, Ambrose (1774). See Sparrow, Robert. E.

Alliston, Bryan. S Feb T Apr 1737. Le.

Allmond, Richard. S Lent T *Thornton* May LC AA Co., Md., Jul 1774. K.

Allum, Thomas. R 14 yrs Mar 1772 LC Bal Co., Md, sold to Joshua Hall. Ha.

Allwright, Richard. S Dec 1772 T *Justitia* Jan 1773. M.

Alner, John. SQS Jan 1737 LC QA Co., Md., from *Amity* Apr 1738. Do.

Alsom, William. S Oct T *Justitia* Dec 1774. L.

Alsop, Margaret. S Sep-Oct 1773 T *Justitia* Jan 1774. M.

Amblet, Edward. S for housebreaking Aug 1758 (WJ). St.

Amblet, John. S for housebreaking Aug 1758 (WJ). St.

Ambrose, Ann. S Sep-Oct T *Justitia* Dec 1774. M.

Ambrose, Samuel. S Carmarthen R 14 yrs May 1775. Wal.

Amor, John. R 14 yrs Jul TB to Va Sep 1741 T *Philleroy* LC QA Co., Md., Apr 1742. Wi.

Amor, William of Egham. SQS Jul T *Phoenix* Oct 1760. Sy.

Amos, Absalom. S Summer 1739 T Jan 1740. Le.

Anderson, Ann. T *Harpooner* to Va Jan 1741. M.

Anderson, Ann. S Jan T *Justitia* May 1745. L.

Anderson, Ann wife of Michael. SQS Newcastle Summer 1759 (AHJ). Nl.

Anderson, Christian. SQS Newcastle Christmas 1749 (AHJ). Nl.

Anderson, Edward. S Jul LC Bal Co., Md., Dec 1783 from Swift. M.

Anderson, Francis. T *Phoenix* Oct 1760. M.

Anderson, George. S May T *Phoenix* Oct 1760. M.

Anderson, Hester, singlewoman. S Bristol Apr 1743 *Raven* LC Knt Co., Md., Feb 1744. G.

Anderson, James. S Jul T *Dolphin* May 1763; runaway. M.

Anderson, Jane. S May-Jul T Sep 1746 *Mary*. M.

Anderson, Jane wife of Andrew. SQS City Easter AT Summer 1758 (AHJ). Nl.

Anderson, John. S Lent T from London Apr 1755. Wa.

Anderson, Luke. S Jan-Jun T Jul 1747 *Laura*. M.

Anderson, Mary. S Apr T May 1750 *Lichfield*. L.

Anderson, Richard. S Summer R 14 yrs Apr 1742. St.

Anderson, Thomas. S May-Jul T Sep 1746 *Mary*. M.

Anderton, Eleanor. S Lent T Jul 1745 *Italian Merchant*. Sy.

Andrews, Amos. S 14 yrs Lent 1750 LC QA Co., Md., from *Catherine* Nov 1750. So.

Andrews, Edward. T May 1751 *Tryal*. Sy.

Andrews, Edward. LC Md from *Isabella* Jul 1775 & sold to John Walker. X.

Andrews, James. S Lent T *Dolphin* May 1763. K.

Andrews, John (1738). *See* Suiton. So.

Andrews, Mary. T *Justitia* Jan 1773. M.

Andrews, Mary. S Lent LC Bal Co., Md., Jul 1771. De.

Andrews, Mary. Jul 1783 LC Bal Co., Md., Dec 1783 from *Swift*. M.

Andrews, Thomas. S & R 14 yrs Lent, escaped from gaol but retaken, LC Bal Co., Md., Jun 1773. Wa.

Angell, Isaac. S Feb T *Thames* Mar 1754. L.

Angell, John. SQS Jul TB Aug 1739. G.

Angus, Daniel. S Lent LC AA Co., Md., from *Thornton* Jul 1775. L.

Angus, William. T *Justitia* Feb 1776. L.

Annasant, Brillia of Newington. S Summer T Oct 1750 *Rachael*. Sy.

Ansley, John. SQS Apr T May 1750 *Lichfield*. M.

Anslow, Jane. S s silver watch Jan T Apr 1735 *Patapsco* LC Annapolis Oct 1735. L.

Anson, Benjamin. SQS Feb T Mar 1750 *Tryal*. M.

Anthony *als* Jennings, Mary. S Mar T *Thames* Mar 1754. L.

Appleton, Francis. S Ruthin Apr 1756 (AHJ). Wal.

Appleton, Mary. S Summer T *Barnard* Oct 1756. Sy.

Appleton, Thomas. S Summer 1738 LC Knt Co., Md., from *Hawk* Apr 1739. Ha.

Apps, Thomas. S Oct 1772 T *Justitia* Jan 1773. L.

Apted, Elizabeth. S Summer T Sep 1751 *Greyhound*. Sy.

Archbold, Joan. SQS Lent 1736 & T from Liverpool. St.

Archer, Isaac. S May-Jul T *Tayloe* Jul 1773. M.

Archer, Jacob. SQS York 1755 (AHJ). Y.

Archer, John. S May-Jul T *Tayloe* Jul 1773. M.

Archer, William. S Lent but pardoned Mar 1774. M.

Aris, Robert. R Feb T May 1746. Sy.

Arkeston, John. S Summer T from London Oct 1755. Wa.

Arland, Thomas. SQS Jul 1732 LC Knt Co., Md., from *Falcon* Mar 1733. So.

Arlinge, Francis. S Dec 1772 T *Justitia* Jan 1773. M.

Arlot, Francis. S Jul 1736 LC QA Co., Md., from *Amity* May 1737. Ha.

Arman, Isabel. S Aberdeen for repeated thefts R for life Jun 1763. Sco.

Armsby, Richard (1737) - *See* Hanslip. No.

Armstrong, Charles. S Lent LC Bal Co., Md., Jul 1772. De.

Armstrong, George. S Lent LC AA Co., Md., from *Thornton* Jul 1773. L.

Armstrong, John. S Summer 1741 R 14 yrs Apr 1742 LC PG Co., Md. Wo.

Armstrong, John. TB Apr 1749. Db.

Armstrong, Mary. SQS & T Sep 1751 *Greyhound*. M.

Armstrong, Mary. S Lent T *Thornton* May LC AA Co., Md., Jul 1774. M.

Armstrong, Mary. SQS Jan T *Thornton* May LC AA Co., Md., Jul 1774. L.

Armstrong, Paul. T Sep 1751 *Greyhound*. M.

Armstrong, Robert. SQS City 1751 (AHJ). Nl.

Armstrong, Robert. S Lent LC AA Co., Md., from *Thornton* Jul 1773. L.

Armstrong, Thomas. S Feb T Oct 1751. Nl.

Armstrong, William, soldier. S for highway robbery in Worcestershire Lent R 14 yrs Summer 1744 (GJ) T Apr 1745. St.

Arney, John. S Summer 1718 LC from *Sophia* QA Co., Md. Mar 1719. So.

Arnold, Jane. S for shoplifting & R 14 yrs Lent 1772 LC Bal Co., Md. & sold to Joshua Hall. Be.

Arnold, Mary. S Lent 1732 LC Knt Co., Md., from *Falcon* Mar 1733. Co.

Arnold, Richard. S Lent LC AA Co., Md., from Thornton Jul 1775. Sy.

Arnold, Samuel. S Jan T *Neptune* Mar 1761. M.

Arnold, Sarah. S Jan T Mar 1750 *Tryal*. M.

Arscott, Richard Jr. S 14 yrs Summer 1743 LC Knt Co., Md., from *Globe* Mar 1744. De.

Arthur, John. SQS Mar 1734 LC Knt Co., Md., Mar 1735 from *Falcon*. Co.

Ash, David. T *Justitia* Feb 1776. L.

Ash, Hannah. S Feb T *Thames* Mar 1754. L.

Ash, John. S Jan-Apr T Jun 1748 *Lichfield*. M.

Ash, Thomas. S for breaking & entering Lent R 14 yrs Jul 1726. Do.

Ashby, John. S Lent R 14 yrs Summer T *Barnard* Oct 1756. K.

Ashby *als* Ashley. Mary. S Dec 1735 T Jan 1736 *Dorsetshire* LC Va Sep 1736. M.

Ashden, William of Wapping. S s looking glass Jan 1717 T 14 yrs May 1718 *Tryal* LC Charles Town Aug 1718. LM.

Asher, Francis. S Lent T Apr 1758. Wa.

Asher, Isaac. S Oct 1772 T *Justitia* Jan 1773. L.

Asher, Levi. S May-Jul T *Tayloe* Jul 1773. M.

Ashford, William. S Summer T Aug 1749 *Thames*. K.

Ashford, William. S 14 yrs Jul T *Tayloe* Jul 1774. L.

Ashley, Ann. S Feb T *Thames* Mar 1754. L.

Ashley, William. SQS Beccles 1758. Su.

Ashman, Charles. S Lent LC AA Co., Md., from *Thornton* May 1771, sold to John Whitacre Jr. M.

Ashman, Isaac. S 14 yrs Summer 1734 LC Knt Co., Md., from *Hawk* Apr 1735. So.

Ashmore, William. S Bristol Lent 1743 LC Knt Co., Md., from *Raven* Feb 1744. G.

Ashton, Katherine. S Lent 1735. Y.

Ashton, Ralph of Ashton in Makerfield. SQS Oct 1728. La.

Ashton, William of Salford. SQS Oct 1718. La.

Ashworth, John. SW Lent T *Thornton* May LC AA Co., Md., Jul 1774. M.

Askew, Anne. S Lent 1721 R Jul T Oct 1723 *Forward* to Va from London. Y.

Askew, Jonathan. S Lent 1750 LC QA Co., Md., from *Catherine* Nov 1750. Wo.

Askew, Mary. S Apr-May T *Tryal* Jul 1754. M.

Askron, Thomas. SQS & T May 1745. Y.

Aspel, William. SQS Chelmsford Jan 1751 (AHJ). E.

Asplin, William of Low Leyton, mariner. SQS Jan T May 1750 *Lichfield*. E.

Aspy, Thomas. S Lent 1741 LC QA Co., Md., from *Philleroy* Apr 1742. He.

Assent, James. R for 14 yrs Oct 1772 T *Justitia* Jan 1773. M.

Astey, John S Mar 1747 R Lent 1749 (GJ). He.

Aston, Jane wife of Walter, "an unfortunate poor woman, to be found a good master." S & R Lent 1775 & sold to Richard Moals.

Atkey, William. S Summer 1732 LC Knt Co., Md., from *Falcon* Mar 1733. De.

Atkins, George. SQS Jan 1772 LC Bal Co., Md., Apr 1773. G.

Atkins, John. S Summer 1737 LC QA Co., Md., from *Amity* Apr 1738. Do.

Atkins *als* Atkinson, Susannah. S May-Jul T *Tayloe* Jul 1774. M.

Atkyns, Thomas. S Summer 1753 T Jan 1754. No.

Atkins, William. S Jul T Sep 1751. No.

Atkinson, Elizabeth. SQS City Christmas 1750 (AHJ). Nl.

Atkinson, George. S May 1770. Li.

Atkinson, Jane wife of John. SQS City Summer 1759 (AHJ). Nl.

Atkinson, John. S Jan-Apr T *Lichfield* May 1749. M.

Atkinson, John. SW Lent but pardoned in Apr 1773. M.

Atkinson, Mary. SQS Apr T May 1750 *Lichfield*. M.

Atkinson, Robert. S May T *Beverly* Aug 1763. M.

Atkinson, Thomas. S Oct T *Justitia* Dec 1774. L.

Atkinson, William. S Summer 1735. Wa.

Atkinson, William. SQS Jan 1773 LC Bal Co., Md., from *Adventure* Mar 1773. Du.

Atkis [Alkis], William. S Lent 1729. Nt.

Atley, Christopher of Newington. SQS Apr T May 1750 *Lichfield*. Sy.

Atwood, Hannah. S Oct 1772 T *Justitia* Jan 1773. L.

Attwood, William. S Dec 1753 (AHJ). Wo.

Atwood, William. S Lent T Aug 1753. Wo.

Atwool, Thomas. S Lent LC Bal Co., Md., Jul 1772. So.

Audless, Margaret. S Apr T Apr 1746 *Laura*. L.

Ausley, Henry. S Summer T *Barnard* Oct 1756. Sy.

Aust, Anthony. S for house breaking Mar R 14 yrs Jul TB to Va Sep 1756. Wi.

Austin, Abraham (John). S s silver spoons & clogs Jul 1735 T Jan 1736 *Dorsetshire* LC Va Sep 1736. M.

Austin *als* Veil, Ann. S Oct 1773 T *Justitia* Jan 1774. L.

Austin, Bryant. SQS Oct T *Justitia* Dec 1774. M.

Austin *als* Thompson, Elizabeth [Eleanor]. S Apr 1733 s in Newtoner Street LC from *Caesar* Va Jul 1734. L.

Austin, Henry. S Lent LC AA Co., Md., from *Thornton* Jul 1775. M.

Austin, Isaac. S Lent LC AA Co., Md., from *Hanover Planter* Jul 1773. L.

Austin, Isaac. S Jul T *Tayloe* Jul 1774. L.

Austin, Robert. SQS Apr LC Bal Co., Md., Dec 1772. G.

Autonreith, William. S for life Aug T *Beverly* Aug 1763. L.

Avenell, John. S Lent T *Thornton* May LC AA Co., Md., Jul 1774. Sx.

Avergirl, Elizabeth of St. George, Southwark. SQS Apr T Sep 1751 *Greyhound*. Sy.

Avery, Jane. S Jan-Apr T *Lichfield* May 1749. M.

Avery, John. S Jul T Aug 1749 *Thames*. L.

Avery, Mary. S 14 yrs Apr-May T *Saltspring* Jul 1775. M.

Avery *als* MacDonald, Patrick. S Jul-Dec 1747 but died. M.

Avery, Thomas. S Lent LC Bal Co., Md., Jul 1774. Wi.

Axell, Ann. SQS Chelmsford Jan 1754 (AHJ). E.

Axted, Elizabeth. S Aug T Sep 1751. Sy.

Ayers, Ann. S Jul-Dec 1747 T *St. George* Jan LC Knt Co., Md., Mar 1748. M.

Aylett als Pallett, William. S Lent T *Thornton* May LC AA Co., Md., Jul 1774. Ht.

Aymer, Thomas. T Summer 1745 T Feb 1746. Ha.

Ayres, John. S Oct T *Justitia* Dec 1774. L.

Ayres, William (1737). *See* Wheeler. So.

Ayris, William. SQS Feb LC AA Co., Md., from *Thornton* Jul 1773. L.

Babb, Thomas. T May 1746. De.

Babes, Patrick. SQS Bristol for s in Peter St. Dec 1760. G.

Back, Thomas (1753) - *See* Batch. He.

Backinstone, John. SQS 1759 (AHJ). La.

Bacon, Samuel. R for life Oct 1751-Jan 1752 T *Thames* Mar 1752. M.

Bacon, Thomas. SQS Lent TB Apr 1741. Y.

Badge, Sarah. S Sep T Oct 1750 *Rachael*. M.

Badger, Mary (1730) - *See* Harwood. M.

Badger, Richard (1771). *See* Brookes. St.

Badger, Thomas. S s at Stoughton Lent 1751 LC QA Co., Md., from *Bideford* Sep 1752. Wo.

Badham, Edward. S for house breaking Mar R 14 yrs Apr LC Bal Co., Md., Jul 1771. He.

Bage, George. Jul 1783 LC Bal Co., Md., Dec 1783 from *Swift*. M.

Baggott, John. S Apr T May 1750 *Lichfield*. M.

Bagnall, John *als* Hamilton, William. S Summer TB Aug 1771; returned before his time, confined at Chester & R for life Jan 1774. Nt.

Bagnall, John. S 14 yrs Lent LC AA Co., Md., from *Hanover Planter* Jul 1773. M.

Bagot, Ann. S Summer LC Bal Co., Md., Dec 1772. Wa.

Bagot, Stephen. S Apr T May 1752 *Lichfield*. L.

Bagshaw, Henry. S May-Jul T Sep 1751 *Greyhound*. M.

Bagshaw, Jeremiah. S Apr 1753. Li.

Baguley, John. S Summer T Oct 1756. Nt.

Bagwell, Margaret. S Dec 1747 LC Knt Co., Md., from *St. George* Mar 1748. L

Bagwell, Mary. S Lent LC Bal Co., Md., Jun 1773. Ha.

Baildon, Thomas. S s horse Lent 1729 R 14 yrs Summer 1730. Y.

Bayley, Charles of Wells, husbandman. R for Barbados Feb 1673 but LC Md 1673. So.

Bayley, Francis, aged 25, dark. AT Jul T Sep 1720 LC Annapolis May 1721 from *Gilbert* (NM). No.

Bailey, Daniel. Jul 1783 LC Bal Co., Md., Dec 1783 from *Swift*. M.

Baily, Elias. R for life Mar LC Md from *Elizabeth* Jun 1775. Ha.

Bailey, Francis (Frances). S Lent 1775 but pardoned and taken from transport ship. M.

Bailey, Henry. R City 14 yrs Summer 1754, "later hanged" (AHJ). Nl.

Bailey, James. S Summer T Sep 1751 *Greyhound*. K.

Baillie, James. S Edinburgh for murder R Feb 1772; R for life for returning Feb 1774. Sco.

Bailey, John. R for life Lent T *Tayloe* Jul 1773. Sy.

Bailey, John. S May-Jul T *Tayloe* Jul 1773. M.

Bailey, John. S May T *Saltspring* Jul 1775. L.

Bailey, Nicholas. S Summer T Nov 1735. De.

Bayley, Rachael. S Feb-Apr T May 1751 *Tryal*. M.

Bailey, Richard. S Feb T *Thames* Mar 1754. L.

Bailey, Richard of St. Saviour, Southwark. SQS Jan LC AA Co., Md., from *Thornton* Jul 1775. Sy.

Bailey, Robert. S Oct 1740 T *Harpooner* Jan 1741. L.

Bailey *als* Satchwell, Sarah. S s breeches & T Jan 1736 *Dorsetshire* LC Va Sep 1736. M.

Bailey, Sarah. S Jun T *Tryal* Jul 1754. L.

Baily, Simon. S Mar R 14 yrs Aug 1742 LC QA Co.,Md., from *Kent* Jun 1743. De.

Bailey, Susannah. S Sep T Oct 1750 *Rachael*. M.

Bailey *als* Bowden, Susannah. S Sep-Oct T *Justitia* Dec 1774. M.

Bailey, Thomas. S Lent T 14 yrs Aug 1752 *Tryal*. K.

Bake, John. S Aug T Sep 1751. Sy.

Baker, Benjamin. S for highway robbery Lent R 14 yrs Summer T Oct 1750 *Rachael*. K.

Baker, Edward of Chard, husbandman. R for Barbados Feb 1673 but LC Md 1673. So.

Baker *als* Moore, Elizabeth. S Jul-Sep T *Ruby* Oct 1754. M.

Baker, Elizabeth. S Lent LC Bal Co., Md., Jul 1771. Sh.

Baker, George. S 14 yrs Lent LC AA Co., Md., from *Thornton* Jul 1775. K.

Baker, Giles. S & R Summer 1768. Nf.

Baker, Henry. S Sep-Oct T Dec 1752 *Greyhound* LC Md Apr 1753. M.

Baker, Isaac. S s horse Lent R 14 yrs Jul 1725. Wi.

Baker *als* Frohen, Johanna. S Sep 1740 T *Harpooner* Jan 1741. L.

Baker, John. S for s & breaking Pontefract Gaol Lent 1724 T Summer 1725 LC from *Supply* Md May 1726. Y.

Baker, John (1742) - *See* Crisp, George. Su.

Baker, John. S Summer T Sep 1753. O.

Baker, John. S Summer T *Phoenix* Oct 1760. K.

Baker, John. S 14 yrs for receiving goods stolen in Essex May T Aug 1769 *Douglas*. M.

Baker, John. S Lent LC AA Co., Md., from *Thornton* Jul 1773. M.

Baker, Joseph. S Lent T Sep 1746 *Mary*. E.

Baker, Lewis (1718). See Thomas, John. De.

Baker, Mary. S Jul-Dec 1747 LC Knt Co., Md., from *St. George* Mar 1748. M.

Baker, Nicholas. T Sep 1737 *Pretty Patsy*. L.

Baker, Roger. SQS Jul TB Oct LC Kent. Co., Md., from *Raven* Nov 1737. So.

Baker, Rowland (1775). *See* Mead, John. E.

Baker, Samuel. S Feb T May 1758. Ha.

Baker, Susanna. SQS Bodmin Aug 1770 LC Bal Co., Md., Jul 1771. Co.

Baker, Thomas. SQS Jan T Mar 1750 *Tryal*. M.

Baker *als* Haywood, Thomas. S s horse Lent R 14 yrs Summer 1756 TB to Va. No.

Baker, William *als* Egerton, Shock. R 14 yrs for returning from T Jan 1740 (IJ). M.

Baker, William. Lent T Jun 1748 *Lichfield*. K.

Baker, William. S Lent T *Tryal* Jul 1754. Sx.

Baker alias Sawcer, William. S 14 yrs Lent LC Bal Co., Md., Jul 1771. De.

Baker, William. S s at Ross Lent LC Bal Co., Md., Jun 1773. He.

Baker [Barker], Christopher. S Summer 1770 but escaped in London. Y.

Bakewell, Thomas. S Dec 1749-Jan 1750 T Mar 1750 *Tryal*. M.

Balch, Roger [Robert]. S Apr 1753. So.

Baldock, Edward Mirrikin. S May 1770. Li.

Baldwin, John of St. Margaret Westminster. S Lent LC AA Co., Md., from *Thornton* Jul 1773. M.

Baldwin, Samuel. SQS Jan T *Thornton* May LC AA Co., Md., Jul 1774. Ht.

Baldwin, Thomas. S May-Jul T *Tayloe* Jul 1774. M.

Ball, Benjamin. S Dec 1754 T *Greyhound* Feb 1755. L.

Ball, Elizabeth. S Jul 1747 LC Knt Co., Md., from *St. George* Mar 1748. L.

Ball, James. S Lent 1769 (AHJ). Wi.

Ball, John. S & R 7 yrs Lent 1728. Bu.

Ball, John Sr. S Lent LC Bal Co., Md., Jun 1773. Do.

Ball, John. SQS Bristol s books from St. Thomas's Church Feb TB to Md May

1763. G.

Ball, William. S s cloth from tenters & R 14 yrs May 1721 (NM). No.

Ball, William. S Summer 1743 R 14 yrs Feb 1744. Co.

Ball, William. S Lent T *Thornton* May LC AA Co., Md., Jul 1774. M.

Ballard, John. S & T Jan 1736 *Dorsetshire* LC Va Sep 1736. L.

Ballard, John. S Lent T *Tryal* Jul 1754. Sx.

Ballmore, John. S Lent 1764 TB to Md. No.

Ballover, Paul. S Apr 1757 (AHJ). Li.

Balmer, John. S Lent 1729. Nt.

Bambrick, Richard. S Apr T May 1750 *Lichfield*. M.

Bamford, John. SQS Dec 1753 T *Thames* Mar 1754. M.

Bampton, George. S Lent R 14 yrs Summer T Sep 1751 *Greyhound*. Ht.

Banfield, Richard. S Lent LC AA Co., Md., from *Thornton* Jul 1775. M.

Banke, Richard of Downham. SQS Jan 1720. La.

Banks, William. R Apr T 14 yrs Dec 1771 *Justitia* . Ht.

Bannell *als* Bland, Hannah. S Feb-Apr T May 1752 *Lichfield*. M.

Banning, James. R Jul T *Tayloe* Jul 1774. M.

Bannister, George. S Jan T *Plain Dealer* Jan 1746. L.

Banister, George. S Lent T May 1750 *Lichfield*. E.

Bannister, George. S Jan T *Neptune* Mar 1761. M.

Bannister, Mary. S Dec 1745 T *Plain Dealer* Jan 1746. L.

Bannister, Mary. S Jul T *Tayloe* Jul 1773. L.

Banstead, Jane. SQS Feb T May 1752 *Lichfield*. M.

Bant, Edward. SQS Plymouth Jul 1755 (AHJ). De.

Banyon, William of St. George, Southwark. SQS Apr T Sep 1751 *Greyhound*. Sy.

Barber, Ann. S Jan T *Justitia* May 1745. L.

Barber, George of St. Giles in Fields. R for Barbados Jun 1671 but LC Md Feb 1672. M.

Barber, Jane. S Feb-Apr T May 1751 *Tryal*. M.

Barber, John. S Lent T Apr 1754. Le.

Barber, Mary. S Jul-Dec 1747 LC Knt Co., Md., from *St. George* Mar 1748. M.

Barber, Robert. S Dec 1753-Jan 1754 T *Thames* Mar 1754. M.

Barber, Susanna. S Sep T Dec 1752 *Greyhound* LC Md Apr 1753. M.

Barber *als* Lane, Thomas. S & T Jan 1736 *Dorsetshire* LC Va Sep 1736. L.

Barber, Thomas. S s watch Lent R 14 yrs Summer 1750 (GJ). Sh.

Barber, Thomas. SQS Jul TB Aug 1758. So.

Barber, William. S Summer T Dec 1736. Wa.

Barber, William. T *Justitia* Feb 1776. L.

Barclay, John. S Sep-Oct T Oct 1749 *Mary*. M.

Barefoot, Charles. S Feb T Mar 1750 *Tryal*. M.

Barew, Lawrence. Jul 1783 LC Bal Co., Md., Dec 1783 from *Swift*. M.

Barfield *als* Bradfield, Ann. S Lent LC AA Co., Md., from *Thornton* May 1771. M.

Bargo, Sarah wife of Peter (or John). S Sep-Oct 1775 T *Justitia* Feb 1776. M.

Barker, Christopher. S s at Scarborough Summer TB Aug 1770 but escaped in London. Y.

Barker *als* Wade, Elizabeth. SQS Jan 1726. La.

Barker, Elizabeth. S Aug T *Beverly* Aug 1763. L.

Barker, Isaac of Cold Norton. S Lent R 14 yrs Summer T *Phoenix* Oct 1760. E.

Barker, John of St. Nicholas. S Bristol s shirt Sep 1752. G.

Barker, Mary. S Apr T May 1751 *Tryal*. L.

Barker, Mary. T *Tayloe* Jul 1774. M.

Barker, Samuel. S for highway robbery & R Lent LC Md from *Isabella* Jul 1775 &

sold to Waters & Gartrall. Wa.

Barker, Susanna. S Feb T *Thames* Mar 1752. L.

Barker, Thomas. S Jan T *Justitia* May 1745. L.

Barker, Thomas. S Feb-Apr T May 1751 *Tryal*. M.

Barlat, Thomas. SQS Apr T May 1750 *Lichfield*. M.

Barlow, John. S Lichfield Lent 1738. St.

Barlow, John. S Lent R 14 yrs Summer T *Maryland Packet* Oct 1761. E.

Barlow, Margaret. S & T Jan 1736 *Dorsetshire* LC Va Sep 1736. L.

Barlow, Thurstan of Stretford, yeoman. SQS Apr 1725. La.

Barnard, Daniel. S 14 yrs Lent 1731 LC Knt Co., Md., from *Falcon* Apr 1732. Co.

Barnard, Joseph (1783). *See* Phasoo. M.

Barnard, Sarah. S Lent T Jun 1752. G.

Barnard, Thomas. S Sep T *Maryland Packet* Oct 1761. M.

Barnes, Ann. S Mar 1731 AT Jan 1732. Wa.

Barnes, Benjamin. SWK Jan LC AA Co., Md., from *Thornton* Jul 1775. K.

Barnes *als* Carrol, Bridget. S Southwark Mar LC AA Co., Md., from *Thornton* Jul 1774. Sy.

Barns, Due. S 14 yrs Lent LC Bal Co., Md., Jun 1773. Ha.

Barnes, Elizabeth. SQS Oct 1754 T *Greyhound* Feb 1755. M.

Barnes, Ezekiel. S May-Jun T Aug 1752 *Tryal*. M.

Barnes, Henry of St. Luke. S s stewpan etc. Jul 1740 T *Harpooner* Jan 1741. M.

Barnes, John. S Jan-Apr T Jun 1748 *Lichfield*. M.

Barnes, John. SQS for perjury Apr T *Thornton* May LC AA Co., Md., Jul 1774. M.

Barnes, Mary. T Aug *Owners Goodwill* LC Md Nov 1720. K.

Barnes, Stephen. S for life Feb T *Thames* Mar 1754. M.

Barnes, Thomas. S Feb-Apr T May 1752 *Lichfield*. M.

Barnett, Betty wife of William. S 14 yrs Summer LC Bal Co., Md., Dec 1772. So.

Barnett, John. T Sep 1746. Ha.

Barnet, Joseph. S & T Aug 1752 *Tryal*. L.

Barnet, Joseph. S Lent T *Dolphin* May 1763. Ht.

Barnet, Stair. S Apr T *Dolphin* May 1763. M.

Barnett, William. S Feb T *Tryal* Mar 1757. M.

Barnham, Henry. S Lent 1724 but escaped & no further record found. Li.

Barnsides *als* Downing, Michael. S Sep-Oct T Oct 1749 *Mary*. M.

Barnsley, Joseph. S Dec 1782 LC Bal Co., Md., Dec 1783 from *Swift*. L.

Barrett, Ann. S Apr T Jun 1748 *Lichfield*. L.

Barrett, Elizabeth. S Apr T *Phoenix* Oct 1760. M.

Barrett, James. S Lent T *Thornton* May LC AA Co., Md., Jul 1774. M.

Barrett, John. T Sep 1737 *Pretty Patsy*. L.

Barret, John. S Lent 1741 (IJ). Su.

Barrett, John, a boy. S s at Siston Lent 1763. G.

Barrett, Matthew. T Sep 1746. Ha.

Barrett, Nathaniel. S Lent R 14 yrs Summer T *Phoenix* Oct 1760. Sy.

Barrett, Peter. S May T *Saltspring* Jul 1775. L.

Barratt, Robert. S Sep 1752 (AHJ). Li.

Barrett, Sampson of Sheffield. R for Africa or America Jul 1705. Y.

Barrett, Susannah. T May 1752 *Lichfield*. L.

Barrett, Thomas. S Lent R Jun 1724, died on passage in *Rappahannock* 1726. Li.

Barrett, Thomas. S Summer T Aug 1749 *Thames*. K.

Barrett, William. S Jan-Apr T *Lichfield* May 1749. M.

Barrett, William. S May-Jul T *Tayloe* Jul 1773. M.

Barrett, William. R 14 yrs Jul T *Saltspring* Jul 1775. M.

Barrington, Mary. S Lent R 14 yrs Summer T *Phoenix* Oct 1760. K.

Barrington, Thomas. S Apr LC Md from *Elizabeth* Jun 1775. So.

Barrow, John. S Jul 1734. Wi.

Barrow, John. SQS Shrewsbury s a ram Jul 1766. Sh.

Barrowcliff, John. S May 1772. Li.

Barrows, John of Heaton Norris. SQS Jan 1722 TB Apr 1723. La.

Barry, Ann. S Lent T *Thornton* May LC AA Co., Md., Jul 1774. M.

Barry, Barnard. S Apr T May 1752 *Lichfield*. L.

Bartelott, George (1773). *See* Ridgely. Wi.

Bartelott, Robert (1773). *See* Long. Wi.

Barter, Mark. T *Randolph* Sep 1768. De.

Bartlet, Nicholas. S Lent 1744 LC Knt Co., Md., from *Susannah* Aug 1744. De.

Barton, Anne of Salford, spinster. SQS Jan 1722 TB Apr 1723. La.

Barton, John. S Jun-Dec 1745 T *Plain Dealer* Jan 1746. M.

Barton, John. T Oct 1750 *Rachael*. K.

Barton, John. S Lent R 14 yrs Summer T *Maryland Packet* Oct 1761. Bu.

Barton, John-Jolly. SQS Ipswich Apr 1722. Su.

Barton, William. S Dec 1745 T *Plain Dealer* Jan 1746. L.

Bartram, Anthony. SQS Dec 1772 LC AA Co., Md., from Thornton Jul 1773. M.

Basely, John. SQS & T Apr 1742 LC PG Co., Md. Do.

Basely, William. S Summer 1738 LC QA Co., Md., from *Amity* Mar 1739. Co.

Basey, Ann. S Sep T *Phoenix* Oct 1760. M.

Basil als Boswell, Henry. S Lent LC Bal Co., Md., Jun 1773; runaway. Wo.

Basil als Boswell, Timothy. S s shoes at Shipston on Stour Lent LC Bal Co., Md., Jun 1773. Wo.

Bass, George. S Bury St. Edmunds s at Wickhambrooke Summer 1771. Su.

Bassett, Elisha. S Sep-Oct 1775 T *Justitia* Feb 1776. M.

Bassett, Elizabeth. S Sep-Dec 1746 T Jan 1747 *George William*. M.

Bassett, Joseph. T May 1751 *Tryal*. Ht.

Bastin, William. SQS & T May 1750 *Lichfield*. Ht.

Baston, James. S Dec 1749-Jan 1750 T Mar 1750 *Tryal*. M.

Baswicke, George of St. George, Southwark. SQS Apr T Sep 1751 *Greyhound*. Sy.

Batch *als* Back, Thomas. S & R s sheep Aug 1753. He.

Bate, Benjamin. S Lent LC Bal Co., Md., Jun 1773. Wa.

Bateman, Jeremiah. SQS Leeds Lent 1738. Y.

Bateman, Peter. S Sep T Oct 1750 *Rachael*. M.

Bateman, Samuel of Manchester, webster. SQS Apr 1723 T Apr 1724. La.

Bateman, Sarah. T *Tayloe* Jul 1774. M.

Bateman, Thomas. S 14 yrs for receiving goods stolen at Huntingdon Feb T Apr 1735 *Patapsco* LC Annapolis Oct 1735. M.

Bateman *als* Bates, Thomas. SQS Oct 1772 T *Justitia* Jan 1773. M.

Bates, Joseph. S Summer T Oct 1756. Nt.

Bates, Robert. S for highway robbery & R 14 yrs Jun 1740. No.

Bates, Susannah. S Jun T *Maryland Packet* Oct 1761. M.

Bates, William. S May-Jul T Aug 1749 *Thames*. M.

Bath, William. S & T Sep 1751 *Greyhound*. M.

Batson, Mordecai. S Apr-Jun 1739 T *Sea Nymph* to Md. M.

Batt, George. S May R 14 yrs Aug 1731 LC Md from *Falcon* Mar 1733. So.

Batterson, John. S s at Newport Pagnell Lent LC AA Co., Md., from *Thornton* Jul 1775. Bu.

Batton, Francis of St. Saviour, Southwark. SQS May T *Tryal* Jul 1754. Sy.

Batten, John . S Summer 1770 LC Bal Co., Md., Jun 1771. De.

Batton, Mary. S Apr T May 1749 *Lichfield*. L.

Batty, James. S Lent LC AA Co., Md., from *Thornton* Jul 1773. L.

Bavin, Thomas. S Dec-Jan T Mar 1750 *Tryal*. M.

Bavington, Ann. S Summer 1773 T *Justitia* Jan 1774. Bu.

Bawcock, John. T May 1751 *Tryal*. E.

Bawden, Henry. S Lent T May 1746 from Appledore. Co.

Bax, Jeremiah. S Lent T *Tryal* Jul 1754. K.

Baxall, William (1774) - *See* Boxwell. Ha.

Baxson, Mordecai. S Jun T Jul 1747 *Laura*. L.

Baxter, Elizabeth. S Jan T May 1746. Wi.

Baxter, Elizabeth. SQS City Michaelmas 1761 (AHJ). Nl.

Baxter, Hope. S Summer 1735 T Lent 1736. Le.

Baxter, James. SQS Sep 1772 T *Justitia* Jan 1773. M.

Baxter, John. SQS Apr 1728. La.

Baxter, John. S Oct 1757. Li.

Bayes, John. S s clothing Apr T Dec 1735 *John* LC Annapolis Sep 1736. M.

Baylis, Abraham. S s at Kidderminster Aug LC Bal Co., Md., Dec 1770. Wo.

Bayliss, James. R for life for highway robbery in Ledbury, Herefordshire, Jul 1736. M.

Baylis, James. S Lent 1761 (AHJ). Wo.

Baylis, John. S Lent LC Annapolis Nov 1733 from *Patapsco* . Wa.

Bailiss, John of Tooting. SQS Jan T *Thornton* May LC Md Jul 1774. Sy.

Baylis, Joseph. S May T *Beverly* Aug 1763. M.

Bayliss, Richard. S 14 yrs s sheep Lent LC Bal Co., Md., Jul 1771. Wa.

Baylis, Sarah. S s clothing Apr 1760 (WJ). G.

Baylis, Thomas. S Lent T Aug 1753. Wo.

Bayliss, William. S & R 14 yrs Mar 1768. Wo.

Baynham, Anthony. S s sheep Lent R 14 yrs Summer 1748 (GJ). He.

Baynham, Henry. S Apr T *Dolphin* May 1763. L.

Baythorne, James. R May T for life Sep T *Tryal* Mar 1757. M.

Baythorn, William. S & T Aug 1752 *Tryal*. L.

Bazely [Beazley], John. S & R 14 yrs Lent LC Md from *Elizabeth* Jun 1775. Wo.

Beach, John. S Lent LC AA Co., Md., from *Thornton* May 1771. M.

Beacham, George. S 14 yrs Lent LC Bal Co., Md., Dec 1772; runaway. De.

Beedle, Laurence. R for Barbados Feb 1672 but LC AA Co Md Nov 1673. M.

Beadle, William. S Feb-Apr T May 1752 *Lichfield*. M.

Beal, Samuel of Wethersfield. SQS Oct 1773 to be T 5 yrs for running away from his family after being judged an incorrigible rogue T *Justitia* Jan 1774. Bu.

Bealing, John (1737). *See* Pitman. Do.

Beam, William. T *Justitia* Dec 1774. L.

Bean, Daniel. S Lent 1774 but pardoned and removed from transport ship. M.

Bean, John. S Dec 1782 LC Bal Co., Md., Dec 1783 from *Swift*. L.

Been, Timothy. S May-Jul T Aug 1749 *Thames*. M.

Bear, William. S Jan T Apr 1735 *Patapsco* LC Annapolis Oct 1735. L.

Beard *als* Butcher, Charlotte. S May-Jul T *Tayloe* Jul 1773. M.

Beard, John. T Apr 1735 *Patapsco* LC Annapolis Oct 1735. K.

Beard, Richard. S May-Jul T Sep 1751 *Greyhound*. M.

Beard, Samuel. S s sheep Summer 1772 LC Bal Co., Md., Apr 1773. G.

Beards, Joseph. S Lent LC Bal Co., Md., Jul 1771. Wa.

Beare, Elizabeth of St. Martin in Fields, spinster. R Sep 1671 LC Md Jun 1673. M.

Beare, Josiah. S Lent 1735. De.

Beasley, John. S Apr T May 1751 *Tryal*. L.

Beason, William. S Jun-Dec 1745 T *Plain Dealer* Jan 1746. M.

Beaton, James. S Apr T May 1751 *Tryal*. L.

Beeton, Maryon (Margaret). S Lent LC AA Co., Md., from *Hanover Planter* Jul 1773. M.

Beattie?, William. Jul 1783 LC Bal Co., Md., Dec 1783 from *Swift*. M.

Beaumont, Elizabeth wife of Thomas. T *Maryland Packet* Oct 1761. M.

Beaumont, Samuel. S Lent 1724 but escaped & no further record found. Li.

Beamont, Thomas. R & T Apr 1735 *Patapsco* LC Annapolis Oct 1735. M.

Beaumont, William of St. Olave, Southwark. SQS Feb T Apr *Thornton* LC AA Co., Md., Jul 1771. Sy.

Beaumont, William. S Summer T *Barnard* Oct 1756. K.

Beauty, John (1757) - *See* Crawford. O.

Beaver, John. S 14 yrs s at Woburn Lent LC AA Co., Md., from *Thornton* Jul 1775. Bu.

Beaver, Joseph. S Lent 1733. Wa.

Beavis, William. S Summer 1741 LC QA Co., Md., from *Philleroy* Apr 1742. De.

Beezley, Ann. S Feb T *Thames* Mar 1754. L.

Beazley, John (1775) - *See* Bazely.

Beazor, John. S Lent LC AA Co., Md., from *Hanover Planter* Jul 1773. M.

Beazor, Richard. S Lent LC AA Co., Md., from *Hanover Planter* Jul 1773. M.

Beck, John. T *Justitia* Jan 1774. M.

Beck, Mary. S Jan T *Plain Dealer* Jan 1746. L.

Beck, Richard. T Aug 1749 *Thames*. L.

Beckett, Ann. S Aug 1771. Li.

Beckett, Rose. S s at Stokenchurch Summer 1752 as accomplice of Nicholas Delafield (*q.v.*). O.

Beddington, Edward. S Lent LC AA Co., Md., from *Thornton* May 1771. M.

Bedford, Walter. S Dec 1753-Jan 1754 T *Thames* Mar 1754. M.

Bednam, Mary. S Summer T from London Oct 1755. Wa.

Bednell, Sarah. S s cloth in Birmingham Aug T Oct 1757 (WJ). Wa.

Bee, Mary. S Oct 1757. Li.

Beedle - *See* Beadle.

Been - *See* Bean.

Beer, Hugh, *als* Thomas, William. R 14 yrs Jan 1736. So.

Beesley, William. S s 2 shillings Dec 1735 T Jan 1736 *Dorsetshire* LC Va Sep 1736. M.

Beeson, James. S Oct T *Justitia* Dec 1774. L.

Beetley *als* Duggan, John. S Mar T *Thames* Mar 1754. L.

Beeton - *See* Beaton

Beets, Joseph. S Jun 1753 (AHJ). Wo.

Beford, Thomas of Buckingham. R for Barbados Feb 1664. Bu.

Behoe, Moses. S s wigs & hair at Reading Summer 1722 LC from *Forward* Md Jun 1723. Be.

Bell, James. S Jan T *Justitia* May 1745. L.

Bell, James. S Jul T *Maryland Packet* Oct 1761. L.

Bell, John. S Lent T Jun 1748 *Lichfield*. E.

Bell, John. S Dec 1753-Jan 1754 T *Thames* Mar 1754. M.

Bell, Joseph. S for receiving from William Vaughton (*qv*) Summer 1760. Wa.

Bell, Margaret. T *Sea Nymph* to Md. M.

Bell, Mary. S 14 yrs Feb-Apr 1746 T Apr 1746 *Laura*. M.

Bell, Thomas. S Summer 1762 R 14 yrs Lent T *Dolphin* May 1763. K.

Bell, William of Clapham. SQS Apr T Sep 1751 *Greyhound*. Sy.

Bellamy, John. S Lent LC Bal Co., Md., Jul 1771. So.

Bellamy, Thomas. S Hull Oct 1732 T Dec 1733. Y.

Bellenger, Henry. S Jul T Sep 1751 *Greyhound*. L.

Bellisford, William. S Jun T Sep 1751 *Greyhound*. L.

Belmorshed, Humphrey. S s gowns Oct 1735 T Jan 1736 *Dorsetshire* LC Va Sep 1736. M.

Belt, William (1748). *See* Forster, John. Nl.

Bendall, Thomas. S 14 yrs Lent 1750 LC QA Co., Md., from *Catherine* Nov 1750. So.

Bendyfield, Sarah. S s handkerchief etc Sep 1735 T Jan 1736 *Dorsetshire* LC Va Sep 1736. M.

Benford (Belford), Alice. R for Barbados Dec 1671 but LC Md from *William & Mary* Mar 1672. M.

Benison, Joseph. S Summer 1731 LC Knt Co., Md., from *Falcon* Apr 1732. So.

Benjamin, Abraham. S Apr T May 1752 *Lichfield*. L.

Benjamin, Samuel. S May-Jul T *Tayloe* Jul 1773. M.

Benjamin *als* Sanders, Simon. S Lent LC AA Co., Md., from *Thornton* May 1771. L.

Benn, William.S Lent LC AA Co., Md., from *Thornton* Jul 1773. M.

Bennett, Alexander. S 14 yrs Lent LC Bal Co., Md., Jul 1771. De.

Bennett, Ann. S Lent T *Thornton* May LC AA Co., Md., Jul 1774. M.

Bennet, Eleanor. S Feb-Apr 1746 T Apr 1746 *Laura*. M.

Bennett, Elizabeth. S Dec 1747 LC Knt Co., Md., from *St. George* Mar 1748. L.

Bennett, Elizabeth. S Jan T Mar 1750 *Tryal*. L.

Bennett, Elizabeth. S May-Jul T Sep 1751 *Greyhound*. M.

Bennett, George. S Summer 1718 LC from *Sophia* QA Co., Md. Mar 1719. De.

Bennett, George. S s sheep at Chelmarsh & R 14 yrs Jul T *Restoration* LC Bal Co., Md., Oct 1771. Sh.

Bennett, Henry. S Lent LC Bal Co., Md., Jul 1772. So.

Bennett, John. R for Barbados Sep 1672 but LC AA Co Md Nov 1673. L.

Bennett, John. S Summer 1741 LC QA Co., Md., from *Philleroy* Apr 1742. Co.

Bennett, John. S Sep 1747 LC Knt Co., Md., from *St. George* Mar 1748. L.

Bennett, John. S Oct 1751-Jan 1752 T *Thames* Mar 1752. M.

Bennet, John. SQS Exeter Jun 1762 (AHJ). De.

Bennett, Mary (1733). See Kerril. So.

Bennett, Mary. T Oct 1750 *Rachael*. M.

Bennet, Richard. SQS Launceston May 1755 (AHJ). Co.

Bennett, Robert. R & T Aug 1748. Mo.

Bennet, Samuel. S Summer 1718 LC from *Sophia* QA Co., Md. Mar 1719. Co.

Bennett, Sarah. S Jan T Mar 1750 *Tryal*. L.

Bennett, Thomas. S Sep-Oct T Oct 1749 *Mary*. M.

Bennett *als* Baker, Thomas. S Lent LC Bal Co., Md., Jul 1772. De.

Bennett, Thomas. S Lent LC Bal Co., Md., Jul 1772. Sh.

Bennett, Thomas. S 14 yrs Lent LC Bal Co., Md., Jun 1773. G.

Bennett, Walter. S Lent LC Bal Co., Md., Jul 1772. Do.

Bennett, William *als* Dodd, Ezekiel. SQS Jan 1732 LC Knt Co., Md., from *Falcon* Mar 1733. Do.

Bennett, William. S Lent LC Bal Co., Md., Jul 1772. Do.

Benoit, Joseph. S Apr-May T *Saltspring* Jul 1775. M.

Benson, Benjamin. S Summer 1753 R 14 yrs Lent T *Tryal* Jul 1754. E.

Benson, George. S Lent LC AA Co., Md., from *Thornton* May 1771. M.

Bentley, William. S Feb T Apr 1735 *Patapsco* LC Annapolis Oct 1735. M.

Berckham, James. SQS Ipswich 1754. Su.

Bergenhow, Peter. S Oct T *Justitia* Dec 1774. L.

Berk, Sarah wife of Thomas. S Summer T from Bristol Sep 1751. St.

Berk, Thomas (1772). *See* Hollis. M.

Berkett, George. S Lent 1737. St.

Berkley, Elizabeth. S & T Jan 1736 *Dorsetshire* LC Va Sep 1736. L.

Berkshire, John. R & T Apr 1735 *Patapsco* LC Annapolis Oct 1735. M.

Berriball, Pasche. S Lent 1737 LC Knt Co., Md., from *Hawk* Nov 1737. Co.

Berriman, William. T 14 yrs Aug LC Md. from *Reformation* Aug 1722. De.

Berrow, Joseph. S Summer 1757 R 14 yrs Lent 1758 but died on passage to America (AHJ). Wo.

Berry, Alice. S May T *Saltspring* Jul 1775. L.

Berry, Ann. S Feb T *Neptune* Mar 1761. L.

Berry, James. S Dec 1754 T *Greyhound* Feb 1755. L.

Berry (Bury), James. S Lent LC AA Co., Md., from *Thornton* May 1771. K.

Berry, John. S Summer 1732 LC Knt Co., Md., from *Falcon* Mar 1733. De.

Berry, John. T 1746. Sy.

Berry, Margaret. S Apr-May T *Saltspring* Jul 1775. M.

Berry, Michael. S Apr-Jun 1739 T *Sea Nymph* to Md. M.

Berry, Robert. S 14 yrs Lent 1744   LC Knt Co., Md., from *Susannah* Aug 1744. De.

Berry, Samuel. SQS & T Apr 1742 LC PG Co., Md. De.

Bertie, George. S Apr T May 1751 *Tryal*. L.

Best, George. S 14 yrs Summer 1772 LC Bal Co., Md., Apr 1773. So.

Best, Hannah S Summer T Oct 1752. Wa.

Best, John. SW Jan LC AA Co., Md., from *Thornton* Jul 1775. M.

Best, Mary. SQS Launceston Feb 1758 (AHJ). Co.

Best, Richard. S Dec 1772 T *Justitia* Jan 1773. M.

Bettesworth, Thomas. S Mar TB to Va Apr 1742 LC PG Co., Md. Wi.

Betts, William. S for highway robbery & R Summer LC Md from *William* Dec 1774 & sold to Frederick Myers. Wa.

Bevan, Matthew. S Lent LC AA Co., Md., from *Hanover Planter* Jul 1773. M.

Beverley, William. S Apr T May 1750 *Lichfield*. L.

Beverton, Simon. S Lent T May 1750 *Lichfield*. K.

Bew, Robert. SQS Wells Jan LC Bal Co., Md., Apr 1773. So.

Bewley, Mary. S & T Aug 1752 *Tryal*. L.

Bexter, John. S Lent R 14 yrs Summer T *Phoenix* Oct 1760. K.

Bibby, Sarah. S Dec 1745 T *Plain Dealer* Jan 1746. L.

Bickerton, George. S s sheep & R 14 yrs Summer LC Md from *William* Dec 1774 & sold to James Frazer; runaway. He.

Bickerton, John. S Oct 1751-Jan 1752 T *Thames* Mar 1752. M.

Bickford, Mary. SQS Exeter Oct 1754 (AHJ). De.

Biddell, John. S & R Lent T May 1755. St.

Biddesford, Thomas. S Lent LC Bal Co., Md., Jun 1773. St.

Biddle, John. S 14 yrs Summer LC Bal Co., Md., Dec 1772. Wa.

Biggs, John. S s sheep Lent R 14 yrs Summer T *Barnard* Oct 1756. Bu.

Biggs, Samuel. T *Justitia* Feb 1776. L.

Biggs, Stephen. S for highway robbery at Hardwick & R Summer 1773 T *Justitia* Jan 1774. Bu.

Biggs, Susanna. S Oct-Dec 1752 LC Md from *Greyhound* Apr 1753. M

Biggs, Thomas. S & T Aug 1752 *Tryal*. L.

Biggs, Thomas. S Apr-May T *Tryal* Jul 1754. M.

Bigley, Richard. S Lent T Sep 1766. Db.

Bignell, Joseph. S s mare at Emberton Lent LC AA Co., Md., from *Thornton* Jul 1773. Bu.

Bigwood, James. SQS Bristol Mar TB May LC Md from *Isabella* Jul 1775 & sold to Waters & Gartrall. G.

Bilby, Richard. S Lent LC AA Co., Md., from *Hanover Planter* Jul 1773. M.

Bilby, William. S Oct 1747 LC Knt Co., Md., from *St. George* Mar 1748. L.

Bill, William. S Apr T Sep 1751. Sy.

Billens, William. S for life Lent LC AA Co., Md., from *Thornton* Jul 1775. Sy.

Billingham, Thomas. S s iron at Kingswinford Summer LC Bal Co., Md., Dec 1772. St.

Billings, John. S Lent T *Thornton* May LC AA Co., Md., Jul 1774. M.

Billings, William. R Summer 1728. Db.

Billingsley, Elizabeth. S Lent T Apr 1756. Wa.

Billis, John. S Lent T *Thornton* May LC AA Co., Md., Jul 1774. Ht.

Bills, William. S Lent R 14 yrs Summer T *Ruby* Oct 1754. K.

Bilson, William. S Feb T *Thames* Mar 1752. L.

Bilth, James. SQS Feb LC AA Co., Md., from *Thornton* Jul 1773. M.

Bince, William. S Lent LC Bal Co., Md., Jul 1772. So.

Binfield [Benfield], David. SQS s in St. Thomas's parish, Oxford, Oct 1770. O.

Binghall, John. S Lent 1756 (AHJ). No.

Binn, Mary. S Summer LC Bal Co., Md., Dec 1772. De.

Binney, James. R 14 yrs Jul 1738 LC QA Co., Md., Jun 1739. De.

Binns, Mary. S Sep-Oct 1775 T *Justitia* Feb 1776. M.

Birch, Bridges. S Lent 1735. Li.

Birch, George of Openshaw, carpenter. SQS Oct 1725 , escaped & recaptured Oct 1726. La.

Birch, Hannah. S Lent R 14 yrs Summer 1758. Wa.

Birch, John. S Oct T Oct 1749 *Mary*. L.

Birch, Mary. S Apr-Jun 1739 T *Sea Nymph* to Md. M.

Birch, Moses. S Jul T *Phoenix* Oct 1760. M.

Birch, Richard. S & R for life for a shooting Mar, escaped from gaol but retaken, LC Bal Co., Md Jun 1773. Wa.

Birch, William. SQS at Gloucester Jul 1754 (WJ). G.

Birchill, John. S 1753 (AHJ). Y.

Birchmall, Isabella *als* Elizabeth. SQS Easter T Sep 1760. Db.

Bird, Anthony. S s at St. Peter, Hereford, Mar LC Bal Co., Md., Jul 1772. He.

Bird, Barnaby. SQS Ipswich Jan 1722. Su.

Bird, Bertram *als* Bartholomew. S Apr-Jun 1739 T *Sea Nymph* to Md. - runaway. M.

Bird, Eleanor. S Apr T *Phoenix* Oct 1760. M.

Bird, George *als* Baby *als* Day of St. Clement Danes. R on petition for returning from transportation & T May 1736 *Patapsco* to Md; returned & S Jun 1739 to be T *Sea Nymph* to Md for life. M.

Bird, John, coast waiter of Liverpool. S Summer R 14 yrs Dec 1738. La.

Bird, John. T *Tayloe* Jul 1773. M.

Bird, John als Holton, Griffith. SWK Jan T *Thornton* May LC AA Co., Md., Jul 1774. K.

Bird, John. S s blankets at Ludlow Summer LC Md from *William* Dec 1774 & sold to John Gordon. Sh.

Bird, John. S Lent LC AA Co., Md., from *Thornton* Jul 1775. L.

Bird, Matthew. S Lent T *Tryal* Jul 1754. Sy.

Bird, Thomas. SQS Ipswich Jan 1722. Su.

Bird, Thomas. S Mar T from Liverpool Dec 1746. St.

Bird, Thomas. S & TB to Va 1757. No.

Bird, Thomas. R 14 yrs Lent 1761. Li.

Bird, Thomas. S Lent LC AA Co., Md., from *Thornton* Jul 1773. M.

Bird, William. S s coat at Bisley Summer 1772 LC Bal Co., Md., Apr 1773. G.

Birdworth, Mary. S Summer T Sep 1751 *Greyhound*. Sy.

Birkett, Samuel. SQS Feb T Mar 1750 *Tryal*. M.

Birks, John. S Sep-Oct 1772 T *Justitia* Jan 1773. M.

Birmingham, Ellen wife of Gerrard. SQS Jul 1725. La.

Bisbee, James. S Apr T May 1751 *Tryal*. L.

Bishop, Daniel. R for life for murder Bristol Apr 1752; whipped in New York s
shirts from clergyman. G.

Bishop, George. S Lent LC AA Co., Md., from *Thornton* Jul 1775. Sy.

Bishop, Henry. S Mar LC Md from *Elizabeth* Jun 1775. Ha.

Bishop, John. S Summer 1740 R 14 yrs Jan 1741. So.

Bishop, Mary. SQS Oct 1774 TB Apr LC Md from *Elizabeth* Jun 1775. So.

Bishop, Roger of Great Maplestead, husbandman. SQS Jul 1773 T *Justitia* Jan 1774.
E.

Bishop, William. T Apr 1735 *Patapsco* LC Annapolis Oct 1735. K.

Bishop, William. S Feb-Apr T May 1751 *Tryal*. M.

Bissett, James. S Oct 1751-Jan 1752 T *Thames* Mar 1752. M.

Black, Andrew. T *Justitia* Feb 1776. M.

Black, Eleanor wife of William. S Sep-Oct 1775 T *Justitia* Feb 1776. M.

Black, Elizabeth SQS City Christmas 1749 (AHJ). Nl.

Black, Joseph. S Jan-Apr T Jun 1748 *Lichfield*. M.

Blackbourn, Elizabeth. S May T Jul 1745 *Italian Merchant*. M.

Blackbourne, John of Camberwell. SQS Jan T *Thames* Feb 1751. Sy.

Blackbourn, William. S & T Apr 1761. Li.

Blackbourne, Lydia, spinster of St. George, Southwark. SQS Apr T May 1752
Lichfield. Sy.

Blackburn, Benjamin. S 14 yrs Sep-Oct 1772 T *Justitia* Jan 1773. M.

Blackburn, Thomas. SQS Newcastle Jul 1772 LC Bal Co., Md., from *Adventure*
Mar 1773. Nl.

Blackdon, George. S Lent 1751 (AHJ). Wi.

Blackerby, Ann. S Jul T Dec 1735 *John* LC Annapolis Sep 1736; when sentenced
she cursed the court: "My curse and God's curse go with ye, and the prayers of my
children fall upon ye." M.

Blackford, Thomas. LC Md from *Isabella* Jul 1775 & sold to Thomas Samuel Pole. X.

Blackford, William. S Summer 1772 LC Bal Co., Md., Apr 1773. Co.

Blackhood, John. S Jan-Jun T Jul 1747 *Laura*. M.

Blackman, William (1773). *See* Blackmore. St.

Blackmore, Edmond. R Jul T *Saltspring* Jul 1775. M.

Blackmore, James. S 14 yrs Summer 1737 LC QA Co., Md., from *Amity* Apr 1738. Ha.

Blackmore, Robert. S Lent LC Bal Co., Md., Jun 1773. Ha.

Blackmore, Thomas. SQS Jul 1741 LC QA Co., Md., from *Philieroy* Apr 1742. De.

Blackmore *als* Blakeman (Blackman), William. S s at Walsall Mar LC Bal Co.,
Md., Jun 1773. St.

Blackston, John. S Dec 1749-Jan 1750 T Mar 1750 *Tryal*. M.

Blackwell, John. S s at St. Michael, Oxford, Summer 1760. O.

Blackwell, William. S Lent s horse R 14 yrs Summer T *Barnard* Oct 1756. Sy.

Blackwood, Hamilton. S Summer 1751 R 14 yrs Lent T May 1752 *Lichfield*. K.

Blair, Mary. S Lent LC Md from *Elizabeth* Jun 1775. Wa.

Blair, Thomas. S & TB to Md. 1753. No.

Blake, Daniel. S Jul T Jul 1748 *Mary*. L.

Blake, Henry. S Aug 1732 LC Md from *Falcon* Mar 1733. De.

Blake, Jane. S Oct 1772 T *Justitia* Jan 1773. L.

Blake, John. S Lent T *Thornton* May LC AA Co., Md., Jul 1774. L.

Blake, Philip. S Feb-Apr T May 1751 *Tryal*. M.

Blake, Richard. S s dray iron Apr T Aug 1718 *Eagle* LC Charles Town Mar 1719. L.

Blakeman, William (1773) - *See* Blackmore. St.

Blanchett, William. SEK Dec 1772 LC AA Co., Md., from *Thornton* Jul 1773; runaway. K.

Bland, Thomas. S Lent T *Dolphin* May 1763. E.

Blandell, Eleanor. S Lent LC AA Co., Md., from *Thornton* Jul 1775. M.

Blanden, Larance. SQS Bury St. Edmunds Sep 1766 T Mar 1767. Su.

Blandford, John. SQS Jul 1737 LC QA Co., Md., from *Amity* Apr 1738. Do.

Blandford, John. S for poaching deer & assaulting keeper Jul 1758. Do.

Blandford, William. S for life Lent LC AA Co., Md., from *Thornton* Jul 1775. Sy.

Blaney *als* Evans, William. S May-Jul T *Tayloe* Jul 1773. M.

Blanthorn, James. S Apr T May 1750 *Lichfield*. M.

Blatherhose, William. Jul 1783 LC Bal Co., Md., Dec 1783 from *Swift*. M.

Blay, John. T *Justitia* Feb 1776. L.

Blee, John. S Feb T *Thames* Mar 1752. L.

Bleson, William. S Jan-Apr T *Lichfield* May 1749. M.

Blewit, Charles. S s at Wolverhampton Lent 1750 LC QA Co., Md., from *Chester* Dec 1752. St.

Blimstone, Robert (1770). *See* Bold. Ch.

Blind Michael (1769) - *See* Pricket, Michael. O.

Blinkin, Thomas. S Apr T Jun 1748 *Lichfield*. L.

Blissed, Guido. S Lent T *Thornton* May LC AA Co., Md., Jul 1774. M.

Blith, Robert. S s horse Summer R 14 yrs Nov 1724. Su.

Blizerd, Joseph. S Jan-Apr T *Lichfield* May 1749. M.

Blofield, Robert Jr. T 1746. Nf.

Bloom, David. S & T Sep 1751 *Greyhound*. M.

Bloome, John of East Dereham. R for Barbados Aug 1671 but LC Md Feb 1672. Nf.

Bloomley, John. S Summer T Aug 1749 *Thames*. K.

Bloss, Sarah. S Sep T *Ruby* Oct 1754. L.

Bloss, William. S Summer 1738 T Jan 1739. Su.

Blunt, Edward. S s money Aug 1764 (WJ). He.

Bluyman, Hannah wife of John, *als* Blindman, Anna. S Apr-Jun 1739 T *Sea Nymph* to Md. M.

Bly, Thomas. T Summer 1745 T Feb 1746. Ha.

Boardman, Charles. S s at Stoke upon Trent Lent 1750 LC QA Co., Md., from *Chester* Dec 1752. St.

Boardman, Margaret of Manchester, spinster. SQS Jan 1724 T Apr 1725. La.

Boatson, Michael. S Summer T Sep 1751 *Greyhound*. Sy.

Bobell *als* Fletcher, William. SQS & T Oct 1730 *Lime* to Jamaica but died there 1732. La.

Bodden, Samuel. S Lent T *Thornton* May LC AA Co., Md., Jul 1774. M.

Boddington, William. S & R Lent 1754. Wa.

Bodenham, George. S Mar T May 1746. Wi.

Bodnam, Thomas. S & TB May 1736. G.

Bodray, Paul (1728) - *See* Boardrey. M.

Bodway, William (1737). *See* Body. Co.

Body *als* Bodway, William. S Lent 1737 LC Knt Co., Md., from *Hawk* Nov 1737. Co.

Boff, John. S Summer LC Bal Co., Md., Dec 1772. Wa.

Boger, Richard. S Summer 1733. Mo.

Boggs, Robert. SWK Jan T *Greyhound* Feb 1754. K.

MORE EMIGRANTS IN BONDAGE

Bolas, Jeremiah, an old convict. S for life Apr 1742. Sh.

Bold *als* Blimstone, Robert. S s heifer Jul 1770 R Mar LC Bal Co., Md., Jul 1771 & sold to Patrick Rock. Ch.

Bolden, Ann. S 1757 (AHJ). La.

Bolden, William. S 1756 (AHJ). La.

Boley, James. SQS Woodbridge 1771. Su.

Bolingbroke, Mary, *als* wife of James Deal. S 14 yrs Apr-Jun 1739 T *Sea Nymph* to Md. M.

Bollard, Richard. T May 1750 *Lichfield*. Sx.

Bolsover, Paul. S Apr 1757. Li.

Bolt, James. S Feb T *Thames* Mar 1752. L.

Boulton, Ann, spinster. SQS Bristol Mar TB May LC Md from *Isabella* Jul 1775 & sold to Waters & Gartrall. G.

Bolton, Bartholomew. S Lent T from Liverpool Aug 1738. St.

Bolton, John. S Feb T *Thames* Mar 1752. L.

Boulton, Thomas. S for killing a buck Mar R 14 yrs Summer 1754 (RM). Ha.

Bond, Elisha. S Summer 1746 T Jan 1747. De.

Bond, Joseph of Bermondsey. S Summer T Oct 1750 *Rachael*. Sy.

Bond, Nicholas. S Dec 1749-Jan 1750 T Mar 1750 *Tryal*. M.

Bond, Stephen. S Oct 1760. Li.

Bond, Thomas. S Lent LC AA Co., Md., from *Hanover Planter* Jul 1773. M.

Bone, Ann. T Summer 1745 T Feb 1746. Ha.

Bones, Elizabeth. S Dec 1749-Jan 1750 T Mar 1750 *Tryal*. M.

Bonner, William. S Jul 1733 R 14 yrs TB Dec 1734. Bd.

Bonneval, John. S Lent 1734 LC Knt Co., Md., Mar 1735 from *Falcon*. De.

Bonney, Joseph. SQS May T Jul 1773 *Tayloe* to Va. M.

Bonney, Julia (Judith). SW Apr 1774 but pardoned and taken from transport ship. M.

Bonniface, William. S Sep-Oct 1772 T *Justitia* Jan 1773. M.

Boon, John. S Bristol Jan T Mar 1757 (AHJ). G.

Boot, Daniel. S s at Hodnet Lent LC Bal Co., Md., Jul 1772. Sh.

Booth, Ann. S Lent 1771 But shown as taken from transport ship and pardoned. M.

Booth, Elizabeth. S Dec T *Justitia* Dec 1774. M.

Booth, Hannah. S Feb-Apr T *Justitia* May 1745. M.

Booth, Henry of Manchester. SQS Apr 1720. La.

Booth, John. S Oct 1758. Li.

Booth, Lucy. S Feb T *Thames* Mar 1752. L.

Booth, William. S 14 yrs Lent LC AA Co., Md., from *Hanover Planter* Jul 1773. M.

Boothman, Jonathan. S May-Jul T *Tayloe* Jul 1773; runaway. M.

Borcham, George of Writtle. SQS Oct 1751 T May 1752 *Lichfield*. E.

Boreham, George. SQS Chelmsford Jan 1752 (AHJ). E.

Borrett, Robert. S Aug 1752. Li.

Bosely, Thomas. S Oct-Dec 1750 T *Thames* Feb 1751. M.

Boss, Robert. S Lent 1750 LC QA Co., Md., from *Catherine* Nov 1750. So.

Bossom, Charles. SQS s meat in Oxford Jan 1763 (OJ). O.

Bostock *als* Head, Mary. S Oct 1721 R Jan 1722. L.

Bostock, William. S for burglary Summer 1763 R 14 yrs Apr 1764. Sh.

Boswell, Ann. S Jul-Dec 1747 to be T 14 yrs LC Knt Co., Md., from *St. George* Mar 1748. M.

Boswell, Samuel. S Lent LC AA Co., Md., from *Hanover Planter* Jul 1773. M.

Botterill, John. S & TB to Md 1775. No.

Bottles, Sarah. S Jul-Dec 1747 LC Knt Co., Md., from *St. George* Mar 1748. M.

Boucher, Thomas. SQS Oct 1754 T *Greyhound* Feb 1755. M.

Bouden, William. S Bristol Mar 1750 LC QA Co., Md., from *Catherine* Nov 1750. G.

Boulin, Honor. S Apr-Jun 1739 T *Sea Nymph* to Md. M.

Boulter, Sarah. T May 1751 *Tryal*. E.

Boulton - *See* Bolton.

Bounce, Sarah. S Sep-Oct 1773 T *Justitia* Jan 1774. M.

Bounds, John. S Summer T Oct 1752. Wa.

Bourn, James. SQS Sep 1735. La.

Bowden *als* Pike, Arthur. SQS Exeter s cake Apr LC Bal Co., Md., Jul 1771. De.

Bowden, Edward. TB Aug 1735 T *Squire* LC Md Apr 1736. Db.

Bowden, Elizabeth. R for Barbados Jun 1671 but LC Md Feb 1672. L.

Bowden, John. T May 1751 *Tryal*. K.

Bowden, Richard. S Aug T from Appledore Dec 1751. Co.

Bowden, Samuel. SQS Warminster Jul 1741 LC QA Co., Md., from *Philleroy* Apr 1742. Wi.

Bowden, William *als* Hill, John. S 14 yrs Lent LC Bal Co., Md., Jul 1772. De.

Bowen, Charles. S Apr T May 1751 *Tryal*. L.

Bowen, Rachel. S Mar T Apr 1746. Sh.

Bowen, William. S Oct-Dec 1754 T *Greyhound* Feb 1755. M.

Bowen, William. S Aug T *Phoenix* Oct 1760. L.

Bowens, Oliver (1773). *See* Bower. Ha.

Bower *als* Bowens, Oliver. S Lent LC Bal Co., Md., Jun 1773. Ha.

Bowerman, Edward, an old offender. S Bristol Mar TB to Md Apr 1765. G.

Bowers, Ann. S Summer T from London Sep 1754. Wa.

Bowers, Elizabeth wife of Ralph of Manchester. SQS Jan 1724 TB Apr 1725. La.

Bowers, Robert. S Apr-May T *Saltspring* Jul 1775. M.

Bowers, Sarah. S Summer T Sep 1751 *Greyhound*. Sy.

Bowge *als* Bowse, Mary. S Jan T Feb 1719 *Worcester* to Md. L.

Bowker, John of St. Saviour Southwark. SQS Jan LC AA Co., Md., from *Thornton* Jul 1775. Sy.

Bowle, John. S & T Sep 1751 *Greyhound*. M.

Bowler, Hannah. S s at Wolstanton Summer 1750 LC Md from *Chester* Dec 1752. St.

Bowler, Mary. S Jul 1757 (RG). Ha.

Bowles (Bowels), Elizabeth. S Lent T *Thornton* May LC AA Co., Md., Jul 1774. M.

Bowles, Samuel. S Feb T *Thames* Mar 1752. L.

Bowles, Thomas. S Summer LC Bal Co., Md., Dec 1770. He.

Bowlton, Richard. S Lent T *Tryal* Jul 1754. E.

Bowman, George. SQS Bristol Aug 1753. G.

Bowman, John. S Lent T Jun 1739. Wa.

Bowman, John. S Sep-Oct T Dec 1752 *Greyhound* LC Md Apr 1753. M.

Bowman, Samuel. S Oct T *Justitia* Dec 1774. L.

Bowman, William. T *Justitia* Feb 1776. L.

Bown, Lydia. S Lent 1734. Nt.

Bown, Sarah. S 14 yrs Lent LC Bal Co., Md., Jul 1771. Do.

Bowse, Mary (1719) - *See* Bowge. L.

Bowyers, Catherine. S Apr T *Justitia* May 1745. L.

Boxall, James. S Lent s sheep R 14 yrs Summer T Aug 1749 *Thames*. Sx.

Boxall, John. S Lent LC AA Co., Md., from *Thornton* Jul 1775. Sx.

Boxall, Robert. S Lent T *Lichfield* May 1749. Sy.

Boxwell alias Baxall, William. S Jul LC Md from *William* Dec 1774 & sold to James Hutchings. Ha.

Boyce, James. SQS New Sarum Jan TB to Va Apr 1742 LC PG Co., Md. Wi.

Boyd, Denis. S Bristol Mar 1755 (AHJ). G.

Boyd, James. S Lent LC AA Co., Md., from *Thornton* Jul 1773. M.

Boylan, William of St. Saviour, Southwark. SQS Apr T Sep 1751 *Greyhound*. Sy.

Boyle, Alice. S Dec 1772 T *Justitia* Jan 1773. M.

Boyle, James. T May 1751 *Tryal*. K.

Boyle, Mark. Jul 1783 LC Bal Co., Md., Dec 1783 from *Swift*. M.

Boyle, Mary. S Nov T Dec 1752 *Greyhound* LC Md Apr 1753. L.

Boys, Stephen. S Apr 1754 (AHJ). Li.

Brace, Richard. S s geese & ducks at Hentland Aug 1770 R Lent LC Bal Co., Md., Jul 1771. He.

Brackleyhurst, William (1762) - *See* Brocklehurst. M.

Brade, James. S Jul T *Beverly* Aug 1763. M.

Bradfield, Ann (1771). *See* Barfield. M.

Bradfield, John. SQS Monmouth Oct 1738. Mo.

Bradford, Elizabeth. T Sep 1737 *Pretty Patsy*. L.

Bradford, Richard. SQS Jan LC AA Co., Md., from *Thornton* Jul 1775. M.

Bradley, Charles. S Lent LC Bal Co., Md., Jun 1773. Ha.

Bradley, Hannah. S May-Jul T Aug 1749 *Thames*. M.

Bradley, John. S Jan s sheets T Apr 1735 *Patapsco* LC Annapolis Oct 1735. M.

Bradley, John. S Summer 1736. Y.

Bradley, John. S s naval stores Summer T Aug 1749 *Thames*. K.

Bradley, John. R 14 yrs Mar 1763 (OJ). Bu.

Bradley, Joseph. T Oct 1750 *Rachael*. M.

Bradley, Richard. R Dec 1773 T *Justitia* Jan 1774. M.

Bradley, Thomas of Hornchurch. S Lent T Jul 1745 *Italian Merchant*. E.

Bradley, Thomas. S s gelding at Beaconsfield S & R 14 yrs Mar T Apr LC AA Co., Md., from *Thornton* Jul 1771. Bu.

Bradley, Thomas. S Lent 1734. No.

Bradley, Thomas. R for life Summer 1772 for being at large after sentence of T & T *Justitia* Jan 1773. Ht.

Bradshaw, William. S Lent LC AA Co., Md., from *Thornton* Jul 1775. M.

Brady, Henry of Necton. R for Barbados Aug 1671 but LC Md from *Baltimore* 1672. Nf.

Braechan, Thomas (1719) - *See* Branchin. E.

Bragg, William. S Summer 1743 LC Knt Co., Md., from *Globe* Mar 1744. De.

Bragg, William. SQS Chelmsford Jan 1755 (AHJ). E.

Brain, Elizabeth. S Feb T *Thames* Mar 1754. M.

Brainford, Thomas (1773) - *See* Brinsford. Sh.

Braley, Mary (1761) - *See* Osborne (AHJ). E.

Bramingham, Elizabeth. S Jun-Dec 1745 T *Plain Dealer* Jan 1746. M.

Bramsby *als* Bramsey, Thomas. S s clothing Apr T Dec 1735 *John* LC Annapolis Sep 1736. M.

Bramston, John. S Feb-Apr 1746 T Apr 1746 *Laura*. M.

Bramstone *als* Benham, Mary, spinster of Maidstone. S Lent T May 1750 *Lichfield*. K.

Branchin (Braechan), Thomas. T May *Margaret* LC Md Sep 1719; sold to William Orrick. E.

Brandling, Elizabeth. T *Plain Dealer* Jan 1746. M.

Branklyn, James. S Summer T *Ruby* Oct 1754. Bu.

Brannon, Catherine. T Jun 1748 *Lichfield*. M.

Brannon, Michael. R for life Dec T *Justitia* Dec 1774. M.

Branston, John. SQS Feb LC AA Co., Md., from *Thornton* Jul 1773. M.

Brassington, Samuel. S Jan-Apr T *Lichfield* May 1749. M.

Bravier, John. S Nov 1762 (AHJ). Wo.

Bray, Benjamin. S Feb T *Thames* Mar 1754. L.

Bray, James. S Lent LC AA Co., Md., from *Hanover Planter* Jul 1773. M.

Bray, Thomas. SQS Apr 1730. La.

Bray, Timothy. S Oct 1773 T *Justitia* Jan 1774. L.

Breakspear, Jane wife of John. S Lent but pardoned May 1773. M.

Bremer, Jacob. T May 1751 *Tryal*. K.

Brenan, William. T from Dublin by *Hercules*, LC Bal. Co., Md., Aug 1773, sold
to James Wilson of Augusta Co., Virginia. Ir.

Brenton, John. S Jul 1718 LC Md *from Sophia* Mar 1719. Co.

Brett, James. T May 1751 *Tryal*. E.

Brewer, Edward. S Lent 1733 LC Knt Co., Md., from *Hawk* Apr 1735. So.

Brewer, George. T Sep 1737 *Pretty Patsy*. L.

Brewer, Richard of Great Leighs. SQS Jan T *Dolphin* May 1763. E.

Brewett, William of Stepney. PT Oct 1672 R Oct 1673 LC Md from *Charles* May
1674. M.

Brewin, William. S Jun-Dec 1745 T *Plain Dealer* Jan 1746. M.

Brewton, Thomas. S 14 yrs s sheep Summer 1772 LC Bal Co., Md., Apr 1773. Wo.

Bride, Ann. S Dec 1735 T Jan 1736 *Dorsetshire* LC Va Sep 1736. M.

Bride, Thomas. S Jun-Dec 1745 T *Plain Dealer* Jan 1746. M.

Bridgen (Bridger), John. S Lent LC AA Co., Md., from *Thornton* Jul 1775. Sx.

Bridgman, Francis Swanston. SQS Bristol Dec 1774 TB May LC Md from
Isabella Jul 1775 & sold to Waters & Gartrall. G.

Bridgman, John. S May-Jun T Aug 1752 *Tryal*. M.

Bridgman, Susannah. S May-Jul T *Tayloe* Jul 1774. M.

Bridle *als* Froome, Henry. SQS & T Apr 1742 LC PG Co., Md. Do.

Briggs *als* Boys, John (William). R for Barbados Oct 1673 but LC Md from
Charles May 1674. L.

Briggs, Mary. S Pontefract Summer 1736. Y.

Briggs, Mary. S Sep T *Barnard* Oct 1756. M.

Briggs, Sarah. S May-Jul T Aug 1749 *Thames*. M.

Briggs, Thomas. S May T *Phoenix* Oct 1760. M.

Bright, Thomas. S Lent 1774 but pardoned and taken from transport ship. M.

Bright, William. S Jan-Jun T Jul 1747 *Laura*. M.

Brightman, William. S Feb-Apr T May 1751 *Tryal*. M.

Brightwell, Elizabeth. S Nov T Dec 1752 *Greyhound* LC Md Apr 1753. L.

Brightwell, William. T Summer 1745 T Feb 1746. Ha.

Brilston, Jonathan (1751). *See* Marriott. No.

Brimley, John Jr. S Lent T Jul 1747 *Laura*. Bu.

Brindley, Elizabeth. S Sep-Oct 1773 T *Justitia* Jan 1774. M.

Brindlow, Stafford. S Summer 1739 (IJ). Su.

Brinklow, John. S Aug T *Beverly* Aug 1763. L.

Brinsford [Brainford], Thomas. S & R 14 yrs Mar LC Bal Co.,Md., Jun 1773. Sh.

Briscoe, Elizabeth, spinster. SQS City Christmas 1766 (AHJ). Nl.

Brisk, John. S Summer 1721 LC Md from *Reformation* Aug 1722. De.

Brittain, Thomas. S s cock at Bredon Lent 1750 LC QA Co., Md., from *Catherine*
Nov 1750. Wo.

Broad, Robert. S Sep-Oct 1773 T *Justitia* Jan 1774. M.

Broadas, Joseph. S Oct 1773 T *Justitia* Jan 1774. L.

Broadbent, Richard. SQS Sep T *Justitia* Dec 1774. M.

Broadfield, William. S s watch at Bridgenorth Summer LC Md from *William* Dec 1774 & sold to Brittingham Dickinson. Sh.

Broadway, Edward. S Apr T Jun 1748 *Lichfield*. L.

Broadway, Robert (1724) - *See* Wright, Joseph. Sh.

Brocas, Thomas. S s gown Jan T Apr 1735 *Patapsco* LC Annapolis Oct 1735. L.

Brockell, Richard. SQS Oct T from Liverpool Nov 1772. Y.

Brockington, Philip. SQS Jul 1743 LC Knt Co., Md., from *Globe* Mar 1744. De.

Brocklehurst or Brackleyhurst, William. S May TB Nov 1762 *Prince William* but pardoned for Army service in Jamaica. M.

Brockley, Thomas. S Apr T May 1752 *Lichfield*. L.

Brockman, John. S Summer T Aug 1749 *Thames*. K.

Brockwell, Thomas. S Lent T *Dolphin* May 1763. E.

Brodfield, William. S s watch at Bridgenorth Summer LC Md from *William* Dec 1774. Sh.

Bromall [Bromwell], Thomas. S 14 yrs for receiving goods stolen by John Serjeant (*q.v.*) Lent 1769. St.

Brome, Elizabeth. S Feb-Apr T May 1752 *Lichfield*. M.

Bromidge, James. S Summer but pardoned & taken from transport ship at Bristol. Wa.

Bromley, Mary *als* wife of Francis Griffith, of St. Margaret Westminster. PT Apr R Oct 1673 LC Md from *Charles* May 1674. M.

Bronkee *als* Bunker, Abraham. S Feb T *Thames* Mar 1754. M.

Brook, William. S Summer 1718 LC Md *from Sophia* Mar 1719. De.

Brookes, Ann. S Sep-Oct T Oct 1749 *Mary*. M.

Brooks, Edward. R for life Oct 1751-Jan 1752 T *Thames* Mar 1752. M.

Brooks, George. S Mar R Apr LC Bal Co.,Md., Aug 1772 & sold to George Payne. Wi.

Brookes, Joseph. S Lent T Apr 1753. Wa.

Brooks, Joseph. S 1757 (AHJ). La.

Brooks *als* Delany, Mary. S Sep T *Phoenix* Oct 1760. M.

Brookes *als* Badger, Richard. S Lent LC Bal Co., Md., Jul 1771. St.

Brookes, Samuel. S Summer T Oct 1756. Wa.

Brookes *als* Brooker, Susanna. S Lent LC Bal Co., Md., Jul 1772. He.

Brooks, Thomas. S Lent 1736 T Lent 1737. Wa.

Brooks, Thomas. R Lent R 14 yrs Summer T Sep 1751 *Greyhound*. K.

Brookes, William. S Feb T *Thames* Mar 1752. L.

Brooks, William. S Summer LC Bal Co., Md., Dec 1770 from *Trotman* & sold to Jeremiah Johnson. No.

Brooking, Samuel. S Nov T Dec 1752 *Greyhound* LC Md Apr 1753. L.

Broom, Jeremiah. SQS Chelmsford Jan 1756 (AHJ). E.

Broom, Robert. S Lent 1758 & TB to Md. No.

Broomfield, Thomas. S & R 14 yrs Summer LC Md from *William* Dec 1774 & sold to Abram Vanbibber. O.

Broughton, William. S May-Jul T Sep 1746 *Mary*. M.

Brown *als* Morley, Mary. S Jan-Apr T *Lichfield* May 1749. M.

Brown, Andrew. S Sep-Oct 1773 T *Justitia* Jan 1774. M.

Brown, Ann. S Summer T *Barnard* Oct 1756. K.

Brown, Ann. S Sep-Oct 1773 T *Justitia* Jan 1774. M.

Brown, Benjamin. S Lent 1750 (AHJ). Wi.

Brown, Catherine. S Dec 1753-Jan 1754 T *Thames* Mar 1754. M.

Brown, Charles. T May 1751 *Tryal*. K.

Brown, Christian. S Summer T *Ruby* Oct 1754. Sy.

Brown, Edward. S Lent LC Bal Co., Md., Jul 1772. Do.

Brown, Elizabeth (1725). *See* Russell. L.

Brown, Elizabeth. S Feb-Apr T *Justitia* May 1745. M.

Brown, Elizabeth. S Feb-Apr 1751 T May 1751 *Tryal*. M.

Brown, Elizabeth. S 14 yrs Feb T *Thames* Mar 1754. M.

Brown, Elizabeth. S Sep T *Maryland Packet* Oct 1761. M.

Brown, Elizabeth (1775). *See* Hoare. M.

Brown, Francis. T Aug 1747. No.

Brown, Francis. S s horses Lent R 14 yrs Summer T *Barnard* Oct 1756. Sy.

Brown, George. SQS Apr 1750 LC QA Co., Md., from *Catherine* Nov 1750. So.

Brown, George. R Dec 1773 T *Justitia* Jan 1774. M.

Brown *als* Scott, Hannah. S Lent T *Thornton* May LC AA Co., Md., Jul 1774. L.

Brown, Henry. SQS Apr T May 1750 *Lichfield*. M.

Browne, James. S Jan-Apr T *Lichfield* May 1749. M.

Brown *als* Thompson, James. S May-Jul T Aug 1749 *Thames*. M.

Brown, James. T May 1751 *Tryal*. E.

Brown, James. S May 1751 *Tryal*. Sy.

Brown, James. S s silver tumbler at St. Mary, Stafford, Lent 1761 T *Atlas* from Bristol; found at large & pardoned for sea service Aug 1761; again found at large & to be transported for life Jul 1763 St.

Brown, James. S Lent T *Thornton* May LC AA Co., Md., Jul 1774. Sx.

Brown, Jane. S Feb T Mar 1750 *Tryal*. M.

Brown, John. S Lent LC Potomac, Va., from *Martha* Dec 1724. So.

Brown, John. SQS Apr 1728. La.

Brown, John. T 1746. Nf.

Brown, John. S Jan-Apr T *Lichfield* May 1749. M.

Brown, John. S Jul T Aug 1749 *Thames*. L.

Brown, John. S Oct-Dec 1750 T *Thames* Feb 1751. M.

Brown, John. SQS Jul T Sep 1751 *Greyhound*. M.

Brown, John *als* Henry. S Jan T *Greyhound* Feb 1755. M.

Brown, John. S Summer 1755 (AHJ). Wo.

Brown, John. S Summer T Oct 1761. Li.

Brown, John. R 14 yrs s sheep Summer 1762. Li.

Brown, John. S Summer LC Bal Co., Md., Dec 1770 from *Trotman* & sold to William Baker. Wi.

Brown, John. S Lent T *Thornton* May LC AA Co., Md., Jul 1774. L.

Brown, John. S Summer 1754 R 14 yrs Lent 1755 (WJ). Wo.

Brown, John. S s at Wolstanton Lent LC Bal Co., Md., Jul 1772. St.

Brown, Joseph. S Oct 1772 T *Justitia* Jan 1773. L.

Brown, Katherine. S Jun 1718 T Feb 1719 *Worcester* LC Annapolis Jun 1719. L.

Brown, Mark. S Lent but pardoned and taken from transport ship in April 1774. M.

Brown, Mary wife of Daniel. T for shoplifting Jan 1747. Wi.

Brown, Mary. S Oct-Dec 1750 T *Thames* Feb 1751. M.

Brown, Mary. S Oct 1751-Jan 1752 T *Thames* Mar 1752. M.

Brown, Mary. S Feb-Apr T May 1752 *Lichfield*. M.

Brown, Peter. S Sep T Nov 1746. Le.

Brown, Peter. S Oct T Oct 1749 *Mary*. L.

Brown, Peter. SQS City 1751 (AHJ). Nl.

Brown, Richard. S Lent 1773 but pardoned. L.

Brown, Robert, *als* Glenton, John. S s horse Lent 1719 R 14 yrs Summer 1721 T Oct 1723 *Forward* from London. Y.

Brown, Robert. S Lent LC Bal Co., Md., Jul 1771. De.

Brown, Robert. S Summer 1772 LC Bal Co., Md., from *Adventure* Mar 1773. Nl.

Brown, Sarah. S Sep 1740 T *Harpooner* Jan 1741. L.

Brown, Thomas. S Oct 1757. Li.

Brown, Thomas. S Jan 1763 (AHJ). E.

Brown, Thomas. S Summer 1772 T *Justitia* Jan 1773. Sy.

Brown, Thomas. S Oct T *Justitia* Dec 1774. L.

Brown, Thomas. Jul 1783 LC Bal Co., Md., Dec 1783 from *Swift*. M.

Browne, William. S Oct T Dec 1735 *John* LC Annapolis Sep 1736. L.

Brown, William. T May 1751 *Tryal*. M.

Brown, William. S Summer T Sep 1754. Wa.

Brown, William. S Jul-Sep T *Ruby* Oct 1754. M.

Brown, William. S s horse Summer 1772 LC Bal Co., Md., from *Adventure* Mar
  1773. Nl.

Brown, William. S Lent T *Thornton* May LC AA Co., Md., Jul 1774. L.

Browning, Joseph. SQS Bury St. Edmunds 1766. Su.

Browning, Joseph. S Lent LC AA Co., Md., from *Thornton* Jul 1775. M.

Broxham [Broxholm], Jane. S Summer 1765. Li.

Bruce, Charles. S Feb-Apr T May 1751 *Tryal*. M.

Bruce, John. S 14 yrs Jul-Dec 1747 LC Knt Co., Md., from *St. George* Mar 1748. M.

Brugmore, Lucy. S Aug T *Beverly* Aug 1763. L.

Brumley, Mary. S May-Jul T Sep 1746 *Mary*. M.

Bryan, Catherine. S 14 yrs Lent LC AA Co., Md., from *Hanover Planter* Jul 1773. M.

Bryan, George. S Jan T Apr 1735 *Patapsco* LC Annapolis Oct 1735. M.

Bryan, James. S Apr T *Dolphin* May 1763; wife Sarah acquitted. M.

Bryan, John. S Feb-Apr T May 1752 *Lichfield*. M.

Bryan, Stephen *als* Thomas. S Summer LC Bal Co., Md., Dec 1772. Wa.

Bryan, Thomas. S Jul 1783 LC Bal Co., Md., Dec 1783 from *Swift*. M.

Bryand *als* Bryant *als* Bryan, Rowland of St. Clement Danes. SW Apr LC AA
  Co., Md., from *Hanover Planter* Jul 1773. M.

Bryant, Ann. S Lent LC AA Co., Md., from *Thornton* Jul 1775. K.

Bryant, John. S Dec 1753-Jan 1754 T *Thames* Mar 1754. M.

Bryant, Michael. S Sep-Oct 1773 T *Justitia* Jan 1774. M.

Bryant, Patrick. SQS Sep 1771T *Justitia* Jan 1772. M.

Bryant, Samuel. SQS Jul T *Justitia* Dec 1774. M.

Bryant, Samuel. S May T *Saltspring* Jul 1775. L.

Bryant, Thomas. T *Justitia* Feb 1776. L.

Buck, George. T May 1751 *Tryal*. Sy.

Buck, John. S Lent LC AA Co., Md., from *Thornton* Jul 1775. K.

Buckeridge, James of Bermondsey. SQS Apr T May 1750 *Lichfield*. Sy.

Buckeridge, Ruth. S Jul T *Barnard* Oct 1756. M.

Buckingham, John. S Lent 1743 (GJ). Be.

Buckingham, Joseph. S s sheep at Dinton Lent LC AA Co., Md., from *Thornton*
  Jul 1775. Bu.

Buckingham, Thomas. S s sheep at Dinton Lent LC AA Co., Md., from *Thornton*
  Jul 1775. Bu.

Buckland, Thomas, *als* Buckley, Humphrey. S Jul-Sep T *Ruby* Oct 1754. M.

Buckle, Benjamin. S Jan-Jun T Jul 1747 *Laura*. M.

Buckle, Daniel of Broxbourne. S for infanticide Summer 1745 R 14 yrs Lent T
  Sep 1746 *Mary*. Ht.

Buckles, Dorothy. S Feb-Apr T *Justitia* May 1745. M.

Buckley, Butler. T Jan 1736 *Dorsetshire* LC Va Sep 1736. Sy.

Buckley, Daniel. S Dec 1750 T *Thames* Feb 1751. L.

Buckley, Elizabeth. S Lent LC Bal Co., Md., Jul 1771. Wa.

Buckley, James. S Oct 1740 T *Harpooner* Jan 1741. L.

Buckley, John. T Dec 1752 *Greyhound* LC Md Apr 1753. M.

Buckley, Joseph. S s horse Lent R 14 yrs Summer 1739. Sh.

Buckley, Thomas. S Lent 1758 & TB to Md. No.

Buckley, Timothy. R Jul TB Sep LC Md from *William* Dec 1774 & sold to James Hutchings. Wi.

Bucknole, Joseph. SQS Jan 1750 LC QA Co., Md., from *Catherine* Nov 1750. De.

Bucktrout, Martha. T Dec 1752 *Greyhound* LC Md Apr 1753. M.

Budbrook, John (1744). *See* Preston. De.

Budden, Elias. R 14 yrs Sep T *Randolph* Sep 1768. Ha.

Budwell, John. S Lent R 14 yrs Summer 1739 (IJ). Nf.

Bulbeck, Thomas. S for assault on Customs officer Summer 1773 T *Justitia* Jan 1774. Sx.

Buley, John. S Sep-Oct T Oct 1749 *Mary*. M.

Bull, John. S Summer 1773 T *Justitia* Jan 1774. Sy.

Bull, John. S Dec 1782 LC Bal Co., Md., Dec 1783 from *Swift*. L.

Bull, Susanna. T *Justitia* Jan 1774. M.

Bull, William. S Apr-Jun 1739 T *Sea Nymph* to Md. M.

Bullen, Richard. Removed from Nottingham to London & S Feb-Apr T May 1752 *Lichfield*. M.

Bullock, Catherine. S Feb T *Thames* Mar 1754. L.

Bullock, James. S Feb-Apr 1746 T Apr 1746 *Laura*. M.

Bulmer, Roger. S s sheep at North Frodingham, R 14 yrs Lent LC Md Aug 1772 & sold to Samuel Worthington. Y.

Bulney, John. S Summer 1734 R 14 yrs Feb T Apr 1735 *Patapsco* LC Annapolis Oct 1735. Sy.

Bult, Robert. R s cloth from a rack Mar LC QA Co., Md from *Catherine* Nov 1750. So.

Bulwinkle, Thomas. S Nov T Dec 1752 *Greyhound* LC Md Apr 1753. L.

Bunn, Oliver. S & R Summer T from London Sep 1754. Wa.

Bunnett, William. S Summer 1747 T *St. George* LC Knt Co., Md., Mar 1748. K.

Burbridge, Elizabeth. S Dec T *Justitia* Dec 1774. M.

Burch, Thomas. SQS Apr T May 1751 *Tryal*. M.

Burchall, Earle. SQS Warminster Summer 1741 LC QA Co., Md., from *Philleroy* Apr 1742. Wi.

Burchall, Thomas. SQS Jan LC Bal Co., Md., Jun 1771. Ch.

Burcher *als* Cane, Sarah. S Jun 1718. L.

Burchett, John of Mitcham. SQS Oct 1773 T *Justitia* Jan 1774. Sy.

Burchett, Mary. S Sep 1740 T *Harpooner* Jan 1741. L.

Burdell, James. S Lent T *Thornton* May LC AA Co., Md., Jul 1774. M.

Burden, John. S Summer 1739 T Jan 1740. Le.

Burford, Thomas. S Lent LC Bal Co., Md., Jul 1774. Wi.

Burge, John. Indicted Jul 1752 for returning from transportation. G.

Burge *als* Shelton, Mary. S Summer T Sep 1751 *Greyhound*. Sy.

Burge, Thomas Jr. S Lent LC Bal Co., Md., Jun 1773. So.

Burgess, Edward. S & T Aug 1752 *Tryal*. L.

Burgess, Elizabeth wife of Samuel. S Sep-Dec 1746 T Jan 1747 *George William*. M.

Burgess, Hannah. S Apr T May 1747. So.

Burgess, John. S Lent T Jul 1745 *Italian Merchant*. Sy.

Burgess, John (1773). *See* Evans. St.

Burgess, John. S Dec 1782 LC Bal Co., Md., Dec 1783 from *Swift*. L.

Burgiss, Joseph. S Feb-Apr T May 1752 *Lichfield*. M.

Burk, Ann. S May-Jun T Aug 1752 *Tryal*. M.

Burk, Catherine. S Feb-Apr 1746 T Apr 1746 *Laura*. M.

Burke, Catherine. Jul 1783 LC Bal Co., Md., Dec 1783 from *Swift*. L.

Burk, Walter. T from Dublin by *Hercules*, LC Bal. Co., Md., Aug 1773, sold to William Walters & Richard Guttrell of Frederick Co. Ir.

Burk, William. S Lent T May 1750 *Lichfield*. K.

Burke *als* Johnson, William. S Mar LC Bal Co.,Md Jun 1773. Ha.

Burle, Jane. S Jan T *Plain Dealer* Jan 1746. M.

Burleigh, Thomas. SQS & T *Justitia* Feb 1776. M.

Burling, Michael. S Feb-Apr T May 1751 *Tryal*. M.

Burling, Thomas. S Sep-Oct 1772 T *Justitia* Jan 1773. M.

Burne, George. S Feb-Apr 1746 T Apr 1746 *Laura*. M.

Burn, Jeremiah. S May-Jul T *Tayloe* Jul 1774. M.

Burn, Lawrence. T *Thames* Feb 1751. M.

Burn, Mary, spinster. S City Summer 1756 (AHJ). Nl.

Burn, Mary. S Oct T *Phoenix* Oct 1760. M.

Burn, Patrick. S Dec 1749-Jan 1750 T Mar 1750 *Tryal*. M.

Burn, Patrick. S Aug T *Beverly* Aug 1763. L.

Burn, Tanglis. S Summer T *Barnard* Oct 1756. Ht.

Burn, Thomas. R Jul T *Tayloe* Jul 1773. M.

Burn, Timothy. S Lent LC AA Co., Md., from *Thornton* Jul 1773. M.

Burne, Tobias. S Dec 1745 T *Plain Dealer* Jan 1746. L.

Burn, Walter, mariner. S Bristol s silver tankard Sep 1759 (BJ). G.

Burn, William. S May-Jul T Sep 1746 *Mary*. M.

Burnby, Thomas. S s sheep Summer 1755 R 14 yrs Lent 1756 & TB to Md. No.

Burnell, Thomas. S Jan 1751 T *Thames* Feb 1751. L.

Burnett, Elizabeth. S Jan-Apr T *Lichfield* May 1749. M.

Burnet, Mary. T Apr 1761. De.

Burnet, Robert. S s mare Lent 1721 R Jul T Oct 1723. Y.

Burnett, William. S 14 yrs & T *Tayloe* Jul 1774. L.

Burnham, John. S Dec 1750 T *Thames* Feb 1751. L.

Burnham, John. SQS Feb LC AA Co., Md., from *Thornton* Jul 1773. M.

Burnham, Mary. S Sep-Oct 1773 T *Justitia* Jan 1774. M.

Burnham, Solomon. S Lent T *Thornton* May LC AA Co., Md., Jul 1774. Sy.

Burrell, George *als* Black George *als* Othello. S Lent LC Bal Co., Md., Jul 1772. Wi.

Burrell, Mathew. S Summer T Oct 1739. Hu.

Burrill, Thomas. S Lent LC AA Co., Md., from *Thornton* Jul 1773. M.

Burrell, Thomas. S for highway robbery at Hardwick & R for life Summer 1773 T *Justitia* Jan 1774. Bu.

Burridge, Archibald. SQS & T *Justitia* Feb 1776. M.

Burridge, Robert. S for highway robbery & R for life Nov 1750 T *Thames* Feb 1751. M.

Burridge, Thomas. S Mar T *Amity* Sep 1735 LC QA Co., Md., Mar 1736. So.

Burrough, Samuel. S Dec 1754 T *Greyhound* Feb 1755. L.

Burrows, Benjamin. S for highway robbery & R Lent LC Md from *Isabella* Jul 1775 & sold to Waters & Gartrall. Wa.

Burrows, Richard. S 14 yrs Lent LC Bal Co., Md., Jun 1773. St.

Burse, Bridges. S Lent 1734. Li.

Burt, Ann. S Jan T May 1746. Wi.

Burt, Robert. S Mar 1736. Do.

Burt, Robert. S Lent T Nov 1746. Do.

Burton, Abraham. S Feb T *Neptune* Mar 1761. L.

Burton, Benjamin. R & T Feb 1748. O.

Burton, Catherine. S May T *Beverly* Aug 1763. M.

Burton, Edmund. R 14 yrs Oct 1772 T *Justitia* Jan 1773. M.

Burton, Elizabeth. AT Jul T Sep 1720 LC Annapolis Md Jun 1723 from *Forward* (NM). No.

Burton, William. S Lent T Apr 1758 *Lux* from London. Db.

Burwell, Richard *als* Nash, John. S 14 yrs Lent LC AA Co., Md., from *Thornton* Jul 1773. K.

Bury, ----. SQS Apr 1735. La.

Bury, William. S Lent R 14 yrs Summer T *Maryland Packet* Oct 1761. E.

Busby, Elizabeth, spinster of St. George, Southwark. SQS Apr T Sep 1751 *Greyhound*. Sy.

Busby, John. SQS Feb T Mar 1750 *Tryal*. M.

Busby, William. S Dec 1782 LC Bal Co., Md., Dec 1783 from *Swift*. L.

Bush, Ann. S Jan T *Neptune* Mar 1761. M.

Bush *als* Bertie, Elizabeth. S & T 14 yrs Aug 1752 *Tryal*. L.

Bush, Margaret. S & T 14 yrs Aug 1752 *Tryal*. L.

Bush, Martha. S & T Aug 1752 *Tryal*. L.

Bush, Mary. S Lent R 14 yrs Summer 1742 (IJ). Su.

Bush, Nathaniel. S Jun 1718 T Feb 1719 *Worcester* but died on passage. L.

Bush, Richard. SQS Bury St. Edmunds Jan 1724 but discharged by King's pardon before transportation. Su.

Bushman, Armenia. SQS &T *Justitia* Feb 1776. M.

Butcher, John. S Lent LC Potomac, Va., from *Martha* Dec 1724. De.

Butcher, John. S Lent T *Thornton* May LC AA Co., Md., Jul 1774. M.

Butcher, Judith. S Jan T Mar 1750 *Tryal*. L.

Butcher, Richard of Lambeth. SQS Jan T *Thames* Feb 1751. Sy.

Butcher, Susanna. S Feb T *Thames* Mar 1752. L.

Butcher, Thomas. S Dec 1772 T *Justitia* Jan 1773. M.

Butler, Abigail. S Apr T May 1749 *Lichfield*. L.

Butler, Alice wife of William. S May-Jul T Sep 1746 *Mary*. M.

Butler, Carolina. S Dec 1754 T *Greyhound* Feb 1755. L.

Butler, Charles. S Jan T *Tryal* Mar 1757. L.

Butler, Edward. S May-Jul T *Tayloe* Jul 1773; runaway. M.

Butler, Elizabeth, spinster, *als* wife of William Longman. R for Barbados Oct 1673 but LC Md from *Charles* May 1674. L.

Butler, George. S Feb T *Thames* Mar 1754. L.

Butler, John. R for life Lent T *Tayloe* Jul 1773. Sy.

Butler, Joseph. T *Justitia* Jan 1774. L.

Butler, Thomas. S Jan-Jun T Jul 1747 *Laura*; runaway. M.

Butler, Thomas. T from Dublin by *Hercules*, LC Bal. Co., Md., Aug 1773, sold to William Walters & Richard Guttrel. Ir.

Butler, William. T *Saltspring* Jul 1775. M.

Butsell (Botsell), William. S Feb T Mar 1729 *Patapsco* LC Annapolis Dec 1729. M.

Butt, William. S Bristol s gelding at Bisley Mar & R 14 yrs Summer T *Restoration* LC Bal Co., Md., Oct 1771. G.

Buttenshaw, Thomas. S Lent T May 1750 *Lichfield*. E.

Butterfield, Abraham. S Dec T *Justitia* Dec 1774. L.

Butters, William. S Summer T Oct 1750 *Rachael*. K.

Butterworth, Joseph. S Feb-Apr T May 1752 *Lichfield*. M.

Butterworth, Robert of Castleton. SQS Oct 1718. La.

Butterworth, Thomas. S Apr 1757. Li.

Button, Mary. S 14 yrs for receiving Lent LC Md from *Elizabeth* Jun 1775. Wa.
Button, Richard. S Jan 1754 (AHJ). E.
Butts, William. S Lent LC AA Co., Md., from *Thornton* Jul 1775. L.
Byall, John. S Dec 1750 T *Thames* Feb 1751. L.
Byatt, Elizabeth. S Lent T *Tryal* Jul 1754. Ht.
Byde, Mary. S Feb T *Thames* Mar 1754. L.
Byles, John. S for highway robbery Lent R 14 yrs Summer 1753 & TB to Va. No.
Bym *als* Bom, William. T *George William* Nov 1743. M.
Byrne, Anthony. R & T Apr 1735 *Patapsco* LC Annapolis Oct 1735. M.
Byrne, Arthur. R Oct 1772 T *Justitia* Jan 1773. M.
Byrom *als* Byron, William. S s stockings Jul 1735 T Jan 1736 *Dorsetshire* LC Va Sep 1736. M.
Bywell, Robert. SQS Richmond Jan 1744. Y.

Cabbage, Edward (1733) - *See* Powers. LM.
Cable, Elizabeth. SQS Ipswich 1758. Su.
Cable, Isabella. S Feb-Apr T *Justitia* May 1745. M.
Cadman, James. S Lent LC Md from *Elizabeth* Jun 1775. Wa.
Cadman, Thomas. S Lent 1735. No.
Cadugan, Philip. SQS Jan 1772 LC Bal Co., Md., Jun 1773. De.
Cahill, Thomas. T from Dublin by *Hercules*, LC Bal. Co., Md., Aug 1773, sold to William Walters & Richard Guttrell. Ir.
Cain *als* Kayne, Patrick. S Apr T May 1751 *Tryal*. L.
Cain, Ann. S Lent R 14 yrs Summer 1752 (BJ). So.
Cakebread, John. S Jul 1771 (HJ). O.
Caldwell, John. S Lent T May 1754. St.
Calebna, Jane (1773). *See* Uren. Co.
Calendar, Robert. S Lent R 14 yrs & T Sep 1761. De.
Calkin, Timothy. S Apr T Dec 1735 *John* LC Annapolis Sep 1736. M.
Callden, Robert. S May-Jun T Aug 1752 *Tryal*. M.
Calleson, Joan, widow. S Plymouth Jul 1759 (AHJ). De.
Calyhan, John. S Jun T *Maryland Packet* Oct 1761. M.
Callihan, John. SWK Oct 1772 T *Justitia* Jan 1773. K.
Callow, Agatha. S s from mansion house Lent R 14 yrs Nov 1724. Su.
Callup, Alice? of Manchester, spinster. SQS Jan 1730. La.
Camell *als* Masey, William. S Mar T Apr 1746. Sh.
Cameron, John. S Lent T 14 yrs Summer 1747 LC Knt Co., Md., from *St. George* Mar 1748. Sy.
Cameron, John. T 14 yrs Jan 1748. Sy.
Cammell, George. S Jan T Mar 1750 *Tryal*. L.
Cammen, Elizabeth. S Apr T May 1747. So.
Camp, Thomas. R 14 yrs Jul 1721 LC Md from *Reformation* Aug 1722. De.
Camp, William. R 14 yrs Mar 1721 LC Md from *Reformation* Aug 1722. De.
Campbell, Alexander. SQS Jan 1726. La.
Campbell, Charles. T for life Aug 1752 *Tryal*. Sy.
Campbell, Edward. S Apr-Jun 1739 to be T 14 yrs T *Sea Nymph* to Md. M.
Campbell, Hugh. S Jan-Apr T Jun 1748 *Lichfield*. M.
Campbell *als* Wilson, Jane. SQS City 1751 (AHJ). Nl.
Campbell, John. S s horse July 1723 R 14 yrs Jul 1723. Y.
Campbell, Peter. S & T Mar 1750 *Tryal*. L.
Campbell, Robert. S Lent T *Thornton* May LC AA Co., Md., May 1774. M.

Campbell, Timothy. T from Dublin by *Hercules*, LC Bal. Co., Md., Aug 1773, sold to William Walters & Richard Guttrell. Ir.

Campion, George. S Lent 1741 (IJ). Su.

Campion, Hyder. S Sep-Oct 1775 T *Justitia* Feb 1776. M.

Cane, James. S Lent T May 1749 *Lichfield*. K.

Cane, Robert of St. Margaret Westminster. SW Jan LC AA Co., Md., from *Thornton* Jul 1775. M.

Cane, Sarah (1718) - *See* Burcher. L.

Cane, Thomas. S Sep 1740 T *Harpooner* Jan 1741. L.

Cane, William. S Jan-Apr T *Lichfield* May 1749. M.

Canfield, Thomas of St. Saviour, Southwark. SQS Jan T *Tayloe* Jul 1773. Sy.

Cannew, James. S Sep-Dec 1746 T Jan 1747 *George William*. M.

Canning, Elizabeth. S Jul 1754, married in Philadelphia, returned to England in 1761 & received £500 in legacy from Mrs. Honeywood of Newington Green in 1761 (BG). L.

Cannon, Bridget. SQS Sep T *Justitia* Dec 1774. M.

Cantrell, Joseph. S Summer 1772, died on passage to Va on *Trimly* 1773. Db.

Cape, Joseph. S Jun T Jul 1747 *Laura*. L.

Capell, Mary. S Jan-Jun T Jul 1747 *Laura*. M.

Capon, Robert. S Lent 1765. Li.

Cappock, John. S Lent T May 1749 *Lichfield*. Ht.

Cardell, William. R & T 14 yrs Feb 1740 *York*. L.

Cardiff, Thomas of St. Martin in Fields. SW Lent LC AA Co., Md., from *Hanover Planter* Jul 1773. M.

Cardinall, Thomas. S Apr-May T *Tryal* Jul 1754. M.

Care, Henry. SQS Launceston May 1763 (AHJ). Co.

Care, William. S Summer 1729 R 14 yrs Feb 1730. Wi.

Cary, Henry. S Apr-Jun 1739 T *Sea Nymph* to Md. M.

Carey, James. S s at Week & Abston Lent TB Mar LC QA Co.,Md from *Catherine* Nov 1750. G.

Carey, James. T Aug 1752 *Tryal*. M.

Carey, Margaret. S Oct T *Justitia* Dec 1774. L.

Cargrove, Nicholas. T from Dublin by *Hercules*, LC Bal. Co., Md., Aug 1773, sold to James Wilson of Augusta Co., Virginia. Ir.

Carle, Thomas. S Aug T *Phoenix* Oct 1760. L.

Carmichael, Mary. S Sep-Oct T Oct 1749 *Mary*. M.

Carmody, Michael. S Sep 1772 T *Justitia* Jan 1773. M.

Carnall, Samuel. S Epiphany TB Sep 1750 (AHJ). Db.

Carne, John. S s box of goods Aug 1755 (BJ). G.

Carnegie, John. S Summer T Sep 1746. Ha.

Carnes, Amos. S Lent T *Lichfield* May 1749. Sy.

Carnes, Mary. S Jul-Dec 1747 T *St. George* Jan LC Knt Co., Md., Mar 1748. M.

Carnes, Thomas. T Sep 1737 *Pretty Patsy*. L.

Carney, John. SQS Dec 1772 LC AA Co., Md., from Thornton Jul 1773. M.

Carney, Michael. S Feb T *Thames* Mar 1754. M.

Carpenter, Joseph. S s sheep Summer 1772 T *Justitia* Jan 1773. K.

Carpenter, Martha. S Lent 1775 but pardoned and removed from transport ship. L.

Carr, Ann. S Apr-May T *Tryal* Jul 1754. M.

Carr, Elizabeth. S Dec 1745 T *Plain Dealer* Jan 1746. L.

Carr, George. S 14 yrs s cow at Tickhill Lent LC Bal Co., Md., Dec 1770 from *Trotman* & sold to William Randall. Y.

Carr, John. S Apr T May 1752 *Lichfield*. L.

MORE EMIGRANTS IN BONDAGE

Carr, Lewis. S Lent LC AA Co., Md., from *Thornton* Jul 1775. M.

Carr, Priscilla. S Oct-Dec 1750 T *Thames* Feb 1751. M.

Carr, William of St. Olave, Southwark. SQS Oct 1750 T *Thames* Feb 1751. Sy.

Carr, William. T from Dublin by *Hercules*, LC Bal. Co., Md., Aug 1773, sold to William Walters & Richard Guttrell. Ir.

Carradice, Mary (1749) - *See* Kethering. Db.

Carragan, James. S Lent LC AA Co., Md., from *Hanover Planter* Jul 1773. L.

Carrodice *als* Bateman, John. S Summer 1746 T 1747. Db.

Carroll *als* Dutton, Andrew. S Sep-Oct T Dec 1752 *Greyhound* LC Md Apr 1753. M.

Carroll, Ann. S Feb-Apr T May 1752 *Lichfield*. M.

Carrol, Bridget (1774). *See* Barnes. Sy.

Carroll, Jane. S Jan T *Tryal* Mar 1757. L.

Carroll, John. R Sep T for life Oct 1750 *Rachael*. M.

Carroll, John. S Jan T *Thames* Feb 1751. M.

Carroll, Timothy. S Apr-May T *Tryal* Jul 1754. M.

Carryson, Sarah. S Jan 1759 (AHJ). E.

Carsey, Jeremiah. S Jan-Apr T *Lichfield* May 1749. M.

Cartee, William. S Lent 1733. Le.

Carter, Ann. S Feb-Apr T May 1752 *Lichfield*. M.

Carter, Elizabeth. S Jun T *Tryal* Jul 1754. L.

Carter, George. S 14 yrs Summer 1732 LC Knt Co., Md., from *Falcon* Mar 1733. Do.

Carter, Henry. S Lent LC Potomac, Va., from *Martha* Dec 1724. Wi.

Carter, James. S Jul T Sep 1746 *Mary*. L.

Carter, James. S Lent LC AA Co., Md., from *Thornton* Jul 1773. L.

Carter, Jane. S Feb-Apr 1746 T Apr 1746 *Laura*. M.

Carter, John. S 14 yrs Lent LC AA Co., Md., from *Thornton* Jul 1775. E.

Carter, Joseph. S s wheat at Skenfrith Mar LC Bal Co.,Md Jul 1772. Mo.

Carter, Martha. S Lent T *Lichfield* May 1749. Sy.

Carter, Mary. S Jul T *Tayloe* Jul 1773. L.

Carter, Nathaniel. S for grand larceny Lent T May 1750 *Lichfield*. Ht.

Carter, Philip. S 14 yrs LC AA Co., Md., from *Thornton* Jul 1775 E.

Carter, Robert. S for life Jan T *Justitia* May 1745. L.

Carter, Robert. S Southwark Lent T *Thornton* May LC AA Co., Md., Jul 1774. Sy.

Carter, Sarah. S Bristol Lent 1743 LC Knt Co., Md., from *Raven* Feb 1744. G.

Carter, Thomas. S Feb-Apr T May 1751 *Tryal*. M.

Carter, Timothy. S Lent R 14 yrs Summer 1756 (RG). Be.

Carter, William. Pardoned for T on petition of inhabitants of Hoddesdon Apr T Oct 1723 *Forward*. Ht.

Carter, William. S May T Jul 1745 *Italian Merchant*. M.

Carter, William. SWK Jan LC AA Co., Md., from *Thornton* May 1771. K.

Cartwright, Ann. S Apr-May T *Tryal* Jul 1754. M.

Cartwright, Matthew. S & T Aug 1752 *Tryal*. L.

Carty, Daniel. T from Dublin by *Hercules*, LC Bal. Co., Md., Aug 1773, sold to James Wilson of Augusta, Virginia. Ir.

Carver, Ann. S May T *Beverly* Aug 1763. M.

Carver, John. R for life Feb T May 1758. Ha.

Carwithen, Mary. S Aug 1731 LC Md from *Falcon* Apr 1732. De.

Carwithy, Thomas. SQS Apr 1737 LC Knt Co., Md., from *Hawk* Nov 1737. Co.

Cary - *See* Carey.

Case, James. SQS Bridport Oct 1732 LC Md from *Falcon* Mar 1733. Do.

Caseley, Samuel. S Apr s iron bars T Dec 1735 *John* LC Annapolis Sep 1736. L.

Casemore, Richard. S Mar T Apr 1737. Wa.

Casemore, William. S Mar T Apr 1737. Wa.

Casey, John. S Oct T Oct 1749 *Mary*. L.

Casey, John. S Jul T *Beverly* Aug 1763. M.

Casey, John. SQS Feb LC AA Co., Md., from *Thornton* Jul 1775. M.

Casey, Mary. S Lent LC AA Co., Md., from *Thornton* Jul 1773. M.

Cash, James. T Lent 1750. Li.

Cash, Robert. S Lent 1737. Li.

Cashbolt, John. S Jan T *Greyhound* Feb 1755. M.

Cashmore, Edward. S Summer LC Bal Co., Md., Dec 1772. Wa.

Cason, Barnard. S Dec 1745 T *Plain Dealer* Jan 1746. L.

Cass, Thomas. S Lent LC Potomac, Va., from *Martha* Dec 1724. Do.

Cassander, William. S Oct-Dec 1754 T *Greyhound* Feb 1755. M.

Castelow, Thomas. S Jan T *Plain Dealer* Jan 1746. L.

Castle, Eleanor. S Sep-Oct T Dec 1752 *Greyhound* LC Md Apr 1753. M.

Castle, John. S May T *Saltspring* Jul 1775. L.

Castleton, Robert. R for Barbados Sep 1672 but LC Md Jun 1673. L.

Caswell, John. S Apr T May 1749 *Lichfield*. L.

Catenach, William. S Lent R for life Summer LC Md from *William* Dec 1774 &
    sold to James Hutchings. G.

Cato, William. SQS Apr LC AA Co., Md., from *Hanover Planter* Jul 1773. M.

Caton *als* Cathorne, Jane. S Jun-Dec 1745 T *Plain Dealer* Jan 1746. M.

Caton, Nicholas. SW Lent LC AA Co., Md., from *Hanover Planter* Jul 1773. M.

Catstre, Vincent. T Apr 1742 LC PG Co., Md. Wo.

Catterton, Robert. S Lent 1735. Y.

Cattle, John. S May 1759 (AHJ). Co.

Catton, John of Stepney, Mddx. R Sep 1671 AT May 1672 & Oct 1673 LC AA
    Co. Md 1674. M.

Cave, Patrick. S 14 yrs Jan T *Plain Dealer* Jan 1746. M.

Cavenagh, Hannah. S Lent LC AA Co., Md., from *Thornton* May 1771. L.

Cavendish, Margaret. S Apr T May 1752 *Lichfield*. L.

Cavill, William. S Apr T May 1747. So.

Cawley, Thomas Jr. S Lent 1751 (AHJ). Wi.

Cayton, William. S Lent LC AA Co., Md., from *Thornton* Jul 1773. M.

Certain, Daniel. S May 1754 (AHJ). Co.

Chadwick, John. S Apr T Jun 1748 *Lichfield*. L.

Chalkley, Thomas. S for perjury May T *Saltspring* Jul 1775. L.

Chamberlain, Richard. R 14 yrs Jul 1746 TB Jan 1747 T *St. George* LC Knt Co.,
    Md., Mar 1748. Wi.

Chamberlain, Samuel. S Lent LC Bal Co., Md., Jul 1772. So.

Chambers, Elizabeth. SQS Bristol s clothes Sep 1757 (BJ). G.

Chambers, John. S Summer 1733 R Lent 1734. Mo.

Chambers, John. T Oct 1750 *Rachael*. M.

Chambers, Margaret. S Sep T *Barnard* Oct 1756. M.

Chambers, Mary. S Jul T *Maryland Packet* Oct 1761. L.

Chambers, Thomas. S 14 yrs for receiving Lent T Apr 1773 TB to Md.. No.

Chambers, William. S 14 yrs Lent 1774 LC AA Co., Md., from *Thornton* Jul 1775.
    Bu.

Chameron, Mary Catherine. S Lent LC AA Co., Md., from *Thornton* Jul 1773. M.

Champion, John. S s mare at Marshfield Summer 1737 R 14 yrs & TB Mar 1738. G.

Chandler, Mary. S & R Lent 1735 T Jan 1736 *Dorsetshire* LC Va Sep 1736. Bu.

Chaplin, Samuel. S. Summer 1731 LC Knt Co., Md., from *Falcon* Apr 1732. So.

Chaplow, James. S Lent T May 1750 *Lichfield*. K.

Chapman, Charles. T May 1752 *Lichfield*. Ht.

Chapman, Isabella of Wellingborough. S Jul 1720 for shoplifting & whipped, died 1721 on passage in *Gilbert* (NM). No.

Chapman, Jacob. S Lent T May 1752 *Lichfield*. Sy.

Chapman, John. S Apr T May 1749 *Lichfield*. L.

Chapman, John. S Lent T May 1752 *Lichfield*. Sy.

Chapman, Mary. T 1745. Y.

Chapman, Peter. S Feb-Apr T *Justitia* May 1745. M.

Chapman Richard. SQS Apr 1772 LC Bal Co., Md., Dec 1772. Co.

Chapman, Robert. S Sep 1750 T Jan 1751. Ha.

Chapman, Samuel. S Lent T *Thornton* May LC AA Co., Md., Jul 1774. L.

Chapman, Stephen. S Lent LC AA Co., Md., from *Thornton* Jul 1775. M.

Chapman, Stephen. S Jan-Feb LC Md Jul T *Saltspring* Jul 1775. M.

Chapman, William. SQS Jan 1772 LC Bal Co., Md., from *Adventure* Mar 1773, sold to Vincent Trapnall. Hu.

Chapman, William. T Jun 1747. E.

Chapman, William. T May 1751 *Tryal*. K.

Chappell, Grace. SQS Warminster Jul TB Sep 1741 LC QA Co., Md from *Philleroy* Apr 1742. Wi.

Chapple als Sampson, Ambrose. S Summer 1731 LC Knt Co., Md., from *Falcon* Apr 1732. So.

Chaple, Henry. T Apr 1735 *Patapsco* LC Annapolis Oct 1735. E.

Chappel, John. SQS Exeter Apr 1749 (AHJ). De.

Chapple, Joseph. S Lent 1737 LC Knt Co., Md., from *Hawk* Nov 1737. De.

Charles, John. R 14 yrs Jul T *Tayloe* Jul 1774. M.

Charlock or Chelew, Nicholas. SQS Jul 1737 LC QA Co., Md., from *Amity* Apr 1738. Co.

Chatham, Ann. S Dec 1773 T *Justitia* Jan 1774. M.

Cheek, William. T Jun 1747. Ha.

Cheeke, William. S Lent T *Tryal* Jul 1754. Sy.

Cheer, John. S 14 yrs as food rioter in Abingdon Dec 1766 (OJ). Be.

Chelcote, John [Joan]. S s in St. Philip & Jacob parish Lent R 14 yrs Summer 1739 (SP). G.

Chelew, Nicholas. S for perjury Mar 1734 LC Knt Co., Md, from *Falcon* Mar 1735. Co.

Chelew, Nicholas (1737). *See* also Charlock. Co.

Cheney, William. S Lent T *Thornton* May LC AA Co., Md., Jul 1774. E.

Cherey, John. S Apr T Sep 1751. Sy.

Cherry, William. S Jul T *Tayloe* Jul 1773. L.

Chessam, Thomas. S Dec 1749-Jan 1750 T Mar 1750 *Tryal*. M.

Chester, Mary. S Jan T *Thames* Feb 1751. M.

Cheswell [Chiswell], William. S Mar s colt at High Clare, Hants, & TB Aug 1738. G.

Cheventum, Thomas of Low Leyton. S Lent T Jul 1745 *Italian Merchant*. E.

Chevys, George. S May-Jul T *Tayloe* Jul 1774. M.

Chew, William. S 14 yrs Lent LC Bal Co., Md., Jun 1773. G.

Chilcott, John. S for highway robbery Summer R 14 yrs Nov 1724 T Apr 1725 *Sukey* LC Md Sep 1725. Bu.

Chilcot, John. S Lent 1750 LC QA Co., Md., from *Catherine* Nov 1750. So.

Child, Edward. S Feb-Apr T May 1752 *Lichfield*. M.

Child, Henry. S May-Jun T Aug 1752 *Tryal*. M.

Child, John. S May-Jun T Aug 1752 *Tryal*. M.

Child, Richard. S Lent AT Jul 1761. Sh.

Childs, William. S Lent T *Thornton* May LC AA Co., Md., Jul 1774; runaway. M.

Chillingworth, Isabella. S 14 yrs for receiving Mar 1763 (OJ). Wo.

Chilman, George Jr. S Lent LC AA Co., Md., from *Thornton* May 1771. K.

Chilton, John. S for perjury Dec 1773 T *Justitia* Jan 1774. L.

Chinery, John of Stanningfield, incorrigible rogue. SQS Bury St. Edmunds 1766. Su.

Chinn, Robert. SW Jan LC AA Co., Md., from *Thornton* Jul 1775. M.

Chisling, William. T Jun 1747. E.

Chittey, Simon. S Apr T May 1752 *Lichfield*. L.

Chorey, John of St. George, Southwark. SQS Apr T Sep 1751 *Greyhound*. Sy.

Chresty, James. S May-Jul T *Tayloe* Jul 1773. M.

Christian, Hannah. S Apr T May 1749 *Lichfield*. L.

Christian, John. T from Dublin by *Hercules*, LC Bal. Co., Md., Aug 1773, sold to James Wilson of Augusta Co., Va. Ir.

Christopher, John. S Jan T *Greyhound* Feb 1755. M.

Christopher, John. S Lent LC AA Co., Md., from *Hanover Planter* Jul 1773. M.

Christie *als* Ware, Agnes. S Jul s silver spoon T Dec 1735 *John* LC Annapolis Sep 1736. M.

Christy, Elizabeth. S Lent R 14 yrs Summer T *Phoenix* Oct 1760. Sy.

Chubb, Honor. S Summer 1731 LC Knt Co., Md., from *Falcon* Apr 1732. De.

Chubb, John. S Lent LC Knt Co., Md., from *Unity* Nov 1733. De.

Church, Elizabeth. S May-Jul T Sep 1746 *Mary*. M.

Church, John. S & R 7 yrs s sheep Summer T Sep 1773 TB to Md. No.

Churchill, Jane wife of William. S Summer 1732 LC Knt Co., Md., from *Falcon* Mar 1733. Do.

Churchman, Walter of St. Margaret Westminster. SW Jun 1775 but respited. M.

Claridge, James. S s horse Summer 1753 R 14 yrs Lent T Apr 1754. Wa.

Clark, Alice. S Feb T *Neptune* Mar 1761. L.

Clarke, Andrew. S Jan-Apr T *Lichfield* May 1749. M.

Clarke, Ann. S Feb T *Thames* Mar 1754. M.

Clarke *als* Green, Ann. S May-Jul T *Tayloe* Jul 1774. M.

Clarke, Arabella. S Dec 1735 s gown T Jan 1736 *Dorsetshire* LC Va Sep 1736. M.

Clark, David. S Lent T *Lichfield* May 1749. Sy.

Clarke, Edmund. S for life Lent LC AA Co., Md., from *Thornton* Jul 1773. K.

Clark, Eleanor. S City 1760 (AHJ). Nl.

Clark, Elijah. S Lent T *Thornton* May LC AA Co., Md., Jul 1774. L.

Clarke, Emanuel. S Oct 1751-Jan 1752 R for life & T *Thames* Mar 1752. M.

Clarke, George. S Feb T *Thames* Mar 1754. L.

Clarke, Isabel wife of Robert. S City 1751 (AHJ). Nl.

Clarke, James. S Summer 1718 LC from *Sophia* QA Co., Md. Mar 1719. De.

Clarke, James. R 14 yrs Jul 1746 TB Jan 1747 T *St. George* LC Knt Co., Md., Mar 1748. Wi.

Clarke, James. SQS & T May 1750 *Lichfield*. Ht.

Clarke, James. S 1753 TB to Va. No.

Clark, James. S Summer T Oct 1756. No.

Clark, James. SQS Apr T *Thornton* May LC AA Co., Md., Jul 1774. M.

Clarke, Jane. S for housebreaking May 1721 (NM). No.

Clarke, John. S 14 yrs for receiving goods stolen at Huntingdon Feb T Apr 1735 *Patapsco* LC Md Oct 1735. M.

Clarke, John. S Oct 1740 T *Harpooner* Jan 1741. L.

Clarke, John (brother of William, Thomas & Walter *q.v.*). S s geese Lent 1742. St.

Clarke, John. SQS Jan 1750 LC QA Co., Md., from *Catherine* Nov 1750. De.

Clark, John of St. Olave, Southwark. S Summer T Oct 1750 *Rachael*. Sy.

Clark, John. T May 1751 *Tryal*. Sx.

Clarke, John. SQS 1753 TB to Md. No.

Clark *als* Checkley, John. S s mare Lent R 14 yrs Summer 1755 TB to Va. No.

Clarke, John. S Lent 1763 (AHJ). E.

Clarke, John. S s sheep Lent R 14 yrs Summer T *Justitia* Sep 1767. Bu.

Clark, John. S Lent T *Thornton* May LC AA Co., Md., Jul 1774. M.

Clarke, John. S Lent LC AA Co., Md., from *Thornton* Jul 1775. Sx.

Clarke, Joseph. S Lent 1732 LC Knt Co., Md., from *Falcon* Mar 1733. De.

Clarke, Joseph. S Lent T Apr 1739. Le.

Clark, Joseph. SQS Exeter Oct 1754 (AHJ). De.

Clarke, Leonard. S for assault in St. James Park Feb T *Tryal* Mar 1757. M.

Clarke *als* Grigge, Margaret. S 14 yrs Jul-Sep T *Ruby* Oct 1754. M.

Clark *als* Bush, Mary. LC Va Sep 1736 from *Dorsetshire*. X.

Clarke, Mary of St. Nicholas, Colchester, widow. SQS Jul 1747 LC Knt Co., Md., from *St. George* Mar 1748. E.

Clarke, Mary. S Jan-Apr T Jun 1748 *Lichfield*. M.

Clarke, Mary. S Jan-Apr T *Lichfield* May 1749. M

Clarke, Mary. S Apr T Sep 1751. Sy.

Clarke, Mary. S Apr-May T *Tryal* Jul 1754: one of this name arrested in 1758 for returning from transportation. M.

Clark, Mary. T *Justitia* Jan 1773. M.

Clark, Mary. T from Dublin by *Hercules*, LC Bal. Co., Md., Aug 1773, sold to James Wilson of Augusta Co., Virginia. Ir.

Clarke, Phillis. S Lent LC Bal Co., Md., Jul 1771. De.

Clarke, Richard. S Lent LC AA Co., Md., from *Thornton* Jul 1775. Bu.

Clark, Robert. S City 1751 (AHJ). Nl.

Clark, Samuel. S Summer 1739. Nf.

Clark, Samuel. SQS May T Jul 1773 *Tayloe* to Va. M.

Clarke, Sarah. S Sep-Oct 1775 T *Justitia* Feb 1776. M.

Clark, Susanna. S Plymouth Nov 1763 (AHJ). De.

Clarke, Thomas, (brother of William, John & Walter *q.v.*). S s corn Lent 1742. St.

Clark, Thomas. SQS Oct T *Justitia* Dec 1774. M.

Clarke, Valentine. T 1747 from Whitehaven. Cu.

Clarke, Walter (brother of William, Thomas & John *q.v.*). S Lent 1742. St.

Clarke, William Jr. (brother of Thomas, John & Walter, *q.v.*). S s sheets Lent 1742. St.

Clarke, William. S Dec 1747 LC Knt Co., Md., from *St. George* Mar 1748. L.

Clarke, William. S Jan T Mar 1750 *Tryal*. L.

Clarke, William. T 1751. Nt.

Clarke, William. S Lent 1752. No.

Clarke, William. S May-Jun T Aug 1752 *Tryal*. M.

Clarke, William. SQS Feb T *Tryal* Jul 1754. M.

Clarke, William. S Lent LC AA Co., Md., from *Thornton* Jul 1775. K.

Clarkson, John of Haighton. SQS Jul 1721. La.

Clarkson, Richard. R Summer 1773 T *Justitia* Jan 1774. Sy.

Clavier, William. LC Md from *Isabella* Jul 1775 & bought his freedom. X.

Claxton, William. T May 1751 *Tryal*. K.

Clay, Elizabeth. S 14 yrs May T *Maryland Packet* Oct 1761. M.

Clay, Granger. T May 1751 *Tryal*. Sx.

Clay, John. S Summer T *Barnard* Oct 1756. E.

Clay, Percival. S Hull Oct 1745 T Mar 1746. Y.

Claymore *als* Clymer, Margaret. S Dec 1735 T Jan 1736 *Dorsetshire* LC Va Sep 1736. M.

Clayton, John of Newington. SQS Apr T May 1752 *Lichfield.* Sy.

Clayton, John. T from Dublin by *Hercules*, LC Bal. Co., Md., Aug 1773, sold to James Wilson of Augusta Co., Virginia. Ir.

Clayton, Martha. S Lent 1731. Bd.

Clayton, Thomas. S Oct T Oct 1749 *Mary.* L.

Clayton, William. S Lent 1731. Bd.

Clayton, William. S s silk Lent 1768. Wa.

Clayton, William. S Lent LC AA Co., Md., from *Thornton* Jul 1775. M.

Cleaton, John. S Lent R Jul 1761. Sh.

Cleaver *als* Temple, Robert. S s horse Summer 1738 R 14 yrs Lent 1739; T *St. George* Jan LC Knt Co., Md., Mar 1748. Wa.

Cleeve *als* Hammet, Joseph. T May 1746. De.

Cleford, Thomas. S Summer T Oct 1750 *Rachael.* K.

Cleham, Elizabeth. T *Tryal* Jul 1754. M.

Clements, Jona. S Summer 1718 LC from *Sophia* QA Co., Md. Mar 1719. De.

Clements, Mark. S 14 yrs S Lent LC AA Co., Md., from *Thornton* Jul 1773. Ht.

Clements, Samuel Felix. S Lent LC Bal Co., Md., Jun 1773. Co.

Cleveland, John. S Summer 1773 T *Justitia* Jan 1774. K.

Clewes, Mary. S Oct T *Phoenix* Oct 1760. M.

Clewley, Joseph. T *Thornton* May LCAA Co., Md., Jul 1774. M.

Clews, Richard. S Lent LC Bal Co., Md., Jul 1771. Wa.

Clifford, William. S Mar 1759 s heifer R 14 yrs Jun 1760 T Nov 1761. Ha.

Clifton, James. S Lent T May 1739. Li.

Clifton, William. R 14 yrs Jul T *Saltspring* Jul 1775. M.

Cloden, Garrett of Stebbing, cordwainer. SQS Jul T *Ruby* Oct 1754. E.

Cloe, James. S Jan 1751 (AHJ). E.

Clogg, Robert Jr. S 14 yrs Summer 1740 LC QA Co., Md., from *Philleroy* Apr 1742. De.

Clogg, William. S Summer 1741 LC QA Co., Md., from *Philleroy* Apr 1742. De.

Cloore, Agnes, spinster. SQS Oct 1738 LC QA Co., Md., *from Amity* Mar 1739. Co.

Clover, Mary. S s fowls Jul 1766. Wa.

Clow, Samuel. S 14 yrs Summer 1770. Wa.

Clowes, Elizabeth. S Jan T Mar 1750 *Tryal.* L.

Clymer, Sarah wife of John. S for shoplifting R 14 yrs Lent 1773 but not taken to Bristol in Apr 1773 because of precarious health. Wo.

Coate, Leonard of North Petherton, tailor. R for Barbados Jul 1672 but LC Md 1673. So.

Coats, James. SQS Sep T Oct 1750 *Rachael.* M.

Coates, Thomas. S Hull Jul T Oct 1733. Y.

Coaton, William. S for burglary & R 14 yrs Jun 1740. Le.

Cobb, Samuel. S Jan-Jun T Jul 1747 *Laura.* M.

Coburne, Robert. S Lent 1729. Nt.

Cock, Barnard. S Launceston Jan 1757 (AHJ). Co.

Cock, Prudence. S Launceston Jan 1757 (AHJ). Co.

Cock, Richard. S for forgery Summer 1733 R 14 yrs Jan 1734 LC Knt Co., Md, from *Falcon* Mar 1735. Ha.

Cockburn, James (1751) - *See* Cowburn (AHJ). Nl.

Cockington, William. S Lent 1731. Bd.

Cockram, George. S 14 yrs Lent 1742 LC QA Co., Md., from *Kent* Jun 1743. De.

Cockran, Francis. S Lent R Jul T Dec 1736 *Dorsetshire* . Sy.

Cockran, Joshua. T from Dublin by *Hercules*, LC Bal. Co., Md., Aug 1773, sold to William Walters & Richard Guttrell. Ir.

Coe, Anthony. S Feb T *Neptune* Mar 1761. L.

Coe, William. S Summer T Oct 1738. Hu.

Cohen, John. SQS Jan LC AA Co., Md., from *Thornton* Jul 1775. M.

Coke, William. AT Aug 1764. Db.

Coker, John. SQS Jan LC AA Co., Md., from *Thornton* Jul 1775. M.

Colbrath, John. S Lent LC AA Co., Md., from *Thornton* Jul 1775. E.

Colding, William. S for breaking gaol Mar 1754 (OJ). O.

Cole, Elizabeth. S Jan-Apr T *Lichfield* May 1749. M.

Cole, George. T *Tryal* Jul 1754. M.

Cole, George. T *Barnard* Oct 1756. M.

Cole, Henry. S Aug 1738. G.

Cole, Henry. T Apr 1739 *Forward* . Sy.

Cole, James. S Lent T Sep 1746 *Mary*. K.

Cole, James. T May 1751 *Tryal*. E.

Cole, James. SQS Oct 1754 T *Greyhound* Feb 1755. M.

Cole, John. S Feb-Apr T May 1751 *Tryal*. M.

Cole, John. S Lent LC AA Co., Md., from *Thornton* Jul 1775. Ht.

Cole, Joseph. S Sep 1750. Li.

Cole, John. SQS Feb LC AA Co., Md., from *Thornton* Jul 1773. M.

Cole, Joseph. S Sep 1751 (AHJ). Li.

Cole, Judith. S Sep-Dec 1746 T Jan 1747 *George William*. M.

Cole *als* Johnson, Mary. SQS May T Sep 1751 *Greyhound*. M.

Cole, Richard. S Sep T Oct 1750 *Rachael*. M.

Cole, Richard. R 14 yrs Oct 1772 T *Justitia* Jan 1773. M.

Cole, Robert. S Lent T *Tryal* Jul 1754. Ht.

Cole, Ulalia. S Lent 1737 LC Knt Co., Md., from *Hawk* Nov 1737. De.

Coleman, Henry. S Sep-Oct 1772 T *Justitia* Jan 1773. M.

Coleman, Isaac of Faversham. S Lent T May 1750 *Lichfield*. K.

Coleman, John. S s mare Lent R 14 yrs Summer 1756 TB to Va. No.

Coleman, John. S Lent LC AA Co., Md., from *Hanover Planter* Jul 1773. M.

Coleman, Joseph. S Apr-Jun 1739 T *Sea Nymph* to Md. M.

Coleman, Thomas. S Apr-Jun 1739 T *Sea Nymph* to Md. M.

Coleman, Thomas. S s sheep & R 14 yrs Lent T Jul 1747 *Laura*. Bu.

Coles, Benjamin. SQS Jan T *Thornton* May LC AA Co., Md., Jul 1774. Sy.

Coles, Elizabeth. S Lent 1737 LC Knt Co., Md., from *Hawk* Nov 1737. Ha.

Coles, Jonathan. S 14 yrs Lent LC Bal Co., Md., Jul 1771. Do.

Coles als Diggle, Richard. SQS Jan 1731 LC Knt Co., Md., Apr 1732. So.

Coley, William. S Summer T from London Sep 1754. Wa.

Collett, Elizabeth. T Jun 1747. Ha.

Collett *als* Collard, Stephen. S Apr T May 1749 *Lichfield*. L.

Colley *als* Farmer, Ann. S Feb-Apr T May 1751 *Tryal*. M.

Colley, Joseph. S 14 yrs Lent LC Bal Co., Md., Jun 1773. St.

Collier, Benjamin. T May 1752 *Lichfield*. K.

Collier, Edward. R 14 yrs Dec 1723. Be.

Collyer, Elizabeth. S Jan-Apr T *Lichfield* May 1749. M.

Collier, John. S Jul-Sep T *Ruby* Oct 1754. M.

Collier, John. S 1762 (AHJ). La.

Collyer, John. S Lent LC AA Co., Md., from *Thornton* May 1771. E.

Collier, Nathaniel. S Dec 1782 LC Bal Co., Md., Dec 1783 from *Swift*. L.

Collier, Sarah wife of John. S May-Jul T *Tayloe* Jul 1774. M.

Collier, William. R 14 yrs Dec T *Justitia* Dec 1774. M.

Collings, James. S Summer 1741 R 14 yrs Lent 1742. He.

Collings, John. S Jan-Jun T Jul 1747 *Laura*. M.

Collings, Uriah. S Jul 1766. Wa.

Collins, Alice. S Dec 1773 T *Justitia* Jan 1774. M.

Collins, Ann. S Dec 1749-Jan 1750 T Mar 1750 *Tryal*. M.

Collins, Ann. S Apr-May T *Tryal* Jul 1754. M.

Collins, Daniel. S Bristol Jan 1758 (AHJ). G.

Collins, Hugh. S Sep T *Phoenix* Oct 1760. M.

Collins, Hugh. S Jul T *Beverly* Aug 1763. M.

Collins, Jane. S Sep T Nov 1746. Sh.

Collins, John. SQS Exeter Jul 1734 LC Knt Co., Md, from *Falcon* Mar 1735. De.

Collins, John. S Mar T Sep 1747. Ha.

Collins, John. S s sheep Lent R 14 yrs Summer T *Ruby* Oct 1754. Bu.

Collins, John. S Sep-Oct 1772 T *Justitia* Jan 1773. M.

Collins, John. S Lent LC Bal Co., Md., Jun 1773. So.

Collins *als* Tilly *als* Burroughs, Mary. S Jan T Apr 1735 *Patapsco* LC Annapolis Oct 1735. L.

Collins, Richard. S Dec 1772 T *Justitia* Jan 1773. M.

Collins, Thomas. S Oct 1772 T *Justitia* Jan 1773. L.

Collins, Timothy. S Lent LC AA Co., Md., from *Thornton* Jul 1773. L.

Collins, Walter. S Summer 1718 LC from *Sophia* QA Co., Md. Mar 1719. De.

Collins, William. S s horse & R 14 yrs Jun 1741. Wa.

Collins, William. S Jan-Apr T Jun 1748 *Lichfield*. M.

Collins, William. S May-Jul T Jul 1748 *Mary*. M.

Collins, William. S Jul T *Beverly* Aug 1763. M.

Collins, William. S Summer LC Bal Co., Md., Dec 1772. So.

Collipress, William. S & R Jul 1740 (GJ). G.

Collipriest, John. S 14 yrs Lent 1737 LC Knt Co., Md., from *Bideford* Nov 1737. So.

Collis, Thomas. S Sep T *Ruby* Oct 1754. L.

Collop, George. S Dec T *Justitia* Dec 1774. M.

Collyer - *See* Collier.

Colnet, Isaac. S Jul T *Beverly* Aug 1763. M.

Colwell, Hannah. SQS Exeter Apr 1753 (AHJ). De.

Colwell, Ufan. S Oct-Dec 1750 T *Thames* Feb 1751. M.

Combe, William. S Mar 1734 LC Knt Co., Md, Mar 1735 from *Falcon*. De.

Comber, Richard. S Jan T May 1746. Sx.

Comberlidge, Thomas. S s at Leek Lent 1750 LC QA Co., Md., from *Chester* Dec 1752. St.

Combes, James. SQS Jan T *Thornton* May LC AA Co., Md., Jul 1774. Sy.

Comer, Charles. S Summer T Sep 1746. Ha.

Comley, Benjamin. S Bristol Jan 1758 (AHJ). G.

Comley, Thomas. S Lent LC Bal Co., Md., Jul 1774. Wi.

Commins, Nicholas. S Summer LC Md from *Reformation* Aug 1722. De.

Commons, Thomas. S 14 yrs Summer 1738 LC QA Co., Md. Jun 1739. So.

Compton, James. S Lent LC AA Co., Md., from *Hanover Planter* Jul 1773. L.

Compton, Mary. T *Maryland Packet* Oct 1761. M.

Compton, Walter. S Feb-Apr T May 1752 *Lichfield*. M.

Condren, Thomas. S 14 yrs May-Jul T Jul 1748 *Mary*. M.

Conduit, John. S Jul T Aug 1749 *Thames*. L.

Coney, Elizabeth. S & T May 1745. Y.

Coney, George. S Oct-Dec 1754 T *Greyhound* Feb 1755. M.

Confield, Thomas. SQS Jan LC AA Co., Md., from *Thornton* Jul 1773. Sy.
Congdon, Elizabeth wife of Faithful. S Summer 1772 LC Bal Co., Md., Apr 1773. Co.
Conibeer (Cunebeer), Anthony. S Jan LC QA Co., Md., from *Leopard* May 1738. De.
Conn, John of High Ongar. S Lent R 14 yrs Summer T *Phoenix* Oct 1760. E.
Connell, Alexander. S May T Jul 1745 *Italian Merchant*. M.
Connell, Collumb. S Sep 1740 T *Harpooner* Jan 1741. L.
Connell, Thomas. 1746 T 14 yrs Apr 1746 *Laura*. M.
Connolly, Dennis. S Lent LC AA Co., Md., from *Hanover Planter* Jul 1773. L.
Connerly, Eleanor. S May-Jul T *Tayloe* Jul 1774. M.
Connerly *als* Connolly, John. S Jan T *Thames* Feb 1751. M.
Connolly, Patrick. S Jan-Jun T Jul 1747 *Laura*. M.
Connor, David. SQS Feb T May 1752 *Lichfield*. M.
Connor, Francis. S Jun T *Tryal* Jul 1754. L.
Connor, Hugh. S 14 yrs Jan T *Plain Dealer* Jan 1746. M.
Connor, Mary. S Feb T *Thames* Mar 1754. M.
Conner, Mary. S Jul-Sep T *Ruby* Oct 1754. M.
Connor, Mary. T from Dublin by *Hercules*, LC Bal. Co., Md., Aug 1773, sold to
    William Walters & Richard Guttrell. Ir.
Conner, Temperance, wife of George. S as pickpocket Lent R 14 yrs Jun 1734 LC
    Knt Co., Md from *Falcon* Mar 1735. Co.
Conner, William. S Jun 1718 T Feb *Worcester* LC Md Jun 1719. L.
Conson, Ann. S Oct 1751-Jan 1752 T *Thames* Mar 1752. M.
Constable, Elizabeth wife of Samuel. S May-Jul T *Tayloe* Jul 1774. M.
Constable, Sarah. SWK Jul 1772 T *Justitia* Jan 1773. K.
Conway, Ann wife of John. S Sep T *Barnard* Oct 1756. M.
Conybeare, Ann. S 14 yrs Summer 1772 LC Bal Co., Md., Apr 1773. So.
Conyers, Sarah. S Dec 1753-Jan 1754 T *Thames* Mar 1754. M.
Cook, Alexander. S Dec T *Justitia* Dec 1774. L.
Cook, Ann. S Dec 1760 T *Neptune* Mar 1761. M.
Cook, Charles, *als* Holm, George, *als* Peel, James. S s at Colwich Aug T
    Restoration LC Bal Co., Md., Oct 1771. St.
Cooke, Charles. S Lent LC AA Co., Md., from *Thornton* Jul 1775. M.
Cooke, Elizabeth. T 1746. Su.
Cook, Elizabeth. S City 1758 (AHJ). Nl.
Cooke, Elizabeth. S Lent LC AA Co., Md., from *Thornton* May 1771. K.
Cooke, George. S Lent s horse R 14 yrs Aug 1726. De.
Cooke, George. S Feb T *Tryal* Mar 1757. M.
Cooke, George. S Sep-Oct 1772 T *Justitia* Jan 1773. M.
Cooke, Henry. S Lent T Jul 1745 *Italian Merchant*. E.
Cook, Henry. S May 1775. Li.
Cook, James. S Lent R 14 yrs Summer T Sep 1751 *Greyhound*. E.
Cook, James. S Dumfries for rape R Nov 1774. Sco.
Cook, John. S 14 yrs Jan-Apr T Jun 1748 *Lichfield*. M.
Cook, John. S Jan T *Thames* Feb 1751. L.
Cook, John. R 7 yrs Jul T *Tayloe* Jul 1773. M.
Cook, John. S Lent T *Thornton* May LC AA Co., Md., Jul 1774. M.
Cook, Joseph. S Lent LC Bal Co., Md., Jun 1773. Wi.
Cooke, Mary. S Jan-Jun T Jul 1747 *Laura*. M.
Cooke, Mary. S Sep T *Ruby* Oct 1754. L.
Cooke, Miles. S Apr T *Dolphin* May 1763; runaway. M.
Cook, Nathaniel. S Summer 1747 LC Knt Co., Md., from *St. George* Mar 1748. K.
Cook, Richard. S Jan-Apr T *Lichfield* May 1749. M.

Cooke, Robert. T 1746. Su.

Cook, Robert of Merstham. SQS Oct 1750 T *Thames* Feb 1751. Sy.

Cook, Robert. S 1752 TB to Md. No.

Cooke, Samuel of Manchester, callenderer. SQS Apr 1723 T Apr 1724. La.

Cooke, Sarah. S Jan 1717 T 14 yrs May 1718 *Tryal* LC Charles Town Aug 1718. L.

Cooke, Sarah. S Lent R 14 yrs Summer T *Ruby* Oct 1754. Sy.

Cooke, Stephen. S Lent LC AA Co., Md., from *Thornton* Jul 1775. Bu.

Cooke, Susanna. T Sep 1751 *Greyhound.* Sx.

Cook, Thomas. T May 1745. Y.

Cook, Thomas. S Jul-Dec 1747 LC Knt Co., Md., from *St. George* Mar 1748. M.

Cooke, Thomas. S Dec 1753-Jan 1754 T *Thames* Mar 1754. M.

Cook, Thomas. S Sep-Oct 1775 T *Justitia* Feb 1776. M.

Cook, William. S Summer 1762 R 14 yrs Lent T *Dolphin* May 1763. E.

Cook, William. S Lent but pardoned in April 1773. Ha.

Cook, William. S Jul LC Md from *William* Dec 1774 & sold to William Lux. Ha.

Cookson, Lancelot. S s silver cutlery at St. Leonard Bridgnorth Summer 1743. Sh.

Cooley, James. SQS Jan T *Greyhound* Feb 1755. M.

Cooley, John. S Feb-Apr 1746 T Apr 1746 *Laura.* M.

Cooley, John. S Sep 1756 (AHJ). Wo.

Cooley, John. S Lent T *Thornton* May LC AA Co., Md., Jul 1774. M.

Cooley, Robert. S Summer T Sep 1751 *Greyhound.* K.

Cooling, Thomas. T May 1751 *Tryal.* Sy.

Cooper, Charles. S Apr-May T *Saltspring* Jul 1775. M.

Cooper, Elizabeth. S Apr T *Lichfield* May 1749. L.

Cooper, Elizabeth. S Oct-Dec 1754 T *Greyhound* Feb 1755. M.

Cooper, Francis. S Lent 1741 LC QA Co., Md., from *Philleroy* Apr 1742. He.

Cooper, George. SQS Bristol Mar TB May LC Md from *Isabella* Jul 1775 & sold to Waters & Gartrall. G.

Cooper, James (1719). *See* Seddon. La.

Cooper, John. T Sep 1737 *Pretty Patsy.* L.

Cooper, John. S Lent T Jun 1748 *Lichfield.* K.

Cooper, John. S May-Jul T Aug 1749 *Thames.* M.

Cooper, John. T Aug 1752 *Tryal.* K.

Cooper, John. S Lent T Apr 1753. Wa.

Cooper, John. S Lent T *Tryal* Jul 1754. Ht.

Cooper, John. S s ox & cow Lent R 14 yrs Summer 1761 TB to Va. No.

Cooper, John. S Sep-Oct T *Justitia* Dec 1774. M.

Cooper, Joseph. S Feb T Mar 1750 *Tryal.* M.

Cooper, Joseph. S Lent T Apr 1756. Wa.

Cooper, Mary. S Summer 1763 (AHJ). Nl.

Cooper, Sarah. S s clothing Lent 1768. Wa.

Cooper, Thomas. S & T Mar 1750 *Tryal.* L.

Cooper, Thomas. S Oct-Dec 1754 T *Greyhound* Feb 1755. M.

Cooper, Thomas. S Lent LC AA Co., Md., from *Thornton* Jul 1775. K.

Coopes, Charles. S s fowls Feb 1738 (RM). Ha.

Cooter, John. T May 1751 *Tryal.* K.

Cope, Eleanor. S Apr-Jun 1739 T *Sea Nymph* to Md. M.

Cope, John. S for housebreaking Summer 1721 T Jul *Alexander* LC Md Sep 1723. Ht.

Cope, John. S Apr-Jun 1739 T *Sea Nymph* to Md. M.

Cope, John. T Sep 1746. Ha.

Cope, John. S Bristol May 1761 but escaped from prison ; to hang Oct 1761 for returning. G.

Cope, William. S Lent TB Aug 1733. Db.

Copes, John. S 14 yrs Lent LC AA Co., Md., from *Hanover Planter* Jul 1773. M.

Corbet, Edward (Henry). S s deer in Uttoxeter Lent but R for Army service in Jamaica Apr 1762. St.

Corbet, James. SQS Feb LC AA Co., Md., from *Thornton* Jul 1775. M.

Corbett, Mary. S Lent 1762. St.

Corbett, Michael (1764). *See* Croxhall, William. Wa.

Corbishaw, Richard of Manchester, linen weaver. SQS Jul 1719. La.

Corbold, John. T 1746. Su.

Corderoy, Robert. S Jul T *Tayloe* Jul 1774. L.

Cordoza, Aaron. S Apr T 14 yrs May 1752 *Lichfield*. L.

Cordosa, Jacob. S Dec 1770 but R for sea service. M.

Cordoza, Samuel. S Sep T Oct 1750 *Rachael*. L.

Corham, Thomas. SQS Jul 1733 LC Knt Co., Md., from *Falcon* Apr 1734. Co.

Cork, Richard. SQS Oct 1731 LC Knt Co., Md., from *Falcon* Apr 1732. So.

Corledge, William. Jul 1783 LC Bal Co., Md., Dec 1783 from *Swift*. M.

Cormack, Mary. T *St. George* Jan LC Knt Co., Md., Mar 1748. M.

Corner, Richard. S Lent LC AA Co., Md., from *Hanover Planter* Jul 1773. M.

Cornish, Cornelius. SQS Gloucester Jul 1754 (OJ). G.

Cornish, William. S Apr T May 1750 *Lichfield*. L.

Cornewall, Anne, spinster. R for Barbados Sep 1672 but LC AA Co. Md Nov 1673. L.

Cornwall, Elizabeth. S Jan T *Greyhound* Feb 1755. L.

Corp, Edward. S Dec 1746 T Jan 1747 *George William*. L.

Corpe, Richard. S Lent 1773 but received a free pardon.

Corrigan, Hugh. S Oct-Dec 1750 T *Thames* Feb 1751. M.

Cosson, John. S Dec 1750 T *Thames* Feb 1751. L.

Costello, Robert. S Aug T *Beverly* Aug 1763. L.

Coster, James. S for life Lent LC AA Co., Md., from *Thornton* Jul 1775. Sy.

Coster, Joshua. R 14 yrs Jul T *Tayloe* Jul 1774. M.

Coster, William. S Dec 1772 T *Justitia* Jan 1773. M.

Cottam, William. S Summer T Sep 1766. Li.

Cottam, William. S Lent TB Apr 1771; Luke Cottam to be imprisoned for two years. Nt.

Cotteril, William. T Aug 1752 *Tryal*. Sy.

Cotterell, William. S Lent LC AA Co., Md., from *Thornton* Jul 1773. L.

Cotton, John. S Lent 1732. Bd.

Cotton, Joshua. S Oct T *Justitia* Dec 1774. L.

Cotton, Mary. SQS May T Jul 1773 *Tayloe* to Va. M.

Cotton, William of St. Saviour, Southwark. SQS Jun T Aug 1752 *Tryal*. Sy.

Cotton, William. S Apr 1766. Li.

Cotton, William. SQS Apr T *Thornton* May LC AA Co., Md., Jul 1774. M.

Couch, Elianore. S May T *Phoenix* Oct 1760. M.

Couling, William. S Lent T Apr 1754. O.

Coulsey, Thomas. S Oct 1751-Jan 1752 T *Thames* Mar 1752. M.

Coulson, William of Simpson. SQS for leaving his place of settlement Jul 1772 (OJ). O.

Coulson, William. S Jan 1717 T 14 yrs May 1718 Tryal LC Charles Town Aug 1718. L.

Coulton, Jervase. S Lent 1730. Nt.

Counsellor, Jacob. SQS T *Thornton* May Feb LC AA Co., Md., Jul 1774. M.

Court, Eleanor. T *Justitia* Feb 1776. M.

Courtney, James. S Jul 1747 T Jan LC Knt Co., Md., from *St. George* Mar 1748. L.

Courtenay, Mi(chael). T from Dublin by *Hercules*, LC Bal. Co., Md., Aug 1773, sold to James Wilson of Augusta Co., Virginia. Ir.

Covnett, John. S Jul T *Tayloe* Jul 1773. L.

Cowburn *als* Cockburn, James. S City 1751 (AHJ). Nl.

Cowdell, Thomas. S Feb-Apr T May 1751 *Tryal*. M.

Cowe, William. S Lent 1729. Nt.

Cowell, Caleb. S Lent T *Tryal* Jul 1754. K.

Cowell, Joseph. S s sheep Lent R 14 yrs Summer T Oct 1750 *Rachael*. E.

Cowley, Joseph. S Lent LC AA Co., Md., Jul 1774. M.

Cowley, Richard. R for Barbados Oct 1673 but LC Md from *Charles* May 1674. M.

Cowley, William. S Feb T Jun 1751. G.

Cowling, William. S Summer 1752 (BJ). De.

Cown, James. S Summer 1746 T Jan 1747. De.

Cowpland, Thomas. S s horse Lent 1726 R 14 yrs Lent 1729. Y.

Cox, Ann. S s at Dudley Summer 1758. Wo.

Cox, Ann. S 14 yrs Lent LC Bal Co., Md., Jul 1772. So.

Cox, Charles. S Lent T *Thornton* May LC AA Co., Md., Jul 1774. K.

Cox, James. S 14 yrs Summer 1772 LC Bal Co., Md., Apr 1773. So.

Cox, John. S Jan T *Thames* Feb 1751. M.

Cox, John. S s sheep Lent R 14 yrs Summer T *Ruby* Oct 1754. Bu.

Cox, John. S Lent LC Bal Co., Md., Jun 1773. So.

Cox, John. S Sep-Oct 1775 T *Justitia* Feb 1776. M.

Cox, Peter. SQS Sep 1772 T *Justitia* Jan 1773. M.

Cox, Peter. SQS Feb LC AA Co., Md., from *Thornton* Jul 1775. M.

Cox, Robert. SQS 1753. No.

Cox, Samuel. S Lent T Apr 1753. Wa.

Cox, William. S Lent T *Dolphin* May 1763. Sy.

Cox, William. S Lent 1772 LC Bal Co., Md., Apr 1773. Wo.

Coxhill, Henry Joseph. S Lent LC AA Co., Md., from *Thornton* Jul 1775. Sy.

Coyle, James. S Jan-Apr T Jun 1748 *Lichfield*. M.

Coyle, Michael. S Jan-Apr T Jun 1748 *Lichfield*. M.

Crabb, Joseph. S 14 yrs Summer 1738 LC QA Co., Md. Jun 1739. De.

Crackles, Thomas. S Aug T *Phoenix* Oct 1760. L.

Cracy, Ann. S Sep T Nov 1746. Sh.

Craddock, Elizabeth. S 14 yrs Summer LC Bal Co., Md., Dec 1770. He.

Craddock, James (1773). *See* Town. St.

Craddock, William. S Bristol Jan 1756 (AHJ). G.

Craddock, William. S Lent 1770. No.

Cradock, Mary. S Dec 1753-Jan 1754 T *Thames* Mar 1754. M.

Craft, Ann. S Jul s stockings T Dec 1735 *John* LC Annapolis Sep 1736. M.

Craft, John. S 14 yrs S Summer LC Bal Co., Md., Dec 1772. Wa.

Crafts, Francis. S May-Jul T Sep 1751 *Greyhound*. M.

Crafts, Thomas. S Apr T Jun 1748 *Lichfield*. L.

Crags *als* Shaw, Thomas. S Apr T May 1750 *Lichfield*. L.

Craggs, Walter. S 1752 (AHJ). Nl.

Cragy, Charles. S Dec 1750 T *Thames* Feb 1751. L.

Craig, Matthew. S Jan LC QA Co., Md., from *Leopard* May 1738. De.

Craith, Bridget. S Dec 1747 LC Knt Co., Md., from *St. George* Mar 1748. L.

Crammer, William. S Summer T from London Sep 1754. Wa.

Cramphorn, William. S Lent LC AA Co., Md., from *Thornton* Jul 1775. Ht.

Crandon, Abraham. S Lent LC Potomac, Va., from *Martha* Dec 1724. Do.

Crane, Francis. T Jun *Bideford* LC QA Co., Md., Sep 1752. Wo.

Cranford, Mary. S Summer 1721 T Jul *Alexander* LC Md Sep 1723. Sy.

Crapp, Mary. S Summer 1718 LC from *Sophia* QA Co., Md. Mar 1719. Co.

Cranwell *als* Cranaway, John. S for highway robbery Lent R 14 yrs Summer T *Phoenix* Oct 1760. Bu.

Crassley, John. S Lent T Apr 1757. Wa.

Crauty, David . T from Waterford by *Betsy* LC Bal. Co., Md., Aug 1773. Ir.

Craven, Edward. S May-Jul T *Tayloe* Jul 1773. M.

Crawford, Barbara. S City 1749 (AHJ). Nl.

Crawford, John *als* Beauty. SQS s at Godstow Jul 1757 (OJ). O.

Crawford, Susanna. S Jul-Dec 1747 LC Knt Co., Md., from *St. George* Mar 1748. M.

Crawford, Thomas. S Feb T 14 yrs Mar 1750 *Tryal*. M.

Crawley, Jacob. S Lent LC AA Co., Md., from *Thornton* Jul 1773. Ht.

Crew, Ann. S Jun-Dec 1745 T *Plain Dealer* Jan 1746. M.

Cripps, John. S 14 yrs Jul-Dec 1747 T *St. George* Jan LC Knt Co., Md., Mar 1748. M.

Cripps, Michael. S Summer T *Ruby* Oct 1754. Bu.

Crispe, George *als* Baker, John. S s mare Summer 1742 R 14 yrs Lent 1743. Su.

Crisp, Robert. R 14 yrs Summer 1745 AT Lent T *Mary* Sep 1746. Sy.

Crispe *als* Ridge, Sarah. S Jul-Dec 1747 LC Knt Co., Md., from *St. George* Mar 1748. M.

Crisp, Thomas. S Apr T May 1751 *Tryal*. L.

Crocker, Elizabeth, spinster. S Summer 1741 LC QA Co., Md., from *Philleroy* Apr 1742. De.

Crocker, Elizabeth. SQS Bodmin Jan 1734 LC Knt Co., Md Mar 1735 from *Falcon*. Co.

Crockett, William. S Dec 1746 T Jan 1747 *George William*. L.

Croft, John. S Lent R 14 yrs Summer T Sep 1751 *Greyhound*. Ht.

Crofts, Elizabeth. R for Barbados Oct 1673 but LC Md from *Charles* May 1674. L.

Cromby, Andrew. S Mar T Apr 1747. Li.

Crompton, James. S Lent LC AA Co., Md., from *Thornton* Jul 1775. M.

Crompton, Samuel. SQS Apr 1729. La.

Crone, Fergus. S May-Jul T Jul 1748 *Mary*. M.

Crook, John. S 14 yrs Mar TB *Justitia* but pardoned Aug 1768. Wi.

Crook, William. S Lent LC AA Co., Md., from *Thornton* May 1771, sold to Joshua Bond. L.

Croot, Bartholomew. S 14 yrs Lent 1742 LC QA Co., Md., from *Kent* Jun 1743. De.

Cropper, Samuel of Ashton under Lyne. SQS Apr 1729. La.

Crosby, John. S Sep-Oct T Oct 1749 *Mary*. M.

Croscombe, Ann of Barnstaple, spinster. S July 1738 LC Knt Co., Md., from *Hawk* Apr 1739. De.

Croshaw, Elizabeth. S Apr-May T *Tryal* Jul 1754. M.

Cross, Charles. S Jun 1739 T *Sea Nymph* to Md. L.

Cross, Elizabeth. S & T Sep 1751 *Greyhound*. L.

Cross, George. T May 1751 *Tryal*. K.

Cross, James. S Apr T May 1750 *Lichfield*. L.

Cross, John. S Jan 1752 (AHJ). E.

Cross, Samuel. R 14 yrs Jul T *Saltspring* Jul 1775. M.

Cross, Thompson. S Lent 1765. Li.

Cross, William. S Aug T *Restoration* LC Bal Co., Md., Oct 1771. Wa.

Crossing, William. S 14 yrs Lent 1744 LC Knt Co., Md., from *Susannah* Aug

1744. De.

Crost *als* Crowhurst, John. S Summer 1751 R 14 yrs Lent T May 1752 *Lichfield*. E.

Crouch, Isaac. S Summer T Oct 1755. Le.

Croutch, Thomas. S Jan-Apr T *Lichfield* May 1749. M.

Crow, Sarah, spinster, S Bristol Aug 1741 LC QA Co.,Md from *Philleroy* Apr 1742. G.

Crow, Thomas. S Lent 1765. Sh.

Crowder, Thomas. S Apr-May T *Saltspring* Jul 1775. M.

Crowne, John. S as pickpocket & R Lent 1718. Wo.

Crowther, Edward. S Apr 1746 M T Apr 1746 *Laura*. M.

Croxhall, William *als* Corbett, Michael. S Apr 1764. Wa.

Crozier, Thomas. T Jul 1747. O.

Crudge, Margaret wife of Peter, feltmaker. SQS Jan 1750 LC QA Co., Md., from *Catherine* Nov 1750. De.

Cruise, Peter. S Dec 1749-Jan 1750 T Mar 1750 *Tryal*. M.

Crump, Francis. S Oct T *Phoenix* Oct 1760. M.

Cruttenden, Thomas. S Summer 1748 R 14 yrs Lent T *Lichfield* May 1749. Sx.

Cuddy, Sophia. S Jul-Dec 1747 LC Knt Co., Md., from *St. George* Mar 1748. M.

Cue, Edward. S for housebreaking at French Hay Lent TB Jul 1742. G.

Culberson, James. SQS May T Jul 1773 *Tayloe* to Va. M.

Culpepper, Margaret. S & T Sep 1751 *Greyhound*. M.

Cumber, James. T *Justitia* Jan 1774. L.

Cumberland, Thomas. S Lent T Apr 1739. Le.

Cumberleach, Francis. S Lent T Apr 1757. Wa.

Cummings, Joseph. S Apr-May T *Tryal* Jul 1754. M.

Cummins, Elizabeth. S Apr T *Lichfield* May 1749. L.

Cummins, William. S Feb T Apr 1735 *Patapsco* LC Annapolis Oct 1735. L.

Cundit, John. SQS Jan LC Bal Co., Md., Jun 1773. Wi.

Cunnibear, Thomas. S Apr T May 1747. So.

Cunningham, Ann. S Feb-Apr T May 1752 *Lichfield*. M.

Cunningham, Hugh. S Apr-Jun 1739 T *Sea Nymph* to Md. M.

Cunningham, John of Warrington. SQS Apr 1735. La.

Cunningham, Thomas. S Jan T *Thames* Feb 1751. L.

Cunnington, Alice. S Jan T *Plain Dealer* Jan 1746. M.

Curd, Christopher. S Sep-Oct 1772 T *Justitia* Jan 1773. M.

Curie, James. S 1757 (AHJ). La.

Currall, James. S Oct-Dec 1750 T *Thames* Feb 1751. M.

Currie, George. S & T Apr 1751. No.

Curry, James. S & R for highway robbery Lent 1740 (IJ). Su.

Curtain, Joseph. S 1754 (AHJ). La.

Curtis *als* Richardson, Daniel. S Oct-Dec 1750 T *Thames* Feb 1751. M.

Curtis, Henry. S Lent 1750 LC QA Co., Md., from *Catherine* Nov 1750. G.

Curtis, Henry. SQS 1755 TB to Md. No.

Curtis, Mark. S Lent 1737 LC Knt Co., Md., from *Hawk* Nov 1737. Co.

Curtis, Prudence. S s cloth at Cirencester Lent R 14 yrs Summer TB Aug 1739. G.

Curtis, Thomas?, dangerous rogue. SQS Oct 1718. La.

Curtis, Thomas. S Dec 1749-Jan 1750 T Mar 1750 *Tryal*. M.

Curtis, William. S s at Wickwar Lent R 14 yrs Summer TB Aug 1740; to hang for returning Mar 1742. G.

Curtis, William. S Lent T Sep 1754. O.

Cust, Christopher. S Jan T *Plain Dealer* Jan 1746. M.

Custard, Thomas. SQS Apr 1771 LC Bal Co., Md., Jul 1771.

Cuthbert, Ann. S Jan-Apr T Jun 1748 *Lichfield.* M.

Cuthbert, George. S Sep-Oct 1775 T *Justitia* Feb 1776. M.

Cuthbert, Mathew. S City Summer 1751 (AHJ). Nl.

Cuthbertson, James. S City Summer 1756 (AHJ). Nl.

Cutler, Francis. SQS Jan 1735 T *Amity* LC QA Co., Md., Mar 1736. So.

Cutler, Henry. S Apr T *Justitia* May 1745. L.

Cutler, Thomas *als* Weedon. S Lent LC AA Co., Md., from *Thornton* Jul 1773. Ht.

Cutting, Edward. LC Va Sep 1736 from *Dorsetshire.* X.

Cuttridge, Thomas. S Summer T Aug 1749 *Thames.* E.

Da Costa, Antonio. S Feb T Mar 1750 *Tryal.* M.

Dabbs, John. S Lent T *Thornton* May LC AA Co., Md., Jul 1774. Sx.

Dacock, Thomas. T May 1752 *Lichfield.* Sy.

Daffy, Isabella. S May T *Maryland Packet* Oct 1761. M.

Daikins, Anna Maria. S Sep-Oct T *Justitia* Dec 1774. M.

Dailey, Ann. S Sep-Oct 1773 T *Justitia* Jan 1774. M.

Dailey, Charles. S Summer T *Phoenix* Oct 1760. K.

Daily, John. SQS Sep T *Justitia* Dec 1774. M.

Daines, Edward. S Dec 1750 T *Thames* Feb 1751. L.

Dalby, Mary. S Jan T *Justitia* May 1745. L.

Dalby, Susan. S s linen Jul T Dec 1735 *John* LC Annapolis Sep 1736. M.

Dalby, William. S Lent LC Bal Co., Md., Dec 1770 from *Trotman* & sold to John Cockey. Y.

Dale, William. S Summer 1736 T May 1737. St.

Dales, Robert. S Sep-Oct 1773 T *Justitia* Jan 1774. M.

Daley, Mary. S Dec 1773 T *Justitia* Jan 1774. M.

Daley, Rose. S Apr-May T *Saltspring* Jul 1775. M.

Dalfee, David. S Jun T Jul 1747 *Laura.* L.

Dallimore, Benjamin. S Lent 1735 LC QA Co., Md., from *Amity* Apr 1738. Ha.

Dally, John. S Norwich for housebreaking Summer R 14 yrs Dec 1726. Nf.

Dalrymple, Mary. S Lent T Summer 1752. Wa.

Dalrymple, Thomas. S Lent 1738. Li.

Dalton, Edward. T Lent 1750. Li.

Dalton, Thomas. S Oct-Dec 1754 T *Greyhound* Feb 1755. M.

Dalton, William. S Lent LC AA Co., Md., from *Thornton* Jul 1773. M.

Dance, Thomas. SQS Gloucester s fowls Jul 1755 (GJ). G.

Dancey, Thomas. S for burglary Summer 1740 R Lent 1741. St.

Dand, Elizabeth (1761) - *See* Miller. Nl.

Danford, John of St. Helen's. S s silk handkerchiefs Apr T Aug 1718 *Eagle* LC Charles Town Mar 1719. L.

Danford, Richard. SQS Gloucester Jan 1757 (GJ). G.

Dangerfield, Samuel. S s at Handsworth Aug T *Restoration* LC Bal Co., Md., Oct 1771. St.

Daniel *als* MacDonagh, Charles. S Sep 1735 T Jan 1736 *Dorsetshire* LC Va Sep 1736. M.

Daniel, John. S Summer LC Bal Co., Md., Dec 1772. So.

Daniel, Thomas. S Lent LC AA Co., Md., from *Thornton* Jul 1775. L.

Danks, Mary. S Jan T *Plain Dealer* Jan 1746. M.

Dannage, Joseph. Jul 1783 LC Bal Co., Md., Dec 1783 from *Swift.* M.

Darby, Ann. S Feb-Apr 1746 T Apr 1746 *Laura.* M.

Darby, Owen. S Jun 1739 T *Sea Nymph* to Md. L.

Darby, Roger of Reigate. SQS Apr T May 1750 *Lichfield*. Sy.

Darby, William. S Jun T Jul 1747 *Laura*. L.

Dare, Richard. S Summer 1738 LC QA Co., Md. Jun 1739. De.

Darey, Mary. S Summer T *Phoenix* Oct 1760. Bu.

Dark, Joseph. S Lent 1750 LC QA Co., Md., from *Catherine* Nov 1750. G.

Darling, Robert. S Lent LC AA Co., Md., from *Thornton* Jul 1773. M.

Darlington, James. S Apr-Jun 1739 T *Sea Nymph* to Md. M.

Darlow, Thomas. S Apr T May 1750 *Lichfield*. L.

Darnell, Francis. S Lent 1744. No.

Dart, Mary. S Feb-Apr T May 1751 *Tryal*. M.

Dart, William. S Lent 1744 LC Knt Co., Md., from *Susannah* Aug 1744. De.

Darton, Amelia *als* Milicent. S Feb T *Neptune* Mar 1761. L.

Darvey, Andrew. S May-Jul T Aug 1749 *Thames*. M.

Daubigney, Alexander. S Lent LC AA Co., Md., from *Thornton* Jul 1775. M.

Davett, Joseph. S Jan T May 1749 *Lichfield*. E.

Davey - *See* Davy.

David, Daniel. S Lent T *Thornton* May LC AA Co., Md., Jul 1774. L.

Davids, David. T Jan 1748. Sy.

Davids, Joseph. SQS Jul T *Justitia* Dec 1774. M.

Davidson, Anne. S Edinburgh for infanticide R Aug 1762. Sco.

Davidson, Barbara. S Aberdeen for concealing pregnancy R for life Jun 1772. Sco.

Davidson, Catherine. S for life Jul T Aug 1749 *Thames*; runaway. L.

Davison, John. S Sep-Oct T Oct 1749 *Mary*. M.

Davison, John. SQS Lent T *Thornton* May LC AA Co., Md., Jul 1774. M.

Davison, Ralph. S Lent LC Bal Co., Md., Jul 1771. Wa.

Davison, Samuel. S Lent 1724 but escaped & no further record found. Li.

Davison, Samuel. S s cows Lent 1725 AT Summer 1728. Y.

Davidson, William. S Lent 1750 LC QA Co., Md., from *Catherine* Nov 1750. G.

Davidson, William. S Inverness for robbery R for life Jun 1773. Sco.

Davidson, William. S Sep-Oct 1773 T *Justitia* Jan 1774. M.

Davis *als* Boswell, Ann. S May T Jul 1745 *Italian Merchant*. L.

Davis, Ann. S Lent T *Lichfield* May 1749. Sy.

Davis, Ann. T Aug 1752 *Tryal*. K.

Davis, Ann. S May-Jul T *Tayloe* Jul 1773. M.

Davis, Benjamin. SQS & T *Justitia* Feb 1776. M.

Davis, Catherine. S Dec 1753-Jan 1754 T *Thames* Mar 1754. M.

Davis, Charles. S Lent 1750 LC QA Co., Md., from *Catherine* Nov 1750. Mo.

Davis, Charles. S 14 yrs Lent T *Thornton* May LC AA Co., Md., Jul 1774. E.

Davis, David. S Jan T May 1746. Sx.

Davis, David. S for life Jan T *Tryal* Mar 1757. L.

Davis, Edward. S Jul T Sep 1746 *Mary*. L.

Davies, Edward. S s at Shrewsbury & R 14 yrs Jul T *Restoration* LC Bal Co., Md., Oct 1771. Sh.

Davis, Elizabeth. S Apr-Jun 1739 to be T 14 yrs T *Sea Nymph* to Md. M.

Davis, Elizabeth. S Sep 1740 T *Harpooner* Jan 1741. L.

Davis, Elizabeth. S Feb T Mar 1750 *Tryal*. M.

Davis, Elizabeth. S May-Jul T Sep 1751 *Greyhound*. M.

Davis, Elizabeth. S for life Feb T *Thames* Mar 1752. L.

Davis, Elizabeth. S Jul T *Barnard* Oct 1756. M.

Davis, Elizabeth. S Lent LC AA Co., Md., from *Thornton* Jul 1773. M.

Davis, Elizabeth. S Sep-Oct 1773 T *Justitia* Jan 1774. M.

Davis, Evan. S Apr T Sep 1746. Mo.

Davis *als* Davison, Grace. S & T Sep 1751 *Greyhound*. L.

Davis, Henry. S Oct 1740 T *Harpooner* Jan 1741. L.

Davis, James. S Jun-Dec 1745 T *Plain Dealer* Jan 1746. M.

Davis, James. S Sep T *Ruby* Oct 1754. L.

Davis, James. Ordered for T in 1754 but returned, and pardoned to be T for life (BJ). He.

Davis, Jane. S Lent T *Thornton* May LC AA Co., Md., Jul 1774. M.

Davis, John. S Dec 1746 T Jan 1747 *George William*. L.

Davis, John. S Jul-Dec 1747 LC Knt. Co., Md., from *St. George* Mar 1748. M.

Davis, John. S Summer T Sep 1751 *Greyhound*. Sy.

Davis, John. S Feb T *Thames* Mar 1752. L.

Davies, John. S Jul-Sep T *Ruby* Oct 1754. M.

Davis, John. S s horse Lent R 14 yrs Summer 1757 TB to Va. No.

Davis, John. S Dec T *Neptune* Mar 1761. M.

Davies, John. R 14 yrs Sep T *Randolph* Sep 1768. Ha.

Davies, John. S Lent LC Bal Co., Md., Jul 1772. Sh.

Davis, John. S Merioneth for burglary R 14 yrs Apr LC Md from *Isabella* Jul 1775 & sold to Waters & Gartrall. Wal.

Davis, John Evan. SQS Lent LC AA Co., Md., from *Hanover Planter* Jul 1773. M.

Davis, Joseph. S Lent T Sep 1746 *Mary*. E.

Davis, Joseph. S Apr T *Dolphin* May 1763. L.

Davis, Luke. S 14 yrs Lent LC Bal Co., Md., Jun 1773. He.

Davis, Margaret. S s iron hoops Apr T Dec 1735 *John* LC Annapolis Sep 1736. M.

Davis, Margaret wife of Evan (*qv*). S Apr T Sep 1746. Mo.

Davis, Maria. S 1758 (AHJ). La.

Davis, Mary. S Apr T *Justitia* May 1745. L.

Davis, Mary. SQS Jan 1750 LC QA Co., Md., from *Catherine* Nov 1750. De.

Davis, Mary. S Mar 1757 (AHJ). Sh.

Davis, Mary. SQS Jan T *Thornton* May LC AA Co., Md., Jul 1774. M.

Davis, Mary. S Jul T *Tayloe* Jul 1774. L.

Davis, Matthew. SQS Dec 1753 T *Thames* Mar 1754. M.

Davis, Peter. S Aug 1750 (AHJ). Sh.

Davis, Peter. S Jul-Sep T *Ruby* Oct 1754. M.

Davis, Philip. S Bristol for highway robbery in St. Stephen's parish Summer 1754 R 14 yrs Lent 1755 (BJ). G.

Davis, Richard. S Summer 1746 T Jan 1747. De.

Davis, Richard. S Lent T May 1750 *Lichfield*. Bu.

Davies, Richard. S s gelding at Wellington & R 14 yrs Jul T *Restoration* LC Bal Co., Md., Oct 1771. Sh.

Davis, Samuel. S Dec 1753-Jan 1754 T *Thames* Mar 1754. M.

Davis, Sarah of Bristol. SQS Bristol s in Broad St. Oct 1761 TB to Md Sep 1763. G.

Davis, Sarah. S 14 yrs Sep-Oct 1772 T *Justitia* Jan 1773. M.

Davis, Thomas. S Jun 1739 to be T 14 yrs T *Sea Nymph* to Md. L.

Davis, Thomas. S Summer 1741 LC QA Co., Md., from *Philleroy* Apr 1742. He.

Davis, Thomas. S 14 yrs Feb-Apr T Apr 1746 *Laura*. M.

Davies, Thomas. S Lent T *Tryal* Jul 1754. Sy.

Davis, Thomas. S s sheep Jul 1755. G.

Davis, Thomas. S Mar 1759 (AHJ). Sh.

Davis, Thomas. S Sep-Oct 1772 T *Justitia* Jan 1773. M.

Davis, Thomas. S Jul T *Tayloe* Jul 1773. L.

Davies, Thomas. S s yarn at Baschurch Summer pardoned Sep but LC Md from *William* Dec 1774 & sold to James Hutchings. Sh.

Davis, Velvidera, spinster. S Bristol Sep 1741 LC QA Co., Md., from *Philleroy* Apr 1742. G.

Davis, William. S & T for life Mar 1750 *Tryal*. L.

Davis, William. S Summer T *Barnard* Oct 1756. Sy.

Davis, William. S Jul T *Phoenix* Oct 1760. M.

Davis, William. S Lent LC AA Co., Md., from *Thornton* Jul 1773. L.

Davis, William. S Oct 1773 T *Justitia* Jan 1774. L.

Davies, William (1773). *See* Matthews. Co.

Davis, William. S Lent T *Thornton* May LC AA Co., Md., Jul 1774. L.

Davis, William. SQS Bristol Mar TB May LC Md from *William* Dec 1774 & sold to James Hutchings. G.

Davison - *See* Davidson.

Davy, Ann. S for life Lent LC Bal Co., Md., Jul 1771. De.

Davy, Honor. S Summer 1734 LC Knt Co., Md., Mar 1735 from *Falcon*. De.

Davy, John. S Summer 1773 T *Justitia* Jan 1774. Sy.

Davie, Philip. S Bristol Jun 1750 LC QA Co., Md., from *Catherine* Nov 1750. G.

Davey, Robert. S Jun 1739 T *Sea Nymph* to Md. L.

Davy, Robert. S & T for life Sep 1751 *Greyhound*. L. Davey, William. T *Randolph* Sep 1768. De.

Davy, Thomas. S 14 yrs Lent LC Bal Co., Md., Jul 1772. De.

Davey, William. S May 1754 (AHJ). Co.

Davey, William (1773). See Matthews. Co.

Daw, Michael. S Lent LC AA Co., Md., from *Thornton* Jul 1773. L.

Daw, Samuel. S Mar T Apr 1742 LC PG Co., Md. Do.

Dawes, George. S for shopbreaking at Redlingfield Lent 1740 (IJ). Su.

Daws, Robert. T May 1752 *Lichfield*. Sy.

Dawes, Thomas. S Summer T *Ruby* Oct 1754. E.

Dawkins, Ann. S City 1753 (AHJ). Nl.

Dawkings *als* Crispe, George. S Summer 1744 R 14 yrs Lent T Jul 1745 *Italian Merchant*. E.

Dawkins, John. S Lent 1754 R 14 yrs Summer T *Barnard* Oct 1756. Bu.

Dawkins, Richard. T May 1751 *Tryal*. E.

Dawkins, Thomas. S Lent T *Thornton* May LC AA Co., Md., Jul 1774. E.

Dawks, Mary. S Lent 1767. Wa.

Dawley, Francis. S Lent T Apr 1751. St.

Dawley, Francis. S Lent LC AA Co., Md., from *Thornton* Jul 1773. K.

Dawling, Elizabeth. SQS Ipswich Jul 1748. Su.

Dawney, Mary. T May 1745. Y.

Dawsey, James. S Apr T May 1750 *Lichfield*. M.

Dawsey, Patrick. S Dec 1749-Jan 1750 T Mar 1750 *Tryal*. M.

Dawson, Ann. S Lent T *Dolphin* Apr 1761. Sy.

Dawson *als* Dodson, John. S Jul T Sep 1746 *Mary*. L.

Dawson, John. S Lent T *Thornton* May LC AA Co., Md., Jul 1774. M.

Dawson, Mary. S Feb-Apr Apr 1746 *Laura*. .M.

Dawson, Mary. S Lent LC AA Co., Md., from *Thornton* Jul 1775. M.

Dawson, Richard. S s at Leek Summer LC Md from *William* Dec 1774 & bought his freedom. St.

Dawson, Timothy. S Sep-Oct T *Justitia* Jan 1774. M.

Dawson, William. R & T Apr 1747. Li.

Dawson, William. S s oxen Summer 1754 R 14 yrs Lent 1755 (GJ). Sh.

Dawson, William. S s cow & R Lent 1774. Wa.

Day, Elizabeth. S Sep T *Barnard* Oct 1756. M.

Day, James. S s gold ring Summer 1753 R 14 yrs Lent 1754 (GJ). Be.

Day, Robert (1753) - *See* Hickman. Be.

Day, Susanna. S Jul-Sep T *Ruby* Oct 1754. M.

Day, William of Merstham. SQS Oct 1750 T *Thames* Feb 1751. Sy.

Day, Zacariah. S Lent T Jun 1748 *Lichfield*. E.

Dayley, James. T from Dublin by *Hercules*, LC Bal. Co., Md., Aug 1773, sold to
  William Walters & Richard Guttrell. Ir.

Dayley, Thomas. S Lent LC Bal Co., Md., Jul 1772. G.

Deacon, Elizabeth. S Mar T *Neptune* Mar 1761. L.

Deacon, Sarah. T Jan 1747 *George William*. L.

Deakin *als* Peacock, Mary. S May T Dec 1735 *John* LC Annapolis Sep 1736. L.

Deal, Ann. S Lent T Jul 1745 *Italian Merchant*. Sy.

Deale, Edward. SQS Ipswich Oct 1721. Su.

Deal, James. S Jan T *Justitia* May 1745. L.

Dealtry, Abraham. T Summer 1745. Y.

Dean, John. S Jun-Dec 1745 T *Plain Dealer* Jan 1746. M.

Dean, John. S Jan T Mar 1750 *Tryal*. L.

Deane, Joshua. S & T for life Jan 1736 *Dorsetshire* LC Va Sep 1736. L.

Dean, Richard. S Summer T *Ruby* Oct 1754. Sy.

Dean, Samuel. S Lent LC AA Co., Md., from *Hanover Planter* Jul 1773. M.

Deare, Ann. S Jul T *Barnard* Oct 1756. M.

Deasley *als* Deardsley, Howard. S s coat Feb T Apr 1735 *Patapsco* LC Annapolis
  Oct 1735. L.

Death, George. S Lent 1741 (IJ). Su.

Death, Thomas. S for s from mansion house Lent R 14 yrs Nov 1724. Su.

Deay, Thomas. S Summer 1763 T Jan 1764. Le.

Debang, Hugh. S Apr T May 1752 *Lichfield*. L.

Debidge, Ann. S Feb-Apr 1746 T Apr 1746 *Laura*. M.

Deboe, John. T Jan 1736 *Dorsetshire* LC Va Sep 1736. Sy.

Decelie, Samuel. SW Lent T *Thornton* May LC AA Co., Md., Jul 1774. M.

Deeble, John. S Mar 1761 (AHJ). Co.

Deeks, Thomas. R Summer 1772 for pulling down mills T *Justitia* Jan 1773. E.

Deemer, Jeremiah. S Jul-Sep T *Ruby* Oct 1754. M.

Deer, John. S Lent T Apr 1746. E.

Deer, Richard. S Jan T Mar 1750 *Tryal*. L.

Deighton, William. S Bristol Mar 1755 (AHJ). G.

Delafield, Nicholas. S for breaking into the house of his father Rev. Delafield at
Stokenchurch Summer 1752. O.

Delahay, John. S s at Llancillo Summer LC Md from *William* Dec 1774 & bought
  his freedom. He.

Delahunt, Rose. SL Jul T Sep 1755 *Tryal*. Sy.

Delander, Peter. S May T Jul 1745 *Italian Merchant*. L.

Delaney, Dennis. S Jul 1747 LC Knt Co., Md., from *St. George* Mar 1748. L.

Delaney, Mary. S Apr T May 1752 *Lichfield*. L.

Delaney, Mary. R Dec 1773 T *Justitia* Jan 1774. M.

Delany, Richard. S 14 yrs Lent LC AA Co., Md., from *Thornton* Jul 1775. Sy.

Demaine, Rebecca. S Jun-Dec 1745 T *Plain Dealer* Jan 1746. M.

Dempsey, James. R for life Oct 1772 T *Justitia* Jan 1773. M.

Dempsey, Pearce. S Aug T *Phoenix* Oct 1760. L.

Dempsey, Richard. S & T Sep 1751 *Greyhound*. M.

Denman, Robert. S Lent LC AA Co., Md., from *Thornton* Jul 1773. M.

Dennett, Thomas. S Sep 1740 T *Harpooner* Jan 1741. L.

Dennis, Mary (1730) - *See* Rusher. M.

Dennis, Thomas. S Lent T May 1746. Co.

Dennis, William. S Feb T *Thames* Mar 1754. M.

Dennison *als* Lawler, Catherine. S May-Jul T Jul 1748 *Mary*. M.

Dennison, John. S Sep T *Phoenix* Oct 1760. M.

Dennison, Thomas. R Jul T *Tayloe* Jul 1773. M.

Densley, James [Joseph]. SQS Bristol s silver buckles Dec 1765 TB to Md Apr 1766. G.

Denslow, Mary. S Feb-Apr T May 1751 *Tryal*. M.

Desbrieres, Rose Langlais. S Lent LC AA Co., Md., from *Thornton* May 1771. L.

Devenish, Robert. R for Barbados Oct 1673 but LC Md from *Charles* May 1674. L.

Devereux, James. S Summer T Sep 1751 *Greyhound*. K.

Devereaux, James. R 14 yrs Dec 1773 T *Justitia* Jan 1774. M.

Devett, James. S Lent LC AA Co., Md., from *Hanover Planter* Jul 1773. M.

Devill, Valentine. T from Dublin by *Hercules*, LC Bal. Co., Md., Aug 1773, sold to William Walters & Richard Guttrell. Ir.

Devine, Philip. S Jun-Dec 1745 T *Plain Dealer* Jan 1746. M.

Devits, Ann. S for burglary & R 14 yrs Jun 1741. Wa.

Dewe, Henry. SQS s iron in Culham Mar 1770 (WJ). O.

Dew, John. S Jul 1733 R 14 yrs Jun 1734 LC Knt Co., Md, Mar 1735 from *Falcon*. Ha.

Dewdney, William. SQS Oct 1742 LC QA Co., Md., from *Kent* Jun 1743. De.

Dewell, Alexander. S Plymouth Nov 1763 (AHJ). De.

Dewine, William. S 14 yrs Lent LC AA Co., Md., from *Thornton* May 1771. K.

Dewitt, Elizabeth. S Lent T *Thornton* May LC AA Co., Md., Jul 1774. M.

Dewty, Richard. SQS Sep 1735. La.

Dey, Mary, widow. SQS Bristol Feb 1753. G.

Diamond, Mary. S Sep-Oct 1775 T *Justitia* Feb 1776. M.

Diaper, John. S Lent 1771 but pardoned Mar 1771. M.

Dickins, Catherine. S Mar T *Thames* Mar 1754.

Dickens, David. S Summer T Aug 1749 *Thames*. Sy.

Dickens, John. S Oct 1772 T *Justitia* Jan 1773. L.

Dickens, Thomas. SW Lent LC AA Co., Md., from *Hanover Planter* Jul 1773. M.

Dicker, Catherine. S May-Jul T Jul 1748 *Mary*. M.

Dickinson, Abraham. S & R Dec 1736 T Sep 1737. Y.

Dickinson, Amy. S s cloth at Stroud Jul T *Restoration* LC Bal Co., Md., Oct 1771. G.

Dickinson, George. S May 1770. Li.

Dickinson, Guy. SW Jan T *Thornton* May LC AA Co., Md., Jul 1774. M.

Dickenson, Robert. S s harrow teeth at Tettenhall. S & R 14 yrs Aug T *Restoration* LC Bal Co., Md., Oct 1771. St.

Dickinson, William. S Lent LC Bal Co., Md., Jul 1771. Wa.

Dickson, William. S Jun 1718 T Feb 1719 *Worcester* LC Annapolis Jun 1719. L.

Digby (Digsby), George. R Apr on petition of inhabitants of Hoddesdon & T Oct 1723 *Forward* . Ht.

Diggle, Richard (1731). *See* Coles. So.

Dighton, William. SQS Jan T Mar 1750 *Tryal*. M.

Dikes, Henry, *als* Clarke, James. S Jan T *Thames* Feb 1751. M.

Dilling, James. S Lent T Apr 1746. E.

Dillon, John. S Dec T *Justitia* Dec 1774. M.

Diment, Henry. SQS Jan 1750 LC QA Co., Md., from *Catherine* Nov 1750. De.

Dinecombe, Henry. S Summer T Nov 1735. De.

Dingle, William. S Summer 1731 LC Knt Co., Md., from *Falcon* Apr 1732. De.

Dinns, Sarah. S Lent T Jun 1748 *Lichfield*. K.

Ditch, Lydia. T May 1752 *Lichfield*. K.

Dix, Joseph. S Dec 1745 T *Plain Dealer* Jan 1746. L.

Dixon, Benjamin. S Dec 1749-Jan 1750 T Mar 1750 *Tryal*. M.

Dixon, Eleanor. S Sep-Oct T *Justitia* Dec 1774. M.

Dixon, Henry. S May-Jul T Aug 1749 *Thames*. M.

Dixon, Jane. S Sep T *Phoenix* Oct 1760. M.

Dixon, John. T Aug 1752 *Tryal*. E.

Dixon, John. S Lent LC AA Co., Md., from *Hanover Planter* Jul 1773. M.

Dixon, Richard. S Feb-Apr T May 1751 *Tryal*. M.

Dixon, Richard. SQS Oct 1754 T *Greyhound* Feb 1755. M.

Dixon *als* Pope, Sarah. S Feb T *Thames* Mar 1752. L.

Dixon, William. S Lent LC AA Co., Md., from *Thornton* May 1771. Ht.

Dobbikin, John. S Aug 1752. Li.

Dobbins, William. S s at St. Nicholas, Worcester, for s from his master, an apothecary, Lent 1762. Wo.

Dobson, Thomas. S for burglary Lent R Jun 1723 T Jul 1724 *Robert*. Sy.

Dockerday, William. SQS Jan LC AA Co., Md., from *Thornton* Jul 1773. Sy.

Dodd, Anne. S 14 yrs Lent 1742 LC QA Co., Md., from *Kent* Jun 1743. De.

Dodd, Edward. S Summer 1733 T Summer 1734. Li.

Dodd, Ezekiel (1732) - See Bennett, William. Do.

Dod, John. T May 1752 *Lichfield*. Bu.

Dodd, Robert. S for life Lent LC AA Co., Md., from *Thornton* Jul 1775. K.

Dodd, Samuel. S & T 14 yrs Sep 1751 *Greyhound*. M.

Dodd, Thomas. S Summer T Sep 1751 *Greyhound*. Bu.

Dodds, John. S Summer 1772 LC Bal Co., Md., from *Adventure* Mar 1773. Du.

Dodson, John. S Lent T *Thornton* May LC AA Co., Md., Jul 1774. L.

Doe, Mary. S Dec 1745 T *Plain Dealer* Jan 1746. L.

Doggarty, Patrick. S May-Jul T *Tayloe* Jul 1774. M.

Doggett, Jacob of Camberwell. SQS Apr T *Dolphin* May 1763. Sy.

Doggett, Joseph. R Dec T *Justitia* Dec 1774. M.

Doharty, Matthew. S Feb-Apr T May 1752 *Lichfield*. M.

Dollins, John. R Feb T Sep 1730 *Smith*. E.

Dollison, Thomas. S Oct 1751-Jan 1752 T *Thames* Mar 1752. M.

Dolls, James. S Feb T *Thames* Mar 1752. L.

Dolly, James. SQS & T *Justitia* Sep 1767. Sy.

Donaldson, James. S Apr T *Dolphin* May 1763; runaway. M.

Donaldson, John. S City Lent 1761, broke out of gaol (AHJ). Y.

Donaldson, William. S May T *Saltspring* Jul 1775. L.

Donelly, John. SQS & T Sep 1751 *Greyhound*. M.

Dongey, William. S Summer T Aug 1749 *Thames*. K.

Donkin, Ann, spinster. S City 1752 (AHJ). Nl.

Donnahaugh, Dennis. S Summer 1772 T *Justitia* Jan 1773. E.

Donnelly, Bryan. S Apr T *Dolphin* May 1763. M.

Donnilly, Patrick. S Jul T *Phoenix* Oct 1760. M.

Donnington, William. S May-Jul T Sep 1746 *Mary*. M.

Donnohow, David. S Lent T May 1749 *Lichfield*. K.

Doolan, John. S Aug T *Beverly* Aug 1763. L.

Dooley, John . T from Waterford by *Betsy* LC Bal. Co., Md., Aug 1773. Ir.

Dooley, Laurence. SQS Oct T *Justitia* Dec 1774. M.

Dooley *als* Dowley, Valentine. SQS Sep 1772 T *Justitia* Jan 1773. M.

Door, William. S Lent 1764. Mo.

Dorman, George. SQS Jan LC AA Co., Md., from *Thornton* Jul 1775. Sy.

Dormer, Justin. R 14 yrs May 1725. No.

Dorrell, Thomas. SQS Oct 1754 T *Greyhound* Feb 1755. M.

Dotterell, William. SQS Jul T *Justitia* Dec 1774. M.

Doubledee, Mary. S Sep T Nov 1746. Le.

Doughton, Ann. S s cloak Dec 1735 T Jan 1736 *Dorsetshire* LC Va Sep 1736. M.

Doughty, Elizabeth. S Jan T *Plain Dealer* Jan 1746. L.

Doughty, Hormond. SQS Ipswich Jul 1732. Su.

Doughty, Philip. R Jul T *Tayloe* Jul 1774. M.

Douglas, Alexander. S Dec 1750 T *Thames* Feb 1751. L.

Douglas, Daniel. S Apr T Jun 1735. De.

Douglas, John. SQS Lent T Aug 1752. Y.

Dove, Elianor. S Jan-Apr T *Lichfield* May 1749. M.

Dovetrie, James. T *Tayloe* Jul 1774. L.

Dovey, Joseph. S s sheep Aug 1758 (WJ). Wo.

Dowday, John. S Jul T *Saltspring* Jul 1775. L.

Dowdell, William. S Jan 1761 TB *Dolphin* but R for Army service Oct 1761. L.

Dowdle, Thomas of St. Olave, Southwark. SQS Feb T May 1750 *Lichfield*. Sy.

Dowers, Oliver, aged 19. S for breaking into his uncle's house in St. Philip & Jacob Lent R 14 yrs Summer TB Aug 1739. G.

Dowland, Margaret. S Apr T *Dolphin* Apr 1761. M.

Dowland, William, a lad. S s lead Feb LC from Patapsco Annapolis Nov 1733. M.

Dowle, Jacob. S s handkerchiefs Feb T Apr 1735 *Patapsco* LC Annapolis Oct 1735. L.

Dowling, Richard. S Lent LC AA Co., Md., from *Hanover Planter* Jul 1773. M.

Dowling, Silas. S Sep T *Ruby* Oct 1754. L.

Downe, William. S Lent LC AA Co., Md., from *Thornton* May 1771. K.

Downer, Elizabeth. S Lent R 14 yrs Summer T *Ruby* Oct 1754. Sy.

Downes, Charles. S May T *Saltspring* Jul 1775. L.

Downes, James. S Jul T *Restoration* LC Bal Co., Md., Oct 1771. He.

Downes, Joseph. S Oct T Oct 1749 *Mary*. L.

Downey, John. T from Dublin by *Hercules*, LC Bal. Co., Md., Aug 1773, sold to James Wilson of Augusta Co., Virginia. Ir.

Downie, John. S Edinburgh for murder R Dec 1774. Sco.

Downing, John. SQS Feb T May 1751 *Tryal*. M.

Downing, Solomon. S Lent 1724 but escaped & no further record found. Li.

Downing, William Biron. S Lent R 14 yrs Jul T *Ruby* Oct 1754. K.

Dowset, Joseph. T Apr 1735 *Patapsco* LC Annapolis Oct 1735. E.

Doyle, Margaret. S Lent LC AA Co., Md., from *Thornton* Jul 1775. K.

Doyle, Philip. S Dec 1754 T *Greyhound* Feb 1755. L.

Draper, James. S s horse Lent R 14 yrs Summer 1756 TB to Va. No.

Draper, Samuel. S Lent 1756 (AHJ). No.

Draper, Simon. S Lent LC Bal Co., Md., Jun 1773. Wi.

Draper, Thomas. S Summer LC Bal Co., Md., Dec 1770 from *Trotman* & sold to John Cockey. Nf.

Draper, Thomas. S Lent LC Bal Co., Md., Jun 1773. Wi.

Draper, William. SQS & T Jul 1735 *Amity* LC QA Co., Md., Mar 1736. So.

Drayson, Gabriel. S Lent LC AA Co., Md., from *Thornton* Jul 1773. K.

Drayton, Robert. S s yarn Sep 1750 (WJ). Wa.

Drayton, Samuel. S 14 yrs Lent LC Bal Co., Md., Jun 1773. G.

MORE EMIGRANTS IN BONDAGE

Drewe, Mary. SQS Exeter Aug 1762 (AHJ). De.

Drewry, Jane. S for infanticide Summer 1749 R 14 yrs Lent T May 1750 *Lichfield*. Sy.

Drewry, Robert. S Lent 1724 but escaped & no further record found. Li.

Drewry, Thomas. S Apr 1757. Li.

Drinkwater, Elizabeth. S Apr T *Dolphin* Apr 1761. M.

Driscall, John. S Lent 1744. No.

Driver, John. S Sep T *Phoenix* Oct 1760. L.

Dron, Powel of St. Ann Westminster. S Apr 1718. L.

Drown, William. S 14 yrs Lent 1742 LC QA Co., Md., from *Kent* Jun 1743. De.

Drury, Robert. S Summer T Oct 1739. Hu.

Dubden, Valentine. S Oct 1772 T *Justitia* Jan 1773. L.

Duckett, John. S Sep T 14 yrs Oct 1750 *Rachael*. M.

Duckett, Rachael. S Sep 1740 T *Harpooner* Jan 1741. L.

Duckett, Richard. S s at Ellesborough Lent T *Tayloe* Jul 1773. Bu.

Ducret, John Victoire. R for life Dec T *Justitia* Dec 1774. M.

Dudfield, Thomas. Jul 1783 LC Bal Co., Md., Dec 1783 from *Swift*. M.

Dudley, Joseph. S s money Apr 1751 (WJ). Wa.

Dudley, Joseph. S s at Dudley Jul T *Restoration* LC Bal Co., Md., Oct 1771. Wo.

Dudley, Richard. S Oct-Dec 1754 T *Greyhound* Feb 1755. M.

Duffin, Ann. S Dec T *Justitia* Dec 1774. L.

Duffey, James. S Dec 1772 T *Justitia* Jan 1773. M.

Duffee, James. SQS Apr T *Thornton* May LC AA Co., Md., Jul 1774. M.

Duffy, Michael. SW Jan T *Thornton* May LC AA Co., Md., Jul 1774. M.

Duft, Hugh. SW Lent LC AA Co., Md., from *Hanover Planter* Jul 1773. M.

Dugard, Abraham. S Lent LC AA Co., Md., from *Thornton* Jul 1775. M.

Dugard, John. S Lent LC AA Co., Md., from *Thornton* Jul 1775. M.

Duggan, Thomas. S Dec 1773 T *Justitia* Jan 1774. L.

Duke, Henry. S Lent 1732 LC Knt Co., Md., from *Falcon* Mar 1733. So.

Duke, William. S Jul T Oct 1747. Do.

Dukes, John. S Jul-Sep T *Ruby* Oct 1754. M.

Dukes, Richard. S Jul-Sep T *Ruby* Oct 1754. M.

Dumerick, George, *als* Napton, Francis. S Jan-Apr T *Lichfield* May 1749. M.

Dunbar, Jonathan. S May-Jul T *Tayloe* Jul 1773. M.

Duncan, James. S Aberdeen for housebreaking R Sep 1770. Sco.

Duncan, John. S Lent LC AA Co., Md., from *Thornton* Jul 1773. L.

Duncer, Thomas. S Jun 1758 (AHJ). Wo.

Duncomb, Catherine. T *Ruby* Oct 1754. L.

Duncomb, John. S May-Jul T *Tayloe* Jul 1773. M.

Dundass, Elizabeth. S Jun-Dec 1745 T *Plain Dealer* Jan 1746. M.

Dunfield, Edward. S Sep-Oct T Oct 1749 *Mary*. M.

Dunk, Thomas. R Summer T Aug 1749 *Thames*. Sy.

Dunkin, Margaret. S Lent T *Tryal* Jul 1754. K.

Dunmole, Francis. S Jun T *Tryal* Jul 1754. L.

Dunn, Amy. S Lent T May 1750 *Lichfield*. K.

Dunn, Anne. S Lent 1750 LC QA Co., Md., from *Catherine* Nov 1750. G.

Dunn, Barnaby. SQS Jul T *Justitia* Dec 1774. M.

Dunn, Catherine. S Aug T *Phoenix* Oct 1760. L.

Dunn, Elizabeth. S Lent T Jun 1748 *Lichfield*. K.

Dunn, George. S Lent T Apr 1757. Wa.

Dunn, Hugh. S Apr T May 1751 *Tryal*. L.

Dunn, James. T May 1751 *Tryal*. K.

Dunn, James. S Jul T *Saltspring* Jul 1775. M.

Dunn, John. S Oct 1751-Jan 1752 T *Thames* Mar 1752. M.

Dunn, John. S Dec 1772 T *Justitia* Jan 1773. M.

Dunn, Mary. S Jul-Sep T *Ruby* Oct 1754. M.

Dunn, Patrick. S Lent LC AA Co., Md., from *Hanover Planter* Jul 1773. L.

Dunn, Patrick. S Lent LC AA Co., Md., from *Thornton* Jul 1773. M.

Dunn, Paul. S Apr-Jun 1739 T *Sea Nymph* to Md. M.

Dunn, William, yeoman. S City Summer 1751 (AHJ). Nl.

Dunney, William. S Bristol Jan T Oct 1749 (AHJ). G.

Dunning, Ann. S Lent LC Bal Co., Md., Dec 1770 from *Trotman* & sold to William Hunter. Y.

Dunning, William. S Summer 1751 R 14 yrs Lent T May 1752 *Lichfield*. Sy.

Dunnot, John. SQS Ipswich Jan 1723. Su.

Dunwell, Katherine. S & T Jan 1736 *Dorsetshire* LC Va Sep 1736. L.

Durden, Benjamin. S Dec 1772 T *Justitia* Jan 1773. M.

Durgin, James (1766) - *See* Stowers. Be.

Durham, Abraham. SQS Exeter Nov 1760 (AHJ). De.

Durham, Ann. S for burglary & R Aug 1763 (WJ). He.

Durham, John. S Dec 1750 T *Thames* Feb 1751. L.

Durham, Ralph. S s fish at Hedgerley Lent T *Tayloe* Jul 1773. Bu.

Durrant, Susan. S Summer 1739. Nf.

Durrell, Thomas. S Lent 1750 (AHJ). Wi.

Dust, Francis. S Apr-May T *Tryal* Jul 1754. M.

Dutton, Andrew (1752) - *See* Carroll. M.

Dweheen, Stephen. S Bristol Jan 1752 (AHJ). G.

Dwyer, Catherine wife of Mathew. S Sep-Dec 1746 T Jan 1747 *George William*. M.

Dwyer, John. S & T Jan 1736 *Dorsetshire* LC Va Sep 1736. L.

Dwire, Peter. SQS & T Jul 1773 *Tayloe* to Va. M.

Dyal, Sarah. S Jan-Apr T Jun 1748 *Lichfield*. M.

Dyas, Thomas. S Apr 1755. Li.

Dyer, Angelo. S Lent LC AA Co., Md., from *Hanover Planter* Jul 1773. L.

Dyer, Benjamin. S Summer 1743 LC Knt Co., Md., from *Globe* Mar 1744. De.

Dyer, Betty. SQS Bristol s shirt etc. Mar 1759 (BJ). G.

Dyer, Elizabeth. S Bristol Jan T Feb 1759 (AHJ). G.

Dyer, Francis. SQS May T Jul 1773 *Tayloe* to Va. M.

Dyer, James. S 14 yrs Lent 1744 LC Knt Co., Md., from *Susannah* Aug 1744. De.

Dyer, Margaret. S May-Jul T *Tayloe* Jul 1774. M.

Dyster, Edward. S Jan T *Greyhound* Feb 1755. M.

Eabrey,, Edward. S Mar 1754 (AHJ). Sh.

Eades, John. S Lent LC AA Co., Md., from *Thornton* Jul 1773. M.

Eager, Samuel. S Oct 1751-Jan 1752 R for life & T *Thames* Mar 1752. M.

Eagle, Edward. T *Tryal* Mar 1757. M.

Eagle, Edward. S May T *Beverly* Aug 1763; runaway. M.

Eagle, Thomas. SQS 1755 TB to Md. No.

Eales, Richard. S Summer 1737 LC QA Co., Md., from *Amity* Apr 1738. Co.

Eanis, Bryan. S Lent T 14 yrs Jun 1752 *Tryal*. E.

Earle *als* Saunders, Nicholas. S Jul T *Restoration* LC Bal Co., Md., Oct 1771. De.

Early, Ann. S Lent LC Bal Co., Md., Jul 1772. De.

Easam, James. S 14 yrs Summer LC Bal Co., Md., Dec 1772. Co.

Eason, John. S May-Jul T *Tayloe* Jul 1774. M.

East, Daniel. S Sep-Oct 1775 T *Justitia* Feb 1776. M.

East, Jane. S Jul T *Barnard* Oct 1756. M.

East *als* Wiggington, John. SQS Dec 1772 but received a free pardon & removed from transport ship in March 1773. M.

Eastbury, James. S Lent LC Bal Co., Md., Jun 1773. G.

Easthope, Charles. S Aug 1753 (AHJ). Sh.

Eastlake, Pascoe. SQS Aug Summer LC Bal Co., Md., Dec 1772. Co.

Eastmead, John Clement. S Lent R 14 yrs Summer T Sep 1751 *Greyhound*. E.

Easton (Eason), Thomas. S s book May 1735 T Jan 1736 *Dorsetshire* LC Va Sep 1736. M.

Eaton, Catherine. S Oct-Dec 1754 T *Greyhound* Feb 1755. M.

Eaton, Charles. SQS & T May 1750 *Lichfield*. Ht.

Eaton, Elizabeth. S Dec 1753-Jan 1754 T *Thames* Mar 1754. M.

Eaton, John. R Summer 1772 T *Justitia* Jan 1773; runaway. Sy.

Eaton, Joseph. S for coin clipping & R 14 yrs Lent 1728. St.

Eaton, Mary wife of George. S Aug T *Restoration* LC Bal Co., Md., Oct 1771. Wa.

Eatwell, John. R 14 yrs Feb S & R 14 yrs Summer 1752 TB to Va Sep 1753. Wi.

Eatwell [Etwal], William. S Lent 1767. Bu.

Eaves, Edward. S 14 yrs Lent LC Bal Co., Md., Dec 1772. Wa.

Ebblewhite, John. AT Summer T Aug 1774. Li.

Eberal, Samuel. S Summer T Sep 1753. Wa.

Eccleston, Freeman. S 1755 (AHJ). La.

Eddison *als* Lister, John. S Lent 1728 R 14 yrs Lent 1729. Y.

Eddy, Walter. S May 1755 (AHJ). Co.

Edgele *als* Ellford, William. S Oct 1753 T *Thames* Mar 1754. M.

Edgley *als* Hamilton, Ann. S Jul T *Phoenix* Oct 1760. M.

Edgley, Mary Magdalen. S Lent T *Thornton* May LC AA Co., Md., Jul 1774. L.

Edings, John. S Mar T Apr 1747. Li.

Edmonds, Ann. S & T Jan 1736 *Dorsetshire* LC Va Sep 1736. L.

Edmonds, William. S Mar T *Thames* Mar 1754. L.

Edwards *als* Jones, Ann. S Apr-May T *Saltspring* Jul 1775. M.

Edwards, Anthony. S Lent T *Dolphin* Apr 1761. Sy.

Edwards, Daniel Jr. of Farnham. SQS Jan T *Thames* Feb 1751. Sy.

Edwards, Edward. S Dec 1745 T *Plain Dealer* Jan 1746. L.

Edwards, Edward. S Jan-Jun T Jul 1747 *Laura*. M.

Edwards, Elizabeth wife of Joseph. S Feb-Apr 1746 T Apr 1746 *Laura*. M.

Edwards, John of St. John's. SQS Jan T May 1752 *Lichfield*. Sy.

Edwards, John. R Summer 1773 T *Justitia* Jan 1774. Ht.

Edwards, John. S Sep-Oct T *Justitia* Dec 1774. M.

Edwards, Margaret. S Feb-Apr T May 1751 *Tryal*. M.

Edwards, Philip. T Summer 1745 T Feb 1746. Ha.

Edwards, Robert. R 14 yrs Dec T *Justitia* Dec 1774. M.

Edwards, Samuel. S Lent 1731 LC Knt Co., Md., from *Falcon* Apr 1732. De.

Edwards, Thomas. S s money & R 14 yrs Jun 1740. No.

Edwards, Thomas. S for highway robbery Summer 1756 R 14 yrs Lent 1757. Sh.

Edwards, Thomas. S Jul 1758 R Feb T 14 yrs Apr 1759 *Thetis*. E.

Edwards, Thomas. S Lent LC AA Co., Md., from *Thornton* May 1771. L.

Edwards, Thomas. S Lent LC AA Co., Md., from *Thornton* Jul 1775. Ht.

Edwards, William. S s 4 oxen Apr T Sep 1746. Mo.

Edy, William *als* Pascoe, Joseph. S 14 yrs Lent LC Bal Co., Md., Jul 1771. De.

Eeg, Hans. S for life Aug T *Beverly* Aug 1763. L.

Edgerton, Ann wife of Thomas. S Summer LC Bal Co., Md., Dec 1772; runaway. Wa.

Egerton, Isaac. S May T *Maryland Packet* Oct 1761. M.

Egerton *als* Batt, Philip. S May-Jun T Aug 1752 *Tryal*. M.

Egerton, Shock (1740) - *See* Baker, William. M.

Egleston, Joseph. T Sep 1737 *Pretty Patsy*. L.

Eglon, Robert. S Lent LC Knt Co., Md., from *Bideford* Nov 1737. So.

Elam, James. S 1754 (AHJ). Y.

Elam, John. T Oct 1746. Be.

Elber, Henry. S Dec T *Justitia* Dec 1774. M.

Elder, Alexander. S Lent LC AA Co., Md., from *Thornton* Jul 1775. M.

Elder, Andrew. S Dec T *Justitia* Dec 1774. L.

Elias, Margaret. SQS Bristol s money Mar 1755 (BJ). G.

Elinian, Robert. SW Lent LC AA Co., Md., from *Hanover Planter* Jul 1773. M.

Elkington, Lee. SQS s in Oxford Jan 1771 but R for EI Co. service Mar 1771 (OJ). O.

Ellcock, John. S for housebreaking at Madresfield Lent 1755. Wo.

Ellery, John. S Lent LC Bal Co., Md., Jun 1773. So.

Ellett, Robert. S Lent LC Knt Co., Md., from *Unity* Nov 1733. De.

Ellgood, Christopher of Stebbing. SQS Apr T *Tryal* Jul 1754. E.

Elliman, Thomas. S Lent 1741 LC QA Co., Md., from *Philleroy* Apr 1742. He.

Ellinger, Israel [James]. S Mar 1757. Ha.

Elliott, James of Wisley or Send. S for highway robbery Lent R 14 yrs Summer T Oct 1750 *Rachael*. Sy.

Elliott, Mary wife of John. R 14 yrs City Summer 1754 (AHJ). Nl.

Elliot, Michael. S Summer LC Bal Co., Md., Dec 1772. Ch.

Elliott, Richard. S Apr T May 1750 *Lichfield*. M.

Elliott, Sarah wife of Thomas. S s apron Dec 1735 T Jan 1736 *Dorsetshire* LC Va Sep 1736. M.

Elliott, Thomas. S Lent LC AA Co., Md., from *Thornton* Jul 1775. Sy.

Elliott, William. S Oct 1751-Jan 1752 T *Thames* Mar 1752. M.

Ellis, Ann wife of Edward. S 14 yrs Summer 1749 LC QA Co., Md., from *Catherine* Nov 1750. G.

Ellis, Elizabeth. S May-Jul T Sep 1746 *Mary*. M.

Ellis, Elizabeth. S Lent LC AA Co., Md., from *Thornton* Jul 1775. M.

Ellis, Francis. S Summer 1736. Y.

Ellis, George. S Lent T *Thornton* May LC AA Co., Md., Jul 1774. Sy.

Ellis, Jane. S Oct 1747 LC Knt Co., Md., from *St. George* Mar 1748. L.

Ellis, John. T May 1746. De.

Ellis, Joseph. S 14 yrs Summer 1731 LC Knt Co., Md., from *Falcon* Apr 1732. De.

Ellis, Robert. S s horse Lent 1718 R 14 yrs Summer 1721 T Oct 1723 *Forward* from London. Y.

Ellis, Roger. S Lent LC Potomac, Va., from *Martha* Dec 1724. So.

Ellis, Thomas. S Dec T *Justitia* Dec 1774. M.

Ellis, Walter. S Lent LC Potomac, Va., from *Martha* Dec 1724. Do.

Ellis, William. S Sep 1753. Li.

Ellison, Ann. SQS Bristol s silver mug Sep 1757 (BJ). G.

Ellison, John. SQS Bristol s shoes Mar 1755 (BJ). G.

Ellitt, Ann. SQS & T Oct 1759. Y.

Ellston *als* Inman, William. S Lent T Sep 1755. St.

Elsegood, William. S Jan-Apr T *Lichfield* May 1749. M.

Elson, Henry. S Lent LC AA Co., Md., from *Thornton* Jul 1775. Sy.

Elton *als* Reynolds, Martha. R for America Aug 1702 & to be transported at her own charge or else executed: husband Alexander Reynolds executed for counterfeiting. L.

MORE EMIGRANTS IN BONDAGE

Elwood, William of Dereham. R for Barbados Aug 1671 but LC Md 1672 from *Baltimore* of London . Nf.

Emanuel, Ralph. S Dec 1774; sold to Andrew Leitch, Va., "used to the sea", runaway from *Justitia* Apr 1775. L.

Emanuel, Samuel. S Jul T *Saltspring* Jul 1775. M.

Emmerson, Ann. S Sep-Oct 1775 T *Justitia* Feb 1776. M.

Emerson, John. S City 1749 (AHJ). Nl.

Emerton, John. S Lent LC AA Co., Md., from *Hanover Planter* Jul 1773. L.

Emery, George. Respited 1747. Bd.

Emmott, Nathaniel. SQS Jul 1734 LC Knt Co., Md., from *Hawk* Apr 1735. So.

Emmott, William. S Dec 1753-Jan 1754 T *Thames* Mar 1754. M.

Emms, John. S Feb T Jul 1747. Nf.

Emon, David. S Apr-May T *Saltspring* Jul 1775. M.

Emroe, Christopher. SQS Apr T May 1752 *Lichfield*. M.

Emson, John. S for s from house Lent R 14 yrs Summer 1726. Mo.

Emtage, John. S Jun-Dec 1745 T *Plain Dealer* Jan 1746. M.

Endersby, Thomas. S Feb-Apr T May 1752 *Lichfield*. M.

England, Edward. S 1756 TB to Md. No.

England, John. S Jun 1739 T *Sea Nymph* to Md. L.

English, John. SQS Ipswich 1754. Su.

English, William. S Jul T *Beverly* Aug 1763; runaway. M.

Ennis, Brian. S Chelmsford Jan 1752 (AHJ). E.

Enstead, William. S Apr T May 1750 *Lichfield*. M.

Enwood, John. S Oct 1773 T *Justitia* Jan 1774. L.

Enwood, Mary. S Feb-Apr 1746 T Apr 1746 *Laura*. M.

Eppingstall, John. S Lent LC AA Co., Md., from *Thornton* Jul 1775. E.

Erskine als Maxwell als Hamilton, Thomas. S Lent LC AA Co., Md., from *Thornton* May 1771. M.

Erwin, Esther. S May T *Phoenix* Oct 1760. M.

Esbury, James. SQS Summer 1772 LC Bal Co., Md., Apr 1773.

Essex, Richard. S for highway robbery at Shalstone & R Summer 1772 T *Justitia* Jan 1773. Bu.

Esthers, Sarah of St. Saviour, Southwark, spinster. SQS Apr T May 1750 *Lichfield*. Sy.

Etheridge, Francis. T Jul 1747. Wa.

Etheridge, Sarah. S May-Jul T *Tayloe* Jul 1773. M.

Eustice, Thomas. S Oct T *Justitia* Dec 1774. L.

Evans, Catherine. S 14 yrs Feb-Apr 1746 T Apr 1746 *Laura*. M.

Evans, Charles. R Jul T *Tayloe* Jul 1773. M.

Evans, Dorothy. T May 1752 *Lichfield*. L.

Evans, Edward. S Lent LC Knt Co., Md., from *Unity* Nov 1733. De.

Evans, Edward. S Dec 1750 T *Thames* Feb 1751. L.

Evans, Edward. S Summer T Sep 1751 *Greyhound*. Bu.

Evans, Edward. S 14 yrs Summer 1770 LC Bal Co., Md., Jun 1771. Sh.

Evans, Elias. SQS & T *Justitia* Jan 1773. M.

Evans, Elizabeth. SQS Dec 1772 LC AA Co., Md., from *Thornton* Jul 1773. M.

Evans, Evan of Llanarth. S Carmarthen s sheep R 14 yrs May 1770. Wal.

Evans, Henry. SW Apr T *Thornton* May LC AA Co., Md., Jul 1774. M.

Evans, James. S Feb T *Thames* Mar 1754. M.

Evans, Jane. S Jan-Apr T Jun 1748 *Lichfield*. M.

Evans, John. S Mar 1742. He.

Evans, John. S for breaking into his master's house at Ripple Lent R 14 yrs Summer 1755. Wo.

Evans, John. S Oct T *Barnard* Oct 1756. L.

Evans, John. S Anglesey s sheep R Apr 1771. Wal.

Evans *als* Burgess, John. S Lent but taken from ship & pardoned in July 1773. St.

Evans, Jonathan (1766) - *See* Evans, John. Wo.

Evans, Joseph. S Summer T Aug 1749 *Thames*. E.

Evans, Margaret. S Conway for murder R Apr 1763. Wal.

Evans, Richard. S Denbigh s horse R 14 yrs Mar 1767. Wal.

Evans, Richard. S & R 14 yrs Summer LC Md from *William* Dec 1774 & sold to Thomas Rams? Sh.

Evans, Samuel. S Jul-Dec 1747 T *St. George* Jan LC Knt Co., Md., Mar 1748. M.

Evans, Samuel of Lindridge, farmer. S s hops at St. Nicholas, Worcester, Mar LC Bal Co., Md Jul 1772. Wo.

Evans, Samuel. S 14 yrs Lent LC Bal Co., Md., Jun 1773. G.

Evans, Sarah. S May-Jul T Aug 1749 *Thames*. M.

Evans, Susannah. T Oct 1768 *Justitia* . Sx.

Evans, Thomas. S Lent T Oct 1735. Sh.

Evans, Thomas. S Jul 1749 (AHJ). Sh.

Evans, Thomas. S Apr-May T *Saltspring* Jul 1775. M.

Evans, Timothy. S Jan T Mar 1750 *Tryal*. L.

Evans, William. S Feb T Mar 1750 *Tryal*. M.

Evans, William. S Sep-Oct 1772 T *Justitia* Jan 1773. M.

Evans, William. SQS Apr LC Bal Co., Md., Jun 1773. Mo.

Evans *als* Hamilton, William. S & R 14 yrs Summer LC Md from *William* Dec 1774 & sold to Henry Howard. St.

Eve, John. S for ripping lead from a house Sep T *Barnard* Oct 1756. M.

Everitt *als* Everill, Andrew. S Lent T May 1749 *Lichfield*. Ht.

Everett, James. S Lent LC AA Co., Md., from *Thornton* Jul 1775. E.

Everett, Joseph. R 14 yrs Jul T *Tayloe* Jul 1774. M.

Everett, Joseph. S Lent T *Thornton* May LC AA Co., Md., Jul 1774. E.

Everat, Thomas. SQS s cloth Jul 1761 (OJ). G.

Every, Mary wife of John. S Lent LC AA Co., Md., from *Thornton* Jul 1773. M.

Every, Robert. SW Jan LC AA Co., Md., from *Thornton* Jul 1775. M.

Eves, Richard. S Dec 1745 T *Plain Dealer* Jan 1746. L.

Eves, William. S & T Sep 1751 *Greyhound*. M.

Evett, Elizabeth. S Apr-Jun 1739 T *Sea Nymph* to Md. M.

Evins, Richard. R for Barbados Oct 1673 but LC Md from *Charles* May 1674. L.

Ewdall *als* Evedall, Richard. R for Barbados Oct 1673 LC Md from *Charles* May 1674. M.

Ewen, William. T Jan 1736 *Dorsetshire* LC Va Sep 1736. Sx.

Ewens, William. S 14 yrs Lent LC AA Co., Md., from *Thornton* Jul 1773. K.

Ewer, Samuel. S Lent T Apr 1758. Wa.

Ewin, John. T 1746. Nf.

Ewin, John. S Apr T *Dolphin* Apr 1761. M.

Ewing, Samuel. R 14 yrs Mar T Apr 1742 LC PG Co., Md. Do.

Exelby, Mary. T Jun 1748 *Lichfield*. M.

Exell, Ann. S Lent T *Tryal* Jul 1754. E.

Eyles, Mary. S Feb T Mar 1750 *Tryal*. M.

Eyles, William. S Apr 1753. Li.

Eyre *als* Wheeler, James. S 14 yrs Summer 1738 LC Knt Co., Md., *from Hawk* Apr 1739. Wi.

Eyre, Joseph. S Lent 1724 but escaped & no further record found. Li.

Eyther, John. S Summer 1736 R Lent 1737. Sh.

Fagan, Catherine. S Dec 1773 T *Justitia* Jan 1774. M.

Fagan, John. S Jun T *Tryal* Jul 1754. L.

Fagan, John. S Sep-Oct 1775 T *Justitia* Feb 1776. M.

Fahee, Thomas. S Apr T May 1752 *Lichfield*. L.

Fain, James. S Summer T Sep 1763. Wa.

Fairall, John. S Summer 1747 LC Knt Co., Md., from *St. George* Mar 1748. K.

Fairbank, James. S Jan T *Greyhound* Feb 1755. L.

Fairburn, Robert. S Aug T *Beverly* Aug 1763. L.

Fairburn, William. S York City Lent 1735. Y.

Falcon, Jacob. S Apr T *Justitia* May 1745. L.

Fall, John. S Lent R 14 yrs Summer T Sep 1751 *Greyhound*. K.

Fall, Margaret. S City 1751 (AHJ). Nl.

Fancy, Abel. S 14 yrs Aug 1737 S Jul 1736 LC QA Co., Md., from *Amity* May 1737. Do.

Fanis *als* Sturgis, Sarah. S for vagrancy 1773 TB to Md. No.

Fanjoy, William. S Sep-Oct 1773 T *Justitia* Jan 1774. M.

Farfass [Farvis], William. S Lent for burglary R 14 yrs Summer 1722. G.

Farley, John. T Apr 1746 *Laura*. M.

Farleys, Henry. S Lent R 14 yrs Summer T Oct 1750 *Rachael*. K.

Farmer, Edward. S Lent T May 1749 *Lichfield*. K.

Farmer, Elizabeth. T Sep 1737 *Pretty Patsy*. L.

Farmer, Helen, widow. R for Barbados Oct 1673 but LC Md from *Charles* May 1674. L.

Farmer, John. R Mar T May 1746. Sy.

Farmer, John Sr. S s at St. Julian, Shrewsbury, Summer 1764 but broke out of gaol; John Farmer Jr. acquitted. Sh.

Farmer, Robert. T May 1751 *Tryal*. Sx.

Farmer, Thomas. S Summer T Oct 1752. Wa.

Farnaby, Ralph. S Lent LC AA Co., Md., from *Thornton* May 1771. K.

Farncombe als Vencombe, Henry. S 14 yrs Lent LC Bal Co., Md., Jul 1771. So.

Farr, George. S Aug 1735 S Jul 1736 LC QA Co., Md., from *Amity* May 1737. Do.

Farr, George. S Sep T *Ruby* Oct 1754. L.

Farranton, Jasper. S Lent 1743 LC Knt Co., Md., from *Raven* Feb 1744. Wo.

Farraway, Robert. T Aug 1752 *Tryal*. E.

Farrell, Francis. S Dec 1749-Jan 1750 T Mar 1750 *Tryal*. M.

Farrell *als* Forrel, James. R 14 yrs Sep T *Randolph* Sep 1768. Ha.

Farrell, John. S Sep-Oct 1772 T *Justitia* Jan 1773; runaway. M.

Farroll, John. SW Lent LC AA Co., Md., from *Hanover Planter* Jul 1773. M.

Farrell, Margaret. T from Dublin by *Hercules*, LC Bal. Co., Md., Aug 1773, sold to James McDowell of Virginia. Ir.

Farrell, Peter. S Lent T *Thornton* May LC AA Co., Md., Jul 1774. K.

Farrell, Thomas. SQS Apr T May 1751 *Tryal*. M.

Farrall, William. S Lent T from Bristol May 1755. St

Farren, William. S Summer 1718 LC from *Sophia* QA Co., Md. Mar 1719. De.

Farris *als* Farrow, James. S Feb-Apr T 14 yrs May 1751 *Tryal*. M.

Farrow, Elizabeth. T 1745. Y.

Farrow, John. S Apr T *Justitia* May 1745. L.

Farthing, Anne. SQS Oct 1732 LC Knt Co., Md., from *Falcon* Mar 1733. So.

Farthing, Charles. SQS Jan LC AA Co., Md., from *Thornton* Jul 1775. M.

Farthing, John. S Lent LC AA Co., Md., from *Thornton* May 1771. M.

Farthing, Samuel. S Summer 1734 LC Knt Co., Md., from *Hawk* Apr 1735. De.

Fartley, William. S 1754 (AHJ). La.

Faulkner, Ann. S Aug T *Beverly* Aug 1763. L.

Faulkner *als* Howard, Jane. S Oct-Dec 1750 T *Thames* Feb 1751. M.

Faulkner, Richard. SQS & T Sep 1751 *Greyhound*. M.

Falkner, William. S Apr 1753. Li.

Fawcett, Dudley. S Mar T Apr 1747. Li.

Fawcett, Edward. R 14 yrs Mar 1742 LC PG Co., Md. Co.

Fawcett, James. S Apr T *Lichfield* May 1749. L.

Fawdry, John. S Lent 1735. No.

Fazakerly, James of Tarbock. SQS Jan 1737. La.

Fear, Edmund. S for life Lent LC Bal Co., Md., Jun 1773. So.

Fear, George. S Dec 1749-Jan 1750 T Mar 1750 *Tryal*. M.

Fear, John. S Lent R 14 yrs Summer T *Ruby* Oct 1754. K.

Fearn, John. S for housebreaking & R 14 yrs Jun 1726. Wa.

Fell, Edward. S 14 yrs Lent LC AA Co., Md., from *Thornton* Jul 1773. E.

Fell, William. S Summer T Aug 1749 *Thames*; runaway. Sy.

Fellows, Henry. S s sheep Lent R 14 yrs Summer T *Justitia* Sep 1766. Bu.

Felton, John. S Feb T *Thames* Mar 1752. L.

Felton, William. T Jun *Bideford* LC QA Co., Md., Sep 1752. Wo.

Fenby, Thomas. S Dec T *Justitia* Dec 1774. M.

Fenley, Henry. S Oct T *Justitia* Dec 1774. L.

Fenn *als* Welham, James. S for life Lent T *Thornton* May LC AA Co., Md., Jul 1774. K.

Fennell, Richard. S 14 yrs Lent 1758 TB to Va. No.

Fenner, Isaac. T Jun 1747. E.

Fenney, William. S 1760 (AHJ). La.

Fenton, James. S Apr T May 1750 *Lichfield*. M.

Fenton, William. S Jan T *Thames* Feb 1751. M.

Ferand, William. SQS & T Apr 1742 LC PG Co., Md. Co.

Ferriday, Edward. S Lent LC Bal Co., Md., Jul 1774. Sh.

Ferring, Charles. S Apr-May T *Tryal* Jul 1754. M.

Field, Ann. S Apr T Jun 1748 *Lichfield*. L.

Field, Anne. SQS Jul 1756 (OJ). O.

Field, Ann. S Dec 1773 T *Justitia* Jan 1774. L.

Field, Ann. S 14 yrs Jul T *Tayloe* Jul 1774. L.

Field, Hannah. SQS & T Sep 1751 *Greyhound*. M.

Field, Hannah. S Lent LC AA Co., Md., from *Thornton* Jul 1775. L.

Field, James. S Lent LC AA Co., Md., from *Thornton* May 1771. M.

Field, Margaret. S Summer T Aug 1749 *Thames*. Sy.

Field, Mary. S 14 yrs Feb-Apr T Apr 1746 *Laura*. M.

Field, Mary. S s at All Saints, Worcester, Jul T *Restoration* LC Bal Co., Md., Oct 1771. Wo.

Field, William. S May T *Phoenix* Oct 1760. M.

Field, William. SQS Jan LC AA Co., Md., from *Thornton* Jul 1773. Sy.

Fielder, Stephen. S Feb T *Thames* Mar 1754. L.

Fielding, John. S Jul 1720 for s sheep, whipped & died on passage in *Gilbert* 1721 (NM). No.

Fielding, John. S Oct 1772 T *Justitia* Jan 1773. L.

Fife, John. S Apr-Jun 1739 T *Sea Nymph* to Md. M.

Fife, William. S Oct T *Barnard* Oct 1756. M.

Fiford, William. S Lent 1750 LC QA Co., Md., from *Catherine* Nov 1750. Do.

Fill, John. S Dec 1753 (AHJ). Wo.

MORE EMIGRANTS IN BONDAGE

Fillingham, George. S Sep 1751. Li.

Finch, Heneage. S Sep-Dec 1746 T Jan 1747 *George William*. M.

Finch, John. S Jul T Sep 1746 *Mary*. L.

Finch, Samuel. SQS Bury St. Edmunds Jan 1724. Su.

Finder, Joseph of St. Saviour, Southwark. SQS Apr T May 1752 *Lichfield*. Sy.

Finlay, Richard. S Summer T Aug 1749 *Thames*. E.

Finney, Richard. S Sep T Oct 1759. Le.

Firth, Hannah. S 1761 (AHJ). Du.

Firth, James. S Summer LC Dec 1770 from *Trotman* and sold to Daniel Shaw. Nt.

Firth, John. S 1762 (AHJ). Du.

Fish, Thomas. S 14 yrs Jul 1736 S Jul 1736 LC QA Co., Md., from *Amity* May 1737. Ha.

Fisher *als* Casey, Alexander. S Jan-Apr T *Lichfield* May 1749. M.

Fisher, Christopher. S May-Jul T Sep 1751 *Greyhound*. M.

Fisher, James. S Summer 1761. Ca.

Fisher, John. S May-Jul T Sep 1751 *Greyhound*. M.

Fisher, John. S Aug T *Phoenix* Oct 1760. L.

Fisher, John. Jul 1783 LC Bal Co., Md., Dec 1783 from *Swift*. M.

Fisher, Joseph. S s at Kingswinford Summer 1758. St.

Fisher, Joseph. S Lent R 14 yrs Summer T Sep 1751 *Greyhound*. Sy.

Fisher, Joseph. SW Lent LC AA Co., Md., from *Hanover Planter* Jul 1773. M.

Fisher, Joseph. S Lent LC Bal Co., Md., Jun 1773. Ha.

Fisher, Thomas. S Apr-Jun 1739 T *Sea Nymph* to Md. M.

Fisher, William. T Summer 1745 T Feb 1746. Ha.

Fiske, Mary. SQS Bury St. Edmunds Jan 1721. Su.

Fitch, Edward. S Apr-May T *Tryal* Jul 1754. M.

Fitness, Eden. R Summer 1772 T *Justitia* Jan 1773. Sy.

Fitzgerald, Catherine. S Dec 1745 T *Plain Dealer* Jan 1746. L.

Fitzgerald, Eleanor. S Lent LC AA Co., Md., from *Thornton* Jul 1773. M.

Fitzgerald, James. S Sep-Oct 1772 T *Justitia* Jan 1773. M.

Fitzgerald, Martin. S confirmed Apr T Dec 1734 *Caesar* . Sy.

Fitzjohn, Edward. S Summer 1758 TB to Va. No.

Fitzmorris, John. S May-Jul T *Tayloe* Jul 1773. M.

Fitzsimmonds, James. S Dec 1747 LC Knt Co., Md., from *St. George* Mar 1748. M.

Fitzwater, Joseph. S for life Jan T *Justitia* May 1745. L.

Flack, George. S Lent T Jun 1748 *Lichfield*. Ht.

Flack *als* Jones, John of Lambeth. S Lent T May 1750 *Lichfield*. Sy.

Flack, William. S 14 yrs Lent LC AA Co., Md., from *Thornton* Jul 1775. E.

Flake, Sarah. SQS May T Jul 1773 *Tayloe* to Va. M.

Flanders, John. T Aug 1749. Bu.

Flannagan, Andrew. S Apr T *Dolphin* Apr 1761. M.

Flannagan, William. S Lent T *Thornton* May LC AA Co., Md., Jul 1774. M.

Flathers, Edward. S Dec T *Justitia* Dec 1774. L.

Flemming, Thomas. S Lent LC AA Co., Md., from *Thornton* Jul 1775. E.

Fleppen, John. S for perjury Jul LC Md from *William* Dec 1774 & sold to Richard Jacob. Do.

Fletcher, Ambrose. S Jan-Jun T 14 yrs Jun 1728 *Elizabeth* LC Potomack Aug 1729; petition from parents Robert & Mary Fletcher. L.

Fletcher, Eleanor. S Jul T *Barnard* Oct 1756. M.

Fletcher, George. SQS Jul LC Bal Co., Md., Dec 1772. Sh.

Fletcher, John. SQS Apr 1729. La.

Fletcher, John. S Sep T *Ruby* Oct 1754. L.

Fletcher, Joseph of Ardwick. SQS Apr 1730. La.

Fletcher, Joseph of Formby, husbandman. SQS Jan 1737. La.

Fletcher, Sarah wife of Joseph of Ardwick (*qv*). SQS Jan 1730. La.

Fletcher, William (1730) - *See* Bobell. La.

Fletcher, William. S Jan-Jun T Jul 1747 *Laura*. M.

Fletcher, William. S Dec 1773 T *Justitia* Jan 1774. M.

Fleweman, William. S Norwich Sep T Nov 1746. Nf.

Flinders, William. S Lent T Apr 1758 *Lux* from London. Db.

Fling, John. S Jul-Dec 1747 LC Knt Co., Md., from *St. George* Mar 1748. M.

Flint, John. S 14 yrs Lent T *Thornton* May LC AA Co., Md., Jul 1774. Ht.

Flint, Richard. S Lent but taken from transport ship & pardoned in April 1775. M.

Flintham, Mary. S Apr T *Phoenix* Oct 1760. M.

Flood, Frances. SQS Dec 1772 LC AA Co., Md., from *Thornton* Jul 1773. M.

Flood, Francis. S Jan T 14 yrs Feb 1719 *Worcester* LC Annapolis Jun 1719. L.

Flood, Matthew. SW Apr T *Thornton* May LC AA Co., Md., Jul 1774. M.

Flower, James. SQS Jan LC Bal Co., Md., Apr 1773. G.

Flower, Samuel. SW Apr T *Thornton* May LC AA Co., Md., Jul 1774. M.

Flowers, Jane. S Jul-Dec 1747 LC Knt Co., Md., from *St. George* Mar 1748. M.

Flowers, William. S Summer 1746 T Jul 1747. Wa.

Floyd, Anne wife of William. S City Summer 1718 T 14 yrs to Va Aug 1719. Nl.

Floyd, William. S s sheep Summer 1748 R 14 yrs Lent LC Md from LC QA Co.,
    Md., from *Chester* Nov 1749. He.

Fluck, Richard. S Lent LC Bal Co., Md., Jul 1772. G.

Fogarty, Mary. S Feb T *Neptune* Mar 1761. M.

Fogarty, Patrick. S Jun T *Maryland Packet* Oct 1761. M.

Folks [Fowkes] Edward. S s at Maer Summer LC Md from *William* Dec 1774 & sold
    to Thomas Johnson Jr. St.

Follard, James (John). S Jul T 14 yrs Aug 1718 *Eagle* LC Charles Town Mar 1719. L.

Foller, Robert. S Lent but taken from transport ship & pardoned in April 1774. L.

Folwell, John. S Summer T Dec 1737 from London. No.

Food, James. S Lent T *Lichfield* May 1749. Sy.

Foote, Elizabeth. S Feb-Apr 1746 T Apr 1746 *Laura*. M.

Foot, Simon. S Lent LC Bal Co., Md., Jun 1773. Do.

Forbes, Francis. S Sep-Oct T Oct 1749 *Mary*. M.

Forbes, James. S for life Summer 1770 LC Bal Co., Md., Jun 1771. Wo.

Forbess, John. S May-Jul T *Tayloe* Jul 1773. M.

Ford, Amelia. S & T Aug 1752 *Tryal*. L.

Ford, Ann. S Lent T *Thornton* May LC AA Co., Md., Jul 1774. K.

Ford, James (Francis). T Jan 1736 *Dorsetshire* LC Va Sep 1736. Sy.

Ford, Jeremiah of Reigate. SQS Apr T May 1750 *Lichfield*. Sy.

Ford, John. S Sep-Oct 1775 T *Justitia* Feb 1776. M.

Ford, Mary Ann. S Feb-Apr 1746 T Apr 1746 *Laura*. M.

Ford, Patrick. S Lent T *Thornton* May LC AA Co., Md., Jul 1774. E.

Ford, Richard. S Feb T *Thames* Mar 1754. M.

Ford, Thomas. S Dec 1745 T *Plain Dealer* Jan 1746. L.

Ford, Thomas. S Lent LC Bal Co., Md., Jun 1773. Ha.

Ford, William. S Summer LC Bal Co., Md., Dec 1772. St.

Fordham, Jacob. S Jan T *Thames* Feb 1751. M.

Fordham, Thomas. S Lent T *Thornton* May LC AA Co., Md., Jul 1774. E.

Fore, George. SQS Jan T *Thornton* May LC AA Co., Md., Jul 1774. Sy.

Foreman, Mary. S Dec 1753-Jan 1754 T *Thames* Mar 1754. M.

Foreman, Richard (1738). *See* Pointer. Wi.

Foresight, John. S Jul-Sep T *Ruby* Oct 1754. M.

Forey, William. T May 1751 *Tryal*. Sx.

Forest, Henry. S for housebreaking Lent R 14 yrs Summer 1755 (GJ). Sh.

Forrest, Robert. SQS May 1736 LC QA Co., Md., from *Amity* May 1737. Do.

Forrester, John. S Jul T *Beverly* Aug 1763. M.

Forester, Robert. S City Easter 1758 (AHJ).

Forsbrook, Richard. S Lent for housebreaking at Stourbridge R ̱4 yrs Summer 1755. Wo.

Forse, Richard. S Lent 1750 LC QA Co., Md., from *Catherine* Nov 1750. Do.

Forshaw, James. S 1759 (AHJ). La.

Forster - *See* Foster.

Fortescue, John (1754) - *See* Foster. O.

Forth (Firth?), James. S Summer LC Bal Co., Md., Dec 1770 from *Trotman* & sold to Daniel Shaw. Nt.

Forward, Ambrose. S s goat hair May T Dec 1735 *John* LC Annapolis Sep 1736. M.

Fosker, William. SW Apr T *Thornton* May LC AA Co., Md., Jul 1774. M.

Foskett, Henry. S Lent T May 1749 *Lichfield*. Bu.

Fossett, John. S Lent LC AA Co., Md., from *Hanover Planter* Ju ̱ 1773. M.

Foster, Fortune. S s edging Jan T Apr 1735 *Patapsco* LC Annapolis Oct 1735. L.

Forster, George. S Apr-May T *Tryal* Jul 1754. M.

Forster, Henry. S s at Handsworth Aug T *Restoration* LC Bal Co., Md., Oct 1771. St.

Forster, John *als* Bell, William. T Jan 1748. Nl.

Foster, John. S Jan-Apr T *Lichfield* May 1749. M.

Foster, John. T May 1752 *Lichfield*. Sy.

Foster *als* Fortescue, John. S Lent T Sep 1754. O.

Foster, John. SQS Oct 1770 LC AA Co., Md., from *Thornton* May 1771. Ht.

Foster, John. S Lent 1752. No.

Foster, John. S Jan T *Tryal* Mar 1757. L.

Forster, Mary. S Jul T *Tayloe* Jul 1773. L.

Foster, Mary. S Summer LC Bal Co., Md., Dec 1770 from *Trotman* & sold to John Gill Jr. X.

Foster, Thomas. S Jun 1739 T *Sea Nymph* to Md. L.

Forster, William. S s brass stamp May 1735 T Jan 1736 *Dorsetshire* LC Va Sep 1736. M.

Forster, William. S Feb-Apr T May 1752 *Lichfield*. M.

Foster *als* Fosker, William of St. Paul Covent Garden. SW Apr LC Md Jul 1774, respited Apr pardoned Aug 1775. M.

Foulks, Edward. S Sep T *Ruby* Oct 1754. L.

Foulson, Henry. TB Aug 1735 T *Squire* LC Md Apr 1736. Db.

Fountayne, Aaron of Water Newton. R for Barbados Aug 1671 but LC Md Feb 1672. Hu.

Fountaine, John. S Summer 1733 LC Knt Co., Md., from *Falcon* Apr 1734. Do.

Fowke, Hugh. S Apr 1757 R for life Aug 1758 (WJ). Wa.

Fowks, Samuel. S Lent T May 1765. Db.

Fowler, Elizabeth. S Lent R 14 yrs Summer T *Maryland Packet* Oct 1761. Bu.

Fowler, Hester. S 14 yrs Jan T *Plain Dealer* Jan 1746. M.

Fowler, John. S May-Jul T *Tayloe* Jul 1773. M.

Fowler, Thomas. S Dec 1750 T *Thames* Feb 1751. L.

Fowles *als* Fowler, Mary. S May-Jul T Jul 1748 *Mary*. M.

Fox, Andrew. S Summer T Sep 1772 TB to Md. No.

Fox, Ann. T 1747. Db.

Fox, Mary. S Lent T *Thornton* May LC AA Co., Md., Jul 1774. L.

Foxall, Elizabeth. S 14 yrs Lent LC Bal Co., Md., Jul 1771. Do.

Foxall, Joseph. S Mar T Apr 1737. Wa.

MORE EMIGRANTS IN BONDAGE

Foy, James. S Aug T *Beverly* Aug 1763. L.

Foyle, William. S Jul TB Sep LC Md from *William* Dec 1774 & sold to Henry Penny. Wa.

Fraine, James. S for perjury at last Assizes, to stand once in pillory and then to be T 14 yrs Aug 1763 (WJ). Wa.

Frame, Matthias, a soldier. S s money Feb T Apr 1735 *Patapsco* LC Annapolis Oct 1735. M.

Franceys, John. S Oct 1735 T Jan 1736 *Dorsetshire* LC Va Sep 1736. M.

Francis, Christopher of Bristol, mariner. S & R 14 yrs for s from the *Hopewell* in distress & TB to Va Apr 1773. G.

Francis, John. SQS Oct 1773 LC Bal Co., Md., Jul 1774. Do.

Francis, Matthias. S Apr-Jun 1739 T *Sea Nymph* to Md. M.

Francis, Phene (Phebe). S Lent but pardoned May 1773. M.

Francis, Richard of Hendon. S s sheep Oct 1730 LC from *Forward* Potomack Jan 1731. M.

Francis, Thomas. S Lent LC Knt Co., Md., from *Bideford* Nov 1737. So.

Franklin, Catherine. S May T *Saltspring* Jul 1775. L.

Franklin, Charles. S Sep 1747 LC Knt Co., Md., from *St. George* Mar 1748. L.

Francklyn, James. S s sheep Aug 1754 (RG). Be.

Franklin, Thomas. S Lent LC AA Co., Md., from *Thornton* Jul 1773. L.

Franks, John. S Summer T Dec 1737. Le.

Frazer, Charlotte. Respited May 1764 TB *Dolphin* but pardoned same month. Sy.

Fraizier, Elizabeth. S Feb-Apr T *Justitia* May 1745. M.

Frazer, Henry. S Lent LC AA Co., Md., from *Thornton* Jul 1773. K.

Frasier, Sarah. S Lent T *Dolphin* May 1763. K.

Fream, John. S Lent LC Bal Co., Md., Jul 1772. G.

Frederick, John. S Apr T Jun 1748 *Lichfield*. L.

Freeman, Ann. S Apr T May 1750 *Lichfield*. L.

Freeman, James. SQS Feb LC AA Co., Md., from *Thornton* Jul 1775. M.

Freeman, John. S May-Jul T Sep 1746 *Mary*. M.

Freeman, Mary. S May-Jul T Jul 1748 *Mary*. M.

Freeman, Mary. S Feb-Apr T May 1751 *Tryal*. M.

Freeman, Nathaniel. T May 1752 *Lichfield*. E.

Freeman, Samuel. S Apr T May 1751 *Tryal*. L.

Freeman, Thomas. S Feb T *Thames* Mar 1752. L.

Freeman, Thomas. S s wheat Apr 1773 (HJ). G.

Freer, Joseph. S 1754 TB to Md. No.

Freestone, Walter. S Summer 1718 LC from *Sophia* QA Co., Md. Mar 1719. So.

French, Alice. S Jun-Dec 1745 T *Plain Dealer* Jan 1746. M.

French, David. S Sep-Oct 1772 T *Justitia* Jan 1773. M.

French, George. SQS Apr 1732 LC Knt Co., Md., from *Falcon* Apr 1734. So.

French, Richard. S Summer 1741 LC QA Co., Md., from *Philleroy* Apr 1742. De.

French, William. S Dec T *Justitia* Dec 1774. M.

Freney, Elizabeth. SQS Exeter Jul T *Restoration* LC Bal Co., Md., Oct 1771. De.

Frevitt, William. S Lent T *Tryal* Jul 1754. Sy.

Frewin, Mary. SQS Apr T May 1752 *Lichfield*. M.

Frickens, Mary. S Lent LC AA Co., Md., from *Hanover Planter* Jul 1773. L.

Frindly, John. S Jan-Apr T *Lichfield* May 1749. M.

Frizer *als* Smith, Richard. S s horse at Temple Laughern Jul 1769 R 14 yrs Lent 1770. Wo.

Frost, Abraham. S s naval stores Summer T Aug 1749 *Thames*. K.

Frost, Job. LC Md from *Isabella* Jul 1775 & sold to Nathan Jacobs. X

Frost, William, weaver. SQS Jan 1730 & Summer 1732 LC Knt Co., Md., from *Falcon* Mar 1733. De.

Frost, William. S Summer 1738 LC Knt Co., Md., from *Hawk* Apr 1739. Ha.

Fry *als* Hull, Ann. SQS Apr T May 1752 *Lichfield*. M.

Fry, Richard. SQS Feb but taken from transport ship & pardoned in April 1775. M.

Fry, William. S Apr T for life May 1750 *Lichfield*. M.

Fryatt, Bartholomew SQS Ipswich Jan 1738. Su.

Fryer, Henry. T *York* to Md Jun 1740. Bu.

Fryer *als* Turpin, John. S Feb T 14 yrs Mar 1750 *Tryal*. M.

Fryers, John. R 14 yrs Oct 1772 T *Justitia* Jan 1773. M.

Fukes, Thomas. SQS Sep T *Justitia* Dec 1774. M.

Fulford, John. S May-Jul T Sep 1751 *Greyhound*. M.

Fulford, Mary. T May 1746. De.

Fulham, Thomas. S Apr-May T *Tryal* Jul 1754. M.

Fulker, Mary. S Jan-Jun T Jul 1747 *Laura*. M.

Fullagar, John. T May 1751 *Tryal*. K.

Fuller *als* Pulley, Elizabeth. S Apr T *Justitia* May 1745. L.

Fuller, John. S s gelding Norwich Summer R 14 yrs Dec 1726. Nf.

Fuller, John. S Lent T May 1750 *Lichfield*. E.

Fuller, Sarah. S Sep T Oct 1750 *Rachael*. M.

Fuller, Thomas *als* Smith *als* Shorter, William. S 14 yrs Lent LC Bal Co., Md., Jun 1773; runaway. So.

Fuller, William. T 1746. Su.

Fuller, Zachariah. S s sheep Summer 1744 R 14 yrs Lent 1745 (GJ). Be.

Funnell, John. S s shirts Apr T Dec 1735 *John* LC Annapolis Sep 1736. M.

Furber, John. SQS & T Jul 1735 *Amity* LC QA Co., Md., Mar 1736. So.

Furness (Furnace), Amy. S Jun 1718 T Feb 1719 *Worcester* LC Annapolis Jun 1719. L.

Furness, John. T Apr 1735 *Patapsco* LC Annapolis Oct 1735. E.

Furrier, Ann. S Lent T *Thornton* May LC AA Co., Md., Jul 1774. L.

Fyson, Thomas (1747). *See* Lemon. E.

Gaffney, James. S Summer 1731 LC Knt Co., Md., from *Falcon* Apr 1732. So.

Gaffney, Michael. Jul 1783 LC Bal Co., Md., Dec 1783 from *Swift*. M.

Gaffy, Mary. SQS Jul T *Justitia* Dec 1774. M.

Gagey, Samuel. T Jan 1748. Sy.

Gahagan, John. R for life Jul T *Tayloe* Jul 1773. M.

Gailks, Mary. T Jan 1736 *Dorsetshire* LC Va Sep 1736. Sy.

Gaite, Hester. S Bristol Jan T Dec 1757 (AHJ). G.

Gale, Dorothy. S May-Jul T Aug 1749 *Thames*. M.

Gale, John. S Lent LC Potomac, Va., from *Martha* Dec 1724. Wi.

Gale, John. S 14 yrs Lent 1742 LC QA Co., Md., from *Kent* Jun 1743. De.

Gale, Richard. S Summer 1718 LC from *Sophia* QA Co., Md. Mar 1719. Co.

Gale, Richard. SQS Jan LC Bal Co., Md., Jul 1771. Do.

Gallon, Edward. S Summer 1733 R 14 yrs Summer 1734. Nl.

Gallon, Robert. S s sheep Apr 1746 T Feb 1747. Nl.

Galloway, James. S Jan T *Justitia* May 1745. L.

Galloway, John. R 14 yrs Bristol May 1743 LC Knt Co.,Md., from *Raven* Feb 1744. G.

Galpin, William. S Lent LC Bal Co., Md., Jul 1771. Do.

Gambell, James of St. Olave, Southwark. S Lent T May 1750 *Lichfield*. Sy.

Gamble, Thomas. S Lent T *Lichfield* May 1749. Sy.

Gammins, Elizabeth. S Apr 1747: S at Wells to hang Sep 1753 for returning. So.

Gammon, John. S Exeter Sep 1750 (AHJ). De.

Gane, Mary. S Bristol Jan T Mar 1752 (AHJ). G.

Gannon, John. S Lent LC AA Co., Md., from *Thornton* May 1771. M.

Gant *als* Lowe, James of Leyland, miller. PT 1726-1728. La.

Gard, Christopher. SQS Jan LC Bal Co., Md., Jul 1772. So.

Gardner, Anne. SQS Gloucester Jul 1754 (OJ). G.

Gardiner, Ann, spinster. S City Summer 1756 (AHJ). Nl.

Gardner, Elizabeth. S Jun-Dec 1745 T *Plain Dealer* Jan 1746. M.

Gardner *als* Bridgwater, Elizabeth. S Feb-Apr 1746 T Apr 1746 *Laura*. M.

Gardner, Francis. S s shoes Jul 1735 T Jan 1736 *Dorsetshire* LC Va Sep 1736. M.

Gardner, Henry. S Lent T from Bristol May 1754. Sh.

Gardner, James. S 1762 (AHJ). La.

Gardner, Mary. S Lent T May 1749 *Lichfield*. E.

Gardiner, Philis. S Aug 1765 R 14 yrs Feb T Apr 1766 Ann. Sx.

Gardner, Richard. S May-Jul T Sep 1751 *Greyhound*. M.

Gardner, Samuel. S May-Jul T Sep 1746 *Mary*. M.

Gardener, Sarah. S Jan-Apr T *Lichfield* May 1749. M.

Gardiner, William. S Norwich Aug T Sep 1746. Nf.

Gardiner, William. S Norwich & T 1747. Nf.

Gardiner, William. S Summer T *Barnard* Oct 1756. Sy.

Garland, Elizabeth wife of Edward. S s apron Dec 1735 T Jan 1736 *Dorsetshire* LC Va Sep 1736. M.

Garmouth, Edward. S Apr T Sep 1751. Sy.

Garne, Thomas. S 14 yrs Lent LC Bal Co., Md., Jun 1773. G.

Garner, Leda. S May T *Saltspring* Jul 1775. L.

Garner, Samuel. S for highway robbery Lent R 14 yrs Summer 1753 TB to Va. No.

Garnes, Lewis. S Oct 1773 T *Justitia* Jan 1774. L.

Garnett, John. S at Southwark Jan S Lent LC AA Co., Md., from *Thornton* Jul 1773. Sy.

Garnett, Richard. S Apr-Jun 1739 T *Sea Nymph* to Md. M.

Garnon, Judith. S Aug T *Beverly* Aug 1763. L.

Garrard, Robert. S s mare Summer 1750 R 14 yrs Lent T May 1751 *Tryal*. E.

Garratt, Bartholomew. S May-Jul T *Tayloe* Jul 1773. M.

Garrett, John. S Summer T Oct 1739. Hu.

Garrett, John, an old convict. S s sheep Lent R 14 yrs Summer T Aug 1752 *Tryal*. Bu.

Garrett, Joseph. S Lent LC AA Co., Md., from *Thornton* Jul 1775. M.

Garrett, Richard. R for life Jul T *Tayloe* Jul 1774. M.

Garrat, Robert. S & R for highway robbery Sep 1750 (WJ). St.

Garrett, Valentine. S Lent 1732 LC Knt Co., Md., from *Falcon* Mar 1733. Do.

Garrick, Arthur. SQS Apr T May 1751 *Tryal*. M.

Garrison, Elizabeth. S Lent LC AA Co., Md., from *Thornton* Jul 1775. E.

Garth, James. S 14 yrs Lent T *Thornton* May LC AA Co., Md., Jul 1774. M.

Gascoyne, William. S Sep-Oct T Oct 1749 *Mary*. M.

Gaskin, John. S Lent TB Aug 1733. Db.

Gasson, Henry. T Jan 1736 *Dorsetshire* LC Va Sep 1736. Sx.

Gate, Stephen. S Jan T *Thames* Feb 1751. L.

Gates, Samuel of Great Canfield, higler. SQS Oct 1773 T *Justitia* Jan 1774. E.

Gatfield, Margaret. S Lent LC Bal Co., Md., Jul 1772. Wo.

Gauntlett, William. S Summer 1734 LC Knt Co., Md., Mar 1735 from *Falcon*. Ha.

Gay, Richard. S Summer 1731 LC Knt Co., Md., from *Falcon* Apr 1732. De.

Gayer, Andrew. So. S Summer 1718 LC from *Sophia* QA Co., Md. Mar 1719. De.

Gayley, John of Coston, Worcs. S for giving false evidence in King's Bench May

1763 (WJ). L.

Gaywood, John. S Feb-Apr T May 1751 *Tryal.* M.

Gaywood, William. S Feb T *Neptune* Mar 1761. L.

Gazy, Samuel. S Mar T Apr 1737. Wa.

Gazey, Samuel. S Summer 1747 LC Knt Co., Md., from *St. George* Mar 1748. Sy.

Geach, James. S Summer 1731 LC Knt Co., Md., from *Falcon* Apr 1732. Co.

Geary, Jane. S Lent T *Dolphin* Apr 1761. Sy.

Geaton (Gaten), William. R 14 yrs Summer LC Md. from *Reformation* Aug 1722. De.

Gee, George of Enfield. PT Apr R Oct 1673 LC Md from *Charles* May 1674. M.

Gee, John. S Lent T *Thornton* May LC AA Co., Md., Jul 1774. M.

Gent, George. S Summer 1738 LC QA Co., Md. Jun 1739. De.

Gentry, Samuel. S Oct-Dec 1754 T *Greyhound* Feb 1755. M.

George, Andrew. S Apr 1752 (WJ). Wa.

George, Elizabeth wife of Edward. S Feb T *Tryal* Mar 1757. M.

George, George. S s horse Lent R 14 yrs Summer 1759 TB to Va. No.

George, John. S & T Jan 1736 *Dorsetshire* LC Va Sep 1736. L.

George, Joseph. S Chelmsford Jan 1754 (AHJ). E.

George, Little. S Apr-Jun 1739 T *Sea Nymph* to Md. M.

George, Philip. S s sheep & R Summer LC Md from *William* Dec 1774 & sold to James Hutchings. Mo.

George, Richard. S May-Jul T *Tayloe* Jul 1773. M.

George, Thomas. S s sheep & R Summer LC Md from *William* Dec 1774 & sold to James Hutchings. Mo.

George, William. S 14 yrs for receiving sheep stolen at Llanvercha by Thomas & Philip George (*qv*) Summer LC Md from *William* Dec 1774 & sold to Thomas Johnson Jr. Mo.

George, William. S Lent T *Thornton* May LC AA Co., Md., Jul 1774. Sy.

George, William. S Dec T *Justitia* Dec 1774. M.

German, Giles. S Chelmsford Jan 1763 (AHJ). E.

German, Mary. S Summer 1734 LC Knt Co., Md., Mar 1735 from *Falcon*. De.

German, William. T Jul 1747 *Laura*. M.

Gerrade, Robert. S Chelmsford Jan 1751 (AHJ). E.

Gerrard, Rebecca. S Jan T Mar 1750 *Tryal*. L.

Gervise, Gerrard. S Feb T *Thames* Mar 1754. M.

Gibbens, John. S May T Jun 1751. Sy.

Gibbins, Mi(chael). T from Dublin by *Hercules*, LC Bal. Co., Md., Aug 1773, sold to James Wilson of Augusta Co., Virginia. Ir.

Gibbon, John. S for highway robbery Lent R 14 yrs Summer T *Phoenix* Oct 1760. E.

Gibbon, Thomas. S Jun 1718 T Feb 1719 *Worcester* LC Annapolis Jun 1719. L.

Gibbon, William. S Lent 1731 LC Knt Co., Md., from *Falcon* Apr 1732. De.

Gibbons, Charles. S Summer LC Bal Co., Md., Dec 1770. So.

Gibbons, Walter. S Jul T *Saltspring* Jul 1775. M.

Gibbons, William. S Summer LC Bal Co., Md., Dec 1772. Ha.

Gibbs, Benjamin. S Summer 1731 LC Knt Co., Md., from *Falcon* Apr 1732. So.

Gibbs, Frances. S Apr 1755. Li.

Gibbs, Richard. S Summer 1752 T Sep 1753. Wa.

Gibbs, Thomas. S Lent R 14 yrs Summer 1742 (IJ). Su.

Gibbs, William. S Sep T *Phoenix* Oct 1760. L.

Gibson, Alice wife of Robert. S City 1752 (AHJ). Nl.

Gibson, Anne. R Sep 1671 AT Jul 1672 LC Md Jun 1673. M.

Gibson, Isabel, spinster. SQS Jul 1772 LC Bal Co., Md., from *Adventure* Mar 1773. Nl.

Gibson, John. S for life Chelmsford Jan 1750 (AHJ). E.

Gibson, Joseph. S s lead at Tamworth Summer 1750 LC QA Co., Md., from *Chester* Dec 1752. St.

Gibson, Judith. S Apr T May 1752 *Lichfield*. L.

Gibson, Samuel. S Jul T *Tayloe* Jul 1774. L.

Gibson, Thomas. S s horse Summer 1729 R 14 yrs Summer 1730 AT Summer 1732. Nl.

Gibson, Thomas. S Summer 1751 R 14 yrs Lent T May 1752 *Lichfield*. Sy.

Giddins, George. S s horse Lent R 14 yrs Summer 1739. Wo.

Gift, Elizabeth. S Jan T *Greyhound* Feb 1755. L.

Gift, John. S Launceston May 1755 (AHJ). Co.

Gilbee, Ahaz or Alban. S for burglary Lent R 14 yrs Summer T Sep 1757 *Thetis*. Bu.

Gilbert, Frances wife of Thomas. S s watch Oct 1735 T Jan 1736 *Dorsetshire* LC Va Sep 1736. M.

Gilbert, Henry. SQS Bristol Aug 1743 LC Knt Co., Md., from *Raven* Feb 1744. G.

Gilbert, Thomas. S 14 yrs Lent 1750 LC QA Co., Md., from *Catherine* Nov 1750. He.

Gilbert *als* Sparkes, Samuel. S Aug T *Beverly* Aug 1763. L.

Gilchrist, Henry. SQS Jan LC AA Co., Md., from *Thornton* Jul 1775. M.

Giles, Mary wife of Thomas. S Apr-Jun 1739 T *Sea Nymph* to Md. M.

Giles, Mary. T Oct 1746. Be.

Gillham, Michael. SQS & T Apr 1742 LC PG Co., Md. Do.

Gilham, Richard. S Lent LC AA Co., Md., from *Thornton* Jul 1775. K.

Gill, Catherine. SQS Lent LC AA Co., Md., from *Hanover Planter* Jul 1773. M.

Gill, George. S Aug T *Phoenix* Oct 1760. L.

Gill, John. T *Barnard* Oct 1756. M.

Gill, Richard. S & T Sep 1751 *Greyhound*. L.

Gill, William. S Lent 1721 R Oct T Oct 1723 *Forward* from London. Y.

Gillard, George. S Lent LC Bal Co., Md., Jul 1772. So.

Gillard, Scipio (1773). *See* Mitchell. Co.

Gillett, William. S Lent T *Dolphin* May 1763. Ht.

Gilman, Henry. SQS Bury St. Edmunds 1766. Su.

Gilman, Thomas. S Dec T *Justitia* Dec 1774. M.

Gilpin, Thomas. S for breaking & entering Feb T Apr 1735 *Patapsco* LC Annapolis Oct 1735. L.

Gilson, Arthur. S Oct 1751-Jan 1752 T *Thames* Mar 1752. M.

Gilson, William. S Lent R 14 yrs Summer 1764. He.

Gingel, Dinah. S 14 yrs for receiving Mar TB to Va Oct T *Randolph* Sep 1768. Wi.

Ginn, Edward. T May 1752 *Lichfield*. E.

Ginn, Thomas of St. George, Southwark. SQS May T *Tryal* Jul 1754. Sy.

Gladmore, Thomas (1730) - *See* Lanham, John. M.

Gladwin [Gladmin], John. S Mar R Jun T 14 yrs Dec 1758 *The Brothers* Ht.

Glanfield, Sarah. (1722). *See* Griffith. De.

Glascow, Hannah. S Sep T Oct 1750 *Rachael*. M.

Glass, Anthony. S Apr-Jun 1739 T *Sea Nymph* to Md. M.

Glass, Henry. S 14 yrs Lent LC Bal Co., Md., Jul 1772. Wi.

Glasswell, John. S Jan T *Plain Dealer* Jan 1746. M.

Glenton, John (1719) - *See* Brown. Y.

Glesby, Ann. S May-Jul T *Tayloe* Jul 1774. M.

Glibbery, John. T May 1751 *Tryal*. Sy.

Glover, Benjamin. S 14 yrs Summer 1772 LC Bal Co., Md., Apr 1773. Wo.

Glover, Henry. SQS Warminster 1754 (AHJ). Wi.

Glover, John. S Summer 1760 (AHJ). No.

Glover, John. SQS Bristol s silver tankard Dec 1764 (BJ). G.

Glover, John. S 14 yrs Lent LC AA Co., Md., from *Thornton* Jul 1775. K.

Glover, Thomas of Christchurch. SQS Apr T May 1750 *Lichfield*. Sy.

Glynn, John. S Lent 1765. Li.

Glyn, Richard. S Feb T *Neptune* Mar 1761. L.

Glyn, Sarah. S Lent LC AA Co., Md., from *Thornton* Jul 1773. L.

Godbeare, Elizabeth. S Exeter Nov 1760 (AHJ). De.

Godby, Ann wife of Jasper. S Sep-Oct 1773 T *Justitia* Jan 1774. M.

Godby, Jasper. S Jan T *Plain Dealer* Jan 1746 & S Sep 1747 LC Knt Co., Md., from *St. George* Mar 1748. L.

Goddard, Anthony of St. Clement Danes, aged 27. S Mar 1720 T *Honor* but escaped in Vigo, Spain; executed for returning Oct 1720 (NM). L.

Goddard, James Jr. S Lent LC Bal Co., Md., Jun 1773; runaway. Do.

Goddard, John. S 14 yrs Sep-Oct T Oct 1749 *Mary*. M.

Goddard, John. S Apr T May 1751 *Tryal*. L.

Goddard, John of Christchurch. SQS Apr T May 1752 *Lichfield*. Sy.

Goddard, William of Newington. SQS Jan T *Thames* Feb 1751. Sy.

Godfrey, Anthony. S Lent 1724 but escaped & no further record found. Li.

Godfrey, Benjamin. R Jul T *Tayloe* Jul 1774. M.

Godfrey, Elizabeth. S Summer LC Bal Co., Md., Dec 1770 from *Trotman* & sold to Abraham Ensor. Bd.

Godfry, John. SQS Oct 1754 T *Greyhound* Feb 1755. M.

Godfrey, William. S Lent T *Thornton* May LC AA Co., Md., Jul 1774. M.

Godley, Joseph. S Mar T *Thames* Mar 1754. L.

Godman, Elizabeth. S Sep-Dec 1746 T Jan 1747 *George William*. M.

Godstone, William. S Lent LC AA Co., Md., from *Hanover Planter* Jul 1773. M.

Godwin, William. S Lent LC Bal Co., Md., Jun 1773. Mo.

Goff, Ann. S s linen Dec 1735 T Jan 1736 *Dorsetshire* LC Va Sep 1736. M.

Goff, Elias. T Jul 1747 *Laura*. M.

Goff, Richard. S 14 yrs Lent LC Bal Co., Md., Jul 1772. De.

Goff alias Newberry, Thomas. S Lent 1734 LC Knt Co., Md., Mar 1735 from *Falcon*. De.

Goffee, John. S May-Jul T *Tayloe* Jul 1773. M.

Gold, Amey. S Southwark Lent LC AA Co., Md., Jul 1774. Sy.

Gold, John. S Dec 1749-Jan 1750 T Mar 1750 *Tryal*. M.

Gold, Mary. S Lent LC AA Co., Md., from *Thornton* May 1771. Sy.

Goldhawk, Amey. S Southwark Lent T *Thornton* May LC AA Co., Md., from *Thornton* Jul 1775. Sy.

Golding, Thomas. S Bristol Mar 1754.

Goldsmith, Elizabeth. S Aug T *Beverly* Aug 1763. L.

Goldsmith, Samuel. S May T *Saltspring* Jul 1775. L.

Goldup, John. T May 1751 *Tryal*. K.

Goo---, Ann. Jul 1783 LC Bal Co., Md., Dec 1783 from *Swift*. L.

Good, Mary. S Summer T *Ruby* Oct 1754. E.

Goodacre, John. S 14 yrs 1759 (AHJ). Y.

Goodall, Richard SQS s fowls in Dorchester, Oxon, Mar 1770 (OJ). O.

Goodchild, William. S Lent T Sep 1746 *Mary*. E.

Gooden, Thomas. S Summer 1741 (IJ). Su.

Gooderham, Henry. SQS Ipswich 1758. Su.

Gooderham, Levett. SQS Ipswich 1758. Su.

Gooderham, Mary. SQS Ipswich 1758. Su.

Goodhand, Christopher. S Oct 1760. Li.

Goodin, Ann. S Feb-Apr T May 1752 *Lichfield*. M.

Goodman, Francis. S Lent T Apr 1739. Le.

Goodman, Joseph. S Oct 1751-Jan 1752 T *Thames* Mar 1752. M.

Goodman *als* Wallis, Richard. LC Dec 1770 from *Trotman* & sold to Aquila Price. Wa.

Goodman, Thomas. S Jun 1718. L.

Goodman, William. S Lent T Aug 1746. Bu.

Goodman, William. S 1757 TB to Va. No.

Goodman, William. R s horse Lent 1768. Le.

Goodrich, Samuel. S Lent 1734. Li.

Goodrod, Mary. T Jan 1736 *Dorsetshire* LC Va Sep 1736. Sy.

Goodwin, Daniel. S Summer T *Ruby* Oct 1754. E.

Goodwin, Mary. S Lent LC AA Co., Md., from *Thornton* May 1771. M.

Goodwin, Mary. S Lent LC AA Co., Md., from *Thornton* Jul 1773. M.

Goodwyn, Henry. S Oct-Dec 1754 T *Greyhound* Feb 1755. M.

Goodye, John of Lambeth. SQS Apr T Sep 1751 *Greyhound*. Sy.

Goodyear, John. S Lent 1732 LC Knt Co., Md., from *Falcon* Mar 1733. De.

Gordon, Frances. S Apr T May 1750 *Lichfield*. M.

Gorden, James. S Sep-Oct 1775 T *Justitia* Feb 1776. M.

Gordon, John. S Oct T *Barnard* Oct 1756. L.

Gordon, John. S Aberdeen R for life Aug 1767. Sco.

Gordon, John. R for life Summer 1772 T *Justitia* Jan 1773. K.

Gordon, Richard. S Lent T *Thornton* May LC AA Co., Md., Jul 1774. M.

Gordon, Thomas. S Jan-Jun T Jul 1747 *Laura*. M.

Gordon, William. S Jul-Sep T *Ruby* Oct 1754. M.

Gorman, Lawrence. S Feb T *Tryal* Mar 1757. M.

Gorman, Sarah. S Jan T *Thames* Feb 1751. M.

Gorridge, Anthony (1772) - *See* Gutteridge. No.

Gosdin, Mary. S Jan-Jun T Jul 1747 *Laura*. M.

Gosling, Samuel. S 14 yrs Lent LC Bal Co., Md., Jul 1771. De.

Gosling, William. S Sep-Oct 1775 T *Justitia* Feb 1776. M.

Goswell *als* Gosling, James of Duddinghurst. S Summer 1745 R 14 yrs Lent 1746;
   S for returning Lent 1749 R & T for life May 1750 *Lichfield*. E.

Gothard, John Jr. S 14 yrs Lent LC Bal Co., Md., Jul 1772. De.

Gothard, Sarah. S 14 yrs Lent LC Bal Co., Md., Jul 1772. De.

Gotray, Hugh. S Jan-Jun T Jul 1747 *Laura*. M.

Gouge, Richard. S Aug T *Beverly* Aug 1763. L.

Gough, Edward. R for Barbados Jun 1671 but LC Md Feb 1672. L.

Gough, James. S Lent LC AA Co., Md., from *Thornton* Jul 1775. M.

Gough, Mary of St. George, Southwark, spinster. SQS Apr T Sep 1751 *Greyhound*. Sy.

Gould, Elizabeth of Putney, spinster. SQS Apr T May 1752 *Lichfield*. Sy.

Gould, Elizabeth. S Lent T *Thornton* May LC AA Co., Md., Jul 1774. M.

Gould, Mary wife of William, weaver. SQS Apr 1750 LC QA Co., Md., from
   Catherine Nov 1750. De.

Gould, Mary. S Sep-Oct 1773 T *Justitia* Jan 1774. M.

Gould, Thomas. S Jun 1783. M.

Gouldin, George. S Lent T *Tryal* Jul 1754. Sy.

Gouldin, Pearcy. S Jul T *Beverly* Aug 1763. M.

Goulston, Richard. S for life May-Jul T Aug 1749 *Thames*. M.

Govey, George. R 14 yrs Jun 1759 TB *Phoenix* but R to serve in Army or Navy Aug
   1759. Ht.

Govier, Anthony. S Jan LC QA Co., Md., from *Leopard* May 1738. De.

Gower, Philip. S Apr-May T *Tryal* Jul 1754. M.

Gowers, John of Barking. SQS Jan T May 1752 *Lichfield*. E.

Grace, William. S Dec 1745 T *Plain Dealer* Jan 1746. L.

Grace, William. S Jan-Jun T Jul 1747 *Laura*. M.

Grace *als* Frazier, William. S Lent T May 1749 *Lichfield*. Bu.

Grady, Eleanor. S Feb-Apr T May 1752 *Lichfield*. M.

Grady, John. S Lent T *Tryal* Jul 1754. Sy.

Grafton, Henry, *als* Taylor, Harry. S Jul T Jul 1748 *Mary*. L.

Graham, George. S May-Jun T Aug 1752 *Tryal*. M.

Graham, Patrick. S Dec 1760 T *Neptune* Mar 1761. M.

Graham, Robert. S Feb-Apr T *Justitia* May 1745. M.

Graham, Sarah. S Apr T *Dolphin* Apr 1761. M.

Graham, Walter. S Summer T Oct 1761. Li.

Grainger, Francis. S 14 yrs Dec 1773; born Northern England, runaway from *Justitia*, Leeds Town, Va., Apr 1774. L.

Grainger, Mary. S s in Wribbenhall Summer 1759 R 14 yrs Lent 1760. Wo.

Granger, Richard. R 14 yrs Sep T *Randolph* Sep 1768. De.

Grant, Adam. S Feb-Apr T May 1752 *Lichfield*. M.

Grant, Alexander. SL Jul T *Tayloe* Jul 1773. Sy.

Grant, Charles. S & T Jan 1736 *Dorsetshire* LC Va Sep 1736. L.

Grant, Christian. S Dec 1749-Jan 1750 T Mar 1750 *Tryal*. M.

Grant, Elizabeth. T 1751. Li.

Grant, Judith. S Hull Oct 1745 T Mar 1746. Y.

Grant, Margaret wife of John. S May-Jul T *Tayloe* Jul 1773. M.

Grant, Mary. S Summer T Oct 1750 *Rachael*. Sy.

Grant, Mary. S Aug T *Phoenix* Oct 1760. L.

Grant, Sarah. S Bristol Jan T Aug 1754 (AHJ). G.

Grant, Susannah. S Feb-Apr 1746 T Apr 1746 *Laura*. M.

Grantlett, John. S Summer 1718 LC from *Sophia* QA Co., Md. Mar 1719. Co.

Graston, Thomas. SQS Ipswich Summer 1738. Su.

Graves, Elianor, spinster, *als* wife of Thomas of Whitechapel. R for Barbados Jun 1671 but LC Md Feb 1672. M.

Graves, Mary. Jul 1783 LC Bal Co., Md., Dec 1783 from *Swift*. M.

Graves, Thomas. S Summer LC Bal Co., Md., Dec 1770 from *Trotman* & sold to Samuel Worthington Esq. X.

Gravett, James. SQS Jan LC AA Co., Md., from *Thornton* Jul 1773. Sy.

Gravil, John. SQS Jul 1740 (GJ). G.

Gray - *See* Grey.

Grayley, Francis. S Sep-Oct 1772 T *Justitia* Jan 1773. M.

Grayston, Thomas. S Summer 1739. Su.

Grear, Ann. S Sep-Oct 1773 T *Justitia* Jan 1774. M.

Grearson, Thomas. S Sep 1775. Li.

Greasley, Peter. S Lent 1761. Le.

Greatwood, James. S Lent LC AA Co., Md., from *Thornton* Jul 1773. M.

Green, Ann. S Lent 1735. No.

Green, Ann. T Jul 1747. Wa.

Green, Ann. S Bristol Jan 1755 (AHJ). G.

Greaves, Ann. S Summer T *Barnard* Oct 1756. K.

Green, Charles. R Jul T *Tayloe* Jul 1774. M.

Green, Edward. S Summer 1736. Y.

Green, Elizabeth. S & T Jan 1736 *Dorsetshire* LC Va Sep 1736. L.

Green, Francis. S Aug T *Beverly* Aug 1763. L.

Green, Henry. S s horse Summer 1721 T Jul 1723 *Alexander* LC Md Sep 1723. E.

Green, Henry. S Dec 1772 T *Justitia* Jan 1773. M.

Green, John. S for hedge stripping May 1721 (NM). No.

Green, John. S Jul 1736 S Jul 1736 LC QA Co., Md., from *Amity* May 1737. Ha.

Green, John. S Jan-Jun T Jul 1747 *Laura*. M.

Green, John. S Lent R 14 yrs Summer T Aug 1749 *Thames*. E.

Green *als* Gunston, John. S s wheat at St. Aldates Summer 1757. Be.

Green, John. S Feb T *Neptune* Mar 1761. L.

Green, John. S Lent 1770 TB to Md. No.

Green, John. S Lent LC AA Co., Md., from *Thornton* May 1771. K.

Green, Joseph. T May 1751 *Tryal*. Sy.

Green, Margaret. SQS Apr T May 1751 *Tryal*. M.

Green, Marmaduke. S May 1721 for hedge stripping (NM). No.

Green, Mary. S Jan-Apr T *Lichfield* May 1749. M.

Green *als* Collyer *als* Waller, Mary. S Jun T *Maryland Packet* Oct 1761. M.

Green, Richard. S s cordial Apr T Dec 1735 *John* LC Annapolis Sep 1736. L.

Green, Richard. S 1750 (AHJ). Li.

Green, Robert. S Norwich Aug T Sep 1746. Nf.

Green, Robert. S Feb T *Thames* Mar 1752. L.

Green, Robert. S Lent LC AA Co., Md., from *Hanover Planter* Jul 1773. M.

Green, Thomas. S Apr T May 1750 *Lichfield*. M.

Greene, Thomas. SQS 1752 TB to Md. No.

Green, William. T Oct 1749 *Mary*. M.

Green, William. SQS 14 yrs Jan 1750 LC QA Co., Md., from *Catherine* Nov 1750. G.

Green, William. S Dec 1772 T *Justitia* Jan 1773. M.

Greenacres, Ann. S Lent LC Bal Co., Md., Jun 1773. Ch.

Greenaway, Henry. S Apr T *Lichfield* May 1749. L.

Greenaway, Mary. SQS Jun T Aug 1752 *Tryal*. Sy.

Greenhorne, William. S & R Summer T Dec 1733. Nl.

Greenaway, William. S Jun 1739 T *Sea Nymph* to Md. L.

Greenhough, Thomas. S Lent LC Bal Co., Md., Jun 1773. St.

Greening, Thomas. S s clothing Mar 1754. O.

Greenslade, William. R 14 yrs Sep T *Randolph* Sep 1768. De.

Greenwood, Elizabeth. S Sep-Oct 1772 T *Justitia* Jan 1773. M.

Greenwood, Thomas. S 14 yrs Summer 1772 LC Bal Co., Md., Apr 1773. G.

Greeve, Elizabeth Harriot. SQS Oct T *Justitia* Dec 1774. M.

Gregg, Jane, spinster. S City 1751 (AHJ). Nl.

Gregory, Ann. S Jul-Dec 1747 LC Knt Co., Md., from *St. George* Mar 1748. M.

Gregory, Anthony. S Summer 1718 LC from *Sophia* QA Co., Md. Mar 1719. De.

Gregory, Catherine. S Lent LC AA Co., Md., from *Thornton* Jul 1773. M.

Gregory, Daniel. R 14 yrs Jul T *Saltspring* Jul 1775. M.

Gregory, Henry. S s yarn at Baschurch Summer LC from *William* Md Dec 1774 & sold to Thomas Johnson Jr.. Sh.

Gregory, John. S Jan-Apr T *Lichfield* May 1749. M.

Gregory, John. S s horse Lent R & T 14 yrs T Oct 1758 *Lux* from London. Db.

Gregory, Lile. S Lent T *Tryal* Jul 1754. Sy.

Gregson, John. S 1761 (AHJ). La.

Gresham, Charles of Barking. SQS Jan T *Tryal* Jul 1754. E.

Gretton, Cadman. S Oct-Dec 1754 T *Greyhound* Feb 1755. M.

Grew, Joseph. S Sep T Oct 1750 *Rachael*. M.

MORE EMIGRANTS IN BONDAGE

Gray, Ann. T Jun 1747. So.

Gray, Ann, wife of James. S City Christmas 1750 (AHJ). Nl.

Gray, Christopher. S Lent T *Lichfield* May 1749. Sy.

Grey, Henrietta. SQS Lent LC AA Co., Md., from *Hanover Planter* Jul 1773. M.

Gray, James. SQS Jul T Sep 1751 *Greyhound*. M.

Gray *als* Graves, Jane. T *Tayloe* Jul 1774. M.

Grey, Richard. S s mare Lent R 14 yrs Summer 1756 TB to Va. No.

Grey, Richard. S City Easter 1759 (AHJ). Nl.

Grey, Samuel. S Summer 1741 LC QA Co., Md., from *Philleroy* Apr 1742. Co.

Gray, Samuel. S for burglary & R for life Lent T Apr 1773 TB to Md. No.

Grey, Sarah. S Oct 1757. Li.

Gray, Thomas. S Apr T May 1750 *Lichfield*. M.

Gray *als* Jones, William. S Apr-Jun 1739 T *Sea Nymph* to Md. M.

Gray, William. S Jul T *Beverly* Aug 1763. M.

Greystone, Thomas. SQS Ipswich Jan 1738. Su.

Grice, William. S Lent T May 1765. Le.

Griffin, Edward. SQS Oct 1742 LC Knt Co., Md., from *Globe* Mar 1744. De.

Griffin, Edward. S 14 yrs Sep T *Barnard* Oct 1756. M.

Griffin, Harman of St. Saviour, Southwark. SQS Apr T Sep 1751 *Greyhound*. Sy.

Griffin, John. SQS Lent LC AA Co., Md., from *Hanover Planter* Jul 1773. M.

Griffin, Martha. T Aug 1752 *Tryal*. M.

Griffin, Mary. S Aug T *Beverly* Aug 1763. L.

Griffin, Peter. SQS Apr T May 1750 *Lichfield*. M.

Griffin, Robert. S Oct 1740 T *Harpooner* Jan 1741. L.

Griffin, Robert. S Jul T Aug 1749 *Thames*. L.

Griffin, Thomas of Hartwell. S Lent T *Dolphin* May 1763. Bu.

Griffis, Thomas. S s watch at Kidderminster Mar 1754; he was to have pleaded a pardon in May 1754 but his ship had already left. (WJ). Wo.

Griffith *als* Hatch, Ann. S Lent LC AA Co., Md., from *Hanover Planter* Jul 1773. M.

Griffith, Emblin. SQS Feb T May 1752 *Lichfield*. M.

Griffith, Mary. S s cotton Sep 1735 T Jan 1736 *Dorsetshire* LC Va Sep 1736. M.

Griffith, Mary. S Bristol Jan 1750 (AHJ). G.

Griffith, Paul. S Bristol Jan T Mar 1753 (AHJ). G.

Griffith *als* Glanfield, Sarah. S Summer LC Md. from *Reformation* Aug 1722. De.

Griffith, Thomas. S Apr T *Lichfield* May 1749. L.

Griffith, William. S Summer 1772 LC Bal Co., Md., Apr 1773. Mo.

Griffiths, Elizabeth. S Bristol Jan 1760 (AHJ). G.

Griffiths, Elizabeth. S Lent T *Dolphin* Apr 1761. Sy.

Griffiths, Elizabeth. Jul 1783 LC Bal Co., Md., Dec 1783 from *Swift*. L.

Griffiths, James. S Lent T *Thornton* May LC AA Co., Md., Jul 1774. M.

Griffiths, Jane. SQS Bristol s greatcoat in Castle St. Dec 1762. G.

Griffiths, John. S Lent 1750 LC QA Co., Md., from *Catherine* Nov 1750. G.

Griffiths, John. SQS Lent LC AA Co., Md., from *Hanover Planter* Jul 1773. M.

Griffiths, Mary wife of Griffith, cordwainer. S Bristol Jan 1750 LC QA Co., Md., from *Catherine* Nov 1750. G.

Griffiths, Mary. S Jan T *Tryal* Mar 1757. L.

Griffiths (*als* Turner), Mary. S Lent LC Bal Co., Md., Jul 1772. Wo.

Griffiths, Morris. SQS Sep T *Justitia* Dec 1774. M.

Griffiths, Paul. SQS Bristol Mar 1753; father, merchant of Bristol, died shortly after. G.

Griffiths, Thomas. S Summer 1770 LC Bal Co., Md., Jul 1771. He.

Griffiths, William. S s mare & R 14 yrs Summer LC Md from *William* Dec 1774 & sold to Thomas Johnson Jr. Mo.

Griffon, Charles. S Chelmsford Jan 1754 (AHJ). E.

Grigg, James. S Summer 1718 LC from *Sophia* QA Co., Md. Mar 1719. Do.

Grigg, William. S Feb-Apr T May 1751 *Tryal*. M.

Griggs, Thomas. S Jun T Jul 1747 *Laura*. L.

Grimes, George. T May 1752 *Lichfield*. K.

Grimes *als* Graham, Martha. S Apr T *Justitia* May 1745. L.

Grimsby, Richard. S Summer T *Barnard* Oct 1756. Sy.

Grimshaw, Robert. S Mar 1761. Ha.

Grimshire, Josiah. S 14 yrs Lent LC AA Co., Md., from *Thornton* Jul 1775. K.

Grindley, Elizabeth. S & T Jan 1736 *Dorsetshire* LC Va Sep 1736. L.

Grindy, William, formerly keeper of the Red Lion at Nettlebed. S Lent R for life Summer T Sep 1751 *Greyhound* ; committed to Oxford Gaol for returning & executed Oct 1752. Ht.

Grist, Charles. S Lent LC Bal Co., Md., Jun 1773. Wi.

Gritton, John. S Aug T Oct 1751. Nt.

Gritton, John. S s wheat at Walford Mar, escaped but recaptured, LC Bal Co. Md Jun 1773. He.

Groom, Richard. T Lent 1750. Li.

Grose, Simon. S Lent T *Tryal* Jul 1754. Sy.

Gross, Sarah. S 14 yrs Lent T *Thornton* May LC AA Co., Md., Jul 1774. M.

Grove, Ann. S for housebreaking at Wickenford Lent R 14 yrs Summer 1755. Wo.

Grove, Benjamin. Jul 1783 LC Bal Co., Md., Dec 1783 from *Swift*. M.

Grove, Thomas. S Jan 1757 (AHJ). Wo.

Grove, William. T Jun 1747. Ha.

Groves, Ann. S Jul-Dec 1747 LC Knr Co., Md., from *St. George* Mar 1748. M.

Groves, John. Jul 1783 LC Bal Co., Md., Dec 1783 from *Swift*. M.

Groves, Sarah wife of John. S Lent but pardoned Apr 1773. M.

Groves, William. S Jun T Jul 1747 *Laura*. L.

Groves, William. T *Tayloe* Jul 1773. M.

Grubb, Humphrey. S Summer T Aug 1746. E.

Grubb, John. S & T Lent 1761. Mo.

Grubb, William. S Summer T *Justitia* Sep 1767. Bu.

Guest, Elias. S Lent 1765. Sh.

Guest, Joseph. S Jan T *Thames* Feb 1751. L.

Guise, Susanna. S Lent 1761; gaoled for returning in Mar 1762 & executed for robbery at Hampton Lovett. Wo.

Gullaken, James. S Lent T *Thornton* May LC AA Co., Md., Jul 1774. L.

Gullick, William. S Jul-Sep T *Ruby* Oct 1754. M.

Gullocke, Thomas of Newton St. Loe. R for Barbados Jul 1672 but LC Md 1673. So.

Gumm, Ann. T Aug 1752 *Tryal*. Sy.

Gunn, Catherine. S Lent LC AA Co., Md., from *Hanover Planter* Jul 1773. L.

Gunn, John. S Oct T *Justitia* Dec 1774. L.

Gunnele, William. S Jun T *Tryal* Jul 1754. L.

Gunnell, George. S Jan T *Plain Dealer* Jan 1746. M.

Gunnell, John. S Feb T *Neptune* Mar 1761. L.

Gunner [Gunning], Robert. SQS Bristol Aug 1753. G.

Gunner, Sarah. S Summer T Sep 1751 *Greyhound*. K.

Gunston, John (1757) - *See* Green. Be.

Gunter, James. S s cow Lent R 14 yrs Summer 1747 (GJ). Mo.

Gunter, Thomas. R & T Jul 1747. Mo.

Guppy, John. S Lent LC Bal Co., Md., Jul 1771. Do.

Gusseny, Abraham. S Oct T *Justitia* Dec 1774. L.

Gutteridge *als* Gorridge, Anthony. S Summer T Sep 1772, died on passage to Va on *Trimly* 1773. No.

Gutteridge, Charles. S Oct T *Barnard* Oct 1756. M.

Guy, John. S Oct 1751-Jan 1752 T *Thames* Mar 1752. M.

Guy, Sarah. T *Justitia* Feb 1776. L.

Gwatkins, John of Chatham. S Lent T Jul 1745 *Italian Merchant.* K.

Gwillam, John. T *Justitia* Feb 1776. L.

Gwynn, Bryan. S & T Mar 1750 *Tryal.* L.

Gwynn, John. S Apr T May 1751 *Tryal.* L.

Habbertson, John. S Summer R Lent T Oct 1738. Nl.

Hackman, John. S Apr 1759 (WJ). He.

Hackney, John. S Dec 1749-Jan 1750 T Mar 1750 *Tryal.* M.

Hackney, William. S Apr-May T *Saltspring* Jul 1775. M.

Hadden, John. S Summer LC Bal Co., Md., Dec 1770. Wa.

Haddock, William. S Apr T Jun 1748 *Lichfield.* L.

Haden, Samuel. S Apr 1752 (WJ). Wa.

Hadley *als* Watts, Ann. S Lent 1770. Wa.

Hadley, David. S Sep-Oct 1772 T *Justitia* Jan 1773. M.

Hadlow, Hercules. S Lent T *Tryal* Jul 1754. K.

Hagan, Mary. S Lent LC AA Co., Md., from *Thornton* Jul 1773. M.

Hagg, Paul. S Lent T Apr 1758 *Lux* from London. Db.

Haggerty, Matthew . S Lent LC AA Co., Md., from *Thornton* May 1771. M.

Haggett, William. S Lent LC AA Co., Md., from *Thornton* Jul 1773. M.

Haggott, John. S Summer 1770 LC Bal Co., Md., Jun 1771. De.

Hague, James. S s handkerchiefs Apr T Dec 1735 *John* LC Annapolis Sep 1736. M.

Haines - *See* Haynes.

Hainsworth, Benjamin. S Lent LC AA Co., Md., from *Thornton* Jul 1775. M.

Hainsworth, James. S Apr-May T *Saltspring* Jul 1775. M.

Hale, George. S for highway robbery at Whitchurch Lent R 14 yrs Summer T *Justitia* Sep 1767; John Hale hanged. Bu.

Hale, Richard. S Norwich Summer T Sep 1738. Nf.

Hale, William, aged under 20. R Oct 1729. K.

Hale, William of Kirdford. S Summer T Oct 1750 *Rachael.* Sx.

Hale, William. S Lent T May 1754. St.

Hales, Abraham. S Apr T *Lichfield* May 1749. L.

Hales, James. S Lent LC AA Co., Md., from *Thornton* Jul 1775. E.

Hales, John. S Lent 1732. Bd.

Hales, Roger. S Apr T *Lichfield* May 1749. L.

Haley *als* Poor, Jane. S Feb-Apr T May 1752 *Lichfield.* M.

Haley, Richard. S Summer 1764; broke out of Shrewsbury Gaol & found at large in London Lent 1765, condemned to hang but, on petition from Shrewsbury, R 14 yrs Summer 1765. Sh.

Haley, Thomas. S Summer T Sep 1754. Db.

Halford, John (1773). *See* Harefoot. Co.

Halford, Joseph. S Lent LC AA Co., Md., from *Hanover Planter* Jul 1773. L.

Halfpenny, Martha. S Lent T May 1754. St.

Halfpenny, Peter. S Sep-Oct T Oct 1749 *Mary*. M.

Halfwood, James. S 1757 (AHJ). La.

Hall, Elizabeth. S Jul-Sep T *Ruby* Oct 1754. M.

Hall, Elizabeth. S 14 yrs Lent LC Bal Co., Md., Jul 1771. He.

Hall, Francis. R for life T *Tayloe* Jul 1774. M.

Hall, James. S & T Aug 1752 *Tryal*. L.

Hall, John. SQS Apr 1729. La.

Hall, John. SQS Feb T Mar 1750 *Tryal*. M.

Hall, John. S Bristol Jan 1751 (AHJ). G.

Hall, John of Newington. SQS Jan T *Thames* Feb 1751. Sy.

Hall, John. S Dec 1773 T *Justitia* Jan 1774. L.

Hall, Martha. S Jul T Aug 1749 *Thames*. L.

Hall, Mary. SQS Jun T Aug 1752 *Tryal*. M.

Hall, Mary. S Aug T Oct 1757 (WJ). Wa.

Hall, Mary. S Jul T *Tayloe* Jul 1773. L.

Hall, Matthew. S s at Raven Inn, Kidderminster, Aug 1764 (WJ). Wo.

Hall, Richard. S Oct T *Barnard* Oct 1756. L.

Hall, Susanna. S Dec 1745 T *Plain Dealer* Jan 1746. L.

Hall, Thomas. S Dec 1750 T *Thames* Feb 1751. L.

Hall, Thomas. T *Justitia* Jan 1774. M.

Hall, William. S Summer 1734 R 14 yrs Feb 1735. Ht.

Hall, William. S Lent 1738. Li.

Hall, William. S May-Jun T Aug 1752 *Tryal*. M.

Hall, William. S for housebreaking Aug 1753 R 14 yrs Lent 1754 (WJ). St.

Hall, William. S Lent T *Tryal* Jul 1754. K.

Hall, William. T *Maryland Packet* Oct 1761. L.

Hall, William. S Summer LC Bal Co., Md., Dec 1772. De.

Hall, William. S Lent T *Thornton* May LC AA Co., Md., Jul 1774. M.

Hall, William. S Lent LC AA Co., Md., from *Thornton* Jul 1775. Ht.

Hall, William. Jul 1783 LC Bal Co., Md., Dec 1783 from *Swift*. M.

Hallams, John. S for house breaking Lent R 14 yrs Summer 1755 (GJ). St.

Hallett, William. S for life Summer 1770 LC Bal Co., Md., Jun 1771. De.

Halliday, Gabriel. S York City Lent 1735. Y.

Hallier, James. S Bristol Jan T Feb 1757 (AHJ). G.

Halliston, William. S Lent T Jun 1748 *Lichfield*. E.

Halton, William. S Jan-Apr T *Lichfield* May 1749. M.

Halward, William (1764) - *See* Allard. Wo.

Hambleton, William. S Feb T *Thames* Mar 1754. M.

Hamblett, George. S Lent 1732 TB Aug 1733. Db.

Hambridge, Richard. S Jun-Dec T *Plain Dealer* Jan 1746. M.

Hamilton, George. S & T Jan 1736 *Dorsetshire* LC Va Sep 1736. L.

Hamilton, Hamlet. S 1757 (AHJ). La.

Hamilton, Jane. S May-Jul T Aug 1749 *Thames*. M.

Hamilton, John. S Lent LC AA Co., Md., from *Thornton* Jul 1773. M.

Hamilton, Samuel. S Sep T *Ruby* Oct 1754. L.

Hamilton, Thomas (1771). *See* Erskine. M.

Hamilton, William. S Summer 1770 but escaped in London. Sy.

MORE EMIGRANTS IN BONDAGE

Hamilton, William (1771) - *See* Bagnall, John. Nt.

Hammond, Edward. S Jan-Apr T *Lichfield* May 1749. M.

Hammond, Elizabeth, spinster. S Dec 1754 T *Greyhound* Feb 1755. L.

Hammond, James. S Feb T for life Mar 1750 *Tryal.* M.

Hammond, James. S Lent T Apr 1753. Wa.

Hammond, Mary. S Feb T Mar 1750 *Tryal.* M.

Hamond, Thomas. T Jan 1736 *Dorsetshire* LC Va Sep 1736. Sy.

Hammond, Thomas. Jul 1783 LC Bal Co., Md., Dec 1783 from *Swift.* M.

Hampstead, Benjamin. S Summer T Oct 1750 *Rachael.* Sy.

Hampton, John. S Dec 1746 T Jan 1747 *George William.* L.

Hanbury, John. S s nails at Bromsgrove Mar 1754 (WJ). Wo.

Hanby, Richard. S Jul T *Tayloe* Jul 1774. L.

Hanby, Thomas. S Lent T *Thornton* May LC AA Co., Md., Jul 1774. L.

Hancock, Edward. S Jan T Mar 1750 *Tryal.* L.

Hancock, Elizabeth. S Dec 1745 T *Plain Dealer* Jan 1746. L.

Hancock, John. SQS Jan LC Bal Co., Md., Jul 1772. De.

Hancock, John. S & R 14 yrs Summer T Sep 1772 TB to Md. No.

Hancock, John. SQS Jul 1754 (OJ). O.

Hancock, John. S Mar 1762. So.

Hancock, William. SQS Jan LC Bal Co., Md., Jul 1772. De.

Hand, Elizabeth. S May-Jul T Aug 1749 *Thames.* M.

Hand, Harriot. S Apr T *Dolphin* Apr 1761. M.

Hand, Patrick. S Jun-Dec 1745 T *Plain Dealer* Jan 1746. M.

Handen, Richard (1753) - *See* Honden. G.

Handerson, John. S Apr-May T *Tryal* Jul 1754. M.

Handford, Martha. S May-Jul T Sep 1751 *Greyhound.* M.

Handford *als* Gordon, Richard. S Dec 1760 T *Neptune* Mar 1761. M.

Handford, William. S Chelmsford Jan 1748 (AHJ). E.

Handley, James. S Summer 1773 T *Justitia* Jan 1774. Sy.

Handy, John. SQS & T *Amity* LC QA Co., Md., Mar 1736. So.

Handy, John. T Apr 1742 LC PG Co., Md. Wo.

Hanford, Elizabeth. T Jul 1747. Sy.

Hanks, -----. R 14 yrs Mar 1772 (HJ). G.

Hanley, Edward. S Lent 1772 LC Bal Co., Md., Apr 1773. Wo.

Hanley, Peter of Ewell. SQS Jan T *Thames* Feb 1751. Sy.

Hanley, Thomas. T from Dublin by *Hercules,* LC Bal. Co., Md., Aug 1773, sold to
    William Walters & Richard Guttrell. Ir.

Hanlin, James. T from Dublin by *Hercules,* LC Bal. Co., Md., Aug 1773, sold to
    James Wilson of Augusta Co., Virginia. Ir.

Hanna, John. S May-Jun T Aug 1752 *Tryal.* M.

Hannah, William. S Dec 1749-Jan 1750 T Mar 1750 *Tryal.* M.

Hanshaw, William. S & T Sep 1751 *Greyhound.* L.

Hanslip *als* Armsby, Richard. S Lent T Apr 1737. No.

Hanson, William. SQS Pontefract Lent 1738. Y.

Hansow, Mary. SQS Lent T Summer 1735. Db.

Harbin, Joseph. S Lent LC Bal Co., Md., Jul 1772. Do.

Harbourne, Benjamin. SQS Jan T *Greyhound* Feb 1755. M.

Harcot, Peter. S Apr-May T *Saltspring* Jul 1775. M.

Harcourt, Mary. SQS Feb LC AA Co., Md., from *Thornton* Jul 1773. M.

Harcourt, Thomas. S s mare at Hampton Lucy, Warw, Mar 1754 (WJ). Wo.

Hard, John. S Bristol Aug 1741 LC QA Co., Md., from *Philleroy* Apr 1742. G.
Harden, John. S Dec 1773 T *Justitia* Jan 1774. L.
Harden, Samuel. S Lent T Summer 1752. Wa.
Harder, Joseph. S Lent R 14 yrs Summer 1761. Wa.
Harding, Amos. S 14 yrs Lent 1742 LC QA Co., Md., from *Kent* Jun 1743. De.
Harding, Edward. S Summer T *Maryland Packet* Oct 1761. Bu.
Harding, Francis. SW Lent LC AA Co., Md., from *Hanover Planter* Jul 1773. M.
Harding, George. SQS Feb T *Thornton* May LC AA Co., Md., Jul 1774. M.
Harding, James. S Jul T Sep 1751 *Greyhound*. L.
Harding, James. S for life Lent LC Bal Co., Md., Jul 1772. Do.
Harding, Mary. S Jun 1718 T Feb 1719 *Worcester* LC Annapolis Jun 1719. L.
Harding, Mary Ann. T May 1746. De.
Harding, Moses. SQS Calne Oct 1741 TB to Va Apr 1742 LC PG Co., Md. Wi.
Harding, Richard. S Apr 1759 (GJ). G.
Harding, Richard. S Summer T *Maryland Packet* Oct 1761. Bu.
Harding, Robert. S for life Lent LC Bal Co., Md., Jul 1772. Do.
Harding, William. S Lent LC AA Co., Md., from *Hanover Planter* Jul 1773. M.
Harding, William. S 14 yrs Lent LC AA Co., Md., from *Thornton* Jul 1775. Sy.
Hardman, Thomas. S Summer 1737. Y.
Hardware, Charles. S 14 yrs Lent LC Bal Co., Md., Jun 1773. St.
Hardwick, John. S Oct-Dec 1750 T *Thames* Feb 1751. M.
Hardwick, John. S 14 yrs Lent LC Bal Co., Md., Jun 1773. So.
Hardy, John. S for highway robbery Lent R 14 yrs Summer 1728. Nf.
Hardy, Richard. S Sep 1751. Li.
Hardy, William. S Summer T Nov 1746. Do.
Harefoot *als* Halford, John. S Lent LC Bal Co., Md., Jun 1773. Co.
Harford, Hannah. S s shirts Feb T Apr 1735 *Patapsco* LC Annapolis Oct.
Harford, James. S Sep-Oct T Oct 1749 *Mary*. M.
Hargrove, Hester. S s gold ring May T Dec 1735 *John* LC Annapolis Sep 1736. L.
Hargrove, Thomas. T Sep 1737 *Pretty Patsy*. L.
Hargrove, Thomas. S Sep 1747 T *St. George* Jan LC Knt Co., Md., Mar 1748. L.
Harland, Frances. S Jul-Sep T *Ruby* Oct 1754. M.
Harland, Oliver. S 1755 (AHJ). Y.
Harleech, John. S & T Sep 1751 *Greyhound*. L.
Harley, John. T *Justitia* Feb 1776. L.
Harling, Richard. S Dec 1754 T *Greyhound* Feb 1755. L.
Harman, Elizabeth, widow. S Bristol Aug 1743 LC Knt Co., Md., from *Raven* Feb 1744. G.
Harman, John of Kensington. S s lambs Jul 1740 & R on petition. M.
Harman, John. S Jan T *Justitia* May 1745. L.
Harman, William. S s clothing Oct 1733 LC from *Caesar* Va Jul 1734. L.
Harmer, Kinard. S Lent 1750 LC QA Co., Md., from *Catherine* Nov 1750. G.
Harn, Thomas. S Sep 1776. Li.
Harnett, Bartholomew. S for perjury Dec 1732 LC from *Caesar* Va Jul 1734. L.
Harper, Ann. S Oct T *Phoenix* Oct 1760. M.
Harper, Edward. S Lent 1723 R Jun 1724 T *Forward* from London LC Annapolis Jun 1725. Db.
Harper, John. S Summer LC Md from *William* Dec 1774 & sold to John Philpot. Sh.
Harper, Thomas. S Lent T Summer 1752. Wa.
Harper, William. T Jul 1747. Sh.

MORE EMIGRANTS IN BONDAGE

Harper, William. S as pickpocket Summer 1746 R & T Jan 1747. O.

Harpur, Joseph. T Aug 1749. Bu.

Harrad, Martha. S Oct 1772 T *Justitia* Jan 1773. L.

Harrad, Mary. T *Justitia* Feb 1776. L.

Harringan, Neal. S Jan-Apr T Jun 1748 *Lichfield*. M.

Harrington, James. S Oct-Dec 1750 T *Thames* Feb 1751. M.

Harris, Ann. S Lent LC AA Co., Md., from *Thornton* Jul 1773. K.

Harris, Ann wife of Edward. S 14 yrs Lent LC AA Co., Md., from *Thornton* Jul 1775. Sy.

Harris, Daniel. S Sep T *Ruby* Oct 1754. L.

Harris, Elizabeth, spinster. R 14 yrs Lent T *Tryal* Jul 1754. Bu.

Harris, Frances. SQS May T Sep 1751 *Greyhound*. M.

Harris, Francis. SQS Sep 1741 LC QA Co., Md., from *Philleroy* Apr 1742. Co.

Harris, Francis *als* Odgers, Benjamin. S Jul 1761. Co.

Harris, George. S Lent LC Bal Co., Md., Jul 1772. Do.

Harris, George. S s gold ring Mar 1772 (HJ). He.

Harris, George. S Lent LC Bal Co., Md., Jul 1772. Mo.

Harris, George. S May-Jul T *Tayloe* Jul 1774. M.

Harris, James. S s wheat at Claines Lent 1755. Wo.

Harris, James. S 14 yrs Summer 1772 LC Bal Co., Md., Apr 1773. So.

Harris, James. S Jul T *Saltspring* Jul 1775. M.

Harris, John. S 14 yrs Lent 1744 LC Knt Co., Md., from *Susannah* Aug 1744. De.

Harris, John of St. Nicholas, Chelmsford. SQS Jul T Sep 1751 *Greyhound*. E.

Harris, John. S Summer T *Ruby* Oct 1754. K.

Harris, John. SQS Jan LC Bal Co., Md., Jul 1772; sold to Stephen Gill Wood, runaway. De.

Harris, John. S Oct T *Justitia* Dec 1774. L.

Harris, Mary. S for burglary Aug 1724 R 14 yrs Jun 1726. De.

Harris, Mary. S Apr T Apr 1746 *Laura*. L.

Harris, Mary. S Feb-Apr T Apr 1746 *Laura*. .M.

Harris, Matthew. S Apr T Sep 1751. Sy.

Harris, Michael. S Oct-Dec 1754 T *Greyhound* Feb 1755. M.

Harris, Nicholas. S Jul 1761. Co.

Harris, Peter. T *Justitia* Feb 1776. L.

Harris, Richard. S Summer 1732. No.

Harris, Richard. S Lent T *Dolphin* May 1763. E.

Harris, Sarah. S Jun-Dec 1745 T *Plain Dealer* Jan 1746. M.

Harris, Thomas of Staines. PT Oct 1672 R Oct 1673 LC Md from *Charles* May 1674. M.

Harris, Thomas. S Summer 1735. St.

Harris, William. SQS Jul 1738 LC QA Co., Md. Jun 1739. So.

Harris, William. S Jan 1751 T *Thames* Feb 1751. L.

Harris, William of St. George, Southwark. SQS Apr T Sep 1751 *Greyhound*. Sy.

Harris, William. S Lent LC AA Co., Md., from *Thornton* Jul 1775. M.

Harrison, Ann. S Feb-Apr T *Justitia* May 1745. M.

Harrison *als* Johnson *als* Williamson, Ann. S Sep T *Maryland Packet* Oct 1761. M.

Harrison, Ann. S Sep-Oct 1773 T *Justitia* Jan 1774. M.

Harrison, James. S Jan T *Plain Dealer* Jan 1746. L.

Harrison, James. S for perjury Jul 1774 (WJ), Wo.

Harrison, William. R Mar 1747 T Jan 1748. Li.

Harrison, William. S s horse Lent R 14 yrs Summer 1747 LC Knt Co., Md., from *St. George* Mar 1748. Sy.

Harrison, William. T 1751. Nf.

Harrison, William. S Dec 1760 T *Neptune* Mar 1761. M.

Harrison, William. S Jan 1770 but respited Feb 1770. M.

Harrison, William. SQS Jan 1773 LC Bal Co., Md., from *Adventure* Mar 1773. Du.

Harrison, William. S May T *Saltspring* Jul 1775. L.

Harrold, John. S s at Kingwick Lent T *Greyhound* Feb 1754. Bu.

Harry, William, a boy. S Glamorgan s horse R Jan 1765. Wal.

Harry, William. S Carmarthen for burglary R 14 yrs Apr 1775. Wal.

Hart, Arabella. S Oct T *Justitia* Dec 1774. L.

Hart, Fanny. S May T *Saltspring* Jul 1775. L.

Hart, Henry (1783). *See* Wilson, Thomas. M.

Hart, Hester. S Bristol Jan 1757 (AHJ). G.

Hart, John. S Summer LC Knt Co., Md., from *Bideford* Nov 1737. So.

Hart, Joseph. SW Jan LC AA Co., Md., from *Thornton* Jul 1775. M.

Hart, Margaret wife of Daniel. S Sep-Dec 1746 T Jan 1747 *George William*. M.

Hart, Margaret. SQS July 1772 LC Bal Co., Md., from *Adventure* Mar 1773. Nl.

Hart, Mathew. S Sep-Oct 1773 T *Justitia* Jan 1774. M.

Hart, Michael. S Oct T *Barnard* Oct 1756. L.

Hart, Thomas. S Oct T *Justitia* Dec 1774. L.

Hart, William. S for s from mansion house Lent R 14 yrs Nov 1724. Su.

Hart, William. R for life Jan T *Tryal* Mar 1757. M.

Hartcliffe, Alice. S 1761 (AHJ). La.

Hartley, James. S Apr T May 1750 *Lichfield*. M.

Hartley, John. S Feb-Apr T May 1752 *Lichfield*. M.

Hartley, Sarah. S s linen Dec 1735 T Jan 1736 *Dorsetshire* LC Va Sep 1736. M.

Hartley, Thomas. SQS Jan 1729. La.

Hartman, William. S Lent LC AA Co., Md., from *Thornton* Jul 1775. L.

Harvey, Charles. SQS Feb T *Thornton* May LC AA Co., Md., Jul 1774. M.

Harvey, Daniel. S Jun T Jul 1747 *Laura*. L.

Harvey, Edward. S Summer 1749 R 14 yrs Lent T May 1750 *Lichfield*. E.

Harvey, Edward. S Lent LC Bal Co., Md., Jun 1773. Co.

Harvey, Henry. T 1746. Nf.

Harvey, James. T May 1752 *Lichfield*. Ht.

Harvey, John. S Feb T Apr 1746. Sh.

Harvey, John. S Mar T Sep 1747. Ha.

Harvey, John. S Jul-Dec 1747 LC Knt Co., Md., from *St. George* Mar 1748. M.

Harvey, John. S Jan-Apr T Jun 1748 *Lichfield*. M.

Harvey, Richard. S 14 yrs Lent LC Bal Co., Md., Jun 1773. Co.

Harvey, Robert. R for Barbados Sep 1672 but LC AA Co Md Nov 1673. L.

Harvey, Sarah. S Lent LC AA Co., Md., from *Thornton* May 1771. M.

Harvey, Thomas. SQS Oct 1771 LC Bal Co., Md., Jul 1772. So.

Harvey, William. S Feb-Apr T May 1751 *Tryal*. M.

Harwood, Anthony. S Lent 1770. No.

Harwood, Elizabeth. S Apr-May T *Tryal* Jul 1754.1754. M.

Harwood, John. S Jan T *Thames* Feb 1751. M.

Harwood, Leonard, a soldier. S s at St. Mary, Reading, Lent 1756. Be.

Harwood, Sarah. S Apr T *Dolphin* Apr 1761. M.

Haskett, Joseph. S 14 yrs Jul 1736 l S Jul 1736 LC QA Co., Md., from *Amity* May

MORE EMIGRANTS IN BONDAGE

1737. Ha.

Haskin, Frederick. S Summer 1732 AT Lent 1733. Wa.

Haskins, Thomas. SQS Gloucester Lent 1758 (GJ). G.

Haslip, Thomas. S Sep-Oct 1772 T *Justitia* Jan 1773. M.

Haslom, George Jr. SQS & T Apr 1728. La.

Hast, David. Jul 1783 LC Bal Co., Md., Dec 1783 from *Swift*. M.

Hast, Oliva. Jul 1783 LC Bal Co., Md., Dec 1783 from *Swift*. M.

Hastilo, Charles. S Lent T May 1771. Wa.

Hastings, Martha. S Mar T *Thames* Mar 1754. L.

Hastings, William. S Dec 1782 LC Bal Co., Md., Dec 1783 from *Swift*. L.

Hatch, Anne (1773). See Griffith. M.

Hatch *als* Dinham, Joseph. S s sheep Summer 1746 T Jan 1747. De.

Hatch, William. S 14 yrs Lent 1737 LC Knt Co., Md., from *Hawk* Nov 1737. De.

Hatchet, Joseph. S Oct-Dec 1750 T *Thames* Feb 1751. M.

Hatle, William. S Jul 1771 (HJ). O

Hatt, John. S Jan-Apr T *Lichfield* May 1749. M.

Hatton, William. S for life LC AA Co., Md., from *Thornton* Jul 1773. K.

Hatworth, Matthew. S 1750 (AHJ). La.

Haugh, John. S 1757 (AHJ). La.

Haughton, Adolphus James. S Sep T Oct 1750 *Rachael*. M.

Haughton, Elizabeth. S Sep-Oct 1772 T *Justitia* Jan 1773. M.

Haughton, William. S Jul 1747 LC Knt Co., Md., from *St. George* Mar 1748. L.

Haughton, William. S May-Jul T *Tayloe* Jul 1773. M.

Haughton, William. R 14 yrs Jul T *Tayloe* Jul 1774. M.

Hault, William. S 14 yrs s horse Jun 1740 T Aug 1741 *Betty* from Hull. Nt.

Havergill, Elizabeth. S Apr T Sep 1751. Sy.

Havergirl, Nathaniel of St. Saviour, Southwark. SQS Apr T Aug 1752 *Tryal*. Sy.

Hawes, George. S Sep-Oct T *Tayloe* Jul 1774. M.

Hawes, George. S Sep-Oct T *Justitia* Dec 1774. M.

Hawes, James. S Sep T Oct 1750 *Rachael*. M.

Hawes, William. S Lent T May 1749 *Lichfield*. K.

Hawke, Richard. R 14 yrs Jul T *Saltspring* Jul 1775. L.

Hawker, John. S Lent R 14 yrs Summer 1739 (IJ). Nf.

Hawkes, Elizabeth of Warwick, spinster. R for America Jul 1706. Wa.

Hawkes, John. R & T Feb 1748. O.

Hawkesworth *als* Green, John of St. Paul Covent Garden. PT Sep 1672 R Oct 1673 but LC Md from *Charles* May 1674. M.

Hawkins, Ann. S & T Jan 1736 *Dorsetshire* LC Va Sep 1736. L.

Hawkins, Daniel. S Summer T Oct 1755. No.

Hawkins, Diana. SQS Gloucester Jan 1758 (GJ). G.

Hawkins, Elizabeth. S Lent 1750 LC QA Co., Md., from *Catherine* Nov 1750. Do.

Hawkins, Jane. S Summer 1743 LC Knt Co., Md., from *Globe* Mar 1744. De.

Hawkins, John *als* Yellow Jack. S for housebreaking & R for life Lent 1773; returned & S to be T for life Dec 1782. Wa.

Hawkins, John. S Lent LC Bal Co., Md., Jun 1773. Ha.

Hawkins, Margaret. S s clothing Apr TB May 1718. L.

Hawkins, Reubin. SQS Feb S Lent T *Thornton* May LC AA Co., Md., Jul 1774. M.

Hawkins, Richard. S Sep-Oct 1775 T *Justitia* Feb 1776. M.

Hawkins, Thomas. S 1753 TB to Md. No.

Hawkins, Thomas Jr. SQS Bury St. Edmunds 1755. Su.

Hawkins, William. S Lent but pardoned in April 1775. L.
Hawkins, William. S Dec 1782 LC Bal Co., Md., Dec 1783 from *Swift*. L.
Hawky, James. SQS Apr 1729. La.
Haworth, Matthew. S Lancaster 1750 (AHJ).
Hawson, Dennis. T May 1751 *Tryal*. M.
Hay, John. S Lent R 14 yrs Summer 1746. Nt.
Haydon, Eleanor. R Apr T Nov 1747. So.
Hayden, Thomas. S Jan-Apr T *Lichfield* May 1749. M.
Haydon, Thomas. S Apr T May 1750 *Lichfield*. M.
Hays, Ann wife of Christian. S Apr-Jun 1739 T *Sea Nymph* to Md. M.
Hays, Elizabeth. S Apr T Jun 1748 *Lichfield*. L.
Hayes, Frances. S Dec 1753-Jan 1754 T *Thames* Mar 1754. M.
Hayse, John. SQS & T May 1750 *Lichfield*. Ht.
Hays, Mary (1730) - *See* Rusher M.
Hayes, Thomas. S Lent 1738. Li.
Hayes, Thomas. S Jan T *Thames* Feb 1751; runaway. L.
Hayman, Mary. S Sep T Nov 1746. Sh.
Hayman, Thomas. S & T Jan 1736 *Dorsetshire* LC Va Sep 1736. L.
Haymour, Elizabeth. S May-Jul T Jul 1748 *Mary*. M.
Hayne, Philip. S 14 yrs Summer 1772 LC Bal Co., Md., Apr 1773. Co.
Hayne, Thomas. S 14 yrs Lent 1733 LC Knt Co., Md., from *Falcon* Apr 1734. De.
Haines, Ann wife of Samuel. S Sep 1735 T Jan 1736 *Dorsetshire* LC Va Sep 1736. M.
Haynes, Edward. T Jun 1748 *Lichfield*. M.
Haines, Edward. S Bristol Mar 1754.
Haines, Jane. SQS Jul 1741 LC QA Co., Md., from *Philleroy* Apr 1742. Wi.
Haynes, John. S May T Jul 1745 *Italian Merchant*. M.
Haynes, Thomas. S Jun-Dec 1745 T *Plain Dealer* Jan 1746. M.
Haynes, Thomas. S Jul T *Restoration* LC Bal Co., Md., Oct 1771. De.
Hays - *See* Hayes.
Hayward, Thomas. S Lent but taken from ship & pardoned in April 1775. Sy.
Haywarding, John. S Aug 1746 T Jan 1747. Wi.
Haywood, Anne. S Summer 1736 T Dec 1737. Wa.
Haywood, John. R 14 yrs Summer 1767. Wa.
Hayworth, Thomas. S s horse Lent 1729 R 14 yrs Summer 1730. Y.
Hazard, William. SQS Jul T *Justitia* Dec 1774. M.
Hazell, Robert. SWK Oct 1773 T *Justitia* Jan 1774. K.
Head, Anne of Newington, spinster. SQS Apr T May 1750 *Lichfield*. Sy.
Head, Mary (1721) - *See* Bostock. L.
Headdon, William. S Lent LC Knt Co., Md., from *Unity* Nov 1733. De.
Headrick, John. S Stirling s horse R for life Nov 1773. Sco.
Heard, Henry. S Lent 1731 LC Knt Co., Md., from *Falcon* Apr 1732. De.
Hearnden, Thomas. S Lent LC AA Co., Md., from *Thornton* May 1771. K.
Hearne, John. S Dec 1753-Jan 1754 T *Thames* Mar 1754. M.
Heasman, George. S Lent T *Thornton* May LC AA Co., Md., Jul 1774. M.
Heath, Alexander. T *Justitia* Jan 1774. M.
Heath, Charles. S Jul-Dec 1747 LC Knt Co., Md., from *St. George* Mar 1748. M.
Heath, Humphrey. S Summer T Sep 1754. St.
Heath, Mary. S Oct T *Barnard* Oct 1756. L.
Heath, Philip. R to T himself 7 yrs Nov 1775 T *Justitia* Feb 1776. L.
Heath, Samuel. S s from St. John's College Lent 1764. O.

MORE EMIGRANTS IN BONDAGE

Heathcote, Lydia. S 14 yrs Summer 1773; born London, runaway from *Justitia*, Leeds Town, Va., Apr 1774. Sy.

Heathcote, Robert. S 14 yrs Summer 1773 T *Justitia* Jan 1774. Sy.

Heathfield, Thomas of Croydon. S Lent T May 1750 *Lichfield*. Sy.

Heathier, William. S Lent LC Bal Co., Md., Jun 1773. Co.

Heatley or Heathey, John. S 14 yrs for receiving Summer TB Sep T Oct 1759. Db.

Heatley, Ralph. S 14 yrs Lent LC Bal Co., Md., Jul 1772; runaway. St.

Heaverland, William. S Jun T *Tryal* Jul 1754. L.

Heays, Mary. SQS Deal Summer 1747 LC Knt Co., Md., from *St. George* Mar 1748. K.

Hebb, Thomas. S Lent LC Bal Co., Md., Jun 1773. Ha.

Hele, Robert. SQS Oct 1742 LC Knt Co., Md., from *Globe* Mar 1744. De.

Hellier, Richard. S 14 yrs Lent 1742 LC QA Co., Md., from *Kent* Jun 1743. De.

Helmes, Mathew. S Lent 1738. Y.

Hely, Joseph. S Jul-Sep T *Ruby* Oct 1754. M.

Hemingway, John. S Summer 1772, died on passage to Va on *Trimly* 1773. Li.

Hemming, William. S Summer 1772 LC Bal Co., Md., Apr 1773. G.

Hemmis, John. S Lent T May 1754. G.

Henderson, Jane. S Sep-Oct 1775 T *Justitia* Feb 1776. M.

Henderson, William. T May 1751 *Tryal*. K.

Hendy, James. S Feb T May 1758. Ha.

Henley, Mary. S Jan-Apr T *Lichfield* May 1749. M.

Henley, Thomas. Jul 1783 LC Bal Co., Md., Dec 1783 from *Swift*. M.

Henly, William. S Feb T May 1758. Ha.

Hennick, Rachael. S Sep T *Maryland Packet* Oct 1761. M.

Henry, Henry. S Glamorgan s sheep R 14 yrs Feb 1775. Wal.

Henshaw [Hanshaw], John. S Oct 1765 TB *Tryal* but pardoned Nov 1765. L.

Herbert, Arthur. S Apr 1718 TB May 1719. L.

Herbert, John (1783). *See* Kellam. M.

Herbert, Mary of St. Dunstan in West. S s towels Apr 1718 TB May 1719. L.

Herbert, William. S & T Lent 1754. Wa.

Herbert, William. S Lent but pardoned May 1773. M.

Herbert, William. R 14 yrs Jul for shooting at a patrol T *Saltspring* Jul 1775. M.

Herbertson, John. S Lent 1739 T Jan 1740. Nl.

Heritage, Sarah wife of Richard. S Summer LC Bal Co., Md., Dec 1772. Wa.

Herman, Robert. S Lent 1733 LC Knt Co., Md., from *Hawk* Apr 1735. So.

Herne *als* Horne, Pooling. R Jul T *Tayloe* Jul 1774; runaway. M.

Herne, Thomas of Ewell. SQS Jan T *Thames* Feb 1751. Sy.

Heron, Edmund. S City Summer 1727. Nl.

Herring *als* Brown, Catherine. S May T Jul 1745 *Italian Merchant*. M.

Herring, Henry. S Lent LC AA Co., Md., from *Thornton* Jul 1773. M.

Herrop, James. AT from QS Jul 1769. Le.

Herryman, John. S Sep T Oct 1750 *Rachael*. M.

Heskett *als* Hesketh, William. T Oct 1750 *Rachael*. M.

Hessey, Richard. S Feb R 14 yrs Jul T Sep 1758. Ha.

Hestor, William. S 14 yrs Chelmsford Jan 1761 (AHJ). E.

Hewes, John. S Norwich Summer T Sep 1738. Nf.

Hewett, Edward. S Oct 1735 T Jan 1736 *Dorsetshire* LC Va Sep 1736. M.

Hewitt, Mary. S Summer 1736. Y.

Hey, Henry of Prescott, blacksmith. SQS Jul 1719. La.

Heydon, William. S Dec 1749-Jan 1750 T Mar 1750 *Tryal*. M.

Hibbard, Samuel. TB Aug 1735 T *Squire* LC Md Apr 1736. Db.

Hibberd, William. S Lent T *Thornton* May LC AA Co., Md., Jul 1774. M.

Hickey, David. R 14 yrs Sep T *Randolph* Sep 1768. Ha.

Hickman, John. S Summer LC Knt Co., Md., from *Bideford* Nov 1737. So.

Hickman *als* Day, Robert. S Summer T Sep 1753. Be.

Hickman, Seymour. S Lent LC AA Co., Md., from *Thornton* Jul 1775. L.

Hickman, Smith (1775). *See* Smith, John. Ht.

Hickman, Stephen. S Lent R 14 yrs Summer T *Ruby* Oct 1754. K.

Hicks, Elizabeth. S Sep-Oct 1772 T *Justitia* Jan 1773. M.

Hicks, George. SQS Jan LC AA Co., Md., from *Thornton* Jul 1775. M.

Hicks *als* Hilkes, John. S Oct 1751-Jan 1752 T *Thames* Mar 1752. M.

Hicks, John (1761) - *See* Jones.G.

Hicks, John. S Bristol Mar 1773 LC Bal Co., Md., sold to John McCabe. G.

Hicks, William. S Lent LC Bal Co., Md., Jun 1773 & sold to Elias Barniby. Wi.

Hickson, Benjamin. S Sep T *Phoenix* Oct 1760. L.

Hickson, George (1754) - *See* Higgins. Wo.

Hide *See* Hyde.

Higby, Mary. S May-Jul T Jul 1748 *Mary*. M.

Higginbottom, Thomas. S Lent T *Thornton* May LC AA Co., Md., Jul 1774. M.

Higgins, Edward *als* Hickson, George. S s at Moseley and Yardley Mar 1754 (WJ). Wo.

Higgins, Matthew. T *Barnard* Oct 1756. M.

Higgins, William. S Sep-Oct T *Justitia* Dec 1774. M.

Higginson, Charles. S Apr-Jun 1739 T *Sea Nymph* to Md. M.

Higginson, Joseph. S Apr T Jul 1770 *Scarsdale*; native of London, blacksmith aged
   17, runaway from Reuben Daniel of Orange Co. in 1775 . L.

Higgs, John. S Summer LC Bal Co., Md., Dec 1770. Sh.

Highby, Samuel. Jul 1783 LC Bal Co., Md., Dec 1783 from *Swift*. M.

Highfield, Jane. S May T Dec 1735 *John* LC Annapolis Sep 1736. M.

Highmore, Richard. S Jul T Aug 1749 *Thames*. L.

Hill *als* Harrington, Edward. S Oct T Oct 1749 *Mary*. L.

Hill, Elizabeth. S 14 yrs Summer 1732 LC Knt Co., Md., from *Falcon* Mar 1733. De.

Hill, Henry. S May-Jul T Aug 1749 *Thames*. M.

Hill, James. S May-Jul T Aug 1749 *Thames*. M.

Hill, James. T Jun *Bideford* LC QA Co., Md., Sep 1752. Wo.

Hill, Jane. SQS Apr LC Bal Co., Md., Jul 1771. Co.

Hill, John of Thaxted, butcher. SQS for fraud Jul T *Ruby* Oct 1754. E.

Hill, Joseph of Thaxted, butcher. SQS for fraud Jul T *Ruby* Oct 1754. E.

Hill, Mary. S Sep-Dec 1746 T Jan 1747 *George William*. M.

Hill, Mary. S Dec 1749-Jan 1750 T Mar 1750 *Tryal*. M.

Hill, Mary. SQS Lent LC AA Co., Md., from *Hanover Planter* Jul 1773. M.

Hill, Mary. S Apr-May T *Saltspring* Jul 1775. M.

Hill, Robert. S Lent T *Thornton* May LC AA Co., Md., Jul 1774. L.

Hill, Shadrack. SQS Jan LC AA Co., Md., from *Thornton* Jul 1775. Sy.

Hill, Thomas. S Summer LC Md. from *Reformation* Aug 1722. De.

Hill, Thomas. S Apr T Jun 1748 *Lichfield*. L.

Hill, William. SW Lent LC AA Co., Md., from *Hanover Planter* Jul 1773. M.

Hillerton, Edward. T May 1751 *Tryal*. K.

Hilliard, Ann. S Oct-Dec 1750 T *Thames* Feb 1751. M.

Hillier, John. R 14 yrs Sep TB to Va Oct T *Randolph* Sep 1768. Wi.

Hillier, Mary. S Jul 1728 for child murder R after petition & T *Expedition* from

MORE EMIGRANTS IN BONDAGE

Bristol to SC. Bu.

Hillingworth, Richard. S Summer 1772 T *Justitia* Jan 1773. E.

Hills, Daniel. S Lent 1741 (IJ). Su.

Hills, Durham. S City Christmas 1752 (AHJ). Nl.

Hills, Matthew. S Lent but too ill to be T by *Ann* , found at large & R for life Jun T Sep 1766 *Justitia* . K.

Hilton, Ann. S Feb-Apr T May 1752 *Lichfield*. M.

Hind, Mary. T May *Thornton* LC AA Co., Md., Jul 1774. M.

Hindley, Michael. S Summer 1763 T Feb 1764. Wa.

Hindley, William. S Jun T Jul 1747 *Laura*. L.

Hindes, John. S for highway robbery & R 14 yrs Summer LC Md from *William* Dec 1774 & sold to James Hutchings. O.

Hindes, Terence. S Oct 1772 T *Justitia* Jan 1773. L.

Hinds, William. R Dec 1773 T *Justitia* Jan 1774. M.

Hindy, James. S Summer 1738 LC Knt Co., Md., *from Hawk* Apr 1739. Wi.

Hine, Eleanor. S Apr-May T *Tryal* Jul 1754. M.

Hinemore, Ann. S May-Jul T Aug 1749 *Thames*. M.

Hines, John. R 14 yrs Jul T *Saltspring* Jul 1775. M.

Hingston, William. S Lent 1732 LC Knt Co., Md., from *Falcon* Mar 1733. De.

Hinks, Thomas. S Summer LC Bal Co., Md., Dec 1770. Wa.

Hinkson, Richard. S Lent LC from *Patapsco* Annapolis Nov 1733. Bd.

Hinson, Samuel. T Sep 1737 *Pretty Patsy*. L.

Hinton, John. S s at Kempsey Jul T *Restoration* LC Bal Co., Md., Oct 1771. Wo.

Hinton, Thomas. SWK Jan LC AA Co., Md., from *Thornton* Jul 1775. K.

Hinton, Timothy. S Jul-Sep T *Ruby* Oct 1754. M.

Hipditch, William. S Dec T *Justitia* Dec 1774; runaway. M.

Hipkin, Ann wife of Michael of St. George, Southwark. SQS Jan T *Thames* Feb 1751. Sy.

Hippisley, George. S Summer 1731 LC Knt Co., Md., from *Falcon* Apr 1732. So.

Hipps, James. LC Md from *Isabella* Jul 1775 & bought his freedom. X.

Hiscut, Benjamin. S for housebreaking Lent 1735 (GJ). So.

Hitch, Thomas. S Summer LC Bal Co., Md., Dec 1770. He.

Hitchcock, Edward. S May T *Saltspring* Jul 1775. L.

Hitchcock, John. T Aug 1749. Bu.

Hitchcock, Mary. T *Randolph* Sep 1768. De.

Hitchins, Joseph. S Apr-Jun 1739 T *Sea Nymph* to Md. M.

Hitchman, Thomas. S Apr-May T *Tryal* Jul 1754. M.

Hoare, Elizabeth. S Dec 1753-Jan 1754 T *Thames* Mar 1754. M.

Hoare *als* Brown *als* Kirkman, Elizabeth. S Lent LC AA Co., Md., from *Thornton* Jul 1775. M.

Hoar, Hannah. S Oct 1749-Jan 1750 T *Thames* Feb 1751. M.

Hoare, Henry. S for life Lent LC AA Co., Md., from *Thornton* Jul 1775. Sy.

Hoare, Robert. S Mar 1742 LC PG Co., Md. Co.

Hoar, Thomas. S Feb T *Neptune* Mar 1761. L.

Hoare, William. S Jan-Apr T Jun 1748 *Lichfield*. M.

Hobbs, James. S Lent LC AA Co., Md., from *Thornton* Jul 1773. M.

Hobbs, John Jr. SQS Apr 1737 LC LC Knt Co., Md., from *Hawk* Nov 1737. Co.

Hobbs, John. S Lent R Jun T 14 yrs Aug 1752 *Tryal*. K.

Hobbs, Richard. SQS Oct 1749 LC QA Co., Md., from *Catherine* Nov 1750. G.

Hobbs, Robert. SQS Apr T *Thornton* May LC AA Co., Md., Jul 1774. M.

Hobbs, Sarah. S Feb-Apr T Apr 1746 *Laura*. M.

Hobbs, Thomas. S Jul-Sep T *Ruby* Oct 1754. M.

Hobby, John. S & T Jan 1736 *Dorsetshire* LC Va Sep 1736. L.

Hobler, Mary. S May-Jul T *Tayloe* Jul 1774. M.

Hobson, George. S Lent 1752. Nt.

Hobson, Samuel. S Jan-Apr T *Lichfield* May 1749. M.

Hobson, Thomas. S Jan-Jun T Jul 1747 *Laura*. M.

Hockey, Patrick. S Bristol Mar 1755 (AHJ). G.

Hockley, Sarah. T Jun 1748 *Lichfield*. L.

Hocklish, John. S Lent T 14 yrs Aug 1752 *Tryal*. K.

Hoddy, Richard. S Apr T *Dolphin* Apr 1761. M.

Hodge, Francis. S Lent T Apr 1746. Ht.

Hodges *als* Pison, James. S Jul-Dec 1747 LC Knt Co., Md., from *St. George* Mar 1748. M.

Hodges, John. S Dec T *Justitia* Dec 1774. L.

Hodges, Philip. S Summer 1757 R Summer 1758. Wo.

Hodgetts, Aaron. S Lent T Apr 1753. Wa.

Hodgkins, Edward. S Summer T Oct 1738. Le.

Hodgman, Edward. S Oct T *Barnard* Oct 1756. M.

Hodgson, Elizabeth. R 14 yrs Aug 1758 (WJ). Sh.

Hodgson, George. S York 1754 (AHJ). Y.

Hodgson, John. S Summer 1772 LC Bal Co., Md., from *Adventure* Mar 1773. Du.

Hodgson, Samuel. S 14 yrs Aug 1753 (AHJ). We.

Hodgson, Thomas of Coulton. SQS Apr 1735. La.

Hodgson, William. S Dec 1750 T *Thames* Feb 1751. L.

Hodson, John. S Summer T Sep 1754. St.

Hogden, Nehemiah. S Summer 1772 T *Justitia* Jan 1773. K.

Hogg, Andrew. SQS Jan LC AA Co., Md., from *Thornton* Jul 1773. Sy.

Hog, Catherine. S Oct 1773 T *Justitia* Jan 1774. L.

Holbert, Margaret. SL Jul 1773 T *Justitia* Jan 1774. Sy.

Holden, John. S Apr T May 1752 *Lichfield*. L.

Holden *als* Lovegrove, Rebecca. S Sep T *Ruby* Oct 1754. L.

Holden, Richard. S Summer 1724 R Mar 1725. Ht.

Holden, Richard. S Summer 1773 T *Justitia* Jan 1774. K.

Holden, Thomas. S Jul-Dec 1747 LC Knt Co., Md., from *St. George* Mar 1748. M.

Holdsworth, James. S & T Jan 1736 *Dorsetshire* LC Va Sep 1736. L.

Holdturn (Holden), Thomas. S Summer LC Bal Co., Md., Dec 1772, sold to Andrew Hook. St.

Hole, John. S 14 yrs Lent LC Bal Co., Md., Dec 1772. De.

Holl *als* Bowen, Elizabeth. S Sep T *Barnard* Oct 1756. M.

Holl, Elizabeth. S Bristol Lent T Apr 1761 by *Atlas* to Md. G.

Holland *als* Shepherd, Ann. S Oct-Dec 1750 T *Thames* Feb 1751. M.

Holland, Thomas. S Lent T May 1750 *Lichfield*. K.

Holland, Thomas. S Oct 1751-Jan 1752 T *Thames* Mar 1752. M.

Holland, Thomas. S Jan T *Tryal* Mar 1757. L.

Holland, William. S Lent LC AA Co., Md., from *Thornton* Jul 1775. M.

Holliday, James, aged 40 born near Edinburgh. S Apr T May 1720 *Honor* but escaped in Vigo, Spain; executed for returning Oct 1720 (NM). L.

Holliday, Joseph. S Jun 1718 T Feb 1719 *Worcester* LC Annapolis Jun 1719. L.

Hollings, John. S Bristol Jan 1760 (AHJ). G.

MORE EMIGRANTS IN BONDAGE

Hollings, Neomi. S Summer 1739, found pregnant & R 14 yrs Lent 1740. Y.

Hollingsworth, Henry. AT Jul T Sep 1720 (NM). No.

Hollinshead, John. SQS Coventry Aug 1745. Wa.

Hollinshead, William. SQS Coventry Aug 1745. Wa.

Hollis, Alethea. S May-Jun T Aug 1752 *Tryal*. M.

Hollis, Richard. R Summer 1773 T *Justitia* Jan 1774. Sy.

Hollis, William *als* Berk, Thomas. S Dec 1772 but taken from transport ship & pardoned Mar 1773. M.

Holloway, Alice. S Feb T *Neptune* Mar 1761. L.

Holloway *als* Van Gadwey, Jacob. S Dec 1746 T Jan 1747 *George William*. L.

Holloway, William. R for Barbados Sep 1672 but LC Md Jun 1673. L.

Hollows, Elizabeth. S Summer T Aug 1749 *Thames*. Sy.

Hollman, John. T May 1751 *Tryal*. Sy.

Holman, Richard. S Launceston May 1754 (AHJ). Co.

Holmby (Homeby), Thomas. S Jan 1717 T 14 yrs May 1718 *Tryal* LC Charles Town Aug 1718. L.

Holme, Elizabeth - *See* Macereth We.

Holmes, Ann. S Summer T *Barnard* Oct 1756. Sy.

Holmes, Isaac. S Lent LC AA Co., Md., from *Hanover Planter* Jul 1773. M.

Holmes, Jane. T Mar 1750 *Tryal*. M.

Holmes, John. S Jun 1718. M.

Holmes, John, hempdresser. S s flour at St. Helen's Summer 1757 but pardoned Aug 1757. Be.

Holmes, John Jr. S 14 yrs Lent LC Bal Co., Md., Jul 1772. De.

Holmes, Mary. S & T Jan 1736 *Dorsetshire* LC Va Sep 1736. L.

Holmes, Peter. S Lent 1737. Li.

Holmes, Rebecca wife of James. S Lent LC AA Co., Md., from *Thornton* Jul 1775. M.

Holmes, Richard. S Lent LC from *Patapsco* Annapolis Nov 1733. No.

Holmes, Richard. S Sep-Oct 1772 T *Justitia* Jan 1773. M.

Holt, Ann wife of Isaac of Worsley. SQS Jan 1730. La.

Holt, Edmund [Edward]. S Lent R 14 yrs Summer 1757. St.

Holt, John. S Sep T Dec 1746. Nt.

Holt, John. S Lent T May 1750 *Lichfield*. E.

Holt, Ormond. T Apr 1735 *Patapsco* LC Annapolis Oct 1735. E.

Holt, Richard [Edward]. S s cloth at Kidderminster Lent 1774. Wc.

Holt, Thomas of Hundersfield, woollen weaver. SQS Apr 1725. La.

Holt, Thomas. S Lent T *Tryal* Jul 1754. Sy.

Holten, Benjamin. S 14 yrs Lent LC AA Co., Md., from *Thornton* Jul 1773. E.

Holton, Griffith (1774). *See* Bird, John. K.

Home, John. SQS Apr T May 1750 *Lichfield*. M.

Homer, Jonathan. S s mare in Hagley Summer 1759 R 14 yrs Lent 1760. Wo.

Homes, Jonas. S Jan LC QA Co., Md., from *Leopard* May 1738. De.

Honady, William. S 14 yrs Summer 1731 LC Knt Co., Md., from *Falcon* Apr 1732. De.

Honden [Handen], Richard. S & TB 14 yrs Sep 1753. G.

Hone, Ann. SQS Oct 1754 T *Greyhound* Feb 1755. M.

Honey, Joseph. T Apr 1742 LC PG Co., Md. Co.

Honeybond, William. S 14 yrs Lent LC AA Co., Md., from *Thornton* Jul 1773. Ht.

Honour, William. S May-Jun T Aug 1752 *Tryal*. M.

Hood, John Jr. S Lent T Jul 1745 *Italian Merchant*. Sy.

Hood, Samuel. S Bristol Lent 1767. G.

Hooker, Martha. S Lent 1735. Nt.

Hooker, Thomas. S Jul 1736 S Jul 1736 LC QA Co., Md., from *Amity* May 1737. Ha.

Hooker, William. S Jul 1736 S Jul 1736 LC QA Co., Md., from *Amity* May 1737. Ha.

Hooper, Josiah. S s cloth at Stroud Summer LC Md from *William* Dec 1774 & sold to Thomas Johnson. G.

Hooper, Mary. S Lent LC AA Co., Md., from *Thornton* Jul 1775. M.

Hooper, Richard. S 14 yrs Lent 1742 LC QA Co., Md., from *Kent* Jun 1743. De.

Hooper, William. S 14 yrs Lent 1750 LC QA Co., Md., from *Catherine* Nov 1750. He.

Hoot, John. T May 1746. De.

Hooton, John. S Lent T May 1749 *Lichfield*. K.

Hooten, Mary. S 1756 TB to Md. No.

Hopcraft, Robert. S Lent LC AA Co., Md., from *Thornton* May 1771. M.

Hope, John. SQS Bristol s mahogany boards May 1761. G.

Hope, Matthew. S Feb T *Thames* Mar 1752. L.

Hope, Robert. S s sheep R for life May 1771. Sco.

Hope, Thomas. SQS Jul T Sep 1751 *Greyhound*. M.

Hope, William. S Lent LC AA Co., Md., from *Thornton* Jul 1773. K.

Hopes, John. SQS New Sarum or Warminster T *Randolph* Sep 1768. Wi.

Hopkins, Arthur. S Bristol Jan 1757 (AHJ). G.

Hopkins, Elizabeth. S Oct T *Phoenix* Oct 1760. M.

Hopkins, John. S & R 14 yrs for assault on highway Summer 1738. Mo.

Hopkins, John. T Feb 1748. Le.

Hopkins, John. S Lent T *Thornton* May LC AA Co., Md., Jul 1774. K.

Hopkins, Thomas. SQS Jul 1772 LC Bal Co., Md., Apr 1773. Mo.

Hopkins, Thomas. S May-Jul T *Tayloe* Jul 1774. M.

Hopkinson, John. S Sep 1750. Li.

Hopps, Anthony. S May-Jul T Aug 1749 *Thames*. M.

Hopwood, William. S Feb-Apr 1746 T Apr 1746 *Laura*. M.

Horabin, John. S Sep 1740 T *Harpooner* Jan 1741. L.

Horne, Charles, son of an attorney in King Street. S for assault with sword Dec 1735 T Jan 1736 *Dorsetshire* LC Va Sep 1736. M.

Horne, John (1773). *See* Mayhew. Su.

Horner, Robert. S Sep T *Barnard* Oct 1756. M.

Horrabin, James. SQS Oct 1730 & T *Lime* to Jamaica but died there 1732. La.

Horrobin, William. SQS Apr 1729. La.

Horobin, William. S Mar R 14 yrs Summer 1757 (GJ). St.

Horsey, Mary. S Feb-Apr T May 1751 *Tryal*. M.

Horsey, Mary. S Bristol Jan 1756 (AHJ). G.

Horton, Joseph. R 14 yrs Jul T *Saltspring* Jul 1775. M.

Horton, Richard. S for life Jan T *Plain Dealer* Jan 1746. M.

Horton, Thomas. S Oct-Dec 1754 T *Greyhound* Feb 1755. M.

Horton, Thomas. S Lent T *Thornton* May LC AA Co., Md., Jul 1774. M.

Hosegood, George. S Lent 1732 LC Knt Co., Md., from *Falcon* Mar 1733. So.

Hosier, Thomas of St. Giles in Fields. S s quilt Apr T Sep 1718 *Eagle* LC Charles Town Mar 1719. L.

Hoskins, Mary. S Jun 1753 (AHJ). Wo.

Hoskins, Robert. S Exeter Nov 1758 (AHJ). De.

Hosler, William. S Lent R 14 yrs Summer T *Maryland Packet* Oct 1761. E.

Hotchpitch, William. S May-Jul T Aug 1749 *Thames*. M.

Hotton, John. S Apr T *Lichfield* May 1749. L.

Hough, Hugh. S s at Eccleshall Summer LC Md from *William* Dec 1774 & sold to John McCabe. St.

Houghton, James. S Feb-Apr T May 1752 *Lichfield*. M.

Houghton, Martha. R for Barbados Oct 1673 but LC Md from *Charles* May 1674. L.

Houghton, William. S Sep T *Phoenix* Oct 1760. L.

Houlsworth, John. S Oct 1760. Li.

Houlton, Habbacuck. SQS Bristol s silk handkerchiefs in Wine St. Mar TB to Md May 1763. G.

House, James. S Lent LC Bal Co., Md., Jun 1773. Do.

Housely, John. T 1745. Y.

How, Ann wife of James. T Sep 1746. Ha.

How, James. S Feb-Apr T *Justitia* May 1745. M.

How, Joseph. S Summer 1724 R Mar T Nov 1725 *Rappahannock* but died on passage. Ht.

How, Thomas. S Lent 1731 LC Knt Co., Md., from *Falcon* Apr 1732. So.

How, Thomas. S Jan-Apr T *Lichfield* May 1749. M.

Howard, Ann. S Jun 1718 T Feb 1719 *Worcester* LC Annapolis Jun 1719. L.

Howard, Ann. S Feb-Apr 1746 T Apr 1746 *Laura*. M.

Howard, Ann. S Sep T *Phoenix* Oct 1760. L.

Howard, Edward of St. Martin, Colchester. SQS Oct T *Ruby* Oct 1754. E.

Howard, Elizabeth. S Jan T Mar 1750 *Tryal*. L.

Howard, Elizabeth. SQS York Jan T Sep 1763. Y.

Howard, Henry. S Dec 1772 T *Justitia* Jan 1773. M.

Howard, John. S Jul T Sep 1751 *Greyhound*. L.

Howard, John. S Lent LC AA Co., Md., from *Thornton* Jul 1775. M.

Howard, John. Jul 1783 LC Bal Co., Md., Dec 1783 from *Swift*. M.

Howard, Margaret. S Mar T *Thames* Mar 1754. L.

Howard, Mary. S & T Mar 1750 *Tryal*. L.

Howard, Nathaniel. T Jun 1747. E.

Howard, Richard. S Jul T Aug 1749 *Thames*. L.

Howard, Robert. SQS Apr T Aug 1759. Y.

Howard, Samuel. S for highway robbery Lent R 14 yrs Summer T *Justitia* Sep 1766. Bu.

Howard, Samuel. S Glamorgan s sheep R Jun 1766. Wal.

Howard?, William. S Summer LC Bal Co., Md., Dec 1770 from *Trotman* & sold to George Hammond. X.

Howard, William. R Jul T *Saltspring* Jul 1775. M.

Howburn, Sarah. S for murder of her bastard child Apr 1746 T Jan 1748. Nl.

Howell, Francis. S Apr T Jun 1748 *Lichfield*. L.

Howell, John. S Lent LC Bal Co., Md., Jul 1772. G.

Howell, Joseph. S Jun-Dec 1745 T *Plain Dealer* Jan 1746. M.

Howell, Margaret. S Jul T *Barnard* Oct 1756. M.

Howell, Sarah. S Bristol Sep 1741 LC QA Co., Md., from *Philleroy* Apr 1742. G.

Howell, William of Newington. SQS Jun T Aug 1752 *Tryal*. Sy.

Howells, Anthony. S 14 yrs Summer 1741 LC QA Co., Md., from *Philleroy* Apr 1742. He.

Howkins, Daniel. S 1755 TB to Va. No.

Howse, William. T *York* to Md Jun 1740. Bu.

Hoyde, Philip. S & T Mar 1750 *Tryal*. L.

Hoye, Mary. S Lent T Jun 1748 *Lichfield*. K.

Hoyle, John. SQS Jan Summer 1772 LC Bal Co., Md., Apr 1773. Co.

Hoyles, William. S May-Jul T Sep 1746 *Mary*. M.

Huband, Matthew. S Summer T Sep 1751 *Greyhound*. Sx.

Hubbard, John. S Lent T Apr 1746. E.

Hubbard, Samuel (James). S & T Jan 1736 *Dorsetshire* LC Va Sep 1736. L.

Hubbard, William. T Sep 1737 *Pretty Patsy*. L.

Hubbert, Henry. S Lent LC Knt Co., Md., from *Unity* Nov 1733. De.

Hudd, Mary. S Dec 1746 T Jan 1747 *George William*. L.

Huddlestone, Robert. S Apr 1754. Li.

Hudell *als* Hoodell, Thomas. S Jan-Apr T *Lichfield* May 1749. M.

Hudnall, James. S Lent R Jun T 14 yrs Aug 1752 *Tryal*. K.

Hudson, Charles. S Jun 1718 T Feb 1719 *Worcester* to Md; not on LC. L.

Hudson, Jane. S Sep-Dec 1746 T Jan 1747 *George William*. M.

Hudson, John of Heaton Norris, tailor. SQS Oct 1722. La.

Hudson, John. S Apr T May 1750 *Lichfield*. M.

Hudson, John. S Lent LC AA Co., Md., from *Thornton* Jul 1773. M.

Hudson, Thomas of Heaton Norris, weaver. SQS Oct 1722. La.

Hudson, William. S Lent T Jun 1748 *Lichfield*. K.

Hudson, William. SQS Jan T *Greyhound* Feb 1755. M.

Hudswell, William. SQS Oct T from Liverpool Nov 1772. Y

Huggate, Richard of Ewhurst. S Lent T May 1750 *Lichfield*. Sy.

Huggett, Loftius. S Jan T Mar 1750 *Tryal*. L.

Huggins, Benjamin. S May-Jul T Aug 1749 *Thames*. M.

Huggins, John. S Jul T Jul 1748 *Mary*. L.

Hughes, Abraham. S 14 yrs Lent LC AA Co., Md., from *Thornton* Jul 1775. Sy.

Hughes, Ann. SQS & T *Greyhound* Feb 1755. M.

Hughes *als* Dennison, Catherine. S s pinafores Apr T Dec 1735 *John* LC Annapolis
Sep 1736. M.

Hughes, Catherine wife of Jacob. S Oct T *Phoenix* Oct 1760. M.

Hughs, Christopher. S & T Jan 1736 *Dorsetshire* LC Va Sep 1736. L.

Hughes, Deborah. S Jul 1760, taken aboard *Phoenix* but removed to Newgate &
shipped later in 1760. M.

Hughes, Edward. S Jan T *Greyhound* Feb 1755. L.

Hughes, Elizabeth. S s horse Lent R 14 yrs Summer 1754 (GJ). He.

Hughes, Elizabeth. S & T Dec 1759 *Phoenix* . L.

Hughes, Jane. S Apr T *Dolphin* May 1763. L.

Hughes, John. S Apr T May 1751 *Tryal*. L.

Hughs, John. SWK Jan T *Greyhound* Feb 1754. K.

Hughes, John. S Summer T from London Sep 1754. Wa.

Hughes, John. S for life Jan T *Tryal* Mar 1757. L.

Hughes, John. S Oct T *Phoenix* Oct 1760. M.

Hughes, John. S Lent LC Bal Co., Md., Jul 1774. Wi.

Hughes, John. S Lent LC Bal Co., Md., Jul 1774. Sh.

Hughes, John. S Lent LC AA Co., Md., from *Thornton* Jul 1775. M.

Hughes, Peter. R & T Apr 1735 *Patapsco* LC Annapolis Oct 1735. M.

Hughes, William. S Feb-Apr T for life May 1752 *Lichfield*. M.

Hughes, William. S 14 yrs Lent LC AA Co., Md., from *Hanover Planter* Jul 1773. L.

Hughes, William. S Lent T *Thornton* May LC AA Co., Md., Jul 1774. M.

Hughes, William Sr. S s wheat at Llanvihangel Summer LC Md from *William* Dec
1774 & sold to James Hutchings. Mo.

Hughes, William Jr. S s wheat at Llanvihangel Summer LC Md from *William* Dec

1774 & sold to James Hutchings. Mo.

Hull, John. S Lent T May 1750 *Lichfield*. E.

Hull, William. SQS Apr T *Thornton* May LC AA Co., Md., Jul 1774. Sx.

Hullock, Ann. T *Phoenix* Oct 1760. M.

Hullston, Henry. S Oct 1751-Jan 1752 T *Thames* Mar 1752. M.

Hulme?, Richard. Jul 1783 LC Bal Co., Md., Dec 1783 from *Swift*. M.

Humbridge, George. S & T Apr 1751. G.

Hume, Dennison. SQS Bristol Sep LC Bal Co., Md., Dec 1770. G.

Hume, Joseph. S Apr-Jun 1739 T *Sea Nymph* to Md. M.

Humphrey, Edward. S 14 yrs Lent LC AA Co., Md., from *Thornton* May 1771. K.

Humphrey, Elizabeth. S Jul T *Beverly* Aug 1763. M.

Humphrey, William. S Lent R 14 yrs Summer T *Barnard* Oct 1756. K.

Humphreys, Elizabeth. S Dec 1753-Jan 1754 T *Thames* Mar 1754. M.

Humphreys, James. S for life Lent LC AA Co., Md., from *Thornton* Jul 1775. Sy.

Humphreys *als* Russell, Margaret of St. Sepulchre. S s silver cup Apr 1718. L.

Humphrys, Samuel. S Lent LC AA Co., Md., from *Hanover Planter* Jul 1773. M.

Humphreys, Thomas. S Feb T *Thames* Mar 1752. L.

Humphreys, Thomas (1759) - *See* Knightley. Wo.

Hunt, Catherine. S May T *Beverly* Aug 1763. M.

Hunt, Edward. S Apr-Jun 1739 T *Sea Nymph* to Md. M.

Hunt, Edward. S Apr T May 1750 *Lichfield*. L.

Hunt, Francis. R 14 yrs Jul T *Saltspring* Jul 1775. M.

Hunt, Hannah wife of Joseph (*qv*) of St. Albans. S Summer T Aug 1749 *Thames*. Ht.

Hunt, Henry. S Sep-Oct T Oct 1749 *Mary*. M.

Hunt, James. T Apr 1735 *Patapsco* LC Annapolis Oct 1735. Ht.

Hunt, John. S Jun-Dec 1745 T *Plain Dealer* Jan 1746. M.

Hunt, John. S 14 yrs Chelmsford Jan 1752 (AHJ). E.

Hunt, John. S s sheep Lent R 14 yrs Summer 1765: executed in 1768 for returning. He.

Hunt, Joseph of St. Albans. S Summer T Aug 1749 *Thames*. Ht.

Hunt, Mary wife of John S 14 yrs & T *Thames* Mar 1752. M.

Hunt, Samuel. SW Apr T *Thornton* May LC AA Co., Md., Jul 1774. M.

Hunt, Susannah. S Summer T *Barnard* Oct 1756. Sy.

Hunt, Thomas, saddler. R 14 yrs Bristol Aug 1750 LC QA Co., Md., from *Chester* Dec 1752. G.

Hunt, Thomas. SQS Dec 1754 T *Greyhound* Feb 1755. M.

Hunt *als* Symonds, William, brother of John Hunt (q.v.). S s gelding Oct 1770 R 14 yrs Apr LC Md Jul 1771. He.

Hunt, William. S Summer LC Bal Co., Md., Dec 1772. Wa.

Hunter, John. S 14 yrs Oct 1751-Jan 1752 T *Thames* Mar 1752. M.

Hunter, John. S Apr T *Dolphin* May 1763; runaway. M.

Hunter, Peter. SQS Apr T Jun 1754. Y.

Hunter, William. SQS Dec 1753 T *Thames* Mar 1754. M.

Hunter, William. S Lent T *Tryal* Jul 1754. Sy.

Hunton (Hunter), Mary. S s pewter plates May T Dec 1735 *John* LC Annapolis Sep 1736. M.

Hurcan *als* Hurkham, Thomas. R Jul T *Tayloe* Jul 1774. M.

Hurd, William. T *Saltspring* Jul 1775. M.

Hurley, John. SQS Apr T May 1751 *Tryal*. M.

Hurly, John. S Lent T *Thornton* May LC AA Co., Md., Jul 1774. M.

Hurley, Thomas. S Coventry s silver watch Aug 1772. Wa.

Hurley, William. S Aug 1752. So.

Hurlstone, Samuel. T *St. George* Jan LC Knt Co., Md., Mar 1748. Wa.

Hurren, John. SQS Woodbridge 1770. Su.

Hurry, Ann. S Lent LC AA Co., Md., from *Thornton* May 1771. E.

Hurst, Andrew. R for Barbados Sep 1672 but LC Md Jun 1673. L.

Hurst, Elizabeth wife of Emanuel. S Lent LC AA Co., Md., from *Thornton* Jul 1775. M.

Hurst, George. SQS Jan LC Bal Co., Md., Jul 1772. Wi.

Hurst, Hannah. S May-Jul T Sep 1746 *Mary*. M.

Hurst, Henry. S Dec 1772 T *Justitia* Jan 1773; runaway. M.

Hurst, John. S Apr 1746 T Apr 1746 *Laura*. M.

Hurst, John. S Dec 1749-Jan 1750 T Mar 1750 *Tryal*. M.

Hurst, Richard. SQS Bakewell Jul T Dec 1737. Db.

Hurst *als* Smith, Richard. S s mares Lent R 14 yrs Summer 1756 TB to Va. No.

Hurt, John. S Lent R Jun T 14 yrs Aug 1752 *Tryal*. E.

Hussey, Hester. S Feb-Apr 1746 T Apr 1746 *Laura*. M.

Hussey, Mary. S Jan-Jun T Jul 1747 *Laura*. M.

Hussey, Mary. S Oct 1773 T *Justitia* Jan 1774. L.

Hutchford, Elizabeth. S Lent LC AA Co., Md., from *Thornton* May 1771. K.

Hutchins, Ann. S s clothing Oct 1735 T Jan 1736 *Dorsetshire* LC Va Sep 1736. M.

Hutchins, John. S Oct T Oct 1749 *Mary*. L.

Hutchinson, Anthony. S Oct 1757. Li.

Hutchinson, Jane. S May-Jul T Jul 1748 *Mary*. M.

Hutchinson, Ruth. S Bristol s coats Mar 1765 (BJ). G.

Hutsing, John (1765) - *See* Hurring. Su.

Hutton, Samuel. S May-Jul T Aug 1749 *Thames*. M.

Hutton, Susanna. S Oct 1751-Jan 1752 T *Thames* Mar 1752. M.

Huxtable, William. S 14 yrs Lent 1744 LC Knt Co., Md., from *Susannah* Aug 1744. De.

Hyan, William. S Dec 1753-Jan 1754 T *Thames* Mar 1754. M.

Hyde, Elizabeth wife of William. S May-Jul T *Tayloe* Jul 1773. M.

Hyatt, Elizabeth. S Sep-Oct 1773 T *Justitia* Jan 1774. M.

Hyde, Elizabeth. S Jun-Dec 1745 T *Plain Dealer* Jan 1746. M.

Hide, John. SQS Feb LC AA Co., Md., from *Thornton* Jul 1775. M.

Hide, Richard. S & R 14 yrs Summer AT Dec 1738. La.

Hyde, Samuel of Hattersley, Mottram, Cheshire. SQS Lancaster Oct 1735. La.

Ibbetson, Margaret. S York 1757 (AHJ). Y.

Imm, Joseph. S Mar 1742. He.

Immingham, Edward. T Lent 1750. Li.

Impey, Alice. SQS Jun T Aug 1752 *Tryal*. M.

Ingersole *als* Waskett, Ann. S Oct 1740 T *Harpooner* Jan 1741. L.

Ingersole, Thomas. S Lent R 14 yrs Summer 1761. E.

Inglesent, Martha. Jul 1783 LC Bal Co., Md., Dec 1783 from *Swift*. M.

Ingmire, Robert, S Oct-Dec 1754 T *Greyhound* Feb 1755. M.

Ingram, Elizabeth wife of John. S Jun T *Maryland Packet* Oct 1761. M.

Ingram, Elizabeth. S Lent LC AA Co., Md., from *Hanover Planter* Jul 1773. L.

Ingram, Mordecai. S Lent 1750 LC QA Co., Md., from *Catherine* Nov 1750. He.

Ingram, Richard. S Lent LC Knt Co., Md., from *Bideford* Nov 1737. So.

Ingram, Stephen. SQS Apr 1737 LC QA Co., Md., from *Amity* Apr 1738. De.

MORE EMIGRANTS IN BONDAGE

Ingram, William. S s sheep Lent R 14 yrs Summer 1759 TB to Va. No.

Inman, Millicent of St. George, Southwark. SQS Apr T May 1750 *Lichfield*. Sy.

Inman, William (1755) - *See* Ellston. St.

Innis, Ann. SQS Jul 1772 LC Bal Co., Md., from *Adventure* Mar 1773. Nl.

Innes, Solomon. S Sep 1740 T *Harpooner* Jan 1741. L.

Innis, Walter. S Feb-Apr T May 1751 *Tryal*. M.

Inoh, John. S Summer 1752 T Feb 1753. Le.

Ireland, James. S 1757 (AHJ). Du.

Ireland, William of St Giles in Fields. PT Jun R Oct 1673 LC Md from *Charles* May 1674. M.

Ireland, William. S Jan LC QA Co., Md., from *Leopard* May 1738. De.

Ireland, William. S for s sheep Summer 1742 R 14 yrs Lent 1743 (GJ). He.

Irish, Richard. SQS Jan 1735 T *Amity* LC QA Co., Md., Mar 1736. So.

Ironmonger, Robert. SQS Oct T *Justitia* Dec 1774. M.

Irons, William. S for life Feb T *Thames* Mar 1754. M.

Irwin, Susanna. T Jun 1748 *Lichfield*. L.

Isaac, John. S Lent LC Bal Co., Md., Jun 1773. He.

Isaacs, James. S 14 yrs Lent LC AA Co., Md., from *Thornton* Jul 1773. Sy.

Isaacs, Solomon. T *Harpooner* Jan 1741. L.

Isdell, William. S Jul T *Tayloe* Jul 1774. L.

Isted, Edward. S Lent T Jul 1747 *Laura*. Bu.

Iverson, Peter. S Aug T *Restoration* LC Bal Co., Md., Oct 1771. So.

Ivory, Bryan. S Jan-Apr T Jun 1748 *Lichfield*. M.

Izard, Ann. S May-Jul T Sep 1751 *Greyhound*. M.

Jackson, Bryan. S May-Jul T Aug 1749 *Thames*. M.

Jackson, George of Great Birch. SQS Jan T *Dolphin* May 1763. E.

Jackson, James. S for life Feb T *Thames* Mar 1754. M.

Jackson, James. S Sep T *Phoenix* Oct 1760. M.

Jackson, James. S Lent LC AA Co., Md., from *Thornton* May 1771. M.

Jackson *als* Coxe, John. R for Barbados Oct 1673 but LC Md from *Charles* May 1674. L.

Jackson, John of Moston. SQS Apr 1719. La.

Jackson, John. S Jan-Apr T *Lichfield* May 1749. M.

Jackson, Joseph. S Summer T Oct 1750 *Rachael*. K.

Jackson, Mary. S Aug T *Restoration* LC Bal Co., Md., Oct 1771. Wa.

Jackson, Samuel. T Lent 1750. Li

Jackson, Thomas. S Jan-Jun T Jul 1747 *Laura*. M.

Jackson, William. T May 1751 *Tryal*. K.

Jackson, William. S Lent LC AA Co., Md., from *Thornton* Jul 1775. E.

Jacob, Thomas. S Summer 1718 LC from *Sophia* QA Co., Md. Mar 1719. Co.

Jacobs, Cornelius. S Jul-Dec 1747 LC Knt Co., Md., from *St. George* Mar 1748. M.

Jacobs, Samuel. S Dec 1782 LC Bal Co., Md., Dec 1783 from *Swift*. L.

Jacomo, James. S Jan-Apr T Jun 1748 *Lichfield*. M.

Jaffray, Lewis. S Dec 1773 T *Justitia* Jan 1774. M.

James, Diana wife of William. S Lent LC AA Co., Md., from *Thornton* Jul 1775. M.

James, James. S Jul T *Saltspring* Jul 1775. M.

James, John. S Summer LC Summer LC from *Reformation* Aug 1722. De.

James, John. S Apr-Jun 1739 T *Sea Nymph* to Md. but died. M.

James, John. SQS Feb T Mar 1750 *Tryal*. M.

James, John. SQS Gloucester May 1756 (GJ). G.

James, Joseph. S Dec 1745 T *Plain Dealer* Jan 1746. L.

James, Mary. S Lent 1749 (GJ). Mo.

James, Mary. S Dec 1750 T *Thames* Feb 1751. L.

James, Robert (1748) - *See* Smith. Be.

James, Thomas, aged 28. S s oxen at Littleton on Severn Lent TB Mar 1735;
    executed for returning Summer 1736 (GJ). G.

James, Thomas. S for life Jan T *Greyhound* Feb 1755; runaway. L.

James, Thomas. S s wheat at Drayton Dec 1766. Be.

James, Thomas. S Lent LC AA Co., Md., from *Thornton* May 1771. M.

James, William. S Sep-Oct 1772 T *Justitia* Jan 1773. M.

James, William. S Sep-Oct 1773 T *Justitia* Jan 1774. M.

James, William. S s at Magor Summer R for life Aug LC Md from *William* Dec 1774
    & sold to Ely Bailey. Mo.

Jameson, John. S Sep T *Barnard* Oct 1756. M.

Jameson, William. T to Va 14 yrs Aug 1719. Nl.

Jarrett, George. SQS Jan 1772 LC Bal Co., Md., Apr 1773. G.

Jarrett, William. T May 1752 *Lichfield*. Sx.

Jarris, Jane. T Jul 1747. Sy.

Jarvis, Benjamin of Stevenage. S Lent T Jul 1745 *Italian Merchant*. Ht.

Jarvis, Jane. SQS Bristol Nov 1759 (BJ). G.

Jervis *als* Griffiths, John. S Montgomery s horse R Jun 1774. Wal.

Jarvis, Michael. S 14 yrs Summer 1743 LC Knt Co., Md., from *Globe* Mar 1744. De.

Jarvis, Richard. S & T Lent 1754. Wa.

Jervis, Samuel. S Summer T from London Sep 1754. Wa.

Jarvis, Simon. S Jun 1718 T Feb 1719 *Worcester* LC Annapolis Jun 1719. L.

Jervis, William. S Jan T *Greyhound* Feb 1755. L.

Jervis, William. S 14 yrs Summer 1770 LC Bal Co., Md., Jul 1771. St.

Jary, William of Taverham. R for Barbados Aug 1671 but LC Md from *Baltimore* of
    London in 1672. Nf.

Jaunsey, John. S Lent 1741 LC QA Co., Md., from *Philleroy* Apr 1742. He.

Javelow, Charles. S & R 14 yrs Lent 1728. Ca.

Jay, Richard. S Jul T Aug 1749 *Thames*. L.

Jeagles, William. S Summer T 14 yrs Oct 1750 *Rachael*. Sy.

Jebb, John. S 14 yrs Oct 1751-Jan 1752 T *Thames* Mar 1752; runaway. M.

Jebens, Moses. S Jul T *Beverly* Aug 1763. M.

Jefferson, John of Mitcham. SQS Oct 1750 T *Thames* Feb 1751. Sy.

Jefferson, Ralph. S Chelmsford Jan 1763 (AHJ). E.

Jeffery, Francis. S 14 yrs Summer 1771 LC Bal Co., Md., Jul 1772. So.

Jeffery, Mary, spinster. SQS Apr 1750 LC QA Co., Md., from *Catherine* Nov 1750. De.

Jeffery, Mary of Horsham. S Summer 1772 T *Justitia* Jan 1773. Sx.

Jeffery, Richard. SQS Jan 1732 LC Knt Co., Md., from *Falcon* Mar 1733. So.

Jeffery, Susanna. S Summer 1742 LC QA Co., Md., from *Kent* Jun 1743. De.

Jefferys, Ann. T May 1746. De.

Jeffreys, Benjamin. S Feb-Apr T May 1752 *Lichfield*. M.

Jefferies, Catherine. S & T Apr 1751. G.

Jefferys, Elizabeth. S Sep T *Barnard* Oct 1756. M.

Jefferis, Hester. S Bristol Jul 1741 LC QA Co., Md., from *Philleroy* Apr 1742. G.

Jefferies, Jane. S Apr T *Dolphin* May 1763. M.
Jefferys, John. S Apr T May 1750 *Lichfield*. M.
Jefferies, John. R 14 yrs Mar T *Randolph* Sep 1768. Wi.
Jefferies, Luke. S Feb T *Thames* Mar 1754. M.
Jefferis, Margaret. S Bristol Jul 1741 LC QA Co., Md., from *Philleroy* Apr 1742. G.
Jefferys, Samuel. S Launceston Apr 1760 (AHJ). Co.
Jeffs, Thomas. SQS s wood Jan 1759 (OJ). O.
Jeggo, John. S Summer T Oct 1750 *Rachael*. E.
Jenkins, Ann. S Bristol Jan 1756 (AHJ). G.
Jenkins, Edward. S Lent T May 1751 *Tryal*. Bu.

Jenkins, John. S s playhouse tickets Dec 1735 T Jan 1736 *Dorsetshire* LC Va Sep 1736. M.
Jenkins, John. S Lent LC AA Co., Md., from *Thornton* Jul 1775. Sy.
Jenkins, John. S Sep-Oct 1775 T *Justitia* Feb 1776. M.
Jenkins, John. Jul 1783 LC Bal Co., Md., Dec 1783 from *Swift*. M.
Jenkins, Margaret of Fryerning. SQS Jan T May 1749 *Lichfield*. E.
Jenkins, Thomas. S s watch Feb T Apr 1735 *Patapsco* LC Annapolis Oct 1735. M.
Jenkins, Thomas. S Apr-May T *Tryal* Jul 1754. M.
Jenkins, Thomas. S s mare & R 14 yrs Jul T *Restoration* LC Bal Co., Md., Oct 1771. He.
Jenkins, William. SQS s sheep Jul 1740 (GJ). G.
Jenkins, William. S Summer 1741 LC QA Co., Md., from *Philleroy* Apr 1742 & to serve Peter Symons. Mo
Jenkins, William. S Lent T *Thornton* May LC AA Co., Md., Jul 1774. L.
Jenkinson, Edward. S Apr-Jun 1739 T *Sea Nymph* to Md. M.
Jenkinson, George. R Lent 1729. No.
Jenkinson, Paul. S Lent LC AA Co., Md., from *Thornton* May 1771. M.
Jenkinson, William. S Lent T May 1771. Wa.
Jenner, Samuel of Chevening. S Lent T May 1750 *Lichfield*. K.
Jennings, Christopher. S Apr T *Dolphin* May 1763. M.
Jennings, George. S May-Jul T *Tayloe* Jul 1773. M.
Jennings, Henry. S s porringer Jan T Apr 1735 *Patapsco* LC Annapolis Oct 1735. L.
Jennings, Henry. S Summer T *Maryland Packet* Oct 1761. K.
Jennings, John. S Apr T May 1752 *Lichfield*. L.
Jennings, John. S Apr-May T *Tryal* Jul 1754. M.
Jennings, Mary. S Feb-Apr T May 1751 *Tryal*. M.
Jennings, Richard. R 14 yrs Aug LC Md *William* Dec 1774 & sold to James & Joshua Howard. Co.
Jennings, Samuel of Egham. S Lent T May 1750 *Lichfield*. Sy.
Jennings, Thomas, cobbler. SQS Jul 1761 but hanged himself before T (OJ). O.
Jennings, William. S May-Jun T Aug 1752 *Tryal*. M.
Jennings, William. S 14 yrs Lent LC AA Co., Md., from *Thornton* Jul 1775. E.
Jenvey, Peter. S Oct-Dec 1754 T *Greyhound* Feb 1755. M.
Jephson, John. S Jul T Sep 1751 *Greyhound*. L.
Jepp, William. S Lent T *Thornton* May LC AA Co., Md., Jul 1774. E.
Jepson, John. S Lent 1737. Li.
Jepson, John. S Summer 1749 R for life Lent T May 1750 *Lichfield*. E.
Jervis - *See* Jarvis.
Jessup, Thomas. S 14 yrs Lent LC AA Co., Md., from *Thornton* May 1771. K.
Jetter, John. S Sep-Dec 1746 T Jan 1747 *George William*. M.

Jevon, Daniel. S s fowls at Sedgley Aug T *Restoration* LC Bal Co., Md., Oct 1771. St.

Jewell, James. S Sep-Oct T Oct 1749 *Mary.* M.

Jewell [Juel], Laurence. R 7 yrs Aug LC Md *William* Dec 1774 & sold to James Hutchings. Co.

Jewell, William. SQS Oct 1742 LC Knt Co., Md., from *Globe* Mar 1744. De.

Jewel, William. S Lent LC Bal Co., Md., Jun 1773. Co.

Jiggle, William. R for buying stolen wheat & appeal rejected Dec 1750 T *Thames* Feb 1751. Sy.

Jilson, Richard. S Sep-Oct T *Justitia* Dec 1774. M.

Jinks, William. S s horse & R 14 yrs Jun 1741. Wa.

Joban, Joseph. S Summer 1734 T Lent 1735. Wa.

Joban, Joseph. S Lent 1737. Wa.

Jockam, John. S s at Rendcombe Jul T *Restoration* LC Bal Co., Md., Oct 1771. G.

John, Christopher. S Glamorgan s horses R 14 yrs Jun 1772. Wal.

John, Henry. S Haverfordwest s sheep R Oct 1769. Wal.

John, Thomas. S Apr LC Md from *Isabella* Jul 1775 & sold to Waters & Gartrall. Co.

John, William. S s heifer at Redwick & R 14 yrs Jul T *Restoration* LC Bal Co., Md., Oct 1771. Mo.

Johns, Ann. S Feb-Apr T May 1751 *Tryal.* M.

Johns, Elias. S Mar 1742 LC PG Co., Md. Co.

Johns, James (1758) - *See* Rice. De.

Johns, John. S Mar 1742 LC PG Co., Md. Co.

Johns, Robert. S Summer 1733 LC Knt Co., Md., from *Falcon* Apr 1734. De.

Johns, Stephen. S Mar 1742 LC PG Co., Md. Co.

Johns, William. S Summer T Sep 1746. Co.

Johnson, Ann. S Sep-Oct 1773 T *Justitia* Jan 1774. M.

Johnson, Ann. S Lent LC AA Co., Md., from *Thornton* Jul 1775. L.

Johnson, Benjamin. R 14 yrs Oct 1772 T *Justitia* Jan 1773. M.

Johnson, Christopher. S Oct 1773 T *Justitia* Jan 1774. L.

Johnson, David. S Lent LC AA Co., Md., from *Thornton* Jul 1773. L.

Johnson, Elizabeth. S Summer T Sep 1738. Mo.

Johnson, Elizabeth *als* Betty. S Lent R 14 yrs Summer T *Ruby* Oct 1754. Sx.

Johnson, George. S Jul T Aug 1749 *Thames.* L.

Johnson, James, son of Margaret (*q.v.*). SQS Monmouth Oct 1738. Mo.

Johnson, James. S York 1755 (AHJ). Y.

Johnson, James. S Apr T *Dolphin* May 1763. L.

Johnson, John. S Summer 1746 T Jul 1747. Wa.

Johnson, John. S Jan T May 1746. Sx.

Johnson, John. T May 1751 *Tryal.* Sx.

Johnson, John. S May-Jul T Sep 1751 *Greyhound.* M.

Johnson, John. S Lent R 14 yrs Summer T *Ruby* Oct 1754. Ht.

Johnson, John. S Bristol Jan 1756 (AHJ). G.

Johnson, John. S Summer LC Bal Co., Md., Dec 1770 from *Trotman* & sold to James Baker. X.

Johnson, John. S Lent LC AA Co., Md., from *Thornton* May 1771. M.

Johnson, Margaret. SQS Monmouth Oct 1738. Mo.

Johnson *als* Rose *als* Brasie, Mary. S s money Apr T Dec 1735 *John* LC Annapolis Sep 1736. M.

Johnson *als* Maritime *als* Smith, Mary. S & T Jan 1736 *Dorsetshire* LC Va Sep 1736. L.

Johnson, Mary of St. Saviour, Southwark. SQS Apr T May 1750 *Lichfield*. Sy.

Johnson, Mary. S Feb T *Thames* Mar 1752. L.

Johnson, Richard. T May 1751 *Tryal*. K.

Johnson, Robert of St. Olave, Southwark. SQS May T *Tryal* Jul 1754. Sy.

Johnson, Robert. S Lent LC AA Co., Md., from *Thornton* Jul 1775. Bu.

Johnson, Thomas. S Lent LC Bal Co., Md., Jul 1772. Sh.

Johnson, Thomas. S Lent LC AA Co., Md., from *Thornton* Jul 1775. K.

Johnson, Timothy. SQS Feb LC AA Co., Md., from *Thornton* Jul 1773. M.

Johnson, William (1729) - *See* Jones. La.

Johnson, William. S Lent T Apr 1734.

Johnson, William. S & T Jan 1736 *Dorsetshire* LC Va Sep 1736. L.

Johnson, William. S Lent T May 1749 *Lichfield*. Bu.

Johnson, William. S Sep-Oct 1772 T *Justitia* Jan 1773. M.

Johnson, William (1773) - *See* Burke. Ha.

Joiner, Thomas. S Lent T May 1750 *Lichfield*. K.

Joiner, William. S Dec 1749-Jan 1750 T Mar 1750 *Tryal*. M.

Jolland, Elizabeth wife of Robert. S 14 yrs Sep-Oct 1772 T *Justitia* Jan 1773. M.

Jolland, John. S Sep-Oct 1772 T *Justitia* Jan 1773. M.

Jolopp, Mary, spinster. R for Barbados Oct 1673 but LC Md from *Charles* May 1674. L.

Jollop, Samuel. S Lent R Jul T Dec 1736 *Dorsetshire* . Sy.

Jolly, Henry. S Lent T May 1749 *Lichfield*. E.

Jolly, John. S Lent R 14 yrs Jun 1734 LC Knt Co., Md, Mar 1735 from *Falcon*. De.

Jolley, Samuel. S Coventry for highway robbery & R 14 yrs Jun 1741. Wa.

Jones, Anne wife of Thomas (qv).S Lent LC Knt Co., Md., from *Unity* Nov 1733. De.

Jones, Anne. S 14 yrs Bristol May 1743 LC Knt Co., Md., from *Raven* Feb 1744. G.

Jones, Ann. S Feb-Apr T *Justitia* May 1745. M.

Jones, Ann. S Jan-Jun T Jul 1747 *Laura*. M.

Jones, Ann. S Dec 1753-Jan 1754 T *Thames* Mar 1754. M.

Jones, Ann. S Lent T *Thornton* May LC AA Co., Md., Jul 1774. M.

Jones, Ann, spinster. SQS Bristol Dec 1774 TB May LC Md from *Isabella* Jul 1775 & sold to Bazil Ridgley. G.

Jones, Catherine. S Sep T *Barnard* Oct 1756. M.

Jones, Charity. LC Md from *Isabella* Jul 1775 & sold to John Welch. X.

Jones, Charles. S Summer 1734 R 14 yrs Feb T Apr 1735 *Patapsco* LC Annapolis Oct 1735. Ht.

Jones, Charles *als* Waterman, Cober. S Shrewsbury Mar T from Bristol May 1754 (AHJ). Sh.

Jones, Cornelius. S Apr T Jun 1748 *Lichfield*. L.

Jones, Daniel. S Jan T *Tryal* Mar 1757. L.

Jones, David. S Oct 1772 T *Justitia* Jan 1773. L.

Jones, Deborah. S Dec 1772 T *Justitia* Jan 1773. M.

Jones, Edward. S s sheep Lent R 14 yrs Summer 1750 (GJ). St.

Jones, Edward. S Ruthin s horse R 14 yrs Jul 1764. Wal.

Jones, Edward. S s at All Saints, Worcester, Jul T *Restoration* LC Bal Co., Md., Oct 1771. Wo.

Jones *als* Ravell, Edward. R 14 yrs Jul T *Saltspring* Jul 1775. M.

Jones, Edward. S Sep-Oct 1775 T *Justitia* Feb 1776. M.

Jones, Elizabeth of Manchester, spinster. SQS Apr T Jul 1734. La.

Jones *als* Walker, Elizabeth. T Apr 1735 *Patapsco* LC Annapolis Oct 1735. K.

Jones, Elizabeth. S Apr T Dec 1735 *John* LC Annapolis Sep 1736. M.

Jones, Elizabeth. S for life Jul-Sep T *Ruby* Oct 1754. M.

Jones, Elizabeth. S Summer 1757 R 14 yrs Summer 1758. Wo.

Jones, Elizabeth. S Lent LC AA Co., Md., from *Thornton* May 1771. M.

Jones, Elizabeth. SWK Jul 1772 T *Justitia* Jan 1773. K.

Jones, Elizabeth. S Oct 1773 T *Justitia* Jan 1774. L.

Jones, Evan. T Sep 1737 *Pretty Patsy*. L.

Jones, George. S Lent LC Bal Co., Md., Jun 1773. He.

Jones, Henry. S Sep T Oct 1750 *Rachael*. L.

Jones, Henry. S for ripping lead from house Sep T *Barnard* Oct 1756. M.

Jones, Henry. S s sheep at Wolves Newton & R 14 yrs Jul T *Restoration* LC Bal Co., Md., Oct 1771. Mo.

Jones *als* Maunder, Henry. S Dec T *Justitia* Dec 1774. M.

Jones, Hugh. S & T Jan 1736 *Dorsetshire* LC Va Sep 1736. L.

Jones, James. SQS Feb T Mar 1750 *Tryal*. M.

Jones, James. S Apr T May 1750 *Lichfield*. M.

Jones, James. S & T Lent 1754. Wa.

Jones, James. SW Jan LC AA Co., Md., from *Thornton* Jul 1775. M.

Jones, Jane. S Lent LC Bal Co., Md., Jul 1772. Sh.

Jones, Jane. S Lent T *Thornton* May LC AA Co., Md., Jul 1774. L.

Jones, Jane. SQS Jan but pardoned in March 1775. Sy.

Jones, John. S s horse Lent R 14 yrs Summer 1733; executed for returning Summer 1737. St.

Jones, John. S Apr-Jun 1739 T *Sea Nymph* to Md. M.

Jones, John. S s horse & R 14 yrs Jun 1741. Le.

Jones, John. T Aug 1746. Ht.

Jones, John. T *St. George* Jan LC Knt Co., Md., Mar 1748. Wa.

Jones, John. T Jun 1748 *Lichfield*. M.

Jones, John. T Jul 1748 *Mary*. L.

Jones, John. S Lent T May 1749 *Lichfield*. Ht.

Jones, John. S s cloth at Urdesland Lent LC Md from LC QA Co., Md., from *Chester* Nov 1749. He.

Jones, John. S May-Jul T Sep 1751 *Greyhound*. M.

Jones, John. S Feb T *Thames* Mar 1752. L.

Jones, John. S Summer T *Barnard* Oct 1756. K.

Jones, John. S Mar 1761 (AHJ). Sh.

Jones *als* Hicks *als* Lister, John. SQS Bristol s from London Wagon in Peter St. May 1761. G.

Jones, John. S Sep-Oct 1772 T *Justitia* Jan 1773. M.

Jones, John. SQS Jan LC AA Co., Md., from *Thornton* Jul 1773. Sy.

Jones, John (2). S Lent LC AA Co., Md., from *Thornton* Jul 1773. M.

Jones, John. T *Tayloe* Jul 1773. Sy.

Jones, John. S s at Cannock Summer LC Md *William* Dec 1774 & sold to Harry Dorsey Gough. St.

Jones, John. S Jul 1783 LC Bal Co., Md., Dec 1783 from *Swift*. M.

Jones, Joseph. S Apr T May 1747. So.

Jones, Joseph. S Lent LC Bal Co., Md., Jul 1771. Ch.

Jones, Joseph. S Sep-Oct 1775 T *Justitia* Feb 1776. M.

Jones, Lamb. S Jan 1751 T *Thames* Feb 1751. L.

Jones, Margaret. S Mar T *Thames* Mar 1754. L.

Jones, Mary. S Summer 1734 LC Knt Co., Md., Mar 1735 from *Falcon*. De.

Jones, Mary. S & T Jan 1736 *Dorsetshire* LC Va Sep 1736. L.

MORE EMIGRANTS IN BONDAGE

Jones, Mary. S Apr T *Justitia* May 1745. L.

Jones, Mary of St. George, Southwark, spinster. SQS Apr T Sep 1751 *Greyhound*. Sy.

Jones, Mary. S Feb T *Thames* Mar 1752. L.

Jones, Mary. S Feb T *Thames* Mar 1754. M.

Jones, Mary. S Bristol Jan 1756 (AHJ). G.

Jones, Mary. S Feb T *Tryal* Mar 1757. M.

Jones, Mary. S Sep T *Phoenix* Oct 1760. L.

Jones, Mary. S May T *Beverly* Aug 1763. M.

Jones, Mary. S s at Raglan LC Bal Co., Md., Jul 1771. Mo.

Jones, Mary. S May-Jul T *Tayloe* Jul 1773. M.

Jones, Mary. SQS & T *Thornton* May LC AA Co., Md., Jul 1774. M.

Jones, Matthias. S Lent LC AA Co., Md., from *Hanover Planter* Jul 1773. M.

Jones, Moses. S Lent T from London Apr 1755. Wa.

Jones, Nehemiah. S Apr T May 1750 *Lichfield*. M.

Jones, Owen *als* Owen, John. T Jul 1747. Sh.

Jones, Owen. S Lent T May 1749 *Lichfield*. Ht.

Jones, Paul. S Lent 1749 (GJ). He.

Jones, Phillip. S Jul T Aug 1749 *Thames*. L.

Jones, Phillis. S Sep-Oct T Oct 1749 *Mary*. M.

Jones, Phillis. S Bristol Jan 1757 (AHJ). G.

Jones, Ralph. S Feb T 14 yrs Apr 1735 *Patapsco* LC Annapolis Oct 1735. L.

Jones, Rebecca of St. Mary le Bow. S s cloth Apr 1718 T May 1719 *Margaret*; sold
    to Edward Mallux Md Sep 1719. L.

Jones, Richard. S Lent T Apr 1739. Bd.

Jones, Richard. S Jan-Apr T *Lichfield* May 1749. M.

Jones, Richard. S Lent T from Bristol May 1754. Sh.

Jones, Richard. S Summer 1772 LC Bal Co., Md., Apr 1773. G.

Jones, Richard. S Oct T *Justitia* Dec 1774. L.

Jones, Robert. S Summer 1738 LC QA Co., Md. Jun 1739. So.

Jones *als* Mortebois, Robert. S Summer 1751 R 14 yrs Lent T May 1752 *Lichfield*. E.

Jones, Robert. S Jul T *Tayloe* Jul 1774. L.

Jones, Roger. S Glamorgan s sheep R Jun 1766. Wal.

Jones, Roger. S for highway robbery Lent R 14 yrs Summer T *Justitia* Sep 1766. Bu.

Jones, Samuel. S Jun-Dec 1745 T *Plain Dealer* Jan 1746; runaway. M.

Jones, Samuel. S Mar T Sep 1747. Ha.

Jones, Samuel. T Jan 1748. Wa.

Jones, Samuel (2). S Jul T Sep 1751 *Greyhound*. L.

Jones, Samuel. SQS Bristol s coins Aug 1755 (BJ). G.

Jones, Sarah *als* Long Peg. S Ruthin Apr 1756 (AHJ). Wal.

Jones, Sarah. S Lent LC AA Co., Md., from *Thornton* Jul 1773. M.

Jones, Sarah. S May-Jul T *Tayloe* Jul 1773. M.

Jones, Silvester. SQS & T Sep 1751 *Greyhound*. M.

Jones, Susanna. S Dec 1746 T Jan 1747 *George William*. L.

Jones, Thomas. S Lent LC Knt Co., Md., from *Unity* Nov 1733. De.

Jones, Thomas. T Sep 1737 *Pretty Patsy*. L.

Jones, Thomas. S Feb T Apr 1746. Le.

Jones, Thomas. S Mar T Sep 1747. Ha.

Jones, Thomas. T Jul 1747. Wa.

Jones, Thomas. SQS Lent LC AA Co., Md., from *Hanover Planter* Jul 1773. M.

Jones, Thomas. S Dec 1773 T *Justitia* Jan 1774. M.

Jones, Thomas. S Lent LC AA Co., Md., from *Thornton* Jul 1775. Sy.

Jones, Timothy. LC Md from *Isabella* Jul 1775 & sold to John Welch. X.

Jones, Welthian, widow. S 14 yrs Bristol Apr 1743 LC Knt Co., Md., from *Raven* Feb 1744. G.

Jones *als* Johnson, William. SQS Jul 1729. La.

Jones, William. S s hams Apr T Dec 1735 *John* LC Annapolis Sep 1736. M.

Jones, William. T Sep 1737 *Pretty Patsy*. L.

Jones, William. S Sep 1747 LC Knt Co., Md., from *St. George* Mar 1748. L.

Jones, William. S for housebreaking Sep 1750 (WJ). Wa.

Jones, William. S for being at large after sentence of transportation & T 14 yrs Sep 1751 *Greyhound* . Ht.

Jones, William. S Jul T *Tayloe* Jul 1773. L.

Jones, William (2). S May-Jul T *Tayloe* Jul 1774. M.

Jones, William. S Oct T *Justitia* Dec 1774. L.

Jones, William. S Dec T *Justitia* Dec 1774. M.

Jordan, Hugh. S Dec 1750 T *Thames* Feb 1751. L.

Jordan, John. S Summer 1765. K.

Jordan, John. S for highway robbery on Durdham Down & R Aug 1764. G.

Jordan, Rachel. S 14 yrs Summer 1749 LC QA Co., Md., from *Catherine* Nov 1750. Mo.

Jordan, Sarah, *als* wife of Samuel Blythe. S Dec 1772 T *Justitia* Jan 1773. M.

Jordan, Thomas. S Lent LC Bal Co., Md., Jun 1773. Wi.

Jordan, William. T *Randolph* Sep 1768. De.

Joseph, Henry. S 14 yrs Lent LC AA Co., Md., from *Thornton* Jul 1775. L.

Joice, Benjamin. S s sheep Lent R 14 yrs Summer T *Justitia* Sep 1767. Bu.

Joyce, James. S Lent T May 1750 *Lichfield*. K.

Joyce, William. S 14 yrs Jan T *Plain Dealer* Jan 1746. L.

Joyner, John. S s logwood & Tar May 1735 T Jan 1736 *Dorsetshire* LC Va Sep 1736. M.

Joyner, John. S 14 yrs Lent T *Tryal* Jul 1754. Sy.

Jubbs, John of Norwich. R for America Jul 1713 after petition from mother Margaret Jubbs. Nf.

Judah, Isaac. S Dec 1749-Jan 1750 T 14 yrs Mar 1750 *Tryal*. M.

Judd, David. S Summer 1718 LC from *Sophia* QA Co., Md. Mar 1719. De.

Judd, Margaret. S Launceston May 1755 (AHJ). Co.

Judge, Jane wife of William. S s linen Summer T *Ruby* Oct 1754. Bu.

Judge, Judith. S Jul-Dec 1747 LC Knt Co., Md., from *St. George* Mar 1748. M.

Jugular *als* Jugal, Peter of St. Benet Fink. S Jan 1722. L.

Jukes, Benjamin. S Dec 1747 LC Knt Co., Md., from *St. George* Mar 1748. L.

Jumar, William. S Aberdeen for robbing Aberdeen mail R for life Jun 1763. Sco.

Jump, Mary. T Apr 1735 *Patapsco* LC Annapolis Oct 1735. E.

Jump, William. S Jan T *Greyhound* Feb 1755. M.

Juncker, John Lewis. S Jul T Aug 1749 *Thames*. L.

Jury, Ralph. S Lent T May 1750 *Lichfield*. E.

Jury, Richard. S Lent LC Bal Co., Md., Jul 1772. De.

Juson, John. S Feb-Apr T *Laura* Apr 1746. M.

Justice, Henry. S & T May 1736 *Patapsco*, committed for returning Apr 1739 (IJ). L.

Justice, William. T Apr 1735 *Patapsco* LC Annapolis Oct 1735. E.

Juts?, Mary of Manchester, spinster. SQS Jan 1730. La.

MORE EMIGRANTS IN BONDAGE

Kane, Jane wife of Edward. S Sep T *Maryland Packet* Oct 1761. M.

Kaine, Robert. S Jan-Apr T *Lichfield* May 1749. M.

Karrell, Joseph. S Feb T *Thames* Mar 1752. L.

Kasey, Thomas. S Sep-Dec 1746 T Jan 1747 *George William*. M.

Katesmark, James, notorious villain. SQS Bristol s Book of Common Prayer from St. Nicholas Church Feb 1753. G.

Kay, Elizabeth of Manchester, singlewoman. SQS Jan T *Tryal* Mar 1757. La.

Kay, Francis. S for life Oct-Dec 1750 T *Thames* Feb 1751. M.

Kay, Oliver of Tottington, husbandman. SQS Apr 1725. La.

Keather, Stephen. S Lent T Apr 1753. Y.

Keating, John. S Lent R Jun T 14 yrs Aug 1752 *Tryal*. K.

Keatly, Thomas. R Dec 1773 T *Justitia* Jan 1774. M.

Keaton, Michael. S for enlisting British subjects for King of France R 14 yrs Feb T May 1751 *Tryal*. K.

Keays, Daniel. SQS Reading for highway robbery Jan 1769 (RG). Be.

Keeling, Charles. S Jul LC Bal Co., Md., Dec 1783 from *Swift*. M.

Keeling, John (1783). *See* Kellam. M.

Keene, John. S Summer T Sep 1751 *Greyhound*. Bu.

Keen, Richard. S Lent LC Bal Co., Md., Jul 1772. G.

Keene, Thomas. T *Lichfield* May 1749. L.

Keen, William. S Lent T Apr 1757. Wa.

Keightley, Christopher, a boy of St. Giles. S s gold necklace from shop Sep 1733 LC from *Caesar* Va Jul 1734. L.

Keiling *als* Sam, James. S May-Jun T Aug 1752 *Tryal*. M.

Keith, Eleanor. S Feb-Apr T *Laura* Apr 1746. M.

Keith, John. T May 1751 *Tryal*. M.

Keith, Joseph. S Oct T *Barnard* Oct 1756. M.

Kellam *als* Keeling, John *als* Herbert, John S Jul LC Bal Co., Md., Dec 1783 from *Swift*. M.

Kellett, Charles. S Lent R Jun T 14 yrs Aug 1752 *Tryal*. Sx.

Kelly, Andrew. S Aug T *Beverly* Aug 1763. L.

Kelley, Ann. S Sep-Dec 1746 T Jan 1747 *George William*. M.

Kelly, Ann. S Feb T *Neptune* Mar 1761. M.

Kelly, Ann. S May-Jul T *Tayloe* Jul 1774. M.

Kelly, Francis. S Lent LC AA Co., Md., from *Thornton* Jul 1775. E.

Kelly, Hugh. T from Dublin by *Hercules*, LC Bal. Co., Md., Aug 1773, sold to James Wilson of Augusta Co., Virginia. Ir.

Kelly, John. S s iron grate Jan T Apr 1735 *Patapsco* LC Annapolis Oct 1735. M.

Kelly, John. S Bristol Jan 1758 (AHJ). G.

Kelly, Mary. S May-Jul T Jul 1748 *Mary*. M.

Kelly, Mary. S Oct T Oct 1749 *Mary*. L.

Kelly, Mary. S Feb T *Thames* Mar 1754. M.

Kelly, Matthew. S Apr-May T *Tryal* Jul 1754. M.

Kelly, Matthew. S Feb T *Neptune* Mar 1761. M.

Kelly, Patrick. SQS Apr T May 1750 *Lichfield*. M.

Kelly, Patrick. S Sep-Oct T *Justitia* Dec 1774. M.

Kelley, Terence. SQS Apr T May 1750 *Lichfield*. M.

Kelsall, Samuel. S for housebreaking Lent R 14 yrs Summer 1750 (GJ). St.

Kelsall, Samuel. T 14 yrs *Chester* Oct LC QA Co., Md.,. Dec 1752. St.

Kelsey, John. S Sep T *Barnard* Oct 1756. M.

Kelsey, John. S for highway robbery Lent R for life Summer T *Justitia* Sep 1766. Bu.

Kem, George. S Jul 1769 for perjury & to be pilloried before T (RG). Be.

Kem *als* Butcher, George. R 14 yrs Oct 1772 T *Justitia* Jan 1773. M.

Kemp, George. S 14 yrs Lent LC AA Co., Md., from *Thornton* Jul 1773. E.

Kemp, Hannah. SQS Apr S Lent T *Thornton* May LC AA Co., Md., Jul 1774. M.

Kempster, Elizabeth. S Dec 1753-Jan 1754 T *Thames* Mar 1754. M.

Kempster, John. S Summer 1750 R 14 yrs Summer T Sep 1751 *Greyhound*. Bu.

Kempster, John. S 14 yrs S Lent T *Thornton* May LC AA Co., Md., Jul 1774. Ht

Kempton, Thomas. S Sep-Oct T Oct 1749 *Mary*. M.

Kempton, Thomas. S Lent LC AA Co., Md., from *Thornton* Jul 1775. Bu.

Kendall, John. S Lent 1769. No.

Kendall, Mary. S Jul-Dec 1747 LC Knt Co., Md., from *St. George* Mar 1748. M.

Kendall, Thomas. S Lent T *Thornton* May LC AA Co., Md., Jul 1774. E.

Kendall, William. S Norwich Sep T Nov 1746. Nf.

Kendrick, Ann. S Feb-Apr T May 1752 *Lichfield*. M.

Kendrick, William. S Apr T *Lichfield* May 1749. L.

Kennaty, William. S Oct T *Justitia* Dec 1774. L.

Kenneday, Bartholomew. S for highway robbery Lent R 14 yrs Summer T Aug 1749 *Thames*. Sy.

Kennedy, James. S Lent LC AA Co., Md., from *Hanover Planter* Jul 1773. M.

Kennedy, John McIan Bain. S Inverness R for life Jul 1763. Sco.

Kennedy, Peter. S Oct T *Justitia* Dec 1774. L.

Kennewall, Charles. S Jan T *Justitia* May 1745. L.

Kenney, Charlotte. LC Md from *Isabella* Jul 1775 & sold to James Young. X.

Kent, Grace. S Lent LC AA Co., Md., from *Thornton* May 1771. M.

Kent, John. S Jul-Dec 1747 LC Knt Co., Md., from *St. George* Mar 1748. M.

Kent, Richard. T May 1752 *Lichfield*. Sx.

Kent, Stephen. S Summer LC Bal Co., Md., Dec 1772. De.

Kenvin, Evan. S Lent LC Bal Co., Md., Jun 1773. Mo.

Kenyon, John. SQS Apr 1729. La.

Kenyon, Mary of Manchester, spinster. SQS Jan 1730. La.

Kenzer, John. S Jul T *Beverly* Aug 1763. M.

Kenzie, Mary. SQS Jan LC AA Co., Md., from Thornton Jul 1775. Sy.

Kerr *als* Hubbard, Elizabeth. S May-Jul T Jul 1748 *Mary*. M.

Kerril late Bennett, Mary. S Lent 1733 LC Knt Co., Md., from *Hawk* Apr 1735. So.

Kerry *als* Mitchell, John. S for house breaking Lent R 14 yrs Summer 1748 (GJ). Be

Kershaw, Edmund. SQS Jan 1726. La.

Kershaw, Joshua. SQS Apr 1729. La.

Kerslake, William. S 14 yrs Lent 1742 LC QA Co., Md., from *Kent* Jun 1743. De.

Kersley, Simon. SQS Apr 1729. La.

Ketherington *als* Carradice, Mary. S Lent 1749 (AHJ). Db.

Kew, John. S Jul T Oct 1761. Li.

Key, Richard. S Summer 1739 R 14 yrs Feb 1740 LC PG Co., Md. Co.

Key, Silvester of Paston. R for Barbados Aug 1671 but LC Md from *Baltimore* of London in 1672. Nf.

Keys *als* Thornton, John. S Apr T Jun 1748 *Lichfield*. L.

Kibble, John. S Sep 1735 T Jan 1736 *Dorsetshire* LC Va Sep 1736. M.

Kidd, John. S Summer LC Bal Co., Md., Dec 1772. Ha.

Kilburn, Jeremiah. S & TB Sep 1764 *Justitia* but respited Nov 1764. L.

Kilby, John. T Aug 1746. Ht.

Kilgore, Francis. S Lent T Apr 1761. De.

Kilke, Esther. S Dec 1772 T *Justitia* Jan 1773. M.

Killigrew, Elizabeth. S Sep-Oct T Oct 1749 *Mary*. M.

Killegrew, Hannah. S Jul-Dec 1747 LC Knt Co., Md., from *St. George* Mar 1748. M.

Killman, Joseph. S Lent LC Bal Co., Md., Jun 1773. St.

Killy, John. SQS Bristol Dec 1758 (BJ). G.

Kilpack, David. S Jul LC Bal Co., Md., Dec 1783 from *Swift*. M.

Kilroy, Bernard. S Lent LC AA Co., Md., from *Thornton* Jul 1773. L.

Kimmins, Catherine wife of Thomas. S City 1752 (AHJ). Nl.

Kimmins, Thomas. S City 1751 (AHJ). Nl.

Kinder, John. S Mar 1774 LC AA Co., Md., from *Thornton* Jul 1775. Bu.

King, Andrew. S Apr T *Dolphin* May 1763. M.

King, Daniel. S Feb T *Neptune* Mar 1761. M.

King, David. S Jan T *Justitia* May 1745. L.

King, Deborah. S Oct 1751-Jan 1752 T *Thames* Mar 1752. M.

King, Edward. R Summer 1773 T *Justitia* Jan 1774. Sy.

King, Eleanor wife of James. S 14 yrs Feb T *Neptune* Mar 1761. M.

King, Elizabeth. S Feb T *Tryal* Mar 1757. M.

King, James. T May 1752 *Lichfield*. E.

King, Jane. S May-Jul T Sep 1746 *Mary*. M.

King, John. S Mar 1742. He.

King, John of Great Warley. S Lent T Jul 1745 *Italian Merchant*. E.

King, John. T 1746. Su.

King, John. T Jun 1747. Ha.

King, John. S Lent T May 1749 *Lichfield*. K.

King, John. S Summer T *Ruby* Oct 1754. K.

King, John. S Oct 1773 T *Justitia* Jan 1774. L.

King, Joseph. S Jan-Apr T *Lichfield* May 1749. M.

King, Margaret. S Apr T *Phoenix* Oct 1760. M.

King, Margaret. S Jul LC Bal Co., Md., Dec 1783 from *Swift*. M.

King, Mary. S Sep-Dec 1746 T Jan 1747 *George William*. M.

King, Mary. S Jan-Apr T Jun 1748 *Lichfield*. M.

King, Richard. S Lent LC AA Co., Md., from *Thornton* Jul 1773. M.

King, Sarah. T from Dublin by *Hercules*, LC Bal. Co., Md., Aug 1773, sold to
    William Walters & Richard Guttrell. Ir.

King *als* Williams, Sarah. S Sep-Oct T *Justitia* Dec 1774. M.

King, Susan. S Sep 1735 T Jan 1736 *Dorsetshire* LC Va Sep 1736. M.

King, Thomas. S Wells Lent 1736. So.

King, William. S Jan T *Tryal* Mar 1757. L.

King, William. S Lent R 14 yrs Summer T *Maryland Packet* Oct 1761. E.

Kingked, Alexander. S Summer 1718 R 14 yrs & T to Va Aug 1719. Nl.

Kingsborow, Henry. S for shopbreaking at Redlingfield Lent 1740 (IJ). Su.

Kingston *als* Brown, John. S Dec 1750 T *Thames* Feb 1751. L.

Kinsett, Roger. T Aug 1752 *Tryal*. Sx.

Kinsey, John (1751) - *See* Russell. M.

Kipling, Robert. S Lent but pardoned May 1773. L.

Kirby, John. S s sheep Lent R 14 yrs Summer T Sep 1751 *Greyhound*. Bu.

Kirby, Richard. S Lent 1750 LC QA Co., Md., from *Catherine* Nov 1750. G.

Kirby, Thomas. S Dec 1773 T *Justitia* Jan 1774. M.

Kirk, John. S Summer 1762 TB to Va. No.

Kirk, John. S Sep-Oct 1773 T *Justitia* Jan 1774. M.

Kirk, Thomas. S Feb-Apr T *Justitia* May 1745. M.

Kirkman, Elizabeth (1775). *See* Hoare. M.

Kirkman, Sarah. S Sep-Oct 1772 T *Justitia* Jan 1773. M.

Kitchen, George. S Sep-Dec 1746 T Jan 1747 *George William*. M.

Kitchen, Samuel. S 14 yrs Lent LC Bal Co., Md., Jul 1772. Sh.

Kitchenside, Abraham. S Lent LC AA Co., Md., from *Thornton* Jul 1773. M.

Kitchin, John. S Lent T Apr 1739. Le.

Kiteley, Benjamin. S Summer T Sep 1751 *Greyhound*. Sy.

Kitto, William. R 14 yrs Sep T *Randolph* Sep 1768. Ha.

Knafton, Francis. S Apr-Jun 1739 T *Sea Nymph* to Md. M.

Knapp, Edmund. S 14 yrs for receiving Lent 1742 (IJ). Su.

Knapp, James. S Jul-Sep T *Ruby* Oct 1754. M.

Knapton, Robert. S Sep T *Ruby* Oct 1754. L.

Knight, Benjamin. S s horse Lent 1724 R 14 yrs Jul 1726. Do.

Knight, George. S Apr T Jun 1748 *Lichfield*. L.

Knight, Isaac. S 14 yrs Lent LC Knt Co., Md., from *Bideford* Nov 1737. So.

Knight, James. T Apr 1735 *Patapsco* LC Annapolis Oct 1735. K.

Knight, John. S & T Jan 1736 *Dorsetshire* LC Va Sep 1736. L.

Knight, John. S & T for life Aug 1752 *Tryal*. L.

Knight, John. S Bristol Jan 1756 (AHJ). G.

Knight, John. S for life Lent LC Bal Co., Md., Jul 1771. De.

Knight, John. S Lent LC Bal Co., Md., Jul 1772. G.

Knight, John. SQS Lent LC AA Co., Md., from *Hanover Planter* Jul 1773. M.

Knight, Jonathan. S Lent 1733 LC Knt Co., Md., from *Hawk* Apr 1735. So.

Knight, Peter. S Launceston Jan 1757 (AHJ). Co.

Knight, Thomas of St. George, Southwark. SQS Apr T May 1752 *Lichfield*. Sy.

Knight, Thomas. S Lent LC AA Co., Md., from *Thornton* Jul 1775. L.

Knight, Walter. S Apr-May T *Tryal* Jul 1754. M.

Knight, William. S Launceston May 1755 (AHJ). Co.

Knight, William. S Lent T *Dolphin* May 1763. E.

Knightley *als* Humphreys, Thomas. S s sheets at Lower Mitton Summer 1759. Wo.

Knights, Sarah. S Lent T *Dolphin* Apr 1761. E.

Knipe, Robert Sr. of Broughton. SQS Apr 1734. La.

Knock, Thomas. S Jun-Dec 1745 T *Plain Dealer* Jan 1746. M.

Knotsmell *als* Shelton, Elizabeth. S Jan T *Tryal* Mar 1757. L.

Knott, Mary. S Sep T *Barnard* Oct 1756. M.

Knowland, Eleanor. S Jan-Feb T *Tayloe* Jul 1774. M.

Knowles, Clement. S Summer LC Bal Co., Md., Dec 1772; runaway. St.

Knowles, James. R 14 yrs Bristol May 1743 LC Knt Co., Md., from *Raven* Feb 1744. G.

Knowles, John. SQS Wells Jan 1733 LC Knt Co., Md., from *Falcon* Apr 1734. So.

Knox, John. T from Dublin by *Hercules*, LC Bal. Co., Md., Aug 1773, sold to William Walters & Richard Guttrell. Ir.

Laceby, Oliver. S s sheep Summer 1753 R 14 yrs Lent 1754 (WJ). St.

Lacey, John. S Apr T *Phoenix* Oct 1760. M.

Lacey, Martin. S May-Jul T Aug 1749 *Thames*; runaway. M.

Lacey, Michael. S Lent T *Thornton* May LC AA Co., Md., Jul 1774. L.

Lacey, William. S 14 yrs Lent LC Bal Co., Md., Jul 1771. Wi.

Lacey, William. S Jul LC Bal Co., Md., Dec 1783 from *Swift*. M.
Lack, John. S for killing sheep & R 14 yrs Lent T Apr 1774 TB to Md. No.
Lackay, James. S Lent T Apr 1758. Wa.
Lackey, John. T Apr 1735 *Patapsco* LC Annapolis Oct 1735. Sy.
Lackington, James (1737). See Lashington. So.
Ladd, John. S Apr 1766. Li.
Ladd, John. S 14 yrs Lent LC AA Co., Md., from *Thornton* Jul 1773. E.
Lade, Edward. R Jul T *Tayloe* Jul 1773. M.
Ladir, Elizabeth. S Lent 1738. Li.
Ladle, Michael. S Sep-Oct 1772 T *Justitia* Jan 1773. M.
Laidler, Thomas. S Summer 1739 but R to enlist as marine. Nl.
Laidley, Thomas. T from Glasgow but shipwrecked, to be held in Newgate from Dec 1770 for another ship. Sco.
Lake, Lucy. S Sep-Oct T Oct 1749 *Mary*. M.
Lakeland, John. SQS May T Jul 1773 *Tayloe* to Va. M.
Lakey, Hannah. S 14 yrs Lent LC AA Co., Md., from *Thornton* Jul 1775. K.
Lakey, Robert of Bexwell. R for Barbados Aug 1671 but LC Md from *Charles* May 1674. Nf.
Lakin, Francis. S Summer LC Md *William* Dec 1774 & sold to Johr. Christopher. St.
Lakin, Isabella. S Lent LC AA Co., Md., from *Thornton* May 1771. M.
Lakin, Robert. S Summer LC Md *William* Dec 1774 & sold to Thomas Dorsey. St.
Lamb, John. S Oct 1747 LC Knt Co., Md., from *St. George* Mar 1748. L.
Lamb, John. S Sep-Oct 1772 T *Justitia* Jan 1773. M.
Lamberly, John. T Jun 1747. E.
Lambert, Jeremiah *als* Jemiah of Laindon Hills. SQS Jul T *Ruby* Oct 1754. E.
Lambert, Philip of Laindon Hills. SQS Jul T *Ruby* Oct 1754. E.
Lambert, Samuel. S Summer LC Bal Co., Md., Dec 1770 from *Trotman* & sold to Larkin Randall. Y.
Lambert, Thomas. S Lent LC AA Co., Md., from *Thornton* Jul 1775. M.
Lambert, William of Laindon Hills. SQS Jul T *Ruby* Oct 1754. E.
Lambeth, Ann. S Sep T Oct 1750 *Rachael*. M.
Lambath, Ephraim. S Lent LC Bal Co., Md., Jul 1772. Sh.
Lambeth, Thomas. SQS Jul T *Justitia* Dec 1774. M.
Lamsdall, Adam. T Sep 1751 *Greyhound*. K.
Lancher, Joseph. S Dec 1782 LC Bal Co., Md., Dec 1783 from *Swift*.
Landsdown, Sarah. SQS Dec 1754 (BJ). G.
Landwick *als* Lodowick, William. S May-Jun T Aug 1752 *Tryal*. M.
Lane, Edward. S 14 yrs Summer 1731 LC Knt Co., Md., from *Falcon* Apr 1732. De.
Lane, Edward. S Mar T from Liverpool Dec 1746. St.
Lane, Humphrey. S Summer 1732 LC Knt Co., Md., from *Falcon* Mar 1733. De.
Lane, James. S Dec 1749-Jan 1750 T Mar 1750 *Tryal*. M.
Lane, John. R 14 yrs Mar 1742 LC PG Co., Md. Co.
Lane, John. S 14 yrs Lent 1744 LC Knt Co., Md., from *Susannah* Aug 1744. De.
Lane, Robert. S Lent R 14 yrs Jul T Nov 1734 LC Knt Co., Md, Mar 1735 from *Falcon*. Do.
Lane, Sarah wife of Benjamin. S Feb T *Neptune* Mar 1761. M.
Lane, Thomas. S Bristol Aug 1743 LC Knt Co., Md., from *Raven* Feb 1744. G.
Lane, Thomas. S Sep T *Ruby* Oct 1754. L.
Lane, Thomas. S 14 yrs Jul T Aug 1749 *Thames*. L.
Lane, William. S Lent T Jun 1746. Nt.

Lane, William. S s horse brasses at Alfrick Lent 1759. Wo.

Lane, William. S Lent T *Thornton* May LC AA Co., Md., Jul 1774. M.

Lanes, Elizabeth. S Feb-Apr T *Laura* Apr 1746. M.

Lang, James. S Aug 1733 R 14 yrs Jun 1734 LC Knt Co., Md, Mar 1735 from *Falcon*. De.

Langdale, Elizabeth. S & T Summer 1754. Nt.

Langdon, Ann. SQS Apr LC Bal Co., Md., Dec 1772. De.

Langley, Elizabeth. S Lent T May 1749 *Lichfield*. K.

Langley *als* Plaister, George. R for life Jan T *Tryal* Mar 1757. M.

Langley, John. S 14 yrs Lent LC AA Co., Md., from *Thornton* Jul 1775. K.

Langley, Nathaniel. S for murder at Wooburn R 14 yrs Lant 1728. Bu.

Langley, Titus. S s horse at Tamworth Lent R 14 yrs Summer 1762. St.

Langley, William of St. George, Southwark. S Lent R 14 yrs Summer T Oct 1750 *Rachael*. Sy.

Langsden, Mary. S Lent R 14 yrs Summer T Aug 1752 *Tryal*. Sy.

Lanham, John *als* Gladmore, Thomas. S Dec 1730 LC from *Patapsco* Annapolis Jun 1731. M.

Lanman, Philippa. SQS Jul 1738 LC QA Co., Md. Jun 1739. De.

Lanson, Catherine. S Sep T *Barnard* Oct 1756. M.

Laphan, James. S Jun T *Tryal* Jul 1754. L.

Larcy, James. SQS Ipswich 1758. Su.

Lardner, John. S s at Churchill Summer LC Md from *William* Dec 1774 & sold to John Elder. O.

Laremore, Daniel. S Lent but taken from transport ship & pardoned in April 1774. M.

Large, George. S Lent 1732. Wa.

Large, James. S Norwich Jul T Sep 1751. Nf.

Large, Joseph. S Lent T May 1754. St.

Large, Thomas. S Summer T *Barnard* Oct 1756. K.

Largent, Frances S Lent LC AA Co., Md., from *Thornton* May 1771. M.

Larmer, George. S Feb T *Thames* Mar 1754. M.

Larner, Ann. S Lent but pardoned in June 1774. L.

Larose (La Ross), John. S Feb 1772 TB *Thornton* but taken from ship & pardoned on appeal of Hyme Larose. L.

Lasby, James. S Summer 1769 but died in prison. Li.

Lasgent, John. S Jul LC Bal Co., Md., Dec 1783 from *Swift*. M.

Lashington (Lackington), James. S 14 yrs Lent LC Knt Co., Md., from *Bideford* Nov 1737. So.

Lashley, Joseph. S Lent LC AA Co., Md., from *Thornton* May 1771. M.

Lasoach, Baptist. S Jul LC Bal Co., Md., Dec 1783 from *Swift*. M.

Last, Ambrose. SQS Bury St. Edmunds 1760. Su.

Last, Christopher. S Summer 1739 (IJ). Su.

Latham, Thomas. S s at Walsall Summer 1750 LC QA Co., Md., from *Chester* Dec 1752. St.

Latimore, Andrew. SQS Apr T *Thornton* May LC AA Co., Md., Jul 1774. M.

Launder, Philip. S Feb-Apr T *Justitia* May 1745. M.

Laurence, George. S Feb T Apr 1746. Sh.

Laver, James. S 1759 (AHJ). La.

Laver, Richard. S Lent T *Tryal* Jul 1754. E.

Lawin *als* Lawlin, John. S Jan-Jun T Jul 1747 *Laura*. M.

Lawless, Mary Ann. S May-Jul T Jul 1748 *Mary*. M.

Lawrence, John. S Lent 1738. Li.

Lawrence, John. S Apr T Jun 1748 *Lichfield*. L.

Lawrence, John of Bermondsey. SQS Apr T May 1750 *Lichfield*. Sy.

Lawrence, John. SQS Lent LC AA Co., Md., from *Hanover Planter* Jul 1773. M.

Lawrence, John. SL Jul T *Tayloe* Jul 1773. Sy.

Lawrence, John. SL Jul 1773 T *Justitia* Jan 1774. Sy.

Lawrence, Joseph. S Apr 1742. Wo.

Lawrence, Martha. S Lent R 14 yrs Summer T Sep 1751 *Greyhound*. Ht..

Lawrence, Nathaniel. S Sep 1747 LC Knt Co., Md., from *St. George* Mar 1748. L.

Lawrence, Richard. S Mar T Sep 1747. Ha.

Lawrence, William. S Dec 1749-Jan 1750 T Mar 1750 *Tryal*. M.

Lawrence, William. S Lent LC Bal Co., Md., Jul 1771. Wi.

Lawrence, William. S s sheep R 14 yrs Summer LC Md from *William* Dec 1774 &
sold to Arthur Bryan. Sh.

Lawrett, Mary. S Jun-Dec 1745 T *Plain Dealer* Jan 1746. M.

Laws, George. S Lent LC Bal Co., Md., Jun 1773. Ha.

Laws, John. S Apr T *Justitia* May 1745. L.

Laws, John. T May 1752 *Lichfield*. K.

Lawson, Elizabeth. T May 1751 *Tryal*. Sy.

Lawson, Isabella. S Lent LC AA Co., Md., from *Thornton* Jul 1773. M.

Lawson, John. S Oct-Dec 1750 T *Thames* Feb 1751. M.

Lawson, John. SQS Jul 1772 Bal, Md., from *Adventure* Mar 1773. Nl.

Lawson, Ralph. SQS Dec 1773; born London, runaway from *Justitia*, Leeds Town,
Va., Apr 1774. M.

Lawson, Richard. R 14 yrs for s horse at Aylesbury Mar 1716. Bu.

Laycock, Martha wife of Richard. S Apr-Jun 1739 T *Sea Nymph* to Md. M.

Layers, Mary. S Bristol Jan 1757 (AHJ). G.

Lazarus, Isaac. S Lent LC AA Co., Md., from *Thornton* Jul 1773. L.

Le Valley, John. S Jul T Jul 1748 *Mary*. L.

Lea, Edward. T Jul 1747. Sh.

Leach, John. SQS Jul 1732 LC Knt Co., Md., from *Falcon* Mar 1733. So.

Leach, Solomon. S Lent LC Bal Co., Md., Jul 1771. Wa.

Leacock, David (1770) - *See* Allanson. Y.

Leadbeater, Edward. S s gelding Summer 1739 R 14 yrs Lent T *York* Jun 1740. Bu.

Leadley, Robert. T Jun 1748 *Lichfield*. M.

Lean, Richard. S 14 yrs s horse Summer 1730 LC Knt Co., Md., from *Falcon* Apr
1734. De.

Leane, Robert. S Summer 1718 LC from *Sophia* QA Co., Md. Mar 1719. Co.

Leary, John. S May 1770. Li.

Leary, John. S 14 yrs Oct 1772 T *Justitia* Jan 1773. L.

Leathern, James. S Lent LC Knt Co., Md., from *Unity* Nov 1733. De.

Leatherstone, Hannah. S Oct T *Barnard* Oct 1756. L.

Leavers, Patience. S Sep T Oct 1750 *Rachael*. M.

Ledger, Thomas. S Lent T Jul 1745 *Italian Merchant*. Sy.

Lediard, Ann. S Jul-Sep T *Ruby* Oct 1754. M.

Lediard, Sarah wife of John. SQS Bristol Dec 1774 TB LC Md from *Isabella* Jul May
1775 & bought her freedom. G.

Lee *als* Levy, Ann. S Apr-May T *Saltspring* Jul 1775. M.

Lee, Charles. S Launceston May 1755 (AHJ). Co.

Lee, James. S Jun T *Tryal* Jul 1754. L.

Lee, John. S Apr T Jun 1746. Mo.

Lee, John. S Jul T Aug 1749 *Thames*. L.

Lee, John. S Jul T Sep 1751 *Greyhound*. L.

Lee, John. S Lent T *Thornton* May LC AA Co., Md., Jul 1774. M.

Lee, Mary. SQS & TB Jul 1735 T *Amity* LC QA Co., Md., Mar 1736. So.

Lee *als* Branch, Mary. S Summer 1746 T Jan 1747. De.

Lee, Paul. T Jan 1736 *Dorsetshire* LC Va Sep 1736. Ht.

Lee, Richard. S Shrewsbury Aug 1753 (AHJ). Sh.

Lee, Thomas. S Summer LC Bal Co., Md., Dec 1770. Wa.

Lee, William. S Apr T May 1751 *Tryal*. L.

Lee *als* Leeworthy, William. S May T Jul 1753 *Tryal* ; committed Jun 1758 for
   returning before expiry of term but acquitted because brought to England for court
   martial after loss of HMS *Mars*; pardoned Jan 1759. M.

Lee, William. S Oct T *Justitia* Dec 1774. L.

Leech, John. S Mar 1742. He.

Leeder, Nathaniel. SQS Bury St. Edmunds 1766. Su.

Leeman *als* Smith, John. S Dec 1750 T *Thames* Feb 1751. L.

Leer, Abraham. S May-Jul T *Tayloe* Jul 1774. M.

Lees, Jane wife of William. R & T Jan 1748. G.*

Lees, John. S for housebreaking & R 14 yrs Jun 1741. Wa.

Lees, Richard. S Apr 1742. Wo.

Lees, William. S for burglary & R 14 yrs Lent 1725. Nt.

Leeson, Elizabeth. S Apr T *Lichfield* May 1749. L.

Leeson, Esther. S Oct 1773 T *Justitia* Jan 1774. L.

Leeson, Judith. T from Dublin by *Hercules*, LC Bal. Co., Md., Aug 1773, sold to
   John Price Jr. Ir.

Leeward, Joseph. S Summer 1718 LC from *Sophia* QA Co., Md. Mar 1719. Do.

Leeworthy, William (1753) - *See* Lee. M.

Legay, Louis. S Dec T *Justitia* Dec 1774. M.

Legg, Catharine. SQS Jul LC Bal Co., Md., Dec 1772. So.

Legg, Grace. S 14 yrs Summer 1732 LC Knt Co., Md., from *Falcon* Mar 1733. De.

Legg, Henry. SQS Bristol Jun AT Sep 1743 LC Knt Co., Md., from *Raven* Feb 1744. G.

Legg, Jane. S Sep 1735 T Jan 1736 *Dorsetshire* LC Va Sep 1736. M.

Legg, Solomon. S Jul LC Bal Co., Md., Dec 1783 from *Swift*. M.

Legg, William. S Summer 1718 LC from *Sophia* QA Co., Md. Mar 1719. Do.

Leggatt, Thomas. S Lent T Jul 1745 *Italian Merchant*. Sx.

Lego, Charles. S Apr T May 1752 *Lichfield*. L.

Leigh, Edward. S s brass pot Mar 1771 (HJ). Wo.

Leigh, George of Spotland. SQS Oct 1721. La.

Leigh, Richard of Black Notley. R for Barbados or Jamaica Jul 1712 after petition of
   wife Elizabeth. E.

Leighton, James. S s iron at Houghton cum Wyton Lent 1775; runaway aged 20 from
   Marlborough Iron Works, Va., Nov 1775. Hu.

Lelleongreen, Frederick. S Lent T *Thornton* May LC AA Co., Md., Jul 1774. M.

Leman, Henry. S Jul 1735 T Jan 1736 *Dorsetshire* LC Va Sep 1736. M.

Lemon, Robert. T Apr 1761. De.

Lemon *als* Fyson, Thomas. R & T Jan 1748. E.

Lenard, John. SQS Jan LC AA Co., Md., from *Thornton* Jul 1773. Sy.

Lennard, Margaret. R Lent T 14 yrs May 1752 *Lichfield*. Sy.

MORE EMIGRANTS IN BONDAGE

Lennon *als* Fyson, Thomas. S Lent R 14 yrs Summer 1747 LC Knt Co., Md., from *St. George* Mar 1748. E.

Lenthal, Samuel. S Apr T *Lichfield* May 1749. L.

Lenton, John. S 14 yrs for buying stolen silk from William Clayton (*qv*) Lent 1768. Wa.

Lenton, Martha. S Lent 1763 TB to Va. No.

Leo, John William. S Sep-Oct 1772 T *Justitia* Jan 1773. M.

Leonard, Elizabeth. S May-Jul T Aug 1749 *Thames*. M.

Leonard, William. S s brass boiler from workhouse at Wotton Underedge Summer TB Sep 1753. G.

Leonard, William. S Lent but taken from transport ship & pardoned in April 1774. M.

Leppard, James. S Dec 1745 T *Plain Dealer* Jan 1746. L.

Lequint, Lewis. R for life Dec T *Justitia* Dec 1774. M.

Lescallie, William. SQS Jan LC AA Co., Md., from *Thornton* Jul 1775. M.

Lester, Elizabeth of St. Saviour, Southwark. S Summer T Oct 1750 *Rachael*. Sy.

Lett, Thomas. S Lent 1731. Bd.

Letty, James. SQS Monmouth Oct 1738. Mo.

Lever, James. S Lent LC AA Co., Md., from *Thornton* Jul 1773. M.

Levingston, Anna Maria. S Dec 1746 T Jan 1747 *George William*. L.

Levy, Hart. S Jul LC Bal Co., Md., Dec 1783 from *Swift*. M.

Levi, Israel. S Oct T *Barnard* Oct 1756. L.

Levy, Jacob. S May-Jul T *Tayloe* Jul 1773. M.

Levi, Jeremiah. S Apr T Jun 1748 *Lichfield*. L.

Levy, Mordecai. SQS Sep T *Justitia* Dec 1774. M.

Levy, Solomon. S 14 yrs Sep-Oct 1772 T *Justitia* Jan 1773. M.

Lewen, William. S Dec 1746 T Jan 1747 *George William*. L.

Lewes, Abraham. S Jul T *Tayloe* Jul 1773. L.

Lewis, Ann. T for life *Ruby* Oct 1754. L.

Lewis, Ann. S May T *Maryland Packet* Oct 1761. M.

Lewis, Bartholomew. S Aug T *Beverly* Aug 1763. L.

Lewis, Betty of St. Peter's, spinster. SQS Bristol s sheep skins Dec 1752. G.

Lewis, Catherine. S Lent 1750 LC QA Co., Md., from *Catherine* Nov 1750. G.

Lewis, Daniel. S & T Sep 1751 *Greyhound*. L.

Lewis, David. S Aug T Sep 1746. Mo.

Lewis, David. S Montgomery s horse R Mar 1773. Wal.

Lewis, Elizabeth of Lambeth, spinster. SQS Apr T Sep 1751 *Greyhound*. Sy.

Lewis, Elizabeth. SL Jul T *Tayloe* Jul 1773. Sy.

Lewis, Elizabeth. SL Jul 1773 T *Justitia* Jan 1774. Sy.

Lewis, Elizabeth. S Lent T *Thornton* May LC AA Co., Md., Jul 1774. M.

Lewis, Fabius. R for life Dec T *Justitia* Dec 1774. M.

Lewis, Francis. S Dec 1772 T *Justitia* Jan 1773. M.

Lewis, Frank *als* Francis. S Sep-Oct 1773 T *Justitia* Jan 1774. M.

Lewis, Henry. S Summer 1739. Mo.

Lewis, Henry. SW Apr T *Thornton* May LC AA Co., Md., Jul 1774. M.

Lewis, Isaac. S for street robbery in Stafford Lent R 14 yrs Summer 1748. St.

Lewis, Jane. S Sep-Dec 1746 T Jan 1747 *George William*. M.

Lewis, John. S Feb-Apr T May 1752 *Lichfield*. M.

Lewis, John. S Aug T *Beverly* Aug 1763. L.

Lewis, John. SQS Lent LC AA Co., Md., from *Hanover Planter* Jul 1773. M.

Lewis, Joseph. S Coventry for highway robbery & R 14 yrs Jun 1741. Wa.

Lewis, Mary. S Bristol Jul 1741 LC QA Co., Md., from *Philleroy* Apr 1742. G.

Lewis, Mary. S Lent T *Thornton* May LC AA Co., Md., Jul 1774. M.

Lewis, Nathaniel of Newington. SQS Apr T Sep 1751 *Greyhound.* Sy.

Lewis, Phebe. S Lent T Apr 1769. Mo.

Lewis, Robert. S Jan T May 1746. Sx.

Lewis, Robert. S Lent LC AA Co., Md., from *Thornton* Jul 1775. M.

Lewis, William. S Glamorgan s horse R Jan 1765. Wal.

Lewis, William. S May 1765 TB *Justitia* but pardoned same month. M.

Lewis, William. S 14 yrs Lent LC AA Co., Md., from *Thornton* Jul 1773. K.

Ley, Robert. SQS Jul LC Bal Co., Md., Dec 1772. So.

Liddle, Isabella. S Sep-Oct 1773 T *Justitia* Jan 1774. M.

Lidstone, Thomas. S Lent R 14 yrs & T Sep 1761. De.

Light, William. S Lent 1737 LC Knt Co., Md., from *Hawk* Nov 1737. Ha.

Lightbourne, Richard. S for robbery at Ombersley Summer 1750 R 14 yrs Lent 1751 LC QA Co., Md., from *Bideford* Sep 1752. Wo.

Lightfoot, Arthur. S Bristol Mar 1750 LC QA Co., Md., from *Catherine* Nov 1750. G.

Lightwood, John. S for highway robbery Aug 1758 (WJ). Wo.

Lilly, John Patterson. S Oct 1751-Jan 1752 T *Thames* Mar 1752. M.

Lilly, Margaret wife of William of Chelmsford, cordwainer. SQS Jul T *Ruby* Oct 1754. E.

Lilly, Samuel. S Lent 1724 but escaped & no further record found. Li.

Lilley, Samuel. S Summer 1733. No.

Lilly, Timothy. S s iron Lent R 14 yrs Summer 1750 LC QA Co., Md., from *Chester* Dec 1752. St.

Linch - *See* Lynch.

Lincoln, Rose. S Jun-Dec 1745 T *Plain Dealer* Jan 1746. M.

Lindsey, Anthony. R & T Apr 1735 *Patapsco* LC Annapolis Oct 1735. M.

Lindsey, Catherine. S Jul T *Phoenix* Oct 1760. M.

Linsey, Jane. S Feb-Apr T *Justitia* May 1745. M.

Lindsay, John. S Appleby Aug 1757 (AHJ). We.

Linsey, William. S & R Summer T Sep 1773 TB to Md. No.

Lines, Margaret wife of Andrew. T Jun 1748 *Lichfield.* M.

Linford, Samuel. S Dec T *Justitia* Dec 1774. L.

Lingham, John. S Lent T *Lichfield* May 1749. Sy.

Linley, John. S York 1753 (AHJ). Y.

Linnagar, -----. R 14 yrs Sep 1728. Nf.

Linnerton, George. S Summer LC Bal Co., Md., Dec 1772. Ha.

Linnett, Benjamin. S Summer 1729 TB Sep 1730. Db.

Linsley, Robert. S & R 14 yrs Summer 1728. Li.

Linsted, Thomas. S Lent T Jun 1748 *Lichfield.* E.

Linton, Henry. SQS Jan LC AA Co., Md., from *Thornton* Jul 1775. M.

Lipscombe, William. T Jun 1747. Ha.

Lishman, Jane. S Sep-Oct T *Justitia* Dec 1774. M.

Lisle, William SQS Summer LC Md *William* Dec 1774 & sold to James Hutchings. G.

Lister, John (1728) - *See* Eddison. Y.

Lister, John (1761) - *See* Jones. G.

Litchfield, John. S Lent T *Thornton* May LC AA Co., Md., Jul 1774. E.

Litners, Thomas. S Oct 1772 T *Justitia* Jan 1773. L.

Little, Daniel. R for life Sep T *Barnard* Oct 1756. M.

Little, Thomas. S Dec 1750 T *Thames* Feb 1751. L.

Little, William. SQS Apr LC Bal Co., Md., Jul 1774. Wi.

MORE EMIGRANTS IN BONDAGE

Littleboy, John. S Jul T *Tayloe* Jul 1774. L.

Littlebury, Charles. S Lent 1734. Li.

Littlepage, Thomas. S Jul LC Bal Co., Md., Dec 1783 from *Swift*. M.

Littler, Abigail. S Apr T *Phoenix* Oct 1760. M.

Litton, Thomas. S Lent 1731 LC Knt Co., Md., from *Falcon* Apr 1732. De.

Livermore, Mary. S Lent T May 1750 *Lichfield*. E.

Livesson, John. S Lent LC AA Co., Md., from *Thornton* May 1771. M.

Llandovery, a negro man. S Bristol Sep 1759 (BJ). G.

Llewellin, Elizabeth. S May-Jul T *Tayloe* Jul 1773. M.

Lloyd, Deborah. S for life Feb-Apr T *Laura* Apr 1746. M.

Lloyd, Eleanor. S Jul T *Maryland Packet* Oct 1761. L.

Lloyd, Hester. S Summer T Sep 1738. Mo.

Lloyd, John. S May-Jul T Jul 1748 *Mary*. M.

Lloyd, John of St. John's. SQS Oct 1750 T *Thames* Feb 1751. Sy.

Lloyd, Joseph. R 14 yrs Jul T *Saltspring* Jul 1775. M.

Lloyd, Mary. S Oct 1735 T Jan 1736 *Dorsetshire* LC Va Sep 1736. M.

Lloyd, Matthew. S 14 yrs Summer 1772 LC Bal Co., Md., Jun 1773. Sh.

Lloyd, Sarah. S Lent LC AA Co., Md., from *Hanover Planter* Jul 1773. M.

Lloyd, Thomas. SQS Apr LC Bal Co., Md., Dec 1772. St.

Lobly, Joshua of Purleigh. SQS Jan T *Dolphin* May 1763. E.

Lock, John. S May-Jul T *Tayloe* Jul 1773. M.

Lock, William. S & R s horses Jul 1757 (RG). Be.

Lockett *als* Lockington *als* Wilson, Charles. R for life Dec T *Justitia* Dec 1774. M.

Lockier, Elizabeth. S Lent T from London Apr 1754. Be.

Lockwood, John. T 1746. Su.

Lockwood, Martha. T Feb 1748. Le.

Lockwood, Mary. S Lent LC AA Co., Md., from *Thornton* May 1771. M.

Locup, Mary. SQS Dec 1772 LC AA Co., Md., from *Thornton* Jul 1773. M.

Lodowick, Lewis. S Bristol Dec 1749 LC QA Co., Md., from *Catherine* Nov 1750. G.

Loggs, Henry. S Lent R 14 yrs Summer T Oct 1750 *Rachael*. Ht.

Lollard, Barnard. SQS Apr 1738 LC QA Co., Md. Jun 1739. So.

London, John. S Sep-Oct 1775 T *Justitia* Feb 1776. M.

London, Martha. S 14 yrs Jun 1739 T *Sea Nymph* to Md. L.

Lone, Elizabeth. S Dec 1745 T *Plain Dealer* Jan 1746. L.

Lone, John. S May-Jul T *Tayloe* Jul 1773. M.

Long, Ann. S Jan-Apr T Jun 1748 *Lichfield*. M.

Long, Elizabeth. S Summer 1741 LC QA Co., Md., from *Philleroy* Apr 1742. Co.

Long, John. SQS Apr T May 1751 *Tryal*. M.

Long, John. S s mare at Barton Lent R 14 yrs Summer 1761. Nf.

Long, Joseph. S Mar 1735 T *Amity* LC QA Co., Md., Mar 1736. So.

Long, Mary. S Feb T *Neptune* Mar 1761. M.

Long, Moses. T 1745. Y.

Long Peg (1756) - *See* Jones, Sarah. Wal.

Long *als* Bartelott, Robert. S for life Lent LC Bal Co., Md., Jun 1773. Wi.

Long, Sarah. S Sep T *Phoenix* Oct 1760. M.

Long, William. T Jan 1736 *Dorsetshire* LC Va Sep 1736. Ht.

Long, William. S Apr T *Justitia* May 1745. L.

Longbottom, Elizabeth. S Sep T *Ruby* Oct 1754. L.

Longden, Joseph. S Jul-Dec 1747 LC Knt Co., Md., from *St. George* Mar 1748. M.

Longham, Christian. S Oct 1751-Jan 1752 T *Thames* Mar 1752. M.

Longworth, John of Farnworth. SQS Jan 1730. La.

Looms, Michael of Bermondsey. S Summer T Oct 1750 *Rachael*. Sy.

Lorrell, Mathew. S Mar TB to Va Apr 1742 LC PG Co., Md. Wi.

Loseby, Peter. T May 1752 *Lichfield*. Sy.

Loton, Ann. S May-Jul T *Tayloe* Jul 1774. M.

Lound, Sarah. S Summer T Oct 1758. Li.

Love *als* Lloyd, Peter. S Jan T *Thames* Feb 1751. L.

Loveday, William. S Lent 1741 (IJ). Su.

Loveden, Thomas. S 1754 TB to Md. No.

Lovell, James. S Lent T to Va Oct 1763. No.

Lovell, John. S Jul R & T Sep 1747. Ha.

Lovell, John. S Lent 1763 TB to Va. No.

Lovell, Mary, singlewoman. S Bristol Aug AT Sep 1741 LC Queen Anne's Co., Md
   from *Philleroy* Apr 1742. G.

Lovell, Robert. S Lent 1737 LC Knt Co., Md., from *Hawk* Nov 1737. De.

Lovell, William. SQS Feb T Mar 1750 *Tryal*. M.

Lovering, John. S Oct 1751-Jan 1752 T *Thames* Mar 1752. M.

Lovett, Henry. S Jan-Jun T Jul 1747 *Laura*. M.

Lovett, Mary. T *Saltspring* Jul 1775. M.

Lowe, Alexander of Manchester. SQS Jan 1722 TB Apr 1723. La.

Low, Edmund. S Jul 1747 LC Knt Co., Md., from *St. George* Mar 1748. L.

Lowe, Hanna of Manchester, spinster. SQS Jul 1719. La.

Lowe, James (1726-1728) - *See* Gant. La.

Lowe, John of Manchester. SQS Jan 1730. La.

Low *als* Jones *als* Young *als* Blinkhorne, John. S Jul T Aug 1749 *Thames*. L.

Low, Mary. S Apr-May T *Tryal* Jul 1754. M.

Low, Samuel. S Feb T *Thames* Mar 1752. L.

Lowe, Samuel. S Lent 1773 but received a free pardon. M.

Lowe, Sarah. R 14 yrs for highway robbery Summer but respited Sep 1775. Nt.

Low, Thomas. S Lent T Jun 1748 *Lichfield*. Ht.

Low, Thomas. S May T *Beverly* Aug 1763. M.

Lowe, William of Manchester, husbandman. SQS Apr 1720. La.

Lowance, John. SL & T *Tayloe* Jul 1773. Sy.

Lowder, Richard. S May-Jul T Jul 1748 *Mary*. M.

Lown, Sarah. S Oct 1758. Li.

Lowry, Catherine. S 14 yrs May-Jul T *Mary* Sep 1746. M.

Lowry, Edward. S Dec 1746 T Jan 1747 *George William*. L.

Lowry, Edward. S Dec 1749-Jan 1750 T Mar 1750 *Tryal*. M.

Lowther *als* Reachead, Sarah. S for life Dec 1747 LC Knt Co., Md., from *St. George*
   Mar 1748. L.

Lucas, Dorcas. S Bristol Jan 1757 (AHJ). G.

Lucas, George. S Summer LC Bal Co., Md., Dec 1770 from *Trotman* & sold to
George Lytle. X.

Lucas, John. S s horse Lent R 14 yrs Summer 1755 TB to Va. No.

Lucas, Joseph. T Apr 1735 *Patapsco* LC Annapolis Oct 1735. K.

Lucas, Rachael. S 14 yrs Apr-May T *Tryal* Jul 1754. M.

Lucas, Steven. S Lent but taken from ship & pardoned in April 1775. K.

Lucey, James. S Lent R Jun T 14 yrs Aug 1752 *Tryal*. E.

Luck, George. S Summer 1737 R 14 yrs Feb T Oct 1738 *Genoa*. K.

Luckhurst, William. S Summer T Oct 1750 *Rachael*. K.

MORE EMIGRANTS IN BONDAGE

Ludlow, Henry, aged 11. SQS Feb 1768 TB *Thornton* but pardoned Mar 1768 to serve at sea until he is 21. M.

Luelling, Samuel. R & T Apr 1735 *Patapsco* LC Annapolis Oct 1735. M.

Luff, Robert. S Oct 1751-Jan 1752 T *Thames* Mar 1752. M.

Luke, Joseph. T Jun 1747. Ha.

Luke, William. S Summer 1734 LC Knt Co., Md., Mar 1735 from *Falcon*. Ha.

Lumbard, Sarah. S Mar TB to Va Apr 1742 LC PG Co., Md. Wi.

Lumley, Thomas. SQS Feb LC AA Co., Md., from *Thornton* Jul 1775. M.

Lunn, Richard. S Lent 1724 but escaped & no further record found. Li.

Luscombe, John. SQS Exeter Jul T *Restoration* LC Bal Co., Md., Oct 1771. De.

Lush, William. S Lent LC Bal Co., Md., Jul 1772. Do.

Lush, William. S Lent LC Bal Co., Md., Jun 1773. So.

Lushby, William. R Jul T *Tayloe* Jul 1773. M.

Lusty, Andrew. SQS Mar LC Bal Co., Md., Jul 1772. G.

Luthwait, John. T *Dolphin* May 1763. L.

Lux, John. R 14 yrs Summer LC Md. from *Reformation* Aug 1722. De.

Lux, John. S Plymouth Aug 1751 (AHJ). De.

Lyde, Hannah Rutter. SQS & T Sep 1751 *Greyhound*. M.

Lymes, Herman. S Lent LC AA Co., Md., from *Thornton* Jul 1773. M.

Lynch, Disney. SQS Jul T Sep 1751 *Greyhound*. M.

Lynch, Edward. T *Justitia* Feb 1776. L.

Linch, Elizabeth wife of David. T Summer 1745 T Feb 1746. Ha.

Lynch, John. S Jul T *Saltspring* Jul 1775. L.

Lynch, Mary. S May-Jul T Aug 1749 *Thames*. M.

Lyne, Benedictus. SQS Aug LC Bal Co., Md., Dec 1772. Co.

Lynley, Henry. S Sep 1740 T *Harpooner* Jan 1741. L.

Lynsey, Thomas of St. Mary Savoy. R for Barbados Feb 1672 but LC Md Jun 1673. M.

Lyon, Elizabeth *als* Esther. S 14 yrs Aug T *Beverly* Aug 1763. L.

Lyon *als* Darton *als* Carleton, Mary. R for Barbados Dec 1671 but LC Md from *William & Mary* Mar 1672. M.

Lyon, Moses. S Lent T *Thornton* May LC AA Co., Md., Jul 1774. L.

Lyon, Robert. S Jul LC Bal Co., Md., Dec 1783 from *Swift*. M.

Mably, Edward. S Lent 1738. Db.

Maby, Ambrose. S Feb T Apr 1746. Sh.

Mace, William. S Feb-Apr T May 1752 *Lichfield*. M.

Macereth *als* Holme, Elizabeth. S Summer 1731 R 14 yrs Summer 1732 AT Jul 1737. We.

Mackey, George. S Sep-Oct T Oct 1749 *Mary*. M.

Mackey, John. S Oct 1758. Li.

Macklin, Daniel. S Lent 1732. Db.

Maddis, Richard. S Apr 1754. Li.

Maddox, Elizabeth. S Lent LC AA Co., Md., from *Thornton* Jul 1773. K.

Maddox, Elizabeth. S Lent LC AA Co., Md., from *Hanover Planter* Jul 1773. M.

Maddox, Thomas. S Lent 1761. Sh.

Madle, Joseph. S Lent LC AA Co., Md., from *Thornton* Jul 1775. E.

Mager, John. S Lent LC Bal Co., Md., Jul 1772. De.

Magrave, Ralph. S Oct T *Justitia* Dec 1774. L.

Maid, Jane. S May-Jul T *Tayloe* Jul 1774. M.

Maidenought, Michael. S Apr T May 1750 *Lichfield*. M.

Maile, John. S s sheep Summer 1754 R 14 yrs Lent 1755 TB to Md. No.

Mayle, Margaret. S s shirt Jul 1721 after refusing a whipping (NM). No.

Maile, William [Wilmer]. S s sheep Summer 1754 R 14 yrs Lent 1755 TB to Md. No.

Maine, Abraham. SQS Apr 1737 LC Knt Co., Md., from *Hawk* Nov 1737. Co.

Major, Francis. S Lent 1765. Li.

Major, Hannah. S Summer LC Bal Co., Md., Dec 1770. De.

Major, John. S Apr 1752 (WJ). Wa.

Major *als* Markerson, Walter. S Lent LC Bal Co., Md., Jul 1774. Wi.

Malborn, Enoch. S Summer 1741 R 14 yrs Apr 1742 LC PG Co., Md. Wo.

Malcolm *als* Price, Lidia wife of James. S s silver cup Jul T Dec 1735 *John* LC Annapolis Sep 1736. M.

Mallett, Joseph. S 14 yrs Summer 1734 LC Knt Co., Md., Mar 1735 from *Falcon*. De.

Mallick, John. S Lent LC Bal Co., Md., Jun 1773. Co.

Malone, Abraham. S May-Jul T *Tayloe* Jul 1773. M.

Malone, Dennis. T from Dublin by *Hercules*, LC Bal. Co., Md., Aug 1773, sold to Samuel Cox. Ir.

Malone, John. S Feb-Apr T May 1752 *Lichfield*. M.

Malony, Daniel. S Oct-Dec 1754 T *Greyhound* Feb 1755. M.

Maltby, Hannan. S Sep 1750. Li.

Mander, William. S Mar T Apr 1737. Wa.

Manhall, Elizabeth. S May T *Saltspring* Jul 1775. L.

Manifold alias Merry, Joseph. SQS Apr LC Bal Co., Md., Jul 1771; runaway. St.

Manly, John. S Exeter Jun 1758 (AHJ). De.

Mann, Edward *als* William. S Jul-Sep T *Ruby* Oct 1754. M.

Mann, James. T *Justitia* Feb 1776. L.

Man, Mary. T Aug 1752 *Tryal*. M.

Mann, Mary. S Lent T *Thornton* May LC AA Co., Md., Jul 1774. E.

Manners, Ann wife of John. S City Michaelmas 1756 (AHJ). Nl.

Manners, William. SQS Jan LC Bal Co., Md., Jul 1772. So.

Manning, William. SQS Jul 1738 LC QA Co., Md. Jun 1739. So.

Mansell, Humphrey. S Lent T Aug 1734. Wa.

Mansell, Samuel. S Lent LC Bal Co., Md., Jul 1772. Sh.

Manser, Allen. S s lambs Summer 1744 R 14 yrs Lent T Jul 1745 *Italian Merchant*. Sx.

Mansfield, Elizabeth wife of Robert. S Jan T *Neptune* Mar 1761. M.

Mansfield, Peter of Liston. SQS Apr T *Tayloe* Jul 1773. E.

Mantle, Robert. S Lent R 14 yrs Summer 1739 (IJ). Nf.

Manton, Joseph. S Lent 1744. No.

Manton, Samuel. S 14 yrs s ducks Jan T *Neptune* Mar 1761. M.

Manton, Thomas. S Jan T *Neptune* Mar 1761. M.

Maplesden, Mary. S Lent T May 1750 *Lichfield*. K.

Mapleton, John. S Oct T Oct 1749 *Mary*. L.

Mapsey, Joyce. S Apr 1764. Sh.

March, James. S Lent T Jun 1748 *Lichfield*. K.

Maria, James. S Apr T May 1750 *Lichfield*. M.

Marian, Nicholas. S Lent LC AA Co., Md., from *Thornton* Jul 1773. M.

Mark, Robert. S Mar T Apr 1737. Wa.

Markerson, Walter (1774). See Major. Wi.

Markham, James. S Feb T *Thames* Mar 1754. L.

Marks, John. T *Greyhound* Feb 1755. L.

Marks, Nicholas. SQS Launceston Mar 1734 LC Knt Co., Md, Mar 1735 from *Falcon*. Co.

Marlow, James. S 14 yrs Summer 1737 LC QA Co., Md., from *Amity* Apr 1738. Ha.

Marriman, Thomas Jr. S Feb T Mar 1750 *Tryal*. M.

Marriott *als* Brilston, Jonathan. S & T Apr 1751. No.

Marriott, Samuel. R 14 yrs Dec 1773 T *Justitia* Jan 1774. M.

Marsh, Edward. S Lent LC Bal Co., Md., Jul 1772. G.

Marsh, George. S 14 yrs Lent LC Bal Co., Md., Jul 1771. Do.

Marsh, John. S May T *Beverly* Aug 1763. M.

Marsh, Martha. SQS Beccles 1771. Su.

Marsh, Original. S Dec 1746 T Jan 1747 *George William*. L.

Marsh, William. S 14 yrs Lent LC Bal Co., Md., Jun 1773. De.

Marshall, Elizabeth. S May T *Beverly* Aug 1763. M.

Marshall, Elizabeth. S Lent LC AA Co., Md., from *Thornton* May 1771. L.

Marshall, Henry. S Lent LC AA Co., Md., from *Thornton* Jul 1775. K.

Marshall, James. S Feb-Apr T May 1751 *Tryal*. M.

Marshall, John. S Bristol Jan 1756 (AHJ). G.

Marshall, John. S Lent T *Thornton* May LC AA Co., Md., Jul 1774. M.

Marshall, John. S Sep 1776. Li.

Marshall, Martha. S Apr T May 1752 *Lichfield*. L.

Marshall, Thomas. S Summer 1732 LC Knt Co., Md., from *Falcon* Mar 1733. So.

Marshall, William. R for life Summer 1773 T *Justitia* Jan 1774. Sy.

Marsham, James. S 14 yrs Lent LC Bal Co., Md., Jul 1772. So.

Martin, Andrew. S Sep T *Phoenix* Oct 1760. M.

Martin, Benjamin. R Jul T *Tayloe* Jul 1774. M.

Martin, Bryan. S Apr T Jun 1748 *Lichfield*. L.

Martin, Edward. T May 1752 *Lichfield*. Ht.

Martin, Edward. S Exeter May 1757 (AHJ). De.

Martin, Henry. SQS Oct 1772 LC Bal Co., Md., Jun 1773. Wi.

Martin, Hester. S Lent 1737. Wa.

Martin, Hosea. S Lent 1750 LC QA Co., Md., from *Catherine* Nov 1750. So.

Martin, James. S Lent LC AA Co., Md., from *Hanover Planter* Jul 1773. M.

Martin, John. S Lent LC Potomac, Va., from *Martha* Dec 1724. Wi.

Martyn, John. S Summer 1737 LC QA Co., Md., from *Amity* Apr 1738. De.

Marten *als* Martin, John. S s gelding at Drayton Summer 1744 R 14 yrs Lent 1745. Sh.

Martin, John. S Jun-Dec 1745 T *Plain Dealer* Jan 1746. M.

Martin, John. S Dec 1749-Jan 1750 T Mar 1750 *Tryal*. M.

Martin *als* Martain, John of Battle. S for housebreaking Lent R 14 yrs Summer T Oct 1750 *Rachael*. Sx.

Martin, John. S Feb-Apr T May 1751 *Tryal*. M.

Martin, John. S Aug LC Md *William* Dec 1774 & sold to James Hutchings. So.

Martin, Mary. SQS Oct 1754 T *Greyhound* Feb 1755. M.

Martin, Mary. S Jan T *Tryal* Mar 1757. L.

Martin, Oliver. R for life Lent T *Tayloe* Jul 1773; runaway. Sy.

Martin, Richard. S 14 yrs Lent LC Bal Co., Md., Jul 1772. Wi.

Martin, Robert. S Feb-Apr T May 1751 *Tryal*. M.

Martin, Samuel. SQS Beccles 1758. Su.

Martin, Sarah. S Sep-Oct T Oct 1749 *Mary*. M.

Martin *als* Marchant, Thomas. S Summer 1734 R 14 yrs Feb T Apr 1735 *Patapsco*

LC Annapolis Oct 1735. Sx.

Martin, Thomas. S Apr 1766. Li.

Martin, Thomas. S Jul T *Tayloe* Jul 1773. L.

Martin, Thomas. SQS Jul T *Justitia* Dec 1774. M.

Martyn, William. S 14 yrs Lent 1744 LC Knt Co., Md., from *Susannah* Aug 1744. De.

Martin, William. R Lent T May 1749 *Lichfield*. E.

Masbin, Thomas. AT Jul T Sep 1720 (NM). No.

Mascall, Mary. S Sep T Oct 1750 *Rachael*. M.

Mase, Charles. S Aug T Sep 1751. Sy.

Masey, Thomas. R 14 yrs Oct 1772 T *Justitia* Jan 1773. M.

Mash, John. S Lent LC AA Co., Md., from *Thornton* Jul 1773. M.

Mash, Richard. S 14 yrs s from bleaching yard at Middleton Lent 1772 LC Bal Co., Md., sold to William Ambrose. Su.

Mason, Allen. Pardoned Aug 1746. Ha.

Mason, Amey. SQS Lent LC AA Co., Md., from *Hanover Planter* Jul 1773. M.

Mason, Charles. S Lent LC Bal Co., Md., Jun 1773. Wa.

Mason, Edward of St. Saviour, Southwark, baker. SQS Apr T May 1750 *Lichfield*. Sy.

Mason, George. S Lent T May 1763. No.

Mason, James. S s breeches Sep 1750 (WJ). Wa.

Mason, John. S s bottled cyder from his master Jan 1742. G.

Mason, John. S Apr-Jun 1745 T *Plain Dealer* Jan 1746. M.

Mason, John. S Summer 1747 LC Knt Co., Md., from *St. George* Mar 1748. E.

Mason, Joseph. S 14 yrs Feb-Apr T *Laura* Apr 1746. M.

Mason, Mary. S Mar 1742. He.

Mason, Richard. S Lent R & T May 1751. E.

Mason, Robert. S Mar T Apr 1747. Li.

Mason, William. S Sep T *Maryland Packet* Oct 1761. M.

Massey, Ann. S 14 yrs Oct-Dec 1754 T *Greyhound* Feb 1755. M.

Massey, George. S Mar T Sep 1747. Ha.

Massey, Sarah. S 14 yrs Oct-Dec 1754 T *Greyhound* Feb 1755. M.

Masterton, John. S Jan T *Thames* Feb 1751. M.

Matchet, Jane. S Sep 1754. Li.

Mather, John. S 1761 (AHJ). La.

Maton, Ann. S 14 yrs LC Bal Co., Md., Jul 1772. Wi.

Matthews, Clement wife of Michael. S Oct T *Barnard* Oct 1756. M.

Matthews, Edward. S City Michaelmas 1751 (AHJ). Nl.

Matthews, Edward. S Lent 1757 (AHJ). Wi.

Matthews, Hugh. S Apr T *Lichfield* May 1749. L.

Mathews, James. R for Barbados Oct 1673 but LC Md from *Charles* May 1674. L.

Matthews, James. S Summer 1770 LC Bal Co., Md., Jun 1771. De.

Matthews, Margaret. S Jul-Dec 1747 LC Knt Co., Md., from *St. George* Mar 1748. M.

Matthews, Mary wife of John. S 14 yrs for receiving barley Jan T Apr 1735 *Patapsco* LC Annapolis Oct 1735. M.

Matthews *als* Wright, Mary. S s necklace Oct 1735 T Jan 1736 *Dorsetshire* LC Va Sep 1736. M.

Matthews, Moses. S Summer LC Bal Co., Md., Dec 1772. Ha.

Mathews, Thomas. S Summer 1737 LC QA Co., Md., from *Amity* Apr 1738. Ha.

Matthews, Thomas. T May 1751 *Tryal*. K.

Matthews, William. S Summer 1731 LC Knt Co., Md., from *Falcon* Apr 1732. So.

Matthews, William. S Apr T Jun 1748 *Lichfield*. L.

Matthews, William. S Lent LC Bal Co., Md., Jul 1771. Wo.

Matthews *als* Davies *als* Davey, William. S Lent LC Bal Cc., Md., Jun 1773. Co.

Matthews, William. S Lent LC AA Co., Md., from *Thornton* Jul 1775. M.

Mattocks, John. S Lent T *Thornton* May LC AA Co., Md., Jul 1774. M.

Maud *als* Pickington, Grace. S Jan-Jun T Jul 1747 *Laura*. M.

Maud, Joseph. S Summer 1732. No.

Maul, Mary. S Summer 1752. Nt.

Maul, Robert. T 1751. Nt.

Maxey, Benjamin. S for burning a workshop at Wallingford Lent R 14 yrs Summer 1736; hanged himself in gaol. Be.

Maxfield, Mary. S Apr-May T *Tryal* Jul 1754. M.

Maxwell, John. S s horse & R 14 yrs Jun 1740. Li.

Maxwell, Thomas (1771). *See* Erskine. M.

May, Catherine wife of John. S 14 yrs fpr shoplifting Summer 1733 LC Knt Co., Md., from *Falcon* Apr 1734. De.

May, John. T Aug 1747. Le.

May *als* Cross *als* Darby, Mary. S May-Jul T Jul 1748 *Mary*. M.

May, Peter. S Oct 1772 T *Justitia* Jan 1773. L.

May, Richard. S Summer T Aug 1749 *Thames*. Sy.

May, Susanna. S Lent L S Lent LC AA Co., Md., from *Thornton* May 1771. C AA Co., Md., from *Thornton* May 1771. M.

May, Thomas. S for highway robbery & R 14 yrs Lent T Apr LC Md *William* Dec 1774 & sold to Harry Dorsey Gough. No.

May, William. SQS Launceston Mar 1734 LC Knt Co., Md, Mar 1735 from *Falcon*. Co.

May, William. S Lent 1737 LC Knt Co., Md., from *Hawk* Nov 1737. Co.

Maybank, Elizabeth. S Jan-Apr T Jun 1748 *Lichfield*. M.

Maybrick, Charles, *als* Jones, John. S Apr-May T *Saltspring* Jul 1775. M.

Mayes, Robert. S s cloth from tenter Lent 1721 R Jul T Oct 1725 *Forward* to Va from London. Y.

Mayham, James. S Jul-Dec 1747 LC Knt Co., Md., from *St. George* Mar 1748. M.

Mayhan, James. S Apr-Jun 1739 T *Sea Nymph* to Md. M.

Mayhew *als* Horne, John. S s horse at Easton & R Lent 1773 LC Bal Co., Md., sold to William Randall. Su.

Mayle. *See* Mail.

Mayo, Mary, spinster. S Bristol Aug 1743 LC Knt Co., Md., from *Raven* Feb 1744. G.

Mays, Elizabeth. S Jun-Dec 1745 T *Plain Dealer* Jan 1746. M.

Mays, John. SQS Bury St. Edmunds 1766. Su.

McArdell, Henry. S Sep T Oct 1750 *Rachael*. M.

McArter, Alexander John. S Summer T *Barnard* Oct 1756. Sy.

McCahil, Owen. S Summer 1745 R 14 yrs Lent T *Mary* Sep 1746. Sy.

McCall, Elizabeth. S Apr T *Phoenix* Oct 1760. M.

McCan, Sarah. S Lent 1763 TB to Md. No.

McCarter, Mary. S Jan T *Thames* Feb 1751. M.

McCartney, Arthur. S & T Jan 1736 *Dorsetshire* LC Va Sep 1736. L.

McCartney, George. S Aug T *Restoration* LC Bal Co., Md., Oct 1771. Ch.

McCartney, Patrick of Stoke next Guildford. SQS Oct T *Phoenix* Oct 1760. Sy.

McCarty, Bridget. LC Md from *Isabella* Jul 1775 & sold to Elizabeth Harrison. X

McCarty, James. S May-Jul T *Tayloe* Jul 1773. M.

McCarty, Lawrence. S Jul T Aug 1749 *Thames*. L.

McClough, Daniel. S Lent LC AA Co., Md., from *Thornton* Jul 1775. L.

McConey, James. T Sep 1737 *Pretty Patsy*. L.

McConnell, Dominick. S City 1751 (AHJ). Nl.

McCormick, Adam. S Feb-Apr T *Laura* Apr 1746. M.

McCormick, Ann. S Feb T *Thames* Mar 1754. L.

McCoy, John. T May 1752 *Lichfield*. Sx.

McCoy *als* Smith, Sarah. SQS Feb T *Thornton* May LC AA Co., Md., Jul 1774. M.

McCullogh, Margaret. S Dec T *Justitia* Dec 1774. M.

McCullogh, William. S Apr-Jun 1739 T *Sea Nymph* to Md. M.

McDaniel, Elizabeth. S Sep-Oct 1773 T *Justitia* Jan 1774. M.

McDaniel, James. T *Justitia* Feb 1776. L.

McDaniel, James. R 14 yrs Jul T *Tayloe* Jul 1774. M.

McDaniel, Mary. S Dec 1749-Jan 1750 T Mar 1750 *Tryal*. M.

McDaniel, Thomas. S Jul LC Bal Co., Md., Dec 1783 from *Swift*. M.

McDaniel *als* McDonald, William. SQS Apr T Sep 1751 *Greyhound*. Sy.

McDonald, Ann. S Jan-Apr T Jun 1748 *Lichfield*. M.

McDonald, Archibald. S Jul T Sep 1751 *Greyhound*. L.

McDonald, Elizabeth. T 1746. Su.

McDonald, James. T from Dublin by *Hercules*, LC Bal. Co., Md., Aug 1773, sold to
  William Walters & Richard Guttrell. Ir.

McDonald, James. S Summer 1765. K.

McDonald, Matthew. S 1757 (AHJ). Du.

McDonald, William. S Apr T Sep 1751. Sy.

McFarling/McFarlington, Mary of St. Margaret Westminster. S s linen Apr 1718 TB
  to Va May 1719. L.

McGanley, James. SQS Feb T *Thornton* May LC AA Co., Md., Jul 1774. M.

McGinnis, Charles. S Sep-Oct 1775 T *Justitia* Feb 1776. M.

McGuire, Catherine. S Lent T *Thornton* May LC AA Co., Md., Jul 1774. M.

McGuire, Lockland. S Jul-Dec 1747 LC Knt Co., Md., from *St. George* Mar 1748. M.

McGuire, Martin. S Lent LC AA Co., Md., from *Thornton* May 1771. M.

McHalfpen, James. S Oct T *Barnard* Oct 1756. L.

McIntosh, James. T *Justitia* Feb 1776. L.

McKan, John. S May-Jul T *Tayloe* Jul 1774. M.

McKaw, Alexander. S Summer T Oct 1750 *Rachael*. K.

McKenzie, Catherine. SQS Jan 1773 (OJ). O.

McKenzie, Eleanor. S Sep-Oct 1772 T *Justitia* Jan 1773. M.

McKenzie, Penelope. S Apr T Jun 1748 *Lichfield*. L.

McKenzie, Sarah *als* Mary. S Mar T *Thames* Mar 1754. L.

McKinney, Thomas. SW Lent LC AA Co., Md., from *Hanover Planter* Jul 1773. M.

McKoone, Edward. S s gelding at Wells, Som, Lent R 14 yrs Summer TB Aug 1739. G.

McLane, Jane. S Oct T Oct 1749 *Mary*. L.

McLane, William. T Jan 1747 *George William*. L.

McLaughlin, Jeremiah. S Jan-Apr T *Lichfield* May 1749. M.

McLaughlin *als* Mason *als* Thomas, Mary. S 14 yrs Jun-Dec 1745 T *Plain Dealer*
  Jan 1746. M.

McLean, Eleanor. S Oct 1751-Jan 1752 T *Thames* Mar 1752. M.

McLin, Thomas. S Jan-Apr T Jun 1748 *Lichfield*. M.

McLochlen, Cornelius. S Lent T *Thornton* May LC AA Co., Md., Jul 1774. M.

McMahon *als* Clarke, Benjamin. S Dec 1749-Jan 1750 T Mar 1750 *Tryal*. M.

McMulling, Mary wife of James. S s gowns Sep 1735 T Jan 1736 *Dorsetshire* LC
  Va Sep 1736. M.

MORE EMIGRANTS IN BONDAGE

McNamara, Joseph . T from Waterford by *Betsy* LC Bal. Co., Md., Aug 1773. Ir.

McNamara, Mary wife of James. S Feb T *Tryal* Mar 1757. M.

McNamer, Joseph. SQS Dec 1753 T *Thames* Mar 1754. M.

McNara, Simon of Hoo. S Summer T Oct 1750 *Rachael*. Sx.

McOwen, Owen. S Jul LC Bal Co., Md., Dec 1783 from *Swift*. M.

McPhearson, Ann. S May-Jul T Aug 1749 *Thames*. M.

McPhee, Peter. S Inverness for murder R for life Jun 1773. Sco.

McQuin, Daniel. S Apr T *Lichfield* May 1749. L.

McQuin, John. T Jan 1736 *Dorsetshire* LC Va Sep 1736. Sy.

McUllister, Edward. S Dec 1749-Jan 1750 T Mar 1750 *Tryal*. M.

Meacham, William. S Lent 1769. No.

Mead *als* Watts, John *als* Baker, Rowland. S 14 yrs Lent LC AA Co., Md., from *Thornton* Jul 1775. E.

Mead, Edward. S Summer 1751 R 14 yrs Lent T May 1752 *Lichfield*. Ht.

Meed, Mary. S Summer T Dec 1746. Li.

Mead, Methuselah. S Lent 1732 LC Knt Co., Md., from *Falcon* Apr 1734. So.

Mead, Nightingale. S s lead Jul 1735 T Jan 1736 *Dorsetshire* LC Va Sep 1736. M.

Mead, Nightingale. SQS Apr T May 1750 *Lichfield*; to be publicly whipped from the Red Lion to the Upper Flask in Hampstead before transportation. M.

Meed, Samuel. SQS Apr LC Bal Co., Md., Jul 1771. Do.

Mead, Thomas. S Lent R 14 yrs Summer T *Phoenix* Oct 1760. E.

Meadall, William. S Dec 1749-Jan 1750 T Mar 1750 *Tryal*. M.

Meadle, James. S Summer T Aug 1746. E.

Meadows, Thomas. S Dec 1750 T *Thames* Feb 1751. L.

Meads, Mary. S for s £27 Jul 1765. O.

Meager, William. SQS Oct 1756 LC Knt Co., Md., from *Hawk* Nov 1737. Co.

Meakham, Samuel. S May-Jul T *Tayloe* Jul 1773. M.

Meal, John. S Dec 1750 T *Thames* Feb 1751. L.

Meal, Mary. S Sep T Oct 1750 *Rachael*. M.

Mecum, John. S May-Jul T *Tayloe* Jul 1774. M.

Medcalfe, Adam. S Feb T May 1758. Ha.

Medcalf, Joseph. R 14 yrs Jul T *Tayloe* Jul 1774. M.

Medcalf, William. S for life Lent LC AA Co., Md., from *Thornton* Jul 1775. Ht.

Medlicott, John. S Lent T from Bristol May 1754. Sh..

Medlicott, Peter. S Lent R 14 yrs Summer 1754 (GJ). Sh.

Meed - *See* Mead.

Meek, John. S Summer T *Ruby* Oct 1754. K.

Meek, William. S & R 14 yrs Summer LC Md *William* Dec 1774 & sold to Roger Pomfrey. G.

Meers *als* Kirby, Margaret. S Apr T *Justitia* May 1745. L.

Mees, John. S Jul LC Bal Co., Md., Dec 1783 from *Swift*. M.

Meisey, William. SQS Launceston Mar 1734 LC Knt. Co., Md, Mar 1735 from *Falcon*. Co.

Melishaw [Meltshaw], Sarah wife of Thomas. S Apr-Jun 1739 T *Sea Nymph* Jul 1739. M.

Melland, Thomas. S Summer 1741 R 14 yrs Apr 1742. Wo.

Mellar, Francis. SQS Summer 1758. Nt.

Mellor, Anthony. S Lent T from Bristol May 1755. St.

Melone, John. S Jan-Apr T *Lichfield* May 1749. M.

Melvin, Elliot. SW Jan LC AA Co., Md., from *Thornton* Jul 1773. M.

Melvin, Richard. S Aug T *Phoenix* Oct 1760. L.

Mercer, Elizabeth. S Jan-Jun T Jul 1747 *Laura*. M.

Mercer, James. S & T Mar 1750 *Tryal*. L.

Mercer, Jonas. S 14 yrs Lent 1750 LC QA Co., Md., from *Catherine* Nov 1750. So.

Mercer, Joseph. R 14 yrs Dec 1723 T Jul 1724 *Robert* LC Annapolis Jun 1725. Be.

Merchant, Joseph. S Lent but R for sea service to the East Indies in Mar 1771. M.

Merchant, Stephen Jr. S May-Jul T *Tayloe* Jul 1773. M.

Merchant, William. SQS Feb T Mar 1750 *Tryal*. M.

Mercier, Francis. S Lent LC AA Co., Md., from *Hanover Planter* Jul 1773. M.

Mereden, Joseph. S Lent LC AA Co., Md., from *Hanover Planter* Jul 1773. M.

Meredith, Edward. S May-Jul T Sep 1751 *Greyhound*. M.

Meredith, James. S s sheep Lent R 14 yrs Summer 1765. Mo.

Merriman, Thomas. S Dec 1749-Jan 1750 T Mar 1750 *Tryal*. M.

Merrit, Mary wife of Edward, *als* Mary Kipping. S 14 yrs May-Jul T Sep 1746
    Mary. M.

Merry, Joseph (1771). *See* Maniford. St.

Merry, Mary wife of Samuel of Exeter, dyer. SQS Jul 1742 LC QA Co., Md., from
    Kent Jun 1743. De.

Merry, Richard. S Oct 1751-Jan 1752 T *Thames* Mar 1752. M.

Metcalfe, George. SQS Northallerton Jul TB Aug 1737. Y.

Metters, Richard. S Lent 1731 LC Knt Co., Md., from *Falcon* Apr 1732. De.

Metton, George of St. George, Southwark. SQS Apr T May 1750 *Lichfield*. Sy.

Mewdon, William. S Summer 1718 LC from *Sophia* QA Co., Md. Mar 1719. De.

Mewres, Samuel. S s sheep 1747 & T Jan 1748. Nl.

Middleditch, Eleanor. S May T *Maryland Packet* Oct 1761. M.

Middlemass, William. S s gelding Lent 1721 R Jul T Oct 1723 *Forward* to Va
    from London. Y.

Middleton, John. S Lent LC Potomac, Va., from *Martha* Dec 1724. De.

Middleton, Richard. S Lent LC Potomac, Va., from *Martha* Dec 1724. De.

Middleton, Thomas. S Apr T Jun 1748 *Lichfield*. L.

Middleton, William. S Oct 1773 T *Justitia* Jan 1774. L.

Mies, Elizabeth. S Sep T Nov 1746. Sh.

Mildred, Hannah. S Apr T *Lichfield* May 1749. L.

Miles, Briant. R 14 yrs Jul LC Md *William* Dec 1774 & sold to Lancelot Warfield. Do.

Miles, Charles. S Sep 1740 T *Harpooner* Jan 1741. L.

Miles, Mary. S Apr T May 1751 *Tryal*. L.

Miles, William. S Summer 1749 R 14 yrs Lent T May 1750 *Lichfield*. E.

Millage, Mary. S for house breaking at Frampton Cotterell Mar 1771 (HJ). G.

Millar, Elizabeth. S City 1761 (AHJ). Nl.

Millard, Henry. T May 1747. So.

Millard, Thomas. S s cloth at Stroud Jul T *Restoration* LC Bal Co., Md., Oct
    1771. G.

Miller, Andrew. S 14 yrs May T *Maryland Packet* Oct 1761. M.

Miller, Daniel. S Feb-Apr T *Laura* Apr 1746. M.

Miller *als* Dand, Elizabeth. S City Christmas 1761 (AHJ). Nl.

Miller, James. S 14 yrs Chelmsford Jan 1753 (AHJ). E.

Miller, John. S Lent 1737. Li.

Miller, John. S Lent T May 1752 *Lichfield*. Sy.

Miller *als* Sargent, John. S Oct T Oct 1749 *Mary*. L.

Miller, Lawrence. S Aug T *Beverly* Aug 1763. L.

Miller, Margaret. S May T *Saltspring* Jul 1775. L.

Miller, Mary. S Lent T Oct 1739. Wa.

Miller, Mary wife of Thomas. S Lent T Jun 1748 *Lichfield*. Ht.

Miller, Mary of Chelmsford, chapwoman. SQS Jul T Aug 1749 *Thames*. E.

Miller, Maximilian. S Lent LC AA Co., Md., from *Thornton* May 1771. M.

Miller, Robert. S Jul T Jul 1748 *Mary*. L.

Miller, Solomon. S s horse Summer 1752 R 14 yrs Lent 1753 TB to Md. No.

Miller, Thomas. S May-Jul T *Tayloe* Jul 1773. M.

Millett, Ann. S Apr T May 1751 *Tryal*. L.

Millidge, Mary. S Bristol s at Frampton Cotterell Mar T *Restoration* LC Bal Co.,
    Md., Oct 1771. G.

Millikin, Mark. S Lent LC AA Co., Md., from *Thornton* Jul 1775. L.

Millington, John. S Jan-Apr T *Lichfield* May 1749. M.

Mills, Dorothy. S Summer T Oct 1758. Wa.

Mills, Edward. SQS Wakefield Summer 1738. Y.

Mills, Eleanor wife of William. S May-Jul T *Tayloe* Jul 1773. M.

Mills, Elford. S Sep-Oct T Oct 1749 *Mary*. M.

Mills *als* Cassody, Elizabeth. S Feb T *Thames* Mar 1754. M.

Mills, Elizabeth. T May 1761. Ha.

Mills, Emanuel. S Jan-Apr T *Lichfield* May 1749. M.

Mills *als* Pizey, Henry. S for highway robbery Lent R Summer T for life Oct 1750
    Rachael. E.

Mills, Herman. T *Thames* Feb 1751.

Mills, John. T Jan 1736 *Dorsetshire* LC Va Sep 1736. Sy.

Mills, John of Greenwich. S Lent T May 1750 *Lichfield*. K.

Mills, Joseph. S Lent 1733. Wa.

Mills, Margaret. S s kettle Feb T Apr 1735 *Patapsco* LC Annapolis Oct 1735. M.

Mills, Martha. S & T Sep 1751 *Greyhound*. L.

Mills, Mary. S Oct T Oct 1749 *Mary*. L.

Mills, Robert. S Lent LC Bal Co., Md., Jul 1771. So.

Mills, Thomas. S Jan T *Greyhound* Feb 1755. M.

Millson, Thomas. S Sep-Oct 1773 T *Justitia* Jan 1774. M.

Milsham, John. S s horse Lent R 14 yrs Summer 1739. Wo.

Milsom, Abraham, a boy. S s at Siston Lent 1763. G.

Milward, John. S Lent T Apr 1753. Wa.

Mince, John *als* Peter. S May-Jul T *Tayloe* Jul 1774. M.

Minett, Matthew. S Feb T *Thames* Mar 1754. L.

Mingis, Martha. S Dec 1753-Jan 1754 T *Thames* Mar 1754. M.

Minlas, Richard. T May 1745. Y.

Minnett, Christina. S Summer T from London Oct 1738. Wa.

Mitchell, Benjamin. S Lent R 14 yrs Summer T Aug 1752 *Tryal*. Sy.

Mitchell, Elizabeth. S Jul-Dec 1747 LC Knt Co., Md., from *St. George* Mar 1748. M.

Mitchell, George. S Jul-Dec 1747 but died. M.

Mitchell, James. S s watch Feb T Apr 1735 *Patapsco* LC Annapolis Oct 1735. M.

Mitchell, James. S Lent R 14 yrs Summer 1747 LC Md from *St. George* Mar
    1748. Li.

Mitchell, James. T 14 yrs Jan 1748. Sy.

Mitchell, James. S Lent T *Tryal* Jul 1754. K.

Mitchell, James. S Mar T *Thames* Mar 1754. L.

Mitchell, John. S Apr-Jun 1739 T *Sea Nymph* to Md. M.

Mitchell, John. S Lent R Jul T Jul 1747 *Laura*. Sy.

Mitchell, John (1748). *See* Kerry. Be.

Mitchell, John. S 14 yrs Chelmsford Jan 1763 (AHJ). E.

Mitchell, John. SQS Jul TB Aug T *Restoration* LC Bal Co., Md., Oct 1771. So.

Mitchell, Richard. S 14 yrs Summer 1743 LC Knt Co., Md., from *Globe* Mar 1744. De.

Mitchell als Gillard, Scipio. S Lent LC Bal Co., Md., Jun 1773. Co.

Mitchell, Susannah. T *Saltspring* Jul 1775. M.

Mitchell, William. T *Justitia* Feb 1776. L.

Mixon, William. S Lent 1732 LC Knt Co., Md., from *Falcon* Mar 1733. De.

Moate, John. S Lent R 14 yrs Summer T Sep 1751 *Greyhound*. K.

Mogg, John. S Summer LC Bal Co., Md., Dec 1772. Wa.

Mole, John. S Lent T Apr 1753. Le.

Mole, Thomas. S Lent LC AA Co., Md., from *Thornton* Jul 1775. E.

Moles, George. R for Barbados Dec 1671 LC Md from *William & Mary* Mar 1672. M.

Moll, Francisco. S Jan 1761 TB *Dolphin* but pardoned for Army service Oct 1761. L.

Molland, Thomas. T Apr 1742 LC PG Co., Md. Wo.

Molloy, Roger. SQS Jan LC AA Co., Md., from *Thornton* Jul 1775. M.

Moneypenny, Hugh. S Jan TB *Dolphin* but pardoned for Army service Dec 1761. L.

Monk, Ann. S Feb T *Thames* Mar 1754. L.

Monk, Ann. S May-Jul T *Tayloe* Jul 1774. M.

Monke, Elizabeth. S Apr T Dec 1735 *John* LC Annapolis Sep 1736. M.

Monk, George. S Summer 1755 R 14 yrs Summer T *Barnard* Oct 1756. E.

Monk, John. S Apr-May T *Tryal* Jul 1754. M.

Monk, Joseph. S May-Jul T *Tayloe* Jul 1773. M.

Monk, Mary. S 14 yrs Lent 1750   LC QA Co., Md., from *Catherine* Nov 1750. He.

Monk, Rinaldo. S 14 yrs Mar TB to Va Apr 1742 LC PG Co., Md. Wi.

Monro, Margaret. S May-Jul T *Tayloe* Jul 1774. M.

Monro, Mary. SQS Feb T Mar 1750 *Tryal*. M.

Monroe, Joseph. SWK & T May 1750 *Lichfield*. K.

Monteuth, Mary. S Bristol Jun 1753 (AHJ). G

Montford, Robert. S Lent LC AA Co., Md., from *Thornton* Jul 1773. E.

Montgomery, Alexander. R 14 yrs Dec 1773 T *Justitia* Jan 1774. M.

Montgomery, Frances. S Mar T Sep 1747. Ha.

Moody, Elizabeth of St. James Westminster. S s clothing Apr T Aug 1718 *Eagle* LC Charles Town Mar 1719. L.

Moody, Elizabeth *als* Betty. S Aug TB to Va Sep 1767 after being brought to childbed. Wi.

Moody, John. S Lent 1737 & T from London. St.

Moody, John. S Lent T *Dolphin* May 1763. Ht.

Moody, Samuel. S Lent T *Tryal* Jul 1754. K.

Moon *als* Mohun, Catherine. S Jan T *Greyhound* Feb 1755. L.

Mooney, John. S Feb T 14 yrs Mar 1750 *Tryal*. M.

Mooney, Richard. S Jul-Sep T *Ruby* Oct 1754. M.

Moore, Charles. S Oct T Oct 1749 *Mary*. L.

Moore, Dorothy, spinster. R for Barbados Oct 1673 but LC Md from *Charles* May 1674. L.

Moore, Edward. S Mar TB to Va Apr 1742 LC PG Co., Md. Wi.

Moor, Eglantine. S Summer 1736. Y.

Moore, Elizabeth. S Feb T *Thames* Mar 1752. L.

Moor, James of St. John's. S Summer T Oct 1750 *Rachael*. Sy.

Moore, James. T from Dublin by *Hercules*, LC Bal. Co., Md., Aug 1773, sold to Stephen Gill son of John of Baltimore Co. Ir.

Moore, Jane. S Lent T *Thornton* May LC AA Co., Md., Jul 1774. M.

Moore, John. SQS Exeter Jan 1734 LC Knt Co., Md, Mar 1735 from *Falcon*. De.

Moore, John. S Dec 1749-Jan 1750 T Mar 1750 *Tryal*. M.

Moore, John *als* Stone, Samuel. S Summer 1770 LC Bal Co., Md., Jun 1771. So.

Moore, John. S Lent LC AA Co., Md., from *Thornton* May 1771. L.

Moore, Mary. T Jan 1736 *Dorsetshire* LC Va Sep 1736. Sx.

Moore, Peter. S 14 yrs Lent LC AA Co., Md., from *Thornton* Jul 1775. K.

Moore, Robert. S Feb T *Thames* Mar 1754. L.

Moore, William. SQS Jan 1734 LC Knt Co., Md., from *Hawk* Apr 1735. So.

Moore, William. S Apr T Jun 1748 *Lichfield*. L.

Moore, William (*als* Robert). S Lent LC Bal Co., Md., Dec 1770 from *Trotman* & sold to Stephen Gill Jr. Y.

Moore, William. S Lent T *Thornton* May LC AA Co., Md., Jul 1774. M.

Moore, William. S Lent T *Thornton* May LC AA Co., Md., Jul 1774. L.

Moores, John. R for life Sep T *Barnard* Oct 1756. M.

Moores, Mary. S Summer LC Bal Co., Md., Dec 1770. Ch.

Moores, Thomas. R for life Sep T *Barnard* Oct 1756. M.

Moorshall, Edward. S Jul T *Tayloe* Jul 1773. L.

Moorshall, Thomas. S Jul T *Tayloe* Jul 1774. L.

Mopps, Abraham. T Aug 1749 *Thames*. L.

Mopsey, Ann. S for life Lent LC Bal Co., Md., Jul 1771. So.

Morestly *als* Mosely, Joseph. S Feb-Apr T May 1752 *Lichfield*. M.

Moreton - *See* Morton.

Morey, Stephen. S Summer 1741 LC QA Co., Md., from *Philleroy* Apr 1742. De.

Morgan, David. S Brecon for burglary R 14 yrs Jun 1772. Wal.

Morgan, Edward of Newport Pagnell. S for burglary & R 14 yrs Feb 1724 LC from *Robert* Md Jun 1725. Bu.

Morgan, Edward. T Jan 1736 *Dorsetshire* LC Va Sep 1736. Sy.

Morgan, Elizabeth. SQS Gloucester Jan 1758 (GJ). G.

Morgan, James of Brislington, husbandman. R for Barbados Feb 1673 but LC Md in 1673. So.

Morgan, Jane. S Jan-Jun T Jul 1747 *Laura*. M.

Morgan, Job. S Lent 1734 LC Knt Co., Md., Mar 1735 from *Falcon*. De.

Morgan, John. S Aug T *Beverly* Aug 1763. L.

Morgan, John *als* Morris, Thomas. S Lent T *Thornton* May LC AA Co., Md., Jul 1774. M.

Morgan, Martha. S s at Weobley Lent but respited for report Apr 1770. He.

Morgan, Mary. S s shirt Jan T Apr 1735 *Patapsco* LC Annapolis Oct 1735. M.

Morgan, Mary. S Lent R 14 yrs Summer T Aug 1752 *Tryal*. Sy.

Morgan *als* Slade, Moses. S Lent LC Bal Co., Md., Jun 1773. Wi.

Morgan, Richard. S for highway robbery Lent R 14 yrs Summer 1741 LC QA Co., Md from *Philleroy* Apr 1742. He.

Morgan, Sarah. S Sep T *Barnard* Oct 1756. M.

Morgan, Thomas. S Apr T Jun 1746. Mo.

Morgan, Thomas. T Jun 1747. So.

Morgan, Thomas. S Brecon s horse R 14 yrs May 1769. Wal.

Morgan, Thomas. R 14 yrs Jul T *Tayloe* Jul 1774. M.

Morgan, William (1738) - *See* Williams. G.

Morgan, William. S Summer T Sep 1751 *Greyhound.* Sy.

Morgan, William. S s horse Summer 1751 R 14 yrs Lent 1752 (GJ). Mo.

Morgan, William. S s grain on River Wye Lent 1757 (GJ). G.

Morgan, William. S Jul T *Beverly* Aug 1763. M.

Morgan, William. S Lent, respited Apr, LC Md from *Elizabeth* Jun 1775. Wa.

Morland, Eleanor. S Jul T *Tayloe* Jul 1774. L.

Morley, John. S Oct 1751-Jan 1752 T *Thames* Mar 1752. M.

Morrice, Richard. S Lent R 14 yrs Summer T *Ruby* Oct 1754. Ht.

Morris, Ann wife of William. S 14 yrs LC Bal Co., Md., Jul 1772. Do.

Morris, Batchelor. S Lent LC AA Co., Md., from *Thornton* Jul 1775. Sx.

Morris, Daniel. S for life Lent T *Thornton* May LC AA Co., Md., Jul 1774. Sy.

Morris, Edward. S Lent 1752. No.

Morris, Eleanor. S Sep-Oct T Oct 1749 *Mary.* M.

Morris, Elizabeth wife of John of Eagle Court, Strand. S Sep 1735 T Jan 1736 *Dorsetshire* LC Va Sep 1736. M.

Morris, Hannah. S for murder of her bastard child Summer 1724 R 14 yrs Lent 1725. St.

Morris, James. SQS Feb but pardoned in Nov 1773. Sy.

Morris, Jane. S Dec 1745 T *Plain Dealer* Jan 1746. L.

Morris, Jane wife of Thomas. S Lent 1765. Sh.

Morris, John. S Jun-Dec 1745 T *Plain Dealer* Jan 1746. M.

Morris, John. S Jun T *Tryal* Jul 1754. L.

Morris, John. S Lent LC Bal Co., Md., Dec 1770 from *Trotman* & sold to Charles Barker. Y.

Morris, John. S 14 yrs Lent LC AA Co., Md., from *Thornton* Jul 1775. Bu.

Morris, Lloyd. S Coventry s silver watch Aug 1771. Wa.

Morris, Margaret. S Jan-Apr T *Lichfield* May 1749. M.

Morris, Mary. S Apr-Jun 1739 T *Sea Nymph* to Md. M.

Morris, Michael. T from Dublin by *Hercules*, LC Bal. Co., Md., Aug 1773, sold to Darby Lux. Ir.

Morris, William. S Bristol Sep 1741 LC QA Co., Md., from *Philleroy* Apr 1742. G.

Morris, William. S s sheep Lent R 14 yrs Summer 1743 LC Knt Co., Md., from *Raven* Feb 1744. Mo.

Morris, Thomas. S Apr T May 1747. So.

Morris, Thomas. T May 1752 *Lichfield*. E.

Morris, Thomas *als* Matthew. S Glamorgan R Jan 1765. Wal.

Morris, William. S Summer 1770 LC Bal Co., Md., Jul 1771. He.

Morris, William. T *Tayloe* Jul 1773. L.

Morris, Thomas (1774). *See* Morgan, John. M.

Morris, Thomas. S 14 yrs Lent T *Thornton* May LC AA Co., Md., Jul 1774. Sy.

Morrish, William. S Lent LC Bal Co., Md., Jul 1772. De.

Morse, Charles. S Summer T Sep 1751 *Greyhound.* Sy.

Morse, Dinah. S Lent T *Dolphin* Apr 1761. Sy.

Morse, William. S Jan-Apr T Jun 1748 *Lichfield.* M.

Moreton, Christopher. S Lent LC AA Co., Md., from *Thornton* May 1771. L.

Moreton, John. S s deer from enclosed park Lent R 14 yrs Summer 1738 but died in gaol. Db.

Morton, Martha. SQS Jul T Sep 1767. Y.

Morton, Mary wife of Robert. S Sep-Oct 1772 T *Justitia* Jan 1773. M.

Moreton, Rose. S s in St. James Westminster Jun 1733 LC from *Caesar* Va Jul 1734. M.

Moseley, Charles. S Sep-Oct T Oct 1749 *Mary*. M.

Moseley, Joseph. S Lent T *Lichfield* May 1749. Sx.

Moses, Elizabeth wife of Richard, weaver. SQS Apr 1750 LC QA Co., Md., from *Catherine* Nov 1750. De.

Moses, Jacob. S Aug T *Beverly* Aug 1763. L.

Moses, Solomon. S Dec 1773 T *Justitia* Jan 1774. L.

Moss, Charles. S s breeches at Cirencester Jul T *Restoration* LC Bal Co., Md., Oct 1771. G.

Moss, John. S for vagrancy 1774 TB to Md. No.

Moss, Peter. S Jan-Apr T Jun 1748 *Lichfield*. M.

Mosse, Richard. S Mar T Apr 1746. Sh.

Mosten, John. S Apr T May 1750 *Lichfield*. M.

Mott, Joseph. S Lent LC AA Co., Md., from *Thornton* Jul 1775. E.

Mott, Richard. S 14 yrs Lent LC Bal Co., Md., Jun 1773. Ha.

Motty, Henry. S for housebreaking Summer 1730 T Lent 1740. O.

Moule, Edward. S Sep 1747 LC Knt Co., Md., from *St. George* Mar 1748. L.

Moule, Edward. R & T Jan 1748. E.

Mount, John. S 14 yrs Lent LC AA Co., Md., from *Thornton* Jul 1775. K.

Mount, Jonas. S Lent T *Thornton* May LC AA Co., Md., Jul 1774. K.

Mountague, William (1774). *See* Mounty. Wi.

Mountfort, Richard. S Mar 1754 (AHJ). Sh.

Mounty alias Mountague, William. S Lent LC Bal Co., Md., Jul 1774. Wi.

Mowburn, George. S Lent LC Bal Co., Md., Dec 1770 from *Trotman* & sold to ----- Amos. Y.

Mowls, Ann. S Feb T *Neptune* Mar 1761. L.

Moyle, Richard Sr. S Apr LC Md from *Isabella* Jul 1775 & sold to George Scott. Co.

Muckaway Thomas. S Lent LC AA Co., Md., from *Thornton* May 1771. L.

Muggeridge, Joseph. S Summer 1732 LC Knt Co., Md., from *Falcon* Mar 1733. De.

Mulford, David. S 14 yrs Lent LC AA Co., Md., from *Thornton* Jul 1775. Sy.

Mullens, Mary of Croydon, spinster. SQS Apr T *Dolphin* May 1763. Sy.

Mullett, William. S 14 yrs Lent 1736 S Jul 1736 LC QA Co., Md., from *Amity* May 1737. Do.

Mulling, Patrick. S Oct-Dec 1750 T *Thames* Feb 1751. M.

Mullings, Ann. S Jul T Jul 1748 *Mary*. L.

Mullings, William. S Sep 1747 LC Knt Co., Md., from *St. George* Mar 1748. L.

Mullins, James. S Dec 1749-Jan 1750 T Mar 1750 *Tryal*. M.

Mullins, Jane wife of Richard of Tiverton. SQS Tiverton Jul 1733 LC Knt Co., Md., from *Falcon* Apr 1734. De.

Mulloy, Mary. S Oct T *Barnard* Oct 1756. M.

Munckman, John. S Lent AT Summer 1739. Y.

Munday, Frances. S May-Jul T Jul 1748 *Mary*. M.

Munday, James. S Dec 1749-Jan 1750 T Mar 1750 *Tryal*. M.

Munday, John. S Lent 1734. No.

Munday, Thomas (1734). See Williams. Do.

Mungay, Thomas. S Summer T Sep 1772 TB to Md. No.

Munroe, Robert. S Jan T *Thames* Feb 1751. L.

Munrow, John. T from Dublin by *Hercules*, LC Bal. Co., Md., Aug 1773, sold to William Walters & Richard Guttrell. Ir.

Munson, Richard (1733) - *See* Minson. Wi.

Munt, Jane. S for life Lent LC AA Co., Md., from *Thornton* Jul 1775. M.

Murphy, Ann. S Apr 1746 T Apr 1746 *Laura*. M.

Murphy, Eleanor. S Jul T *Tayloe* Jul 1773. L.

Murphy, James. S Lent LC AA Co., Md., from *Thornton* Jul 1775. M.

Murphy, Jeremiah. S Feb-Apr T May 1751 *Tryal*. M.

Murphy, Mary. S Dec 1749-Jan 1750 T Mar 1750 *Tryal*. M.

Murphy, Thomas. S Sep T *Ruby* Oct 1754. L.

Murfey, Timothy. T May 1755 *Rose*. E.

Murphy, William. S Lent R 14 yrs Summer T *Ruby* Oct 1754. K.

Murray, Elizabeth. S Dec 1747 LC Knt Co., Md., from *St. George* Mar 1748. L.

Murray, Matthew. S Lent LC AA Co., Md., from *Thornton* May 1771. M.

Murray, Robert. S 14 yrs Apr T *Dolphin* May 1763. M.

Murray, William. S City 1752 (AHJ). Nl.

Murrow, Mary. S Apr 1746 T Jan 1748. Nl.

Murtogh, Bryan. S Apr-Jun 1739 T *Sea Nymph* to Md. M.

Muston, Richard Joseph. S Lent LC AA Co., Md., from *Thornton* May 1771. M.

Mutkirke, William. SW Lent LC AA Co., Md., from *Hanover Planter* Jul 1773. M.

Muzzle, Joseph (James). S Summer 1747 R 14 yrs Lent T Jun 1748 *Lichfield*. Sy.

Miers, Emanuel. S & R 14 yrs Summer LC Md *William* Dec 1774 & sold to James Hutchings. Wo.

Myers, Mary. S May-Jul T Jul 1748 *Mary*. M.

Myford, Elizabeth. S Jul T *Beverly* Aug 1763. M.

Nabbs, Thomas. S Lent LC Bal Co., Md., Jul 1772. St.

Nagger, Michael. S Lent 1735. Y.

Nainby, John. S for highway robbery & R 14 yrs Jun 1740. Li.

Naish, Susan of Maidstone. S Lent T Jul 1745 *Italian Merchant*. K.

Nammee, Miles. S Feb 1737 T Lent 1739. Bd.

Nary, Andrew. S Lent T *Thornton* May LC AA Co., Md., Jul 1774. L.

Nash *als* Nass, Abraham. S 14 yrs Apr-Jun 1739 T *Sea Nymph* to Md. M.

Nash, John (1773). *See* Burwell, Richard. K.

Nash, Mary wife of John. S Aug , brought to childbed & TB to Va Sep 1767. Wi.

Nash, Mary. S & T Aug T *Restoration* LC Bal Co., Md., Oct 1771. Wa.

Nash, Richard *als* John (1773) -*See* Burvill. K.

Nash, William. S Lent LC AA Co., Md., from *Thornton* Jul 1773. K.

Nason, John. T 1746. Sy.

Nason, William. S Bristol Feb 1754. G.

Natchel, Mary. S May 1770. Li.

Nayler, John. S Coventry for highway robbery & R 14 yrs Jun 1741. Wa.

Naylor, John. S Lent T Jun 1748 *Lichfield*. E.

Naylor, Susannah. S Dec 1772 T *Justitia* Jan 1773. M.

Neal, Daniel. S May-Jul T *Tayloe* Jul 1774. M.

Neal, John. S Jul LC Bal Co., Md., Dec 1783 from *Swift*. M.

Neal, Mary. S s shirts Apr T Dec 1735 *John* LC Annapolis Sep 1736. M.

Neal, Thomas. S Lent R 14 yrs Jun T Aug 1749 *Thames*. Ht.

Neale, William. S Feb-Apr T May 1752 *Lichfield*. M.

Neaton, Edward. S Lent LC AA Co., Md., from *Thornton* Jul 1775. K.

Need, William. S Jun T *Tryal* Jul 1754. L.

Needham, James. S Oct T Oct 1749 *Mary*. L.

Needham, William. S Lent LC AA Co., Md., from *Thornton* Jul 1775. L.

Neill, Mary. T from Dublin by *Hercules*, LC Bal. Co., Md., Aug 1773, sold to William Walters & Richard Guttrell. Ir.

Neilson, Neils. S Sep T *Phoenix* Oct 1760. M.

Nelmes, Mary. S Summer 1772 LC Bal Co., Md., Apr 1773. G.

Nelmes, William. S Mar 1742. He.

Nelson, Thomas. S Sep-Oct 1775 T *Justitia* Feb 1776. M.

Nelson, William. S Summer 1744 R 14 yrs Lent T Jul 1745 *Italian Merchant*. E.

Nesbitt, Elizabeth. S Feb-Apr T May 1751 *Tryal*. M.

Nesbitt, James. S Lent R 14 yrs Jun T Aug 1752 *Tryal*. K.

Nethercliffe, William. S Lent T May 1752 *Lichfield*. Bu.

Netherly, Catherine wife of David. S City Summer 1756 (AHJ). Nl.

Neves, Daniel. S Apr-Jun 1739 T *Sea Nymph* to Md. M.

Nevinson, Peter. S Lent 1735. Y.

Newberry, Elizabeth wife of Thomas Jr. S Jun-Dec 1745 T *Plain Dealer* Jan 1746. M.

Newberry, John. S Lent LC Bal Co., Md., Jul 1772 & sold to James Gittings. De.

Newberry, Thomas (1734). See Goff. De.

Newborn, Thomas. S Summer T Aug 1746. E.

Newbowl, George. T May 1751 *Tryal*. K.

Newell, Daniel. S Summer LC Bal Co., Md., Dec 1770. Ch.

Newel, John. S Lent 1741 (IJ). Su.

Newell, John. S Lent LC AA Co., Md., from *Thornton* Jul 1775. K.

Newell, William. S Sep-Dec 1746 T Jan 1747 *George William*. M.

Newey, John Jr. of Coston, Worcs. S King's Bench for giving false evidence May 1763 (OJ). L.

Newey, John. S Lent LC Bal Co., Md., Jul 1771. Wa.

Newhouse, Cornelius. S 14 yrs Oct 1751-Jan 1752 T *Thames* Mar 1752. M.

Newings, Letitia (wife of John). SW Lent LC AA Co., Md., from *Hanover Planter* Jul 1773. M.

Newman, Ann. T *Thames* Mar 1754. L.

Newman *als* Howard, Bridget. S Oct T *Barnard* Oct 1756. M.

Newman, Maria. S May-Jun T Aug 1752 *Tryal*. M.

Newman, Richard (1717) - *See* Yeoman. L.

Newman *als* Smith, Thomas. S Jun-Dec 1745 T *Plain Dealer* Jan 1746. M.

Newman *als* Smith, Thomas. S Jun-Dec 1745 T *Plain Dealer* Jan 1746. M.

Newman, William. S Jul-Dec 1747 LC Knt Co., Md., from *St. George* Mar 1748. M.

Newman, Willmott wife of William. SQS Jan 1732 LC Knt Co., Md., from *Falcon* Mar 1733. De.

Newport, Richard (1732). See Pearce. Do.

Newstead, William. S s communion cup in Calthorpe church Summer 1764. Nf.

Newth, Thomas. SQS Jan LC Bal Co., Md., Jun 1773. G.

Newton, Daniel. S Summer 1718 LC from *Sophia* QA Co., Md. Mar 1719. De.

Newton, George. SQS Jul 1772 LC Bal Co., Md., from *Adventure* Mar 1773. Nl.

Newton, George. SQS & T *Justitia* Jan 1774; runaway. L.

Newton, James. S Apr-May T *Saltspring* Jul 1775. M.

Newton, Thomas. S Lent TB May 1734 T *Squire* LC Md Aug 1735. Db.

Newton, William. SQS Jul T *Justitia* Dec 1774. M.

Newton, William. S Jul LC Bal Co., Md., Dec 1783 from *Swift*. M.

Nice, Charles. S s coat Apr T Dec 1735 *John* LC Annapolis Sep 1736. L.

Nicholas, George. S Summer 1750 (GJ). Be.

Nicholas, Robin of Staplehurst. S Lent T Jul 1745 *Italian Merchant*. K.

Nicholas, William. S Brecon s sheep R May 1773. Wal.

Nicholls, Ann. S Mar 1742 LC PG Co., Md. Co.

Nicholls, Daniel (1775). *See* Nicholson. M.

Nicholls, Edward. S 14 yrs Sep-Oct T *Justitia* Dec 1774. M.

Nicholls, Emanuel. S Sep-Oct T Oct 1749 *Mary*. M.

Nicholls, George. S Sep T Oct 1750 *Rachael*. L.

Nicholls, George. S Apr T May 1752 *Lichfield*. L.

Nicholls, John. S Lent T May 1750 *Lichfield*. K.

Nichols, John. S Launceston May 1755 (AHJ). Co.

Nicholls, Mark. R 14 yrs Mar 1742 LC PG Co., Md. Co.

Nicholls, Mary. S Mar T from Liverpool Dec 1746. St.

Nicholls, Mary wife of John of Lambeth. S Summer T Oct 1750 *Rachael*. Sy.

Nichols, Mary. S s silver spoons Apr 1751 (WJ). Wa.

Nicholls, Matthias. S for life & T *Thames* Feb 1751. M.

Nicholls, Richard. S Sep 1740 T *Harpooner* Jan 1741. L.

Nicholls, Richard. S Apr T May 1751 *Tryal*. L.

Nicholls, Samuel. S Launceston Feb 1758 (AHJ). Co.

Nicholls, Thomas. S Summer 1746 T Jul 1747. Wa.

Nicholls, Walter. S Mar T *Thames* Mar 1754. L.

Nicholls, William. S Jul T Jul 1748 *Mary*. L.

Nicholls, William. S Launceston Apr 1753 (AHJ). Co.

Nicholls, William. R 14 yrs Mar 1754. O.

Nicholls, William. S Jul T *Beverly* Aug 1763. M.

Nicholson, Anthony. SQS Jul LC Bal Co., Md., Dec 1770.

Nicholson *als* Nicholls, Daniel. S Lent LC AA Co., Md., from *Thornton* Jul 1775. M.

Nicholson, George. S Lent T *Thornton* May LC AA Co., Md., Jul 1774. M.

Nightingale, Peter. S Lent R 14 yrs Summer 1758 TB to Va. No.

Nimmo, John. SQS Feb LC AA Co., Md., from *Thornton* Jul 1773. M.

Nisbee *als* Surrey, Susanna. S Dec 1753-Jan 1774 T *Thames* Mar 1754. M.

Nisbett, Richard. S Lent LC AA Co., Md., from *Thornton* Jul 1775. L.

Nisbett, William. S Lent R 14 yrs Summer T Sep 1751 *Greyhound*. Sy.

Nixon, Francis. S Sep-Oct 1772 T *Justitia* Jan 1773. M.

Nixon, Jane. S City Easter 1759 (AHJ). Nl.

Nixon, Margaret. S Summer 1772 LC Bal Co., Md., from *Adventure* Mar 1773. Du.

Nixon, Robert. S Aug 1737 T Feb 1738. Cu.

Noble, Jonathan. S Southwark Lent T *Thornton* May LC AA Co., Md., Jul 1774. Sy.

Noble, Mark. S s sheep Summer T *Ruby* Oct 1754. Bu.

Noble, Mary. S Lent T Apr 1757. Wa.

Nobody *als* Parsley, Mary of St. George, Southwark, spinster. SQS Jan T *Thames* Feb 1751. Sy.

Nodder, Sarah. S Lent LC Bal Co., Md., Jul 1774. Wi.

Noel, John. S Aug 1720 but then R without conditions. So.

Nolligg, Ephraim. S Lent LC Bal Co., Md., Jul 1774. Wi.

Nolly, Sarah. SQS Lent LC Bal Co., Md., Jul 1774. Wi.

Noon, John. S Oct-Dec 1754 T *Greyhound* Feb 1755. M.

MORE EMIGRANTS IN BONDAGE

Norbury, Elizabeth. S 14 yrs Lent but taken from transport ship & pardoned in April 1774. M.

Norbury, Hester. S Jan T Mar 1750 *Tryal*. L.

Norford, James. S Aug 1746 T Jul 1747. O.

Norgrave, Joseph. S s mare Summer 1755 R 14 yrs Lent 1756 TB to Md. No.

Norman, Anna Maria. S Lent T Jul 1745 *Italian Merchant*; runaway. K.

Norman, Mary. S May-Jul T Sep 1751 *Greyhound*. M.

Norman, Peter. S Jun 1739 T *Sea Nymph* to Md. L.

Norman, Philip. S Lent LC Bal Co., Md., Jul 1771. So.

Norridge, James. T May 1720 for robbing a church (NM). Le.

Norris, Francis. S Oct 1773 T *Justitia* Jan 1774. L.

Norris, John. T Sep 1737 *Pretty Patsy*.

Norris, John. S Oct T *Barnard* Oct 1756. M.

Norris, Richard. S Mar T *Neptune* Mar 1761. L.

Norris, Thomas. S 14 yrs Summer 1734 LC Knt Co., Md., from *Hawk* Apr 1735. So.

Norris, Thomas. SQS Feb T Mar 1750 *Tryal*. M.

North, Catherine. S Dec 1782 LC Bal Co., Md., Dec 1783 from *Swift* LC Bal Co., Md., Dec 1783 from *Swift*. L.

North, James. SQS Mar 1750 T *Happy Jennett* LC Md Oct 1751. Db.

North, John. S Lent but pardoned Jun 1773. M.

North, Thomas of Kidbrook. S Lent T Jul 1745 *Italian Merchant*. K.

North, William. S Jan 1717 T 14 yrs Sep 1718 *Eagle* LC Charles Town Mar 1719. L.

North, William. SQS Sep T *Justitia* Dec 1774. M.

Norton, James. S Apr T May 1750 *Lichfield*. L.

Norton, John. S Feb 1774 but pardoned in same month. L.

Norton, Mary wife of George. S Sep-Oct 1773 T *Justitia* Jan 1774. M.

Norton, Thomas. S May T *Saltspring* Jul 1775. L.

Norwood, Robert. S for life Lent LC AA Co., Md., from *Thornton* Jul 1775. K.

Noss *als* Nurse, William. S 14 yrs Lent 1750 LC QA Co., Md., from *Catherine* Nov 1750. Do.

Notere, Michael. S & T Aug 1752 *Tryal*. L.

Notson *als* Gibbons, Isabella. S Jan-Jun T Jul 1747 *Laura*. M.

Nott, Joan. T May 1746. De.

Nottage, John. S Lent LC AA Co., Md., from *Thornton* Jul 1775. E.

Nowell, Lamprey. S Sep T *Phoenix* Oct 1760. M.

Nowland, Sarah. S Lent T *Thornton* May LC AA Co., Md., Jul 1774. M.

Nugent, Mary of Manchester. SQS Jan 1722 TB Apr 1723. La.

Nunant, William. S Jun 1736. Y.

Nurse, Catherine. S Oct 1772 T *Justitia* Jan 1773. L.

Nurse, William (1750). *See* Noss. Do.

Nutbrown, John. S Jan T *Thames* Feb 1751. M.

Nutbrown, Miles. S Jan T *Thames* Feb 1751. M.

Nuthall, Thomas. S for killing sheep at Penn & R 14 yrs Aug 1770 LC Bal Co., Md., Jul 1771. St.

Nutkins, Thomas. S Jan-Apr T *Lichfield* May 1749. M.

Nutter, Elizabeth. S Apr-May T *Saltspring* Jul 1775. M.

Nutter, James. S for housebreaking R for life Jun 1771. Sco.

MORE EMIGRANTS IN BONDAGE

O'Brien, Loramy. S Jan T *Neptune* Mar 1761. M.

O'Brien, Thomas. S May-Jul T Aug 1749 *Thames*. M.

O'Brien, William. S Sep-Oct 1773 T *Justitia* Jan 1774. M.

O'Conner, Timothy. S Dec 1772 T *Justitia* Jan 1773. M.

O'Marsh, Catherine, spinster, *als* wife of James. S 14 yrs Feb-Apr T *Laura* Apr 1746. M.

O'Marsh, James. S 14 yrs Feb-Apr T *Laura* Apr 1746. M.

O'Marsh, Robert. S Feb-Apr T *Laura* Apr 1746. M.

O'Marsh, Thomas. S Feb-Apr T *Laura* Apr 1746. M.

O'Neal, Charles. S Apr T *Dolphin* May 1763. L.

O'Neil, Charles. SW Lent LC AA Co., Md., from *Thornton* Jul 1773. M.

O'Neal, Owen. SQS May T Sep 1751 *Greyhound*. M.

Oadway *als* Valentine, Mary. S Oct-Dec 1750 T *Thames* Feb 1751. M.

Oakes, Thomas. S Sep-Dec 1746 T Jan 1747 *George William*. M.

Oakley, Samuel. T May 1751 *Tryal*. Sy.

Oakley, Thomas. S Apr T May 1751 *Tryal*. L.

Oatie, William. S Lent LC Bal Co., Md., Jun 1773. Co.

Oatley, Margaret. S Oct T *Phoenix* Oct 1760. M.

Obney, Robert. S Jul T Aug 1749 *Thames*. L.

Obryan, William. S Summer 1718 LC from *Sophia* QA Co., Md. Mar 1719. Co.

Odderway, James. S Jan-Apr T *Lichfield* May 1749. M.

Odford, Thomas. S Lent LC Potomac, Va., from *Martha* Dec 1724. Do.

Odger, William. S Lent LC Bal Co., Md., Jun 1773. Co.

Odgers, Benjamin (1761) - *See* Harris, Francis. Co.

Odgers, John. S Summer 1738 LC QA Co., Md., *from Amity* Mar 1739. Co.

Ogborn, Robert. SQ Jan LC AA Co., Md., from *Thornton* Jul 1775. M.

Ogden, John. S Jun T *Maryland Packet* Oct 1761. M.

Ogden, Thomas of Manchester, linen weaver. SQS Oct 1730. La.

Ogle, Eleanor. S 14 yrs Sep-Oct 1775 T *Justitia* Feb 1776. M.

Ogleby, George. S May-Jul T *Mary* Sep 1746. M.

Oland, William. S Lent 1750 LC QA Co., Md., from *Catherine* Nov 1750. G.

Olborn *als* Osmond, Emanuel. S Exeter Apr 1752 (AHJ). De.

Old, John. S Summer 1741 R 14 yrs Feb T Apr 1742 LC PG Co., Md. Do.

Old, John. Held in prison to plead pardon Aug 1746. Do.

Oldbury, Mark. S Oct T *Justitia* Dec 1774. L.

Oldfield, Margaret wife of Michael, *als* Margaret Grigg. S Jan-Jun T Jul 1747 *Laura*. M.

Oldis, Sarah. S Mar R 14 yrs Aug T *Restoration* LC Bal Co., Md., Oct 1771. Do.

Oldman, Robert. S Apr T *Lichfield* May 1749. L.

Oliver, John. S Feb T Apr 1735 *Patapsco* LC Annapolis Oct 1735. M.

Oliver, John. S 1773 TB to Md. No.

Oliver, Mary. S Lent LC AA Co., Md., from *Hanover Planter* Jul 1773. L.

Oliver, Robert. T Sep 1737 *Pretty Patsy*. L.

Oliver, Sarah, spinster. S City Christmas 1756 (AHJ). Nl.

Oliver, Thomas. S Dec 1753-Jan 1754 T *Thames* Mar 1754. M.

Oliver, William. S Jun T *Tryal* Jul 1754. L.

Onion, Thomas. S Lent T *Dolphin* May 1763. E.

Onman, David. S Lent 1765. Li.

Orchard, Thomas. SQS Apr, respited but T *Thornton* May LC AA Co., Md Jul 1774. M.

Ord, Robert. SQS & T Jul 1773 *Tayloe* to Va. M.

Orgar, Edward. S Lent LC AA Co., Md., from *Thornton* Jul 1775. E.

Orton *als* Holton, John. S Jan T *Thames* Feb 1751. M.

Orton, Thomas. T *Dolphin* May 1763. M.

Orton, William. S Summer 1743 R 14 yrs Feb 1744. So.

Osborne, Elizabeth. S Lent T Dec 1733. Bd.

Osborn, Joseph. S Lent LC AA Co., Md., from *Thornton* Jul 1773. M.

Osborne *als* Braley, Mary of Ardley, spinster. SQS Jan T *Dolphin* Apr 1761; runaway (AHJ). E.

Osborne, Samuel. S Lent 1752 T Feb 1753. Db.

Osborne, William. S Feb-Apr T May 1751 *Tryal*. M.

Osmand, Alice. S Jan T May 1746. Wi.

Osmond, Ann. SQS Oct 1742 LC Knt Co., Md., from *Globe* Mar 1744. De.

Osmond, Emanuel (1752) - *See* Olborn. De.

Osmonds, John. T May 1755 *Rose*. Sy.

Othen, Samuel. S Lent LC AA Co., Md., from *Thornton* Jul 1775. M.

Ottley, Susannah. R for pulling down mills Summer 1772 T *Justitia* Jan 1773. E.

Overan, John. SQS Aug 1773 T *Thornton* May LC AA Co., Md., Jul 1774. Sy.

Overbury, Robert. S Apr 1746 T Apr 1746 *Laura*. M.

Overton, John *als* William. S s at Christchurch Summer LC Md from *William* Dec 1774 & sold to James Hutchings. Mo.

Owen, Edward. S Apr T Jun 1746. Mo.

Owen, Elizabeth. S Jan-Apr T Jun 1748 *Lichfield*. M.

Owen, Hugh. S Jul T *Beverly* Aug 1763. M.

Owen, John. S s mare Summer 1754 R 14 yrs Lent 1755 (GJ). Mo.

Owen *als* Gardner, Margaret. S Feb T 14 yrs Apr 1735 *Patapsco* LC Annapolis Oct 1735. L.

Owen, Mary. S Jun-Dec 1745 T *Plain Dealer* Jan 1746. M.

Owen, Samuel. S Jan T *Justitia* May 1745. L.

Owen *als* Freeman, Thomas. S Jun 1739 T *Sea Nymph* to Md. L.

Owen, William. R 14 yrs s naval stores Lent T May 1750 *Lichfield*. K.

Owen, William. S Summer LC Bal Co., Md., Dec 1770 from *Trotman* & sold to John Price Jr. Y.

Owens, Edward. S Montgomery R 14 yrs Jul 1764. Wal.

Owens, William. S Lent T *Thornton* May LC AA Co., Md., Jul 1774. L.

Oxtoby, William. R 14 yrs Jul T *Saltspring* Jul 1775. M.

Oyer, James. T May 1750 *Lichfield*. K.

Packer, Daniel. S Summer 1773 T *Justitia* Jan 1774. Bu.

Paddison, William. S s sheep Lent R 14 yrs Summer 1747 LC Md from *St. George* Mar 1748. Li.

Paddock, Joseph. S Lent T Apr 1753. Wa.

Pady, Thomas. S Summer T Aug 1749 *Thames*. E.

Pagans, Thomas. S Summer T Aug 1749 *Thames*. Sy.

Page, Ann, *als* Willis, Mary. S Jul-Dec 1747 LC Knt Co., Md., from *St. George* Mar 1748. M.

Page, Benjamin. S Summer 1739. Nf.

Page, Edward. T Apr 1735 *Patapsco* LC Annapolis Oct 1735. Sy.

Page, Jane. S Oct T *Barnard* Oct 1756. L.

Page, John. S Apr-May T *Tryal* Jul 1754. M.

Page, John. S Lent T Apr 1774 TB to Md. No.

Page, Judith. S Oct-Dec 1750 T *Thames* Feb 1751. M.

Page, Mary. S Jul respited Aug but T Nov 1762 *Prince William* . M.

Pagent, Thomas. S s gold rings Feb 1738 (RM). Ha.

Pagett, Edward. S Jul T *Saltspring* Jul 1775. L.

Pagett, John. S for highway robbery Lent 1757, broke out of gaol & R 14 yrs Lent 1760. St.

Pagram, Mary. S Feb-Apr T *Laura* Apr 1746. M.

Pain(e). *See* Payne.

Painter, Samuel. S Summer 1733. No.

Paling, Thomas. S 14 yrs LC Bal Co., Md., Jul 1772. He.

Pallett, William (1774). *See* Aylett. Ht.

Palmer, Ann. S Apr T Jun 1748 *Lichfield*. L.

Palmer, Bridget. S Summer T *Maryland Packet* Oct 1761. K.

Palmer, Catherine. T Sep 1737 *Pretty Patsy*. L.

Palmer [Paliner], Catherine. S s sheep & R 14 yrs Lent T Sep 1768. Li.

Palmer, Diana. T May 1746. De.

Palmer, Elizabeth. S May-Jul T Jul 1748 *Mary*. M.

Palmer, Henry. S Lent LC AA Co., Md., from *Thornton* Jul 1773. M.

Palmer, John. S Lent 1733 LC Knt Co., Md., from *Hawk* Apr 1735. So.

Palmer, John. SQS Jul 1738 LC QA Co., Md. Jun 1739. So.

Palmer, John. SWK Jan LC AA Co., Md., from *Thornton* Jul 1775. K.

Palmer, Robert. S 14 yrs Summer 1734 LC Knt Co., Md., Mar 1735 from *Falcon*. Ha.

Palmer, Thomas. S Apr T May 1750 *Lichfield*. M.

Palmer, William. SQS Wells Jan 1733 LC Knt Co., Md., from *Falcon* Apr 1734. So.

Palmer, William. SQS May respited Jul 1774. M.

Pankhurst, Thomas. R 14 yrs Jul T *Phoenix* Oct 1760. K.

Pankin, Paul. T Jul 1747 *Laura*. M.

Pantall, Thomas. S s sheep Summer 1748 R 14 yrs Lent LC Md from *Chester* Nov 1749. He.

Paradice, Francis Jr. S Jul 1766, appeal rejected & TB to Va Apr 1767. Wi.

Paramour, Phoebe. T May 1751 *Tryal*. K.

Pardo, Mary. S Jan T *Plain Dealer* Jan 1746. L.

Parford, William. S Apr 1746 T Apr 1746 *Laura*. M.

Pargiter, William. S s hog Summer T Aug 1752 *Tryal*. Bu.

Parish, Benjamin. S Summer T *Barnard* Oct 1756. Bu.

Parish, George. S May-Jul T Aug 1749 *Thames*. M.

Parish, James. SW Apr T *Thornton* May LC AA Co., Md., Jul 1774. M.

Parrish, John (1738). *See* Selly. Ca.

Parish, Thomas. SW Lent LC AA Co., Md., from *Hanover Planter* Jul 1773. M.

Parker, Ann. S Apr T *Phoenix* Oct 1760. M.

Parker, Edward. S Lent 1735. No.

Parker, Elizabeth. S Lent LC AA Co., Md., from *Thornton* Jul 1775. M.

Parker, John. S s shirts Apr T Dec 1735 *John* LC Annapolis Sep 1736. M.

Parker, John. S Mar T Apr 1737. Wa.

Parker, John. S for perjury Lent R 14 yrs Summer 1742 (IJ). Su.

Parker, Joseph. S Jan T Mar 1750 *Tryal*. L.

Parker, Joseph. S s wooden hoops at Dudley Summer LC Md *William* Dec 1774 & sold to Joshua Hall; runaway. Wo.

Parker, Mary. S Oct-Dec 1750 T *Thames* Feb 1751. M.

Parker, Mary. S Lent LC Bal Co., Md., Jul 1772. St.

MORE EMIGRANTS IN BONDAGE

Parker, Richard. S Sep T Oct 1750 *Rachael*. L.

Parker, Robert of Chew Magna. SQS Wells Jan 1728 but recommended for pardon as he has 5 children. So.

Parker, Samuel. S Apr T Jun 1748 *Lichfield*. L.

Parker, Susanna. S Jan T Mar 1750 *Tryal*. L.

Parker, William. S Summer 1736 & T from Hull. Y.

Parker, William. S Sep-Oct 1772 T *Justitia* Jan 1773. M.

Parks, George. S Summer 1737 T Jan 1738. Wa.

Parkes, Giles. S Jul T *Tayloe* Jul 1774. L.

Parkes, Joseph. S Summer LC Bal Co., Md., Dec 1772. Wa.

Parks, Sampson. T May 1755 *Rose*. K.

Parks, William. S for house breaking Summer 1749 R 14 yrs Lent 1750 LC QA Co., Md., from *Chester* Dec 1752. St.

Parkhurst, James. S 14 yrs Lent LC AA Co., Md., from *Thornton* May 1771. Sx.

Parle, James. S Lent LC Bal Co., Md., Jun 1773. He.

Parley, Daniel. SQS Jul 1755. Db.

Parlow, James. S s handkerchiefs Mar 1771 (HJ). He.

Parlo, James. S s sheep & R 14 yrs Aug 1772 LC Bal Co., Md., Jun 1773. He.

Parlour, John. S 14 yrs Summer 1749 LC QA Co., Md., from *Catherine* Nov 1750. He.

Parnell, Elizabeth. S Lent T May 1752 *Lichfield*. Sy.

Parnell, Nurse. S May-Jul T *Tayloe* Jul 1773. M.

Parr, Thomas. S Lent T *Dolphin* May 1763. K.

Parratt, Richard. S & R s horse Summer T Oct 1738. Bd.

Parrott, Elizabeth. S Apr T May 1752 *Lichfield*. L.

Parrott, John. S s shirts Apr T Dec 1735 *John* LC Annapolis Sep 1736. M.

Parrott, John. S for life Summer 1771 LC Bal Co., Md., Jul 1772. Wi.

Parrott, John (1774). *See* Sparrow. M.

Parrott, Leonard. T 1745. Y.

Parry, John. S for life Lent T *Thornton* May LC AA Co., Md., Jul 1774. K.

Parry, John. S s oxen & R Summer LC Md *William* Dec 1774 & sold to William Lux. Mo.

Parry, Mary, spinster. SQS Bristol Aug 1743 LC Knt Co., Md., from *Raven* Feb 1744. G.

Parry, Thomas. S for demolishing water mill of John Parry at Kingsland Mar & R 14 yrs Lent 1775; escaped while under guard to join ship and not recaptured (HJ). He.

Parry, William. S for murder Lent 1724 R 14 yrs Lent 1725. Sh.

Parry, William. S Bala s horse R 14 yrs Apr 1768. Wal.

Parsley, Henry. S Feb T *Thames* Mar 1752. L.

Parsons *als* Ruffler, George. T May 1747. So.

Parsons, George. S Jun T Jul 1747 *Laura*. L.

Parsons, John. SQS Jan 1741 LC QA Co., Md., from *Philleroy* Apr 1742. He.

Parsons, John. S Apr T May 1747. So.

Parsons, Margaret. S May-Jul T *Tayloe* Jul 1773. M.

Parsons, Richard. S Lent R 14 yrs Summer T Aug 1749 *Thames*. K.

Parsons, William. S for highway robbery Summer 1761 R 14 yrs Lent 1762 TB to Md. No.

Partin, Thomas. S Lent T *Lichfield* May 1749. Sy.

Partridge, Joseph. S Apr-Jun 1739 T *Sea Nymph* to Md. M.

Partridge, Matthew of Romford. SQS Jan T May 1750 *Lichfield*. E.

Partridge, Richard. S Jul LC Bal Co., Md., Dec 1783 from *Swift*. M.

Pascoe, John. S Summer 1731 LC Knt Co., Md., from *Falcon* Apr 1732. Co.

Pascoe, John. S Plymouth Aug 1751 (AHJ). De.

Pascoe, Joseph (1771). *See* Edy. De.

Paskey, Edith. S Bristol Jan 1757 (AHJ). G.

Passenger, Jonathan. S 14 yrs Lent 1744 LC Knt Co., Md., from *Susannah* Aug 1744. De.

Patch, John. S Sep-Oct 1773 T *Justitia* Jan 1774. M.

Pate, Bernard. T 1751. Li.

Pateman, Ann wife of John. S Apr T *Dolphin* Apr 1761. M.

Patmore, Benjamin. S Lent LC AA Co., Md., from *Thornton* Jul 1775. K.

Patrick, John. SQS Bury St. Edmunds 1766. Su.

Patrickson, Thomas. T 1747 from Whitehaven. Cu.

Patridge, Love. SQS Apr 1732 LC Knt Co., Md., from *Falcon* Apr 1734. So.

Pattenden, John. S for sending threatening letters Summer 1760 R 14 yrs Lent T *Dolphin* Apr 1761. K.

Paterson *als* Anderson *als* Isedale, Isabella. S Oct T *Phoenix* Oct 1760. M.

Patterson, Robert. SQS Jan S Lent LC Bal Co., Md., Jul 1772. De.

Patterson, Robert. S Summer 1772 LC Bal Co., Md., from *Adventure* Mar 1773. Nl.

Patterson, William of Albourne. S Summer 1772 T *Justitia* Jan 1773. Sx.

Pattin *als* Perrin, Elizabeth. S Bristol Nov 1749 LC QA Co., Md., from *Catherine* Nov 1750. G.

Pattin, John. S Jan T *Thames* Feb 1751. L.

Pattison, William. S Jun 1739 T *Sea Nymph* to Md. L.

Pattson, John. S 14 yrs Lent LC AA Co., Md., from *Thornton* Jul 1773. K.

Patty, Charles. S Summer 1718 LC from *Sophia* QA Co., Md. Mar 1719. Co.

Patty, David. S Lent 1737 LC Knt Co., Md., from *Hawk* Nov 1737. De.

Patty, John. SQS Oct 1770 LC Bal Co., Md., Jun 1771. De.

Paul, Aaron. S City Christmas 1749 (AHJ). Nl.

Paul, Elizabeth. S Summer T Sep 1766. Li.

Paul, Ely. S Jan-Apr T Jun 1748 *Lichfield*. M.

Paul, Gabriel. S Jan-Apr T Jun 1748 *Lichfield*. M.

Pavior, John. SQS Jan 1734 LC Knt Co., Md., from *Hawk* Apr 1735. So.

Paxton, Charles. S May-Jul T Aug 1749 *Thames*. M.

Paxton, Elizabeth. S Feb-Apr T May 1751 *Tryal*. M.

Paylin, Frederick William. S Jul LC Bal Co., Md., Dec 1783 from *Swift*. M.

Paine, Abraham. R Apr T Nov 1747. So.

Pain *als* Waldron, Joan. S Summer 1747 R 14 yrs Mar 1748. De.

Payne, Constabella. S s silver caster Jul T Dec 1735 *John* LC Annapolis Sep 1736. M.

Paine, Edward. S Sep 1740 T *Harpooner* Jan 1741. L.

Paine, Edward. S Jan-Jun T Jul 1747 *Laura*. M.

Payne, Edward. S Lent R 14 yrs Summer T *Phoenix* Oct 1760. Sy.

Payne, Martha. S 14 yrs Jul-Dec 1747 T *St. George* Jan LC Knt Co., Md., Mar 1748. M.

Pain, Mary. S 14 yrs Lent 1744 LC Knt Co., Md., from *Susannah* Aug 1744. De.

Paine, Thomas. S s goods from manor house Summer T Oct 1726 *Forward*. Bu.

Payne, William. S & T Mar 1750 *Tryal*. L.

Payne, William. S 14 yrs S Lent LC AA Co., Md., from *Thornton* Jul 1773. K.

Peacock, Jeremiah. S Feb T *Neptune* Mar 1761. L.

Peacock, John. S Lent 1724 but escaped & no further record found. Li.

Peacock, Richard. S Feb-Apr T May 1751 *Tryal*. M.

Peacock, Susannah. S Lent 1759 (BJ). G.

MORE EMIGRANTS IN BONDAGE

Peacock, Thomas. T Jan 1756 *Greyhound*. Ht.

Peacock, William. S s horse Summer 1729 R 14 yrs Summer 1730. Nl.

Peacock, William. S Lent R 14 yrs Summer T Aug 1752 *Tryal*. Sy.

Peacock, William. S Dec 1754 T *Greyhound* Feb 1755. L.

Peacod, Richard. S & T Jan 1736 *Dorsetshire* LC Va Sep 1736. L.

Peake, Dorothy. S Apr T *Dolphin* Apr 1761. L.

Peake, John. S Summer T Sep 1751 *Greyhound*. Sy.

Peak, Sarah. S Oct T Oct 1749 *Mary*. L.

Peak, Thomas. T 1746. Su.

Peake, William. S Lent 1724 but escaped & no further record found. Li.

Peale, Charles. S s gelding & T for life Jan 1736 *Dorsetshire* LC Va Sep 1736. L.

Peale, James. T May 1752 *Lichfield*. Sy.

Pearce, Abram. S Sep 1733 T Jan 1734 *Caesar* LC Va Jul 1734. M.

Pearse, Andrew. T May 1751 *Tryal*. M.

Pearce, Charles. T May 1755 *Rose*. Sy.

Pearce, Elizabeth. S Summer 1733 LC Knt Co., Md., from *Falcon* Apr 1734. De.

Pearce, John. S Summer 1731 LC Knt Co., Md., from *Falcon* Apr 1732. De.

Pearce, John. S Summer 1732 LC Knt Co., Md., from *Falcon* Mar 1733. Co.

Pearse, John. R 14 yrs Mar T Apr 1742 LC PG Co., Md. Co.

Pearce, John. S 14 yrs Summer 1743 LC Knt Co., Md., from *Globe* Mar 1744. De.

Pearce, John. S Plymouth Jul 1755 (AHJ). De.

Pearce, Joseph. S & R Lent T May 1755. G.

Pearce als Newport, Richard. S 14 yrs Summer 1732 LC Knt Co., Md., from *Falcon*
    Mar 1733. Do.

Pearse, Richard. S Summer 1741 LC QA Co., Md., from *Philleroy* Apr 1742. Wi.

Pearce, Sarah. S May-Jun T Aug 1752 *Tryal*. M.

Pearce, Thomas (1732) - *See* Stephens. Co.

Pearce, Thomas. S Jan T Apr 1735 *Patapsco* LC Annapolis Oct 1735. M.

Pearce, Thomas. S Jan T *Neptune* Mar 1761. M.

Pearce, Thomas. S Lent 1774 but removed from transport ship for poor health &
    pardoned. L.

Pearce, William. S Summer 1732 LC Knt Co., Md., from *Falcon* Mar 1733. Co.

Peirse, William. S Summer 1737 LC QA Co., Md., from *Amity* Apr 1738. De.

Peirce, William. S Lent LC AA Co., Md., from *Thornton* May 1771. L.

Peirse, William. S Dec T *Justitia* Dec 1774; runaway. L.

Pearcehouse, Thomas. SQS May T Jul 1773 *Tayloe* to Va. M.

Pearcey, Ann. T Apr 1735 *Patapsco* LC Annapolis Oct 1735. E.

Pearson, Hugh. S s horse Summer 1729 R 14 yrs Summer 1730 AT Summer 1732. Nl.

Peirson, John. S Summer 1736. Y.

Peirson, John. S for life Jan T *Justitia* May 1745. L.

Pearson, John. T May 1751 *Tryal*. K.

Pearson, Nathaniel. S Apr T May 1752 *Lichfield*. L.

Peart, Thomas. S Oct 1751-Jan 1752 T *Thames* Mar 1752. M.

Peate, John. SQS Feb T May 1752 *Lichfield*. M.

Peat, Richard Denton. S Dec 1753-Jan 1754 T *Thames* Mar 1754. M.

Peate, Thomas. S Summer T Sep 1753. St.

Pebworth *als* Smith, Mary. S Jul-Dec 1747 LC Knt Co., Md., from *St. George* Mar
    1748. M.

Peck, Ann. T Oct 1750 *Rachael*. M.

Peck, Mary. T *Tryal* Mar 1757. L.

Pelling, John. T 14 yrs Aug 1752 *Tryal*. K.

Pellingham, Jane. R for Barbados Dec 1671 but LC Md from *William & Mary* Mar 1672. M.

Penchbeck - *See* Pinchbeck.

Pendro, Thomas. S s sheep Summer 1743 R 14 yrs Lent 1744 (GJ). He.

Penfold, Thomas of West Hoathly. S Summer 1772 T *Justitia* Jan 1773. Sx.

Penford, Daniel. S Jul 1736 S Jul 1736 LC QA Co., Md., from *Amity* May 1737. Ha.

Pengelly, Alexander. S Lent 1732 LC Knt Co., Md., from *Falcon* Mar 1733. So.

Pengilly, John. SQS Jul 1738 LC QA Co., Md. Jun 1739. De.

Pengelly, Thomas. S for life Lent LC Bal Co., Md., Jul 1771. De.

Penington, John. SQS Jan LC AA Co., Md., from *Thornton* Jul 1775. Ht.

Penn, John. S Lent T May 1749 *Lichfield*. Ht.

Penn, Matthew. S Summer T Sep 1751 *Greyhound*. Sy.

Penn, Matthew. T for life & T *Grange Bay* Jul 1772. Ht.

Pennell, Thomas. S Dec 1746 T Jan 1747 *George William*. L.

Pennick, Joseph. T *Randolph* Sep 1768. Do.

Penny, George. S for shoplifting Lent 1729 R 14 yrs Mar 1731. Wi.

Penrice, Lawrence. S & T Sep 1751 *Greyhound*. L.

Perceval, James. S Lent 1745 T Jan 1746. No.

Percival, Mary. S Feb T Jul 1747. Nf.

Perigo, Thomas (1740) - *See* Perry. He.

Perkins, Anne wife of John (*qv*). SQS Sep 1741 LC QA Co., Md., from *Philleroy* Apr 1742. Co.

Perkins, Ann. S Jun-Dec 1745 T *Plain Dealer* Jan 1746. M.

Perkins, John. SQS Sep 1741 LC QA Co., Md., from *Philleroy* Apr 1742. Co.

Perkins, Richard. S 14 yrs Summer 1738 LC QA Co., Md. Jun 1739. De.

Perkins, William. S Summer T Sep 1751 *Greyhound*. K.

Perkins, William. S Lent T *Tryal* Jul 1754. K.

Perrier, Peter. S Lent T *Thornton* May LC AA Co., Md., Jul 1774. L.

Perriman, Betty. S Aug T *Restoration* LC Bal Co., Md., Oct 1771. So.

Perrin, Sarah. S Oct T *Maryland Packet* Oct 1761. L.

Perry, Ann. S Jan T *Plain Dealer* Jan 1746. M.

Perry, George. S Sep T Oct 1750 *Rachael*. M.

Perry, James. S Southwark Mar LC AA Co., Md., from *Thornton* Jul 1775. Sy.

Perry, John. S Dec 1782 LC Bal Co., Md., Dec 1783 from *Swift* LC Bal Co., Md., Dec 1783 from *Swift*. L.

Perry, Martha of Wethersfield, spinster. SQS Jul T Aug 1752 *Tryal*. E.

Perry, Peter. S Summer T Aug 1749 *Thames*. Sy.

Perry, Ralph. S Summer LC Knt Co., Md., from *Bideford* Nov 1737. So.

Perry *als* Preece *als* Perigo, Thomas. S for breaking highway toll barrier at Norton Lent 1735; escaped from Stafford & Liverpool Gaols & executed at Stafford in Lent 1743. He.

Perry, Thomas. S & R 14 yrs Lent 1773 but not taken to Bristol in Apr 1773 because dangerously ill. Wo.

Perry, Thomas. S Jan-Apr T *Lichfield* May 1749. M.

Perry, William. S Summer 1765, broke gaol but was recaptured. K.

Perton, Winifred. S 14 yrs for receiving money stolen by Mary Meirick (*q.v.*) Aug 1764. He.

Peryn, Samuel of Axbridge, husbandman. R for Barbados Feb 1673 but LC Md in 1673. So.

Peter, William. S Southwark Lent T *Thornton* May LC AA Co., Md., Jul 1774. Sy.

Peters, Hugh. SQS Jan 1731 LC Knt Co., Md., from *Falcon* Apr 1732. Co.

Peto, Thomas. S Oct T *Justitia* Dec 1774. L.

Petter, William. S Southwark Mar LC AA Co., Md., from *Thornton* Jul 1775. Sy.

Pettin, Ann wife of Robert. S Lent LC AA Co., Md., from *Thornton* Jul 1775. M.

Pettit, Sarah. S Jan T *Neptune* Mar 1761. M.

Petit, Thomas. T May 1752 *Lichfield*. K.

Pettit, William. S City Christmas 1758 (AHJ). Nl.

Pettitt, Sarah. S Lent T *Thornton* May LC AA Co., Md., Jul 1774. E.

Petty, Francis. S Lent R 14 yrs Dec 1726. Su.

Petty, Thomas. S Lent LC Potomac, Va., from *Martha* Dec 1724. Wi.

Pevett *als* Goddard, Elizabeth. S Feb T *Tryal* Mar 1757. M.

Peyton, Ann wife of Richard. S Dec 1760 T *Neptune* Mar 1761. M.

Phasoo, Joseph *als* Barnard. S Jul LC Bal Co., Md., Dec 1783 from *Swift*. M.

Phelps, Mary. S Lent T Jun 1748 *Lichfield*. Sy.

Phillips, Benjamin. S Lent LC Bal Co., Md., Jun 1773. Wo.

Phillips, Edward. S Apr T May 1750 *Lichfield*. M.

Phillips, Edward. S Apr T May 1751 *Tryal*. L.

Phillips, Elizabeth. S Jul T Aug 1749 *Thames*. L.

Phillips, Elizabeth. S Jul T *Tayloe* Jul 1774. L.

Phillips, Evan. S s gelding at Cleobury & R 14 yrs Jul T *Restoration* LC Bal Co., Md., Oct 1771. Sh.

Phillips, Hannah. S Jun-Dec 1745 T *Plain Dealer* Jan 1746. M.

Phillips, Henry. S s horse Lent R 14 yrs Summer 1753 (GJ). Mo.

Phillips, James. R Jul LC Md *William* Dec 1774 & sold to John Stork. Ha.

Phillips, John. S Jan-Apr T *Lichfield* May 1749. M.

Phillips, John. S Apr-May T *Tryal* Jul 1754. M.

Phillips, John. S for highway robbery & R for life Aug 1770 T Aug T *Restoration* LC Bal Co., Md., Oct 1771. Wa.

Phillips, John. S May-Jul T *Tayloe* Jul 1773. M.

Phillips, Moses. S Jul T *Tayloe* Jul 1774. L.

Phillips, Richard of St. David's, blacksmith. S Pembroke s sheep R 14 yrs Jun 1766. Wal.

Phillips, Thomas of St. John's. SQS Apr T May 1750 *Lichfield*. Sy.

Phillips, Thomas. S Mar LC Md *William* Dec 1774 & sold to James Hutchings. So.

Phillips, Thomas. AT Lent T May 1775. Li.

Phillips, William. S Jun 1718 T Feb 1719 *Worcester* LC Annapolis Jun 1719. L.

Philpott, Edward. S Summer T from Bristol Oct 1754. G.

Philpott, Henry. T May 1752 *Lichfield*. K.

Philpot, Mary. S Lent T *Dolphin* May 1763. Sy.

Phipps, Edward. T *Justitia* Dec 1774. M.

Phipps, James. S Lent T *Dolphin* May 1763. Bu.

Phipps, Mary. S Aug T Oct 1751. Wa.

Phipps, Thomas. S as pickpocket & R 14 yrs Jun 1740. Le.

Piceford, Robert. R 14 yrs Mar T Apr 1742 LC PG Co., Md. Do.

Pickell, Henry. R for life Lent T *Tayloe* Jul 1773. Ht.

Pickering, Hannah. S Lent 1735. Y.

Pickering, John. T May 1751 *Tryal*. E.

Pickering, John. SQS Feb T *Thornton* May LC AA Co., Md., Jul 1774. M.

Pickering, Samuel. S Lent 1770. Wa.

Pickett, Henry. S for life Lent LC AA Co., Md., from *Thornton* Jul 1773. Ht.

Pickford, Mark. S 14 yrs Lent LC Knt Co., Md., from *Bideford* Nov 1737. So.

Picraft, John. S Apr 1773 LC Bal Co., Md., sold to Edward Cockey. Nt.

Picton, Margaret. T Apr 1735 *Patapsco* LC Annapolis Oct 1735. Sy.

Piddington, Edward. S for highway robbery Summer 1758 R 14 yrs Lent 1759 TB to Md. No.

Piddon, Edward (1757) - *See* Smith. Ha.

Pidgeon, Mary wife of John, *als* Mary Evatt. S Sep-Dec 1746 T Jan 1747 *George William*. M.

Piercy, Charles. S Summer LC Bal Co., Md., Dec 1772. Wa.

Pierpoint, George. S s silver & plate Aug 1763. Wa.

Pierson?, Mary. S Summer LC Bal Co., Md., Dec 1770 from *Trotman* & sold to John Males. X.

Pierson, William. S & T Sep 1751 *Greyhound*. M.

Pilbean, John. S Sep-Oct 1775 T *Justitia* Feb 1776. M.

Pill, Isaac. S Launceston Jan 1757 (AHJ). Co.

Pillsworth, John of Theydon Garnon. SQS Jul T Sep 1751 *Greyhound*. E.

Pim, Thomas. T May 1752 *Lichfield*. K.

Pinchbeck, Benjamin. S Lent 1724 but escaped & no further record found. Li.

Penchbeck, Richard. S Aug 1752. Li.

Pinchen, Francis. S Lent LC Potomac, Va., from *Martha* Dec 1724. Wi.

Pindar, William. S Lent 1732. Li.

Pinfield, John. S Mar T Apr LC Bal Co., Md., Jul 1771; runaway. Wa.

Pink, Richard. T May 1751 *Tryal*. Sx.

Pinkney, Isaac. SQS Beccles 1771. Su.

Pinkstone, Thomas. S for life Lent LC AA Co., Md., from *Thornton* Jul 1775. M.

Pinn, William of Wimbledon. SQS Summer 1748 R 14 yrs Lent T *Lichfield* May 1749. Sy.

Pinnell, Thomas. SQS s rags May 1754 & respited (OJ). O.

Pinney, John. S Mar T Apr 1746. Sh.

Pinnigar, Joseph. S Lent LC Bal Co., Md., Jul 1771. Wi.

Piper, Richard. S Feb T *Thames* Mar 1752. L.

Pipp, Joseph. S Mar LC Bal Co., Md Jul 1774; George & James Pipp S to 6 months' hard labour. Wi.

Pippen, John. S Summer 1718 LC from *Sophia* QA Co., Md. Mar 1719. So.

Pippin *als* Pepper, Richard. S Apr-May T *Tryal* Jul 1754. M.

Pitchford, John. S Lent T Summer 1752. Wa.

Pitman *als* Bealing, John. SQS Jan 1737 LC QA Co., Md., from *Amity* Apr 1738. Do.

Pitman, Mary. S Jul T oct 1747. Do.

Pitt, John. S Bristol Mar 1754. G.

Pitt, Joseph. S Lent T *Lichfield* May 1749. Sy.

Pitt, Richard. R Jul T *Tayloe* Jul 1774. M.

Pitt, William Moss. S 14 yrs Lent LC Bal Co., Md., Jun 1773; runaway. Wi.

Pittam, John. S Jul T *Beverly* Aug 1763. M.

Pitts, Charles. S Feb T *Thames* Mar 1754. M.

Pixley, John. S Summer 1739. Nf.

Pixley, Thomas. S Jul T *Saltspring* Jul 1775. L.

Place, Joseph. S Norwich Summer T Sep 1739. Nf.

Plackett, John. S Apr T May 1751 *Tryal*. L.

Plaile, Jeremiah. S Lent T Apr 1746. E.

Plaistow, Samuel. R Jul T *Tayloe* Jul 1773. M.

MORE EMIGRANTS IN BONDAGE

Plaize, Elizabeth. T 1751. So.

Plant, John. S Apr 1755. Li.

Plant, Thomas. S for returning from T Lent 1741 (GJ). St.

Platt, John. S Lent T *Thornton* May LC AA Co., Md., Jul 1774. M.

Platt, William. S Lent T Jun 1748 *Lichfield*. E.

Pleasants, Charles. TB Sep 1766 *Justitia* but respited. M.

Plodd, John Henry. S Jul T *Tayloe* Jul 1773. L.

Ploser *als* Plaser, Christopher. R Jun 1737 T Jan 1738 *Dorsetshire* . E.

Plow, Susan. SQS Beccles 1758. Su.

Plowman, Mary. S Mar 1735 T *Amity* LC QA Co., Md., Mar 1736. So.

Plumb, John. S Feb but received a free pardon and taken from transport ship Mar 1773. L.

Plumbtree, John. S Apr 1758. Li.

Plume, Samuel. S for shopbreaking at Redlingfield Lent 1740 (IJ). Su.

Plumer, William. SQS Sep 1772 T *Justitia* Jan 1773. M.

Plummer, Charles. S s coach seat Apr T May 1718 *Tryal* . L.

Plunkett, Ann. S s human hair Sep 1735 T Jan 1736 *Dorsetshire* LC Va Sep 1736. M.

Plunkett, Robert of Christchurch. SQS Jan T *Thames* Feb 1751. Sy.

Plymouth, Susanna. S Jul T Aug 1749 *Thames*. L.

Pobgee, William. S Summer 1772 T *Justitia* Jan 1773. Sy.

Pocock, Robert. S Summer T Sep 1751 *Greyhound*. Sy.

Podmore, John. S for housebreaking Aug 1753 R 14 yrs Lent 1754 (WJ). St.

Poe, George. S Summer 1741 LC QA Co., Md., from *Philleroy* Apr 1742. De.

Poe, John. S & T for life Mar 1750 *Tryal*. L.

Pointer als Foreman, Richard. SQS Jul 1738 LC Knt Co., Md., *from Hawk* Apr 1739. Wi.

Pointon, William of Manchester. SQS Jan 1722 TB Apr 1723. La.

Poker *als* Rand *als* Cole, John. S Jan-Apr T *Lichfield* May 1749. M.

Polkinghorne, Grace. SQS & T Apr 1742 LC PG Co., Md. Co.

Pollard, Andrew. S Lent T *Dolphin* Apr 1761. E.

Pollard *als* Gillett, Mary. S Apr T *Lichfield* May 1749. L.

Pollard, Mary. S Apr-May T *Saltspring* Jul 1775. M.

Pollard, William. S Jan T Mar 1750 *Tryal*. L.

Pollet, William. S Oct T *Justitia* Dec 1774. L.

Polson, Elizabeth. S s clothing Apr T May 1718 *Tryal* . L.

Pomfrett, Edward. S Sep-Oct T Oct 1749 *Mary*. M.

Pomphrey, James. S s shirt Feb but died on passage in *Patapsco* 1730. M.

Pong, Lettice. S Jan T *Plain Dealer* Jan 1746. M.

Poole, Lewis. S & T Jan 1736 *Dorsetshire* LC Va Sep 1736. L.

Pool, Robert. S Lent LC Potomac, Va., from *Martha* Dec 1724. So.

Pope, Isaac, notorious smuggler. S East Grinstead Apr T Jun 1738 *Forward*. Sx.

Pope, Jeremy. S Lent 1737. Li.

Pope, John. S Lent T *Thornton* May LC AA Co., Md., Jul 1774. K.

Pope, William. S Jul T Aug 1749 *Thames*. L.

Porte, Henry. S Dec 1773 T *Justitia* Jan 1774. L.

Porter, John. S Feb-Apr T May 1752 *Lichfield*. M.

Porter, Mary. S Jul T *Tayloe* Jul 1773. L.

Porter, Rebecca. S Jul T Jul 1748 *Mary*. L.

Porter, William of St. Saviour Southwark. R for Barbados Jun 167 but LC Md from *William & Mary* Mar 1672. Sy.

Porter, William of Blackburn. SQS Jan 1719. La.

Porter, William. S but respited for report Mar T 14 yrs Apr 1768 *Thornton* . K.

Porter, William. S Oct 1772 T *Justitia* Jan 1773. L.

Portess, William. S Lent T May 1750 *Lichfield*. K.

Postern *als* Poston, William. S s sheep Summer 1753 R 14 yrs Lent 1754 (GJ). He.

Poston, William (1753) - *See* Postern. He.

Potter, Charles. S Apr T *Phoenix* Oct 1760. M.

Potter, Elizabeth wife of Samuel Jr. SQS Lent T Oct 1751. Y.

Potter, George. S Sep-Oct T Oct 1749 *Mary*. M.

Potter, Jeremiah. S s at Chesham Lent T *Greyhound* Feb 1754. Bu.

Potter, William. S Feb T *Thames* Mar 1752. L.

Pottinger, William. S Summer 1738 LC Knt Co., Md., *from Hawk* Apr 1739. Ha.

Potts, Edmund. S Jan-Apr T *Lichfield* May 1749. M.

Potts, George. S Dec 1750 T *Thames* Feb 1751. L.

Poulson, Elizabeth. S Oct-Dec 1754 T *Greyhound* Feb 1755. M.

Poulsum, Mary. S Lent LC Bal Co., Md., Jul 1772. Wi.

Poulter, John. S 14 yrs Sep-Oct 1746 T Jan 1747 *George William*. M.

Poulton, Isaac. R 14 yrs Oct 1772 T *Justitia* Jan 1773. M.

Poulton, Samuel. S Feb-Apr T *Justitia* May 1745. M.

Pound, John. S 14 yrs Lent LC Bal Co., Md., Jun 1773. Do.

Povey, Thomas. SQS &T *Justitia* Feb 1776. M.

Powell, Ann. S s money Aug 1766. Wo.

Powell, Charles. S for destroying mills at Kingsland & R Mar 1775 (HJ). He.

Powell, Eleanor. S 14 yrs Apr T *Phoenix* Oct 1760. M.

Powell, Eleanor. S Dec 1772 T *Justitia* Jan 1773. M.

Powell, Evan. S s horses & R for life Summer LC Md *William* Dec 1774 & sold to James & Joshua Howard. St.

Powell, James. S Summer 1739. Mo.

Powell, James. T Aug 1752 *Tryal*. Sy.

Powell, Jeremiah. S Lent T *Thornton* May LC AA Co., Md., Jul 1774. L.

Powell, John. S York 1755 (AHJ). Y.

Powell, John. S Lent LC Bal Co., Md., Jun 1773. So.

Powell, John. SW S Lent LC AA Co., Md., from *Thornton* Jul 1773. M.

Powell, Philip. T *Plain Dealer* Jan 1746. M.

Powell, Sarah. S s handkerchief Jan T Apr 1735 *Patapsco* LC Annapolis Oct 1735. M.

Powell, Sarah wife of William. SQS Sep 1772 LC Bal Co., Md., Jun 1773. Ch.

Powell, Susanna. S Lent LC AA Co., Md., from *Thornton* Jul 1775. Bu.

Powell, Thomas of Hackney. R for Barbados Jun 1671 but LC Md Feb 1672. M.

Powers *als* Cabbage, Edward. S s handkerchief Sep 1733 LC from *Caesar* Va Jul 1734. LM.

Powers, Thomas. T Jul 1747 *Laura*. L.

Powis, Ellen. S Lent T August 1738 from Liverpool. St.

Powis, Samuel. S Lent LC Bal Co., Md., Jun 1773. Wo.

Powl, Elizabeth. S Aug 1766. Li.

Powning, John. S Lent T May 1749 *Lichfield*. K.

Pracey, Thomas. S Jul T *Beverly* Aug 1763. M.

Prankitt, Robert. S Jan-Jun T Jul 1747 *Laura*. M.

Pratt, Francis. T Apr 1735 *Patapsco* LC Annapolis Oct 1735. Ht.

Pratt, Francis. S for life Lent 1773 LC Bal Co., Md., sold to John Clement. Ha.

Pratt, Thomas. S Oct 1772 T *Justitia* Jan 1773; runaway. L.

Preditch, John. S & T Apr 1751. G.

Preece, Thomas (1740) - *See* Perry. He.

Prees, Thomas. S Lent T Apr 1755. He.

Prentice, Robert. S for robbery in Hanbury Aug 1759 (WJ). Wo.

Prescott, Mary. SQS Apr T *Thornton* May LC AA Co., Md., Jul 1774. E.

Presgrove, George. T Sep 1737 *Pretty Patsy*. L.

Pressly, John. S s sheep T Jan 1747. Wi.

Presstand, George. SQS Oct T *Justitia* Dec 1774. M.

Preston als Budbrook, John. S 14 yrs Lent 1744 LC Knt Co., Md., from *Susannah* Aug 1744. De.

Preston, Ann. S Aug T *Phoenix* Oct 1760. L.

Preston, John. T Apr 1735 *Patapsco* LC Annapolis Oct 1735. E.

Preston, Paul. S May-Jul T *Tayloe* Jul 1773; runaway. M.

Preston, Thomas. S Apr T *Dolphin* Apr 1761. L.

Price, Alicia [Alisha], spinster. S Bristol Nov 1753. G,

Price, Daniel. S Lent LC Bal Co., Md., Jul 1774. Sh.

Price, Edward. R & T Feb 1748. O.

Price, Edward. S Lent T Sep 1753. He.

Price, Edward. S Jul T *Beverly* Aug 1763. M.

Price, Elizabeth wife of Samuel. S Sep-Oct T *Justitia* Dec 1774. M.

Price, Hugh. S Brecon s sheep R 14 yrs Jun 1772. Wal.

Price, James. S Apr T Jun 1748 *Lichfield*. L.

Price, James. S s sheep Summer 1753 R 14 yrs Lent 1754 (GJ). Sh.

Price, James. S Lent T *Thornton* May LC AA Co., Md., Jul 1774. L.

Price, John. S Apr T *Justitia* May 1745. L.

Price, John. S Apr 1746 T Jan 1748. Mo.

Price, John. S Oct 1750 T Oct 1751. Mo.

Price, John. S s horse Summer 1753 R 14 yrs Lent 1754 (GJ). Sh.

Price, John. S Oct 1753 T Aug 1754. Mo.

Price, Joseph. S Nov, case reviewed unfavourably & T Dec 1770 *Justitia*. L.

Price, Mary. S Oct 1740 T *Harpooner* Jan 1741. L.

Price, Mary. S Summer 1772 LC Bal Co., Md., Apr 1773. G.

Price, Richard. S s horse Lent R Feb 1724. Mo.

Price, Sarah. SW S Lent LC AA Co., Md., from *Thornton* Jul 1773. M.

Price, Thomas. S Sep-Oct 1773 T *Justitia* Jan 1774. M.

Price, Thomas. S for perjury Feb & respited Apr 1774. L.

Price, William. R 14 yrs Nov 1750 T *Thames* Feb 1751; runaway. M.

Price, William. S Apr T *Dolphin* Apr 1761. M.

Price, William. S Lent LC Bal Co., Md., Dec 1770 from *Trotman* & sold to Abraham Ensor. He.

Pricket *als* Tate, Michael, *als* Blind Michael. S & R 14 yrs Lent 1769. O.

Priest, Ann. S Sep T Oct 1750 *Rachael*. M.

Priest, Richard. SQS Bristol s gold rings Sep 1757 (BJ). G.

Priest, Thomas. R for life Summer 1772 T *Justitia* Jan 1773. Sy.

Priest, William. S s sheep Sep 1746 T Aug 1747. Le.

Prior, Ann. S Feb T *Thames* Mar 1752.

Prior, Elizabeth. S May-Jul T *Tayloe* Jul 1774. M.

Prior, Hannah. SQS Dec 1772 LC AA Co., Md., from *Thornton* Jul 1773. M.

Prior, John. S 14 yrs for receiving Lent T May 1750 *Lichfield*. Sy.

Pryor, Samuel. S for smuggling Summer 1747, taken from Maidstone Gaol by Samuel Pritchett *als* Sam the Tinker, LC Knt Co., Md., Mar 1748. K.

Pritchard, Ann. S 14 yrs Summer 1741 LC QA Co., Md., from *Philleroy* Apr 1742. He.

Pritchard, Ann. T *Maryland Packet* Oct 1761. L.

Pritchard, Elizabeth. S Jul-Sep T *Ruby* Oct 1754. M.

Pritchard, Ezekiel. S s horse 14 yrs Summer 1741 LC QA Co., Md., from *Philleroy* Apr 1742. He.

Pritchard, John of Kill. R for Barbados Jul 1672 but LC Md in 1673. So.

Pritchard, John. S May-Jul T *Tayloe* Jul 1773. M.

Pritchard, Martha. S Feb T *Tryal* Mar 1757. M.

Pritchard, Thomas. S Lent 1741 LC QA Co., Md., from *Philleroy* Apr 1742. He.

Pritchard, William. S Bristol Apr 1736 (GJ). G.

Pritchard, William. S Feb-Apr T May 1751 *Tryal*. M.

Pritchard, William. SQS Bristol Dec 1754 (BJ). G.

Pritchard, William. S s butter at St. Owen, Hereford, Lent 1756. He.

Pritchard *als* Williams, William. S Lent LC Bal Co., Md., Jul 1772. He.

Pritchards, John. SQS Jan LC AA Co., Md., from *Thornton* Jul 1775. Sy.

Probart, William. S Feb T *Tryal* Mar 1757. M.

Probeart, Thomas. S Lent T *Thornton* May LC AA Co., Md., Jul 1774. L.

Proctor, Christopher. S Lent 1731. No.

Procter, John. S Lent LC AA Co., Md., from *Hanover Planter* Jul 1773. M.

Prosey, William. S Apr T Jun 1748 *Lichfield*. L.

Prosser, James. R for life Jan T *Tryal* Mar 1757. M.

Prosser, Sarah. S Feb T *Thames* Mar 1754. M.

Prosser, Thomas. S Feb-Apr T May 1752 *Lichfield*. M.

Prosser, Thomas. S s clothing Apr 1773 (HJ), G.

Prosser, William. S Summer 1760 but died in prison. Mo.

Protherow, John. R 14 yrs Mar respited Apr 1774. So.

Proudfoot, Matthew. T Mar 1750 *Tryal*. M.

Pudiphat, Samuel. S Lent LC AA Co., Md., from *Thornton* Jul 1775. Ht.

Pugh, Ann. S Jul T Jul 1748 *Mary*. L.

Pugh, Daniel. S Dec 1753-Jan 1754 T *Thames* Mar 1754. M.

Pugh, Hugh, *als* Hawkins, Henry. S Apr-May T *Tryal* Jul 1754; runaway. M.

Pugh, Joan. S Summer LC Bal Co., Md., Dec 1770. Sh.

Pugh, John. S Shrewsbury Jul 1749 (AHJ). Sh.

Pugh, John William. S Lent but taken from transport ship & pardoned in April 1774. M.

Pugh, Mary. S Feb T *Thames* Mar 1754. L.

Pugh, Simon of Wandsworth. SQS Jan T *Dolphin* May 1763; runaway. Sy.

Pugsley, John. SQS & T *Amity* LC QA Co., Md., Mar 1736. So.

Puin, Richard. S Lent T Jun 1748 *Lichfield*. Sy.

Pullen, Richard. S Lent LC AA Co., Md., from *Thornton* May 1771. M.

Pullen, Samuel. R Summer 1773 T *Justitia* Jan 1774. Sy.

Pullen *als* Smith, Thomas. S s sheep Lent R & T Summer 1753. Be.

Pullenger, William. S Jan-Apr T Jun 1748 *Lichfield*. M.

Pulpitt, William. T May 1751 *Tryal*. Sx.

Pulsevir, Catherine. SQS Jul 1738 LC QA Co., Md. Jun 1739. De.

Puncheon, Lawrence. S Lent LC Bal Co., Md., Jun 1773. Co.

Purcell, Henry. S Lent R Jun 1733 T Jan 1734 *Caesar* LC Va Jul 1734. Sy.

Purdue, Charles. S Oct 1751-Jan 1752 T *Thames* Mar 1752. M.

Purney, Richard. S Feb T *Thames* Mar 1754. M.

Purse, Bernard. SQS Jan LC Knt Co., Md., from *Bideford* Nov 1737. So.

Pursley, John. S 14 yrs Jan T *Thames* Feb 1751. M.

MORE EMIGRANTS IN BONDAGE

Puttenham *als* Putnam, William of Aldenham. R Summer 1772 T *Justitia* Jan 1773. Ht.

Pyburn, Mary. S City Michaelmas 1762 (AHJ). Nl.

Pye, William. S 14 yrs Summer T *Phoenix* Oct 1760. E.

Pike, Arthur (1771) - *See* Bowden. De.

Pyke, Eilzsha *als* Letitia *als* Alicia. S Jun 1739 T *Sea Nymph* to Md. L.

Pyke, Thomas. S 14 yrs Summer 1735 S Jul 1736 LC QA Co., Md., from *Amity* May 1737. Do.

Pyner, John. SQS Jul T *Justitia* Dec 1774. M.

Pyner, Thomas. S Feb-Apr T May 1751 *Tryal*. M.

Pyner, William. SQS Jan LC AA Co., Md., from *Thornton* Jul 1773. Sy.

Quafe, Thomas. T Jul 1747. Sy.

Quainton, Edward. R 14 yrs for s horse at Aylesbury Mar 1716. Bu.

Quelch, Moses. S Lent T May 1751 *Tryal*. Bu.

Quick, Elizabeth. S Summer LC Md. from *Reformation* Aug 1722. De.

Quick, John. SQS Jul 1738 S Summer 1738 LC QA Co., Md. Jun 1739. So.

Quick, Thomas. S Summer 1718 LC from *Sophia* QA Co., Md. Mar 1719. De.

Quickley, Bartholomew. S Sep-Dec 1746 T Jan 1747 *George William*. M.

Quin *als* Bulger, Mary. S Sep-Oct T Oct 1749 *Mary*. M.

Quin, Margaret. S Feb T Mar 1750 *Tryal*. M.

Quin, Margaret (1761) - *See* Solowin. M.

Quint, Crisset. S s sheet Apr T Dec 1735 *John* LC Annapolis Sep 1736. L.

Quinton, Thomas. SQS Woodbridge 1771. Su.

Quittenden, Sarah. S Summer T Sep 1751 *Greyhound*. K.

Rabnett, James. S Feb-Apr T May 1751 *Tryal*. M.

Raby, William. S Lent LC AA Co., Md., from *Thornton* May 1771. M.

Race, Charles. SWK Jan LC AA Co., Md., from *Thornton* Jul 1775. K.

Rack, John. T Apr 1735 *Patapsco* LC Annapolis Oct 1735. Sy.

Radborn, John. S Dec 1753-Jan 1754 T *Thames* Mar 1754. M.

Radborne *als* Ambrose, Thomas. S Dec 1753-Jan 1754 T *Thames* Mar 1754. M.

Radcliff, Joseph. S Lent R Jun T 14 yrs Aug 1752 *Tryal*. E.

Radford, Ann. SQS Jan 1731 LC Knt Co., Md., from *Falcon* Apr 1732. De.

Radford, George. SQS Jul 1738 S Summer 1738 LC QA Co., Md. Jun 1739. De.

Radford, John. S Lent LC AA Co., Md., from *Thornton* Jul 1773. M.

Radford, Matthew. S Lent T Dec 1731

Radford, Sarah. T Jul 1747. Sy.

Radley, Joseph. T Aug 1752 *Tryal*. Ht.

Radman, Hugh. S s sheep Aug 1739 (GJ). G.

Radwell, Robert. S 14 yrs Jul-Dec 1747 LC Knt Co., Md., from *St. George* Mar 1748. M.

Ragan, James. SQS Feb T Mar 1750 *Tryal*. M.

Ragan, William. S Oct 1773 T *Justitia* Jan 1774. L.

Rainbird, Joseph, *als* Garland, Joseph. R for life Nov 1750 T May 1751 *Tryal*. K.

Rainbow, John. S 1775. No.

Rainforth, George Jr. S for burglary Summer 1748 R 14 yrs Lent LC Md from LC QA Co., Md., from *Chester* Nov 1749. He.

Rakes, Weston. S for life Oct 1751-Jan 1752 T *Thames* Mar 1752. M.

Rall, John. S Summer 1718 LC from *Sophia* QA Co., Md. Mar 1719. De.

Rallinson, John (1755) - *See* Rollinson. Y.

Ralph, John. S for s from mansion house Summer 1723 R Nov 1724. Su.

Ralph, John. S Apr-May T *Tryal* Jul 1754. M.

Ramsden, Edward, son of Elizabeth Ramsden (*q.v.*). S s sheep Mar 1742. Bd.

Ramsden, Elizabeth. S s sheep Mar 1742; her husband and one son transported previously. Bd.

Ramsden, John. S Summer 1736. Y.

Ramsey, Ann. S Feb-Apr T May 1751 *Tryal*. M.

Rand, William. S Lent R Jun T 14 yrs Aug 1752 *Tryal*. E.

Randall, Ann. S Lent LC AA Co., Md., from *Thornton* May 1771. M.

Randall, Christopher. R for Barbados Sep 1672 but LC AA Co Md Nov 1673. L.

Randall, John. S Oct 1740 T *Harpooner* Jan 1741. L.

Randall, Mary. S Jun-Dec 1745 T *Plain Dealer* Jan 1746. M.

Randall, Richard. S Lent T *Thornton* May LC AA Co., Md., Jul 1774. Ht.

Randall, Thomas. S Lent 1773 but pardoned. Ha.

Randall, William. S Lent R 14 yrs Summer T Oct 1750 *Rachael*. K.

Ranton, Richard. S Dec 1745 T *Plain Dealer* Jan 1746. L.

Rascowe, William. S Lent T Apr 1737. Le.

Rash, Mary (1734) - *See* Rush. M.

Rassall, Thomas. S Apr-Jun 1739 T *Sea Nymph* to Md. M.

Rathbone, John. S Summer 1732. Wa.

Rathby, Henry. S Lent 1733. Li.

Raven, John. S for life & T *Lichfield* May 1749. M.

Rawle, David. S Mar T Apr 1746. Sh.

Rawles, Joseph. S Lent LC AA Co., Md., from *Thornton* Jul 1775. E.

Rawlett, William. S Apr T May 1750 *Lichfield*. L.

Rawlings, John. S Norwich Sep T Nov 1746. Nf.

Rawlings, John. S Oct T *Barnard* Oct 1756. L.

Rawlings, Thomas. S Mar T May 1746. Sx.

Rawlins, James. S s woodworking tools Feb T Apr 1735 *Patapsco* LC Annapolis Oct 1735. M.

Rawlins, Richard. S s horse Aug 1753 R 14 yrs Lent 1754 (WJ). St.

Raworth, Thomas. S Apr 1753. Li.

Raybourn, Ann. T May 1751 *Tryal*. K.

Rayner, John. R Summer T Aug 1749 *Thames*. Sy.

Rayner, John. S Lent 1753 (AHJ). Db.

Rayner, Martha. T May 1745. Y.

Raynes, Isaac. S s sheep Lent R 14 yrs Summer T Oct 1755. Le.

Raynsdon, John. S Apr T Jun 1748 *Lichfield*. L.

Rea, Matthew. S Lent 1750 LC QA Co., Md., from *Catherine* Nov 1750. Wo.

Rea, Richard. S Summer T Sep 1753. Wa.

Read, Ann. S 14 yrs Lent LC Bal Co., Md., Jul 1771. Do.

Read, Calvin. R for Barbados Dec 1671 but LC Md from *William & Mary* Mar 1672. M.

Read, Christian. S Lent LC AA Co., Md., from *Hanover Planter* Jul 1773. L.

Read, Elizabeth. S Lent T *Dolphin* May 1763. Sy.

Read, Elizabeth. R Summer 1773 T *Justitia* Jan 1774. Sy.

MORE EMIGRANTS IN BONDAGE

Read, Francis. SQS Apr T *Thornton* May LC AA Co., Md., Jul 1774. M.

Read, Jacob. S Lent 1738. Li.

Read, John. S Summer 1739. Nf.

Read *als* Sweep, John. S Jul-Dec 1747 LC Knt Co., Md., from *St. George* Mar 1748. M.

Read, John. S Lent T May 1750 *Lichfield*. Sx.

Read, John. S Lent 1764. Mo.

Read, John. S Lent T *Thornton* May LC AA Co., Md., Jul 1774. Sx.

Read, Mary wife of Archibald. S 14 yrs Lent LC AA Co., Md., from *Thornton* Jul 1775. Sx.

Read, Nicholas. S Lent LC Bal Co., Md., Jul 1774. Wi.

Read, Robert. S Summer 1773 T *Justitia* Jan 1774. Ht.

Read, Samuel. S Jul LC Bal Co., Md., Dec 1783 from *Swift*. M.

Read, Susanna. S Sep-Dec 1746 T Jan 1747 *George William*. M.

Read, Thomas. S Bristol Jan 1758 (AHJ). G.

Read, Thomas, aged under 15. S s from his master Summer 1758 R 14 yrs Lent 1759. He.

Read, William. R 14 yrs Sep T *Randolph* Sep 1768. Ha.

Reams, Harold. S Summer 1736 T Lent 1737. Li.

Rebecco *als* Handford, Jane. S Dec 1753-Jan 1754 T *Thames* Mar 1754. M.

Reddall, John. S Lent T *Greyhound* Feb 1754. Bu.

Reddall, Mary wife of Samuel. S Summer LC Bal Co., Md., Dec 1772. Wa.

Redford, William of Pendleton, whitster. SQS Jan 1730. La.

Redman, Elizabeth. T Jul 1747. Sy.

Redman, John. S Lent LC Bal Co., Md., Jul 1774. Do.

Redmand, Simon. T from Dublin by *Hercules*, LC Bal. Co., Md., Aug 1773, sold to James Wilson of Augusta Co., Virginia. Ir.

Reed, Elizabeth. S Jan T *Plain Dealer* Jan 1746. M.

Reed, Hannah of Springfield. S Lent R 14 yrs Summer T *Phoenix* Oct 1760. E.

Reed, John. S Lent LC Bal Co., Md., Jun 1773. Ha.

Reed, Margaret *als* Sumner. S Lent LC AA Co., Md., from *Thornton* Jul 1773. L.

Reed, Mary. SQS Oct 1772 LC Bal Co., Md., Jun 1773. De.

Reed, Michael. S Summer 1738. Nt.

Reese, Mary. SQS Bristol Mar 1755 (BJ). G.

Reeve, Robert. T Apr 1741 *Speedwell* or *Mediterranean*, condemned for returning Mar 1742 (IJ). E.

Reeves, Joseph. S Summer 1772 T *Justitia* Jan 1773; runaway. K.

Reeves, Joseph. S for life Lent LC AA Co., Md., from *Thornton* Jul 1775. K.

Reeves, Richard. S Lent LC AA Co., Md., from *Thornton* Jul 1773. M.

Remmet, Sarah. SQS Jul 1743 LC Knt Co., Md., from *Globe* Mar 1744. De.

Restal, Thomas. SQS Gloucester for breaking into his father's house at Stroud Jul 1764 (WJ). G

Retford, Obadiah. S Summer 1733 T Summer 1734. Li.

Revell (Rewell), Jane. S Apr 1718 for receiving goods at Enfield R 14 yrs for Carolina May 1719. L.

Revel, John. S Apr 1718 for receiving goods at Enfield. L.

Revers, Robert. S Lent LC Bal Co., Md., Jul 1772. G.

Reynold, Samuel. R for Barbados Sep 1672 but LC AA Co Md Nov 1673. L.

Reynolds, Ann. S Lent LC AA Co., Md., from *Thornton* May 1771. K.

Reynolds, Constantine. S Jan T Mar 1750 *Tryal*. L.

Reynolds, Elizabeth. S 14 yrs Jun 1739 T *Sea Nymph* to Md. L.

Reynolds, John. S Summer T Sep 1746. Ha.

Reynolds, Jonathan. S Norwich s cloth from tenters Summer R 14 yrs Dec 1726. Nf.

Reynolds, Martha (1702) - *See* Elton. L.

Reynolds, Sarah. T from Dublin by *Hercules*, LC Bal. Co., Md., Aug 1773, sold to John Gill Jr. of Baltimore Co. Ir.

Reynolds, Thomas. S 14 yrs LC Bal Co., Md., Jul 1772. St.

Reynolds, Thomas. R Jul LC Md *William* Dec 1774 & sold to Harry Dorsey Gough. Ha.

Reynolds, William. S Summer T Sep 1751 *Greyhound*. Sy.

Reynolds, William. S Feb T *Thames* Mar 1752. L.

Reynolds, William. S & R Summer T *Maryland Packet* Oct 1761. Bu.

Reynolds, William. SQS s from Duke of Marlborough Jan 1766 (OJ). O.

Reyonds, Sampson. S Launceston Mar 1761 (AHJ). Co.

Rhea, David. T from Dublin by *Hercules*, LC Bal. Co., Md., Aug 1773, sold to James Wilson of Augusta Co., Virginia. Ir.

Rhodenhurst, Mary. S Lent LC Bal Co., Md., Jul 1774. Sh.

Rhodes, John. S Feb T Mar 1758 *Dragon* from London. Nt.

Rhodes, Samuel. S Sep-Oct 1772 T *Justitia* Jan 1773. M.

Rhodes, Thomas. R for life for highway robbery Summer 1772 T *Justitia* Jan 1773. Sy.

Rhodes, Thomas. S Lent LC AA Co., Md., from *Thornton* Jul 1773. L.

Rice, David. S Sep T *Ruby* Oct 1754. L.

Rice *als* Johns, James. S Exeter Nov 1758 (AHJ). De.

Rice, John. S Lent T *Thornton* May LC AA Co., Md., Jul 1774; runaway. Ht.

Rice, Mary. S Lent T *Thornton* May LC AA Co., Md., Jul 1774. M.

Rice, Nathaniel. S s lead at Tamworth Summer 1750 LC QA Co., Md., from *Chester* Dec 1752. St.

Rice, William. S Apr T Dec 1735 *John* LC Annapolis Sep 1736. M.

Rice, William. T *Saltspring* Jul 1775. L.

Rich, Daniel. S Apr T May 1750 *Lichfield*. L.

Rich, Elizabeth. S Apr T *Justitia* May 1745. L.

Rich, John. T May 1752 *Lichfield*. Sy.

Rich, Samuel. S Lent LC Bal Co., Md., Jun 1773. So.

Richard, Thomas. S Glamorgan s sheep R 14 yrs Jun 1766. Wal.

Richards, Charles. SQS Jul T *Justitia* Dec 1774. M.

Richards, Elizabeth wife of Henry. S Apr T *Dolphin* May 1763. M.

Richards, John. S s horse Summer 1726. So.

Richards, John. S Summer 1737 LC QA Co., Md., from *Amity* Apr 1738. De.

Richards, John. Executed Sep 1759 for returning from transportation (BJ). G.

Richards, John. SQS Jan 1771 LC Bal Co., Md., Jun 1771. G.

Richards, Joseph. S Summer 1734 T Feb 1735. Le.

Richards *als* Monk, Joseph. S Jul T *Tayloe* Jul 1773. L.

Richards, Margaret. S Aug T *Phoenix* Oct 1760. L.

Richards, Stephen. SQS Apr T May 1751 *Tryal*. M.

Richards, William S Jan 1746 T Sep 1747. St.

Richards, William. T *Justitia* Jan 1773. M.

Richardson, Elizabeth. S Jul T Sep 1751 *Greyhound*. L.

Richardson, John of Aylesbury. S Lent T *Dolphin* May 1763. Bu.

Richardson, John. S Lent LC Bal Co., Md., Jul 1772. St.

Richardson, John. S Lent T *Thornton* May LC AA Co., Md., Jul 1774. M.

Richardson, Joseph. S s horse Lent R 14 yrs Summer T *Barnard* Oct 1756. Sy.

MORE EMIGRANTS IN BONDAGE

Richardson, Nicholas. S Lent LC AA Co., Md., from *Thornton* Jul 1775. Sx.

Richardson, Peter. S Lent 1738. Li.

Richardson, Richard. S May T *Saltspring* Jul 1775. L.

Richardson, Sarah. S s silver buttons Apr 1735 T *John* LC Annapolis Sep 1736. M.

Richardson, William. S Summer LC Bal Co., Md., Dec 1770 from *Trotman* & sold to Thomas Cole Sr. Y.

Richens, John. S Apr T May 1750 *Lichfield*. M.

Richeson, Thomas. T Jan 1736 *Dorsetshire* LC Va Sep 1736. Sy.

Richmond, Edward. SQS Feb LC AA Co., Md., from *Thornton* Jul 1775. M.

Richmond, James. S Glasgow s cow R for life Apr 1772. Sco.

Richmond, John. SQS Apr T *Thornton* May LC AA Co., Md., Jul 1774. M.

Richmond, Mary. S Feb T *Thames* Mar 1754. L.

Richmond, William. S Lent T *Thornton* May LC AA Co., Md., Jul 1774. M.

Rickard, William. S Plymouth Jul 1763 (AHJ). De.

Rickett, William. S Sep T Oct 1750 *Rachael*. L.

Ricketts, John. S Dec 1749-Jan 1750 T Mar 1750 *Tryal*. M.

Ricketts, Thomas. R 14 yrs Lent TB Mar 1738. G.

Rickman, John. S for house breaking & R 14 yrs Jul 1727. Be.

Rider. *See* Ryder.

Ridgely *als* Bartelott, George. S for life S Lent LC Bal Co., Md., Jun 1773. Wi.

Riding, John. S 1753 (AHJ). La.

Ridley, John. R Jul T *Tayloe* Jul 1774. M.

Ridout, Thomas. R for life Jan T *Tryal* Mar 1757. M.

Riell, Robert. S Summer 1748 R 14 yrs Lent T *Lichfield* May 1749. Sy.

Rigby, James. SQS Feb LC AA Co., Md., from *Thornton* Jul 1773. M.

Rigby, Nicholas. S Lent T *Thornton* May LC AA Co., Md., Jul 1774. M.

Rigg, George. LC Md from *Isabella* Jul 1775 & bought his freedom. X.

Riley, Grace. S Dec 1753-Jan 1754 T *Thames* Mar 1754. M.

Riley, John. S Jul-Sep T *Ruby* Oct 1754. M.

Riley, John. SQS Oct 1772 T *Justitia* Jan T *Justitia* Jan 1773.

Riley *als* Barrett, Joseph. S Apr-May T *Tryal* Jul 1754. M.

Ryley, Margaret. S Jan-Apr T Jun 1748 *Lichfield*. M.

Riley, Mary. S May-Jul T Aug 1749 *Thames*. M.

Riley *als* Bulger, Mary. S Oct 1751-Jan 1752 T *Thames* Mar 1752. M.

Riley *als* Barrett, Mary. S 14 yrs Apr-May T *Tryal* Jul 1754. M.

Riley, Michael. S Feb T *Thames* Mar 1754. L.

Ryley, Sarah. S May-Jul T Aug 1749 *Thames*. M.

Ring, Richard. S May-Jul T *Tayloe* Jul 1773. M.

Ring, William. S Lent T *Tryal* Jul 1754. K.

Risdale, William. S Oct 1772 T *Justitia* Jan 1773. L.

Risley, William. S Sep T *Phoenix* Oct 1760. L.

Rison, Martha. S Jul T Jul 1748 *Mary*. L.

Rithock, Sarah. S Apr-Jun 1739 T *Sea Nymph* to Md. M.

Rivers, Elizabeth. S Oct T *Barnard* Oct 1756. M.

Rivers, Robert. R Dec 1773 T *Justitia* Jan 1774. M.

Roache, Eleanor. S 14 yrs Sep-Oct T *Justitia* Dec 1774. M.

Roach, Elias. S Launceston Apr 1760 (AHJ). Co.

Roach, James. S Oct 1751-Jan 1752 T *Thames* Mar 1752. M.

Roach, Richard. SQS Lent LC AA Co., Md., from *Hanover Planter* Jul 1773. M.

Roach, Robert. S s wigs Feb T Apr 1735 *Patapsco* LC Annapolis Oct 1735. L.

Roades, Mary wife of John. S Bristol Jan 1757 (AHJ). G.

Roades, William. T Aug 1752 *Tryal*. Sx.

Roan, Edward. S s saws Lent 1767. Wa.

Robb, Peter. R Summer 1772 T *Justitia* Jan 1773; runaway. Sy.

Robbins, Mathew. S Mar 1746 Jan 1747 T *St. George* LC Knt Co., Md., Mar 1748. Wi.

Roberts, Anthony. S for housebreaking Summer 1735 T Lent 1736. Wo.

Roberts, Charles. S Lent T Apr 1737. No.

Roberts, Charles. S Jul-Dec 1747 LC Knt Co., Md., from *St. George* Mar 1748. M.

Roberts, Edward. S s horse & R 14 yrs Summer LC Md *William* Dec 1774 & sold to John Walker. Sh.

Roberts, George. S Summer 1755 R 14 yrs Summer T *Barnard* Oct 1756. Sx.

Roberts, Henry. S Lent LC Bal Co., Md., Jul 1772. G.

Roberts, Hugh. S Sep 1747 LC Knt Co., Md., from *St. George* Mar 1748; runaway. L.

Roberts, Hugh. S s skins at St. Julian, Shrewsbury, Summer 1771 T *Restoration* LC Bal Co., Md., Oct 1771. Sh.

Roberts, James. S s horse & R 14 yrs Summer LC Md *William* Dec 1774 & sold to James Walker. Sh.

Roberts, Mary. S s flannel Apr 1751 (WJ). Wa.

Roberts, Mary. S Lent LC AA Co., Md., from *Thornton* May 1771. M.

Roberts, Richard Jr. SQS & T Apr 1742 LC PG Co., Md. De.

Roberts, Richard. S Sep-Oct 1772 T *Justitia* Jan 1773. M.

Roberts, Richard. S Lent T *Thornton* May LC AA Co., Md., Jul 1774. K.

Roberts, Sarah wife of John of St. Saviour, Southwark. SQS Apr T Sep 1751 *Greyhound*. Sy.

Roberts, Thomas. S Apr 1758. Li.

Roberts, Thomas. S Jul T *Tayloe* Jul 1774. L.

Roberts, William. S Summer 1749 (AHJ). Wi.

Robertson, Hanna. S s from shop in Oulton Summer 1761. Nf.

Robertson, John. S Mar T *Thames* Mar 1754. L.

Robertson, John. S Lent LC Bal Co., Md., Jul 1772. Sh.

Robertson, John. S 14 yrs Dec T *Justitia* Dec 1774. L.

Robinson, Andrew. S Feb-Apr T *Justitia* May 1745. M.

Robinson, Ann. S s edging Apr T Dec 1735 *John* LC Annapolis Sep 1736. M.

Robinson, Catherine. S & T 14 yrs Aug 1752 *Tryal*. L.

Robinson, Elizabeth *als* Betty, travelling fortune teller. S s at Leigh Lent 1760; her son aged 13 discharged into the care of his grandfather. Wo.

Robinson, Enoch of Bolton le Moors. SQS Jan 1720. La.

Robinson, Hannah. S Dec 1746 T Jan 1747 *George William*. L.

Robinson, Henry. S Apr T Apr 1746 *Laura*. L.

Robinson, James. S Lent 1733 T Jan 1734. Wa.

Robinson, James. S City 1751 (AHJ). Nl.

Robinson, Jane. S Lent LC AA Co., Md., Jul 1774. M.

Robinson, John. S Jan T *Plain Dealer* Jan 1746. M.

Robinson, John. S Lent T Jun 1748 *Lichfield*. E.

Robinson, John. S 1748 (AHJ). Nl.

Robinson, John. S Oct 1751-Jan 1752 T *Thames* Mar 1752. M.

Robinson, John. S Feb T *Thames* Mar 1754. L.

Robinson, John. S 1756 TB to Va. No.

Robinson, John. SQS Feb LC AA Co., Md., from *Thornton* Jul 1773. M.

Robinson, John. S Sep-Oct 1773 T *Justitia* Jan 1774. M.

Robinson, John. S Lent but taken from transport ship & pardoned in April 1774. M.

Robinson, Lancelot. S Lent 1731. Nt.

Robinson, Leonard. SQS Sep T Oct 1743. Y

Robinson, Michael. S Aug T *Beverly* Aug 1763. L.

Robinson, Rose. S May T Jul 1745 *Italian Merchant*. M.

Robinson, Thomas of St. John's. SQS Apr T May 1750 *Lichfield*. Sy.

Robinson, Thomas. S Oct 1751-Jan 1752 T *Thames* Mar 1752; runaway. M.

Robinson, William. S & T Aug 1752 *Tryal*. L.

Robinson, William. S Apr T *Dolphin* May 1763. M.

Robinson, William. S Summer 1773 T *Justitia* Jan 1774. Sy.

Robson, George. S Summer 1772 LC Bal Co., Md., from *Adventure* Mar 1773. Nl.

Robson, John. S Feb 1747 T Jan 1748. Nl.

Robuctine, Hannah. S Apr T *Lichfield* May 1749. L.

Roche, Mary. S Apr T Dec 1735 *John* LC Annapolis Sep 1736. M.

Rock, John. S Apr-May T *Tryal* Jul 1754. M.

Rock, Joseph. S 14 yrs Summer LC Bal Co., Md., Dec 1772. St

Rock, Sarah. S May-Jun T Aug 1752 *Tryal*. M.

Rodbar, Margaret. S for housebreaking Lent 1735 (GJ). So.

Rodd, Robert Sr. S Lent 1732 LC Knt Co., Md., from *Falcon* Mar 1733. De.

Roe, Hannah. S 14 yrs Lent LC AA Co., Md., from *Thornton* Jul 1773. Sy.

Roe, John. S Sep T Oct 1750 *Rachael*. M.

Roe, Nicholas. T May 1747. So.

Rogers, Arnold. T 1746. Sy.

Rogers, Charles. R 14 yrs Jul T *Saltspring* Jul 1775. M.

Rogers, John. S Jun 1718 T Feb 1719 *Worcester* LC Annapolis Jun 1719. L.

Rogers, John. S s butter May T Dec 1735 *John* LC Annapolis Sep 1736. L.

Rogers, John. R 14 yrs Oct 1772 T *Justitia* Jan 1773. M.

Rogers, John. S Lent LC AA Co., Md., from *Thornton* Jul 1775. L.

Rogers, Joseph. S s brass Jan T Apr 1735 *Patapsco* LC Annapolis Oct 1735. L.

Rogers, Philip. S Apr T May 1750 *Lichfield*. M.

Rogers, Thomas. S Summer 1749 R 14 yrs Lent T May 1750 *Lichfield*. K.

Rogers, Thomas of Mitcham. SQS Oct 1750 T *Thames* Feb 175\. Sy.

Rogers, William, servant in King's Confectionary. S s spoons Jan T Apr 1735 *Patapsco* LC Annapolis Oct 1735. M.

Rogers, William. S Apr T May 1752 *Lichfield*. L.

Rohick, Barnaby. S & T Jan 1736 *Dorsetshire* LC Va Sep 1736. L.

Roley *als* Moronie, John. S Sep-Oct 1775 T *Justitia* Feb 1776. M.

Rolfe, Richard (1758) - *See* Rose. O.

Rollinson *als* Rallinson, John. S York 1755 (AHJ). Y.

Rolls, John. S Summer T *Justitia* Jan 1773. Sy.

Rolph, Thomas. S s ewe Summer 1772 T *Justitia* Jan 1773. K.

Roning, John of Reigate. SQS Apr T May 1750 *Lichfield*. Sy.

Roof, John. S May & T 14 yrs Jun 1751. Sy.

Rooke, Henry. S May-Jul T Jul 1748 *Mary*. M.

Rooke, Richard Jr. S for life Summer 1772 LC Bal Co., Md., Apr 1773. G.

Rooker, William. S Lent LC AA Co., Md., from *Thornton* Jul 1775. M.

Rookes, Sarah. T May 1745. Y.

Rooney, John. T from Dublin by *Hercules*, LC Bal. Co., Md., Aug 1773, sold to James Wilson of Augusta Co., Virginia. Ir.

Roper, James. S & T Aug T *Restoration* LC Bal Co., Md., Oct 1771. Wa.

Rose, Edward. S Mar T Sep 1747. Ha.

Rose, Francis. S Lent T Aug 1746. E.

Rose, George. T Aug 1752 *Tryal*. M.

Rose, Jacob. S Oct T *Phoenix* Oct 1760. M.

Rose, John of Newington. SQS Jan T *Thames* Feb 1751. Sy.

Rose *als* Rolfe, Richard. S s tea spoon Jul 1738. O.

Rose, Stephen. S Lent R 14 yrs Jun T Aug 1749 *Thames*. Sx.

Rose, Thomas. S Apr T May 1750 *Lichfield*. L.

Rose, Thomas. S Apr-May T *Tryal* Jul 1754. M.

Roskrogue, Anne. S Summer 1741 LC QA Co., Md., from *Philleroy* Apr 1742. Co.

Ross *als* Bass, Jane. S Apr 1746 T Apr 1746 *Laura*. M.

Rosser, John. S Summer 1741 LC QA Co., Md., from *Philleroy* Apr 1742 & to serve
    Peter Symons. Mo.

Rosseter, Elizabeth. S Jul T *Tayloe* Jul 1773. L.

Rossiter, John. S Summer 1718 LC from *Sophia* QA Co., Md. Mar 1719. So.

Rossiter, Nicholas. SQS & TB Jul 1735 T *Amity* LC QA Co., Md., Mar 1736. So.

Roste, Hannah. S Feb-Apr T *Justitia* May 1745. M.

Rotheram, Joseph. S 14 yrs Summer LC Bal Co., Md., Dec 1770.

Rough, Sarah. S Lent 1734. Li.

Roulson,, Thomas. S Lent 1732. Wa.

Rouse, Edward. S Lent 1741 (IJ). Su.

Rouse, Frances of St. Margaret Westminster. S s rings Apr 1718 TB May 1719. L.

Rouse, James. S Lent 1741 (IJ). Su.

Rouse, James. T Apr 1761. Li.

Rouse, Mary. S Exeter Sep 1751 (AHJ). De.

Row, George. S Lent AT Jul 1761. Sh.

Rowe, Robert of Tildesley cum Shakerley, hatter. SQS Apr 1735. La.

Row, William. S Oct 1772 T *Justitia* Jan 1773. L.

Rowell, Francis. S Apr T May 1752 *Lichfield*. L.

Rowland, Elizabeth. S Summer T Sep 1751 *Greyhound* LC Md Apr 1753. K.

Rowland *als* Rowlin, Hannah. S Jan-Apr T Jun 1748 *Lichfield*. M.

Rowland, John. SQS Feb T *Thornton* May LC AA Co., Md., Jul 1774. M.

Rowland, Philip. S Sep-Oct 1775 T *Justitia* Feb 1776. M.

Rowland, Thomas. S Lent LC Bal Co., Md., Jul 1771. De.

Rowland, William. S Carnarvon s horse R Apr 1768. Wal.

Rowles, Daniel. S Lent LC AA Co., Md., from *Thornton* May 1771. Ht.

Rowles, Thomas. T *Justitia* Jan 1774. M.

Rowley, Ann. S Summer LC Bal Co., Md., Dec 1772. Wa.

Rowley, Edward. S Lent 1736: tried Apr 1738 for returning. Wo.

Rowley, Thomas. S & T Sep 1751 *Greyhound*. M.

Rowling, Richard. S Lent T May 1754. St.

Rowse, John. T May 1751 *Tryal*. Sy.

Royal, Sarah. S Lent 1734. Li.

Royston, Thomas. T May 1745. Y.

Ruby, Thomas. S Oct 1741 T 14 yrs Feb 1742 *Industry* to Md. M.

Rudge, William. SQS Warwick Jul T Aug T *Restoration* LC Bal Co., Md., Oct 1771. Wa.

Rudkin, Edward. S Lent T *Dolphin* May 1763. Sy.

Ruffhead, William. S Oct T *Justitia* Dec 1774. L.

Rumbold, Thomas. SQS Jul T *Randolph* Sep 1768. Ha.

MORE EMIGRANTS IN BONDAGE

Rumbow, Edward. S Jan-Apr T Jun 1748 *Lichfield*. M.

Rumney, Andrew. T 1747 from Whitehaven. Cu.

Rumsey, William als Warwick, Joseph. S 14 yrs Summer 1737 LC QA Co., Md., from *Amity* Apr 1738. Ha.

Rundle, Richard. S Lent 1737 LC Knt Co., Md., from *Hawk* Nov 1737. Co.

Rush (Rash), Mary. S & T Dec 1734 *Caesar* LC Va Jul 1735. M.

Rushbrooke, Benjamin. T Dec 1734 *Caesar* . E.

Rushby, Mary. T *Plain Dealer* Jan 1746. L.

Rusher als Hays als Dennis, Mary. S & T Oct 1730 *Forward* LC Potomack Jan 1731. M.

Rushfield, Fairfax. R 14 yrs & TB Dec 1734. Bd.

Rushing, Jane. S May-Jul T Aug 1749 *Thames*. M.

Rushton, Thomas. S Aug T *Restoration* LC Bal Co., Md., Oct 1771. St.

Ruskin, Thomas of Enfield. S s gate Jul 1740 T Jan 1741 *Harpooner* to Va. M.

Ruslake, John. S Summer 1718 LC from *Sophia* QA Co., Md. Mar 1719. De.

Russ, Mary. S s from parish church at Tetbury Summer 1768. G.

Russ, Thomas. LC Md from *Isabella* Jul 1775 & sold to Henry Howard. X .

Russell, Alexander. S Feb T Apr 1732 *Patapsco* LC Annapolis Oct 1732. M.

Russell, Ann. R for Va Oct 1618. X.

Russell, Ann. S Feb T *Thames* Mar 1752. L.

Russell, Ann. S Jun T Sep 1767 Justitia. L.

Russell, Cornelius. SQS & TB Apr 1774. So.

Russell, David of St. Martin in Fields. SW Jan T Apr 1772 *Thornton*. M.

Russell, Eleanor (1722). *See* Emmett. So.

Russell, Elizabeth. LC from *Forward* Annapolis Jun 1723. X.

Russell als Brown, Elizabeth. S Oct T 14 yrs Nov 1725 *Rappahannock* LC Rappahannock Apr 1726. L.

Russell, Elizabeth. T Apr 1753 Thames. Sy.

Russell als Wright, Frances. R for Barbados May 1676. L.

Russell, Francis. R for Barbados Dec 1681 & Sep 1682. L.

Russell, George of St. Martin in Fields. SW Jun 1775 but pardoned same month. M.

Russell, Hannah. S May T Sep 1765 *Justitia* . M.

Russell, James. AT Oct R & T Dec 1716 Lewis to Jamaica. M.

Russell, James. S Mar TB to Va Apr 1741. Wi.

Russell, Jane of St. Giles in Fields. S s clothing Oct 1742 T Apr 1743 *Justitia* . M.

Russell, John of Westerham. R for Barbados or Jamaica Jul 1710. K.

Russell als Kinsey, John. S Feb-Apr T May 1751 Tryal. M.

Russell, John. TB Apr 1762 Neptune but pardoned for Army service in Jamaica same month. Sy.

Russell, John of St. Mary Major, Exeter, weaver. S s cloth Mar LC Bal Co., Md Jul 1772. De.

Russell, John Jr. SQS New Sarum or Marlborough & TB to Va Jan 1774. Wi.

Russell, Jonathan, aged 21, dark, glassgrinder. S Jan T Feb 1723 *Jonathan* LC Annapolis Jul 1724. M.

Russell, Joseph. S Oct T Dec 1771 *Justitia* . L.

Russell, Margaret (1718) - *See* Humphreys. L.

Russell, Margaret (1718) - *See* Price. L.

Russell, Robert. R 14 yrs Bristol Apr 1742. G.

Russell als Russen, Robert. R Mar 1774. Ha.

Russell, William. S for food riot Dec 1766. Be.

Russell, William. S Lent T *Thornton* May LC AA Co., Md., Jul 1774. L.

Rust, William. S Summer 1753 R 14 yrs Lent T *Tryal* Jul 1754. E.

Ruston, Alice. S & T Aug T *Restoration* LC Bal Co., Md., Oct 1771. Wa.

Rutlege, Thomas. S Lent LC AA Co., Md., from *Hanover Planter* Jul 1773. M.

Rutt, John. S Summer 1733 R 14 yrs Jun 1734 LC Knt Co., Md, Mar 1735 from *Falcon*. Ha.

Rutter, George. S Summer T *Justitia* Sep 1767. Bu.

Ryan, David. SQS Bristol Dec 1754 (BJ). G.

Ryan, Dennis. T from Dublin by *Hercules*, LC Bal. Co., Md., Aug 1773, sold to James Wilson of Augusta Co., Virginia. Ir.

Ryan, John. T from Dublin by *Hercules*, LC Bal. Co., Md., Aug 1773, sold to Stephen Gill son of John of Bal. Co. Ir.

Ryan, Richard. S Jan-Apr T *Lichfield* May 1749. M.

Ryan, Thomas. S Aug T *Beverly* Aug 1763. L.

Rider, Frances. S s ring Apr T Dec 1735 *John* LC Annapolis Sep 1736. L.

Ryder, Jane. S Jan T Mar 1750 *Tryal*. L.

Rider, John. S Apr-Jun 1739 T *Sea Nymph* to Md. M.

Ryder, John. S Jan-Apr T Jun 1748 *Lichfield*. M.

Rider, William. S Aug T *Phoenix* Oct 1760. L.

Ryder, Mary. S May-Jul T Jul 1748 *Mary*; runaway. M.

Rye, George. S Sep-Oct 1772 T *Justitia* Jan 1773. M.

Ryley. *See* Riley.

Rymas, Matthias. S Jan-Apr T *Lichfield* May 1749. M.

Rymer, George. S Sep-Oct 1772 T *Justitia* Jan 1773. M.

Sable, John. S for highway robbery Lent R 14 yrs Summer T *Phoenix* Oct 1760. Ht.

Sack, John Jr. S 14 yrs Lent LC AA Co., Md., from *Thornton* Jul 1773. E.

Sacker, John, *als* Smith, William. S Oct-Dec 1754 T *Greyhound* Feb 1755. M.

Sadd, Thomas. S s sheep Lent T Sep 1746 *Mary*. K.

Sage, James. S May-Jul T *Tayloe* Jul 1773. M.

Sage, Robert. SQS Apr T *Thornton* May LC AA Co., Md., Jul 1774. M.

Sagemuller, John Diederick. S Feb T Mar 1750 *Tryal*. M.

Sago, John. S May-Jun T Aug 1752 *Tryal*. M.

Saint, John. T 1751. Nt.

Saint, John Egerton. S for assault on Earl of Radnor Jul T *Barnard* Oct 1756. M.

Saires, Edward. S Summer 1734 R 14 yrs Feb T Apr 1735 *Patapsco* LC Annapolis Oct 1735. Sx.

Saires, Thomas. T May 1751 *Tryal*. Sx.

Sale, Mary. S May-Jul T Jul 1748 *Mary*. M.

Salisbury, Morris. S Lent 1750 LC QA Co., Md., from *Catherine* Nov 1750. Do.

Sallis [Solis], Andrew. S Summer TB Aug 1740. G.

Salloway, Robert. S Bristol for receiving from his brother John (*q.v.*) Feb R 14 yrs Mar TB to Md Apr 1764. G.

Salmon, Benjamin. SQS Ipswich 1774. Su.

Salmon, Mary. T Jan 1736 *Dorsetshire* LC Va Sep 1736. Sy.

Salmon, Richard. S Jan T *Plain Dealer* Jan 1746. M.

Salmon, Richard. S Jun T Jul 1747 *Laura*. L.

Salt, Samuel. SQS Bristol s watch from a Jew Aug 1757 (BJ). G.

Salt, William. S for housebreaking Summer 1739 R 14 yrs Jun 1740. Le.

MORE EMIGRANTS IN BONDAGE

Salter, Jemima. S & T Apr 1735 *John* LC Annapolis Sep 1736. M.

Salter, Samuel of Bromley. S Lent T Jul 1745 *Italian Merchant*; runaway. K.

Saltmarsh, John of Moulsham, cordwainer. SQS Jan T May 1750 *Lichfield*. E.

Saltonstall, Richard. S Dec 1782 LC Bal Co., Md., Dec 1783 from *Swift* LC Bal Co., Md., Dec 1783 from *Swift*. L.

Salway, John. SQS Jul LC Bal Co., Md., Dec 1770. De.

Sampson, James. S Dec 1760 T *Neptune* Mar 1761. M.

Sampson, Jonathan. S Lent LC AA Co., Md., from *Thornton* May 1771. K.

Sampson, Thomas. S 14 yrs Lent T *Thornton* May LC AA Co., Md., Jul 1774. L.

Sampson, William. S Lent T *Thornton* May LC AA Co., Md., Jul 1774. M.

Sams, Alice wife of Benjamin of St. George, Southwark. SQS Apr T Sep 1751 *Greyhound*. Sy.

Samuel, Robert. S Chelmsford Jan 1763 (AHJ). E.

Sanders. *See* Saunders.

Sands, John of Lambeth. SQS Oct 1750 T *Thames* Feb 1751. Sy.

Sandys, Samuel. S Lent T *Thornton* May LC AA Co., Md., Jul 1774. M.

Sant, William. S Lent 1741 LC QA Co., Md., from *Philleroy* Apr 1742. He.

Sarflick, Benjamin. S Apr 1766. Li.

Satchwell, Samuel. S Summer 1732. Wa.

Sauce, John. S s handkerchiefs Sep 1733 LC from *Caesar* Va Jul 1734. LM.

Saul, John. S s horse Aug R 14 yrs Nov 1726. Cu.

Saul, Robert. S Lent 1738. Li.

Saul, Sarah. S Lent 1732 LC Knt Co., Md., from *Falcon* Mar 1733. De.

Saunders, Abraham. S Jan T Nov 1746. Bd.

Saunders, Catherine. S Feb T *Tryal* Mar 1757. M.

Saunders, Elizabeth of Whitechapel. S s chinaware Apr T Aug 1718 *Eagle* LC Charles Town Mar 1719. L.

Saunders, Elizabeth. S Jan-Apr T Jun 1748 *Lichfield*. M.

Saunders, Hannah. S Oct T *Phoenix* Oct 1760. M.

Saunders, James. S Feb-Apr T May 1751 *Tryal*. M.

Saunders, John. T Apr 1735 *Patapsco* LC Annapolis Oct 1735. Sx.

Saunders, John. S Summer 1753 R 14 yrs Lent T *Tryal* Jul 1754. K.

Saunders, Lucey. S Oct T *Maryland Packet* Oct 1761. L.

Sanders, Mary. S Jul-Sep T *Ruby* Oct 1754. M.

Sanders, Peter. S Lent T *Tryal* Jul 1754. Sx.

Sanders, Simon (1771). *See* Benjamin. L.

Saunders, William. S Summer 1731 LC Knt Co., Md., from *Falcon* Apr 1732. Co.

Saunders *als* Saunderson, William. S City Summer T Sep 1750. Y.

Sanders, William. S Apr-May T *Tryal* Jul 1754; runaway. M.

Sanders, William. S Lent 1769 (AHJ). Wi.

Saunderson *als* Saunders *als* Alexander, Thomas. S Apr-Jun 1739 T *Sea Nymph* to Md. M.

Saunderson, William (1750) - *See* Saunders. Y.

Savage, George. S 14 yrs LC Bal Co., Md., Jul 1772. St.

Savage, Henry. S Dec 1773 T *Justitia* Jan 1774. M.

Savage, James. S Jan T *Tryal* Mar 1757. L.

Savage, Leonard. SQS Gloucester Jan 1756 (GJ). G.

Savage, Richard. S Lent T *Lichfield* May 1749. Sx.

Savage, Sarah. S Feb-Apr T May 1752 *Lichfield*. M.

Savage, Thomas. S Apr-Jun 1739 T *Sea Nymph* to Md. M.

Savory, John. S Jul LC Bal Co., Md., Dec 1783 from *Swift*. M.

Sawcer, William (1771). *See* Baker. De.

Sawyer, Charles. S Jan T *Tryal* Mar 1757. L.

Sawyer, James. R 14 yrs Jul 1746 TB Jan 1747 LC Knt Co., Md., from *St. George* Mar 1748. Wi.

Sawyer, William. R 14 yrs Jul 1746 TB Jan 1747 LC Knt Co., Md., from *St. George* Mar 1748. Wi.

Saxon, John of Manchester, weaver. SQS Apr 1731. La.

Saxton (Sexton), John. S 14 yrs Lent LC AA Co., Md., from *Thornton* May 1771. Bu.

Say, Richard. SQS Warminster Jul TB Sep 1741 LC QA Co., Md from *Philleroy* Apr 1742. Wi.

Say, William. S s horse Lent T Dec 1737. O.

Sayward, Mary. S Apr-Jun 1739 T *Sea Nymph* to Md. M.

Scaisbridge, John. S Lancaster 1755 (AHJ). La.

Scales, John. S Apr 1753. Li.

Scammell, Edward. R 14 yrs Mar TB to Va Apr 1742 LC PG Co., Md. Wi.

Scarborough, James. S Jan T *Greyhound* Feb 1755. M.

Scarborough, James. S Sep-Oct 1773 T *Justitia* Jan 1774; runaway. M.

Scarborough, Joseph. S Summer 1718 LC from *Sophia* QA Co., Md. Mar 1719. De.

Scarborough, Thomas. T May 1751 *Tryal*. Sx.

Scarcity, William. S Sep 1735 T Jan 1736 *Dorsetshire* LC Va Sep 1736. M.

Scarlet, Peter. S s at Pershore Summer 1768, case reviewed unfavourably and to be T. Wo.

Scarlett, Stephen. S Lent T *Thornton* May LC AA Co., Md., Jul 1774. Sy.

Scarrett, George. S Jan-Apr T Jun 1748 *Lichfield*. M.

Scholes, John. S Sep-Dec 1746 T Jan 1747 *George William*. M.

Scholfield, Philip of Manchester. SQS Apr 1731. La.

Scholfield, Thomas of Bolton. SQS Jan 1722 TB Apr 1723. La.

Schults, Gotolph. SW Jan LC AA Co., Md., from *Thornton* Jul 1773. M.

Scolfield, John. S & T Aug 1752 *Tryal*. L.

Scott, Catherine. S Apr-May T *Tryal* Jul 1754. M.

Scott, Edward. S s horse Lent R 14 yrs Summer 1758 TB to Va. No.

Scott, Eleanor. S City Jan 1759 (AHJ). Nl.

Scott, Hannah (1774). *See* Brown. L.

Scott, James. S Sep T *Barnard* Oct 1756. M.

Scott, James. S Exeter 1760 (AHJ). De.

Scott, Jane. S Jun-Dec 1745 T *Plain Dealer* Jan 1746. M.

Scott, John. S s silver pot Jan T Apr 1735 *Patapsco* LC Annapolis Oct 1735. M.

Scott, John. S York 1753 (AHJ). Y.

Scott, Joshua. S Jan T Sep 1736. Y.

Scott, Judith. S Aug T *Phoenix* Oct 1760. L.

Scott, Nicholas. S Lent T *Dolphin* May 1763. E.

Scott, Thomas. S Dec T *Justitia* Dec 1774. M.

Scott, William. S Aug LC Md *William* Dec 1774 & sold to James Hutchings. So.

Scovell, Thomas. S for housebreaking at Barrington Lent R 14 yrs Summer TB Aug 1738. G.

Scowlcroft, William. S 14 yrs Summer LC Bal Co., Md., Dec 1770. Ch.

Scrivener, John. S Apr T May 1752 *Lichfield*. L.

Scruton, Robert. S 14 yrs Apr 1746 T Apr 1746 *Laura*. M.

Scudder, John. R Summer 1772 T *Justitia* Jan 1773. E.

Scully, Ann. S Lent T *Thornton* May LC AA Co., Md., Jul 1774. M.

Sculthorpe, Thomas. S Lent T Apr 1760. Ru.

Scutt, John. S Summer 1751 R Lent T May 1752 *Lichfield*. Sx.

Scutt, William. S Summer 1751 R Lent T May 1752 *Lichfield*. Sx.

Seaborn, William. S Summer T Aug 1749 *Thames*. E.

Seaburn, Sarah. T May 1751 *Tryal*. K.

Seager *als* Boxer, Benjamin. S s at Kinver Summer LC Md *William* Dec 1774 & sold to Aubrey Richardson. St.

Seger, Robert. SQS Bury St. Edmunds 1766. Su,

Seager, Thomas. R Jul LC Md *William* Dec 1774 & sold to James Hutchings. Ha.

Seal, Ann. S Bristol s at English Bicknor & R 14 yrs Jul T *Restoration* LC Bal Co., Md., Oct 1771. G.

Seal, John. T *Justitia* Jan 1774. L.

Seal, William. S Jul-Dec 1747 LC Knt Co., Md., from *St. George* Mar 1748. M.

Sealy, Robert. S Summer 1731 LC Knt Co., Md., from *Falcon* Apr 1732. So.

Seaman, Jane wife of William. S Sep-Oct 1773 T *Justitia* Jan 1774. M.

Seamer, Nicholas. S Lent 1744 LC Knt Co., Md., from *Susannah* Aug 1744. De.

Seers, Bernard. S May-Jun T Aug 1752 *Tryal*. M.

Seers, Constant. T Sep 1737 *Pretty Patsy*. L.

Sears, George. S Apr 1746 T Apr 1746 *Laura*. M.

Sears, Mary Ann. S Sep-Oct T *Justitia* Dec 1774. M.

Sears, Robert. S & T Jan 1736 *Dorsetshire* LC Va Sep 1736. L.

Seddon *als* Cooper, James of Manchester, cloak dresser. SQS Apr 1719. La.

Seddon, John. S Apr T *Dolphin* May 1763. L.

Seddon, Mary of Manchester, spinster. SQS Apr T Jul 1734. La.

Seddon, Thomas of Bolton le Moors, weaver. SQS Jan 1727. La.

Seddon, Thomas of Manchester. SQS Apr 1730. La.

Sedgwick, Richard. S 14 yrs Apr-Jun 1739 T *Sea Nymph* to Md. M.

Sell, Richard. T *Justitia* Feb 1776. L.

Sell, William. S Lent T *Thornton* May LC AA Co., Md., Jul 1774. M.

Seller, Agnes of Tiverton. SQS Tiverton May 1734 LC Knt Co., Md, Mar 1735 from *Falcon*. De.

Seller, William. S Lent LC AA Co., Md., from *Thornton* Jul 1775. L.

Sellersat *als* Selerate, John. S Summer T Oct 1750 *Rachael*. E.

Sellick, Elizabeth. T May 1746. De.

Sellwood, Sarah. S Summer 1718 LC from *Sophia* QA Co., Md. Mar 1719. So.

Selly [Silly] *als* Parrish, John. S s gelding R 14 yrs Lent T Oct 1738. Ca.

Selvie, George. S Apr-May T *Tryal* Jul 1754. M.

Senturelli, Joseph. S Jan T Mar 1750 *Tryal*. L.

Serjeant, Elizabeth. SQS Bristol as accomplice of Sarah Davis Oct 1761 TB to Md Oct 1762. G.

Sergeant, Thomas. S Lent LC AA Co., Md., from *Thornton* May 1771. M.

Servant, Mary. S Sep-Oct 1772 T *Justitia* Jan 1773. M.

Sevier, Elizabeth. S Lent 1732 LC Knt Co., Md., from *Falcon* Apr 1734. So.

Seward, James. S & R 14 yrs Aug 1771, respited for report Mar but LC Bal Co., Md Sep 1772. So.

Sewell, Jeremy. PT Jun R Oct 1673 LC Md from *Charles* May 1674. M.

Sewell, Richard. S Dec 1782 LC Bal Co., Md., Dec 1783 from *Swift* LC Bal Co., Md., Dec 1783 from *Swift*. L.

Sexton, John. R but died Sep 1747. Nf.

Seyers, John. S Jan T *Plain Dealer* Jan 1746. M.

Seymour, Ann. S Apr T *Dolphin* Apr 1761. M.

Seymour, Charles Stewart. S Jun 1739 T *Sea Nymph* to Md. L.

Seymour/Seamour, Thomas. S Summer 1732 AT Lent LC Annapolis from *Patapsco* Nov 1733. Wa.

Shackerly, Henry. S for highway robbery Summer 1722 R Apr 1723. Sy.

Shackerly, Sampson. S for highway robbery Summer 1722 R Apr 1723. Sy.

Shaen, William. S Aug T *Phoenix* Oct 1760. L.

Shakespeare, John. S s horse in Smitherfield Summer 1759 R 14 yrs Lent 1760. Wo.

Shank (Shonk), John. S Summer 1759 R 14 yrs Lent T Apr 1760 *Thetis*. E.

Sharkey, Lewis. S Dec T *Justitia* Dec 1774. L.

Sharman, Thomas. S Aug 1752. Li.

Sharp, Ann. S Lent T Apr 1757. Wa.

Sharpe, Christopher. S Jul T Aug 1749 *Thames*. L.

Sharpe, Elizabeth. T *Industry* Feb 1772. K.

Sharp, Jane, spinster. SCity Michaelmas 1762 (AHJ). Nl.

Sharp, Richard. S Summer 1773. Le.

Sharp, Thomas. S Lent 1758 TB to Md. No.

Sharp, Thomas. SQS Oct 1771 LC Bal Co., Md., Jul 1772. So.

Sharpells, Henry. S s iron hoops Feb T Apr 1735 *Patapsco* LC Annapolis Oct 1735. M.

Sharpless, Joseph. S Aug 1752. Li.

Sharpley, James. S Apr-May T *Saltspring* Jul 1775. M.

Shaston, Henry. S Summer 1738. Nt.

Shaw, Charles. R 14 yrs Dec T *Justitia* Dec 1774. M.

Shaw, James. S Lancaster 1751 (AHJ). La.

Shaw, Jane. S Sep T *Maryland Packet* Oct 1761. M.

Shaw, John. S Lent, R Summer T Sep 1753. Wa.

Shaw, Mary. S Jun-Dec 1745 T *Plain Dealer* Jan 1746. M.

Shaw, Mary. SQS Yarmouth Summer 1747 LC Knt Co., Md., from *St. George* Mar 1748. Nf.

Shaw, Robert. S Lent 1731. Li.

Shaw, Robert. S May 1770. Li.

Shaw, Thomas of St. Olave, Southwark. SQS Jan T *Thames* Feb 1751. Sy.

Shaw, Thomas. S Lent T Apr 1774 TB to Md. No.

Shay, Jarvis *als* Gervase. S Apr T May 1752 *Lichfield*. L.

Sheaf, William. S Jan-Apr T *Lichfield* May 1749. M.

Shean, James. S Lent LC AA Co., Md., from *Hanover Planter* Jul 1773. L.

Shean, Joseph. S Mar T Apr 1742 LC PG Co., Md. Do.

Shearing, Mary. R Summer 1772 T *Justitia* Jan 1773. Sy.

Shears, Isaac. S Sep-Oct 1775 T *Justitia* Feb 1776. M.

Shears, Leonard. S Summer LC Bal Co., Md., Dec 1772. So.

Shears, Mary. S Mar T *Neptune* Mar 1761. L.

Sheen, William. S Lent T *Thornton* May LC AA Co., Md., Jul 1774. M.

Sheerman, William. SQS Jan T *Greyhound* Feb 1755. M.

Sheers, Elizabeth. S Aug 1752. So.

Sheers, John. S Jan LC QA Co., Md., from *Leopard* May 1738. De.

Sheffield, Thomas. S May-Jun T Aug 1752 *Tryal*. M.

Sheirs, Richard. SW Lent LC AA Co., Md., from *Hanover Planter* Jul 1773. M.

Sheldon, Mary. S Sep-Oct 1772 T *Justitia* Jan 1773. M.

Shelley, John. S Lent LC AA Co., Md., from *Thornton* Jul 1775. Sx.

Shelly, Mary. S 14 yrs Chelmsford Jan 1763 (AHJ). E.

Shelley, Philip. S Summer 1760 R 14 yrs Lent T *Dolphin* Apr 1761. E.

Shelly, Thomas. S Chelmsford Jan 1763 (AHJ). E.

Shelmerdine, Jonathan of Manchester, weaver. SQS Jan 1724 T Apr 1725. La.

Shelock, James. R for life Sep T *Barnard* Oct 1756. M.

Shelton, James. S Feb T *Neptune* Mar 1761. L.

Shelton, John. SQS Jan LC AA Co., Md., from *Thornton* Jul 1775. M.

Shelton, Jonah. S Lent T Apr 1758 *Lux* from London. Db.

Shelvern, Robert. S Sep T Dec 1746. Nt.

Shepherd, Charles. S s sheep Summer 1750 R 14 yrs Lent 1751 (GJ). He.

Shepherd, Charles. S for life S Lent LC Bal Co., Md., Jun 1773. Wo.

Shepherd, Elizabeth. S 14 yrs Exeter Mar 1758 (AHJ). De.

Shepherd, John. S s wooden drawer Sep 1735 T Jan 1736 *Dorsetshire* LC Va Sep 1736. M.

Shepperd, Philip. SQS Jan LC Bal Co., Md., Apr 1773. G.

Sheppard, Robert. S Apr 1774 but taken from transport ship & pardoned in same month. M.

Shepherd, William. S Feb T 14 yrs Mar 1750 *Tryal*. M.

Sheppard, William. R Jul LC Md *William* Dec 1774 & sold to James Hutchings; runaway. Ha.

Sherlock, Ralph. S Sep T Oct 1750 *Rachael*. M.

Sherlock, William. S Jan T *Thames* Feb 1751. M.

Sherrard, George. S Summer LC Bal Co., Md., Dec 1770. St.

Sherrard, John. S Dec 1753-Jan 1754 T *Thames* Mar 1754. M.

Sherrard, Nathaniel. S Oct 1751-Jan 1752 T *Thames* Mar 1752. M.

Sherrard *als* Harwood, Robert. S Apr T *Lichfield* May 1749. L.

Sherwood, William. S Hull Oct 1732 T Jul 1733. Y.

Sherwood, William. S & T Apr 1751. No.

Shettleworth, Thomas. S Summer T Oct 1750 *Rachael*. E.

Shields, Mary. S Lent LC AA Co., Md., from *Hanover Planter* Jul 1773. M.

Shields, Patrick. S May-Jul T *Tayloe* Jul 1774. M.

Shipper, William. S Jan T *Justitia* May 1745. L.

Shipton, William. S s money Mar R 14 yrs Summer 1757. St.

Shirley, John. R 14 yrs Jul T *Tayloe* Jul 1774. M.

Shoebotham, Thomas. S s at Leek Lent 1750 LC QA Co., Md., from *Chester* Dec 1752. St.

Shonk, John (1759) - *See* Shank. E.

Shoran, Ann. T from Dublin by *Hercules*, LC Bal. Co., Md., Aug 1773, sold to James Wilson of Augusta Co., Virginia. Ir.

Shore, Isaac. S Summer T Sep 1751 *Greyhound*. Sx.

Shore, John. T Oct 1750 *Rachael*. M.

Shores, Edward. S & T for life Mar 1750 *Tryal*. L.

Short, Ann. S Summer T from London Dec 1737. No.

Short, Nicholas. S s lead Jan T Apr 1735 *Patapsco* LC Annapolis Oct 1735. M.

Short, Philip. R 14 yrs Dec 1773 T *Justitia* Jan 1774. M.

Shorter, William (1773). See Fuller. So.

Shortoe, George. S Lent LC Bal Co., Md., Jun 1773. So.

Shrieve, John. S Lent R 14 yrs Summer 1747 LC Knt Co., Md , from *St. George* Mar 1748. E.

Shrimplin, John. S Summer T Aug 1749 *Thames*. E.

Shrobb, Edward. R Summer 1773 T *Justitia* Jan 1774. Ht.

Shrons, Godfrey. S Lent T *Dolphin* May 1763. K.

Shute, Henry. S Summer 1718 LC from *Sophia* QA Co., Md. Mar 1719. De.

Shute, John Jr. T *Tayloe* Jul 1773. L.

Sibballs, Robert. S s pewter pots Dec 1735 T Jan 1736 *Dorsetshire* LC Va Sep 1736. M.

Sibre, Samuel. S Apr T Jun 1748 *Lichfield*. L.

Sibthorpe, William. S Jul T *Barnard* Oct 1756. M.

Siday, Elizabeth wife of William. S 14 yrs Lent LC AA Co., Md., from *Thornton* May 1771. L.

Siday, John. S Lent T *Tryal* Jul 1754. E.

Sidebotham, Peter of Salford. SQS Jan 1724 T Apr 1725. La.

Sidey, Jane. SQS Jul 1772 LC Bal Co., Md., from *Adventure* Mar 1773. Nl.

Sidwell, Jonathan. S Lent LC Bal Co., Md., Jun 1773. So.

Sikes, John. T 1745. Y.

Silcock *als* Chamber, Ann. S Jan-Apr T Jun 1748 *Lichfield*. M.

Silcox, Susan. S Lent LC Potomac, Va., from *Martha* Dec 1724. Wi.

Silver, Ann. R 14 yrs Oct 1772 T *Justitia* Jan 1773. M.

Silvester, Richard. S & R 14 yrs Summer LC Md *William* Dec 1774 & sold to Elisha Warfield; runaway. St.

Silvester, Thomas. S Lent but pardoned Apr 1773. M.

Silvey, Aaron. S Oct 1772 T *Justitia* Jan 1773. L.

Simberell *als* Simberlen, Francis. R 14 yrs Dec 1773 T *Justitia* Jan 1774. M.

Simcock, Theophilus. S s at Penn Lent T *Tayloe* Jul 1773. Bu.

Simcox, Thomas. S Summer T Sep 1753. Wa.

Simmonds, Charles, a little boy. S May 1735 T Jan 1736 *Dorsetshire* LC Va Sep 1736. M.

Simmons, Anne. S Apr T *Justitia* May 1745. L.

Simmons, John. S s sheep Lent R 14 yrs Summer 1760 TB to Va. No.

Simmons *als* Symonds, John. S Lent LC AA Co., Md., from *Hanover Planter* Jul 1773. M.

Simmons, Joseph [John]. S Lent 1764. Li.

Simmons, Love. S Oct 1751-Jan 1752 T *Thames* Mar 1752. M.

Simmons, Mark. S Summer 1770 T Apr 1771. Li.

Simmons, Nicholas. S Lent LC AA Co., Md., from *Thornton* Jul 1773. Sy.

Simmons, Thomas. S & T 14 yrs Jan 1736 *Dorsetshire* LC Va Sep 1736. L.

Simmons, William. S Summer T Sep 1751 *Greyhound*. K.

Simms, Elizabeth, *als* wife of William Terry. S Jul-Sep T *Ruby* Oct 1754. M.

Simms, Henry. S May T Jul 1745 *Italian Merchant*. M.

Simms, Jane. S May-Jul T Jul 1748 *Mary*. M.

Simms, John. S Apr T May 1750 *Lichfield*. M.

Simon, John, private soldier. S Jan-Feb T Apr 1753 *Thames*. M.

Simon, Mark. S Apr 1771. Li.

Simonds, Elizabeth. S Lent T *Thornton* May LC AA Co., Md., Jul 1774. L.

Simons, Abraham. S Sep-Oct 1772 T *Justitia* Jan 1773. M.

Simons, David. S May-Jul T *Tayloe* Jul 1774. M.

Simons, Humphrey. S Lent R Summer T Sep 1754. Wa.

Simons, Simon. S Sep-Oct 1772 T *Justitia* Jan 1773. M.

Simpkin, Ruth. S Lent T Jun 1748 *Lichfield*. Sx.

Simpkinson, Robert. S Dec 1749-Jan 1750 T Mar 1750 *Tryal*. M.

Simpson, Ann. S Dec 1746 T Jan 1747 *George William*. L.

Simpson, Ann. S Lent LC AA Co., Md., from *Thornton* Jul 1775. L.

MORE EMIGRANTS IN BONDAGE

Simpson, Daniel. S for highway robbery & R 14 yrs Summer 1772, died on passage to Va on *Trimly*. O.

Simpson, Daniel. S Summer 1751 R 14 yrs Lent T May 1752 *Lichfield*. Sy.

Simpson, Edward. SQS Devizes 1750 (AHJ). Wi.

Simpson, James. S Lent T *Dolphin* May 1763. Ht.

Simpson, William. S Apr T Jun 1748 *Lichfield*. L.

Simpson, William. S Summer 1749 R 14 yrs Lent T May 1750 *Lichfield*. K.

Sinclair, William. T May 1751 *Tryal*. Sy.

Singer, Isaac. SQS & T Jul 1773 *Tayloe* to Va. M.

Singer, Michael. S May-Jul T *Tayloe* Jul 1774. M.

Singer, Thomas. S May-Jul T *Tayloe* Jul 1774. M.

Singleton, Bridget. S Feb but pardoned in Apr 1773. L.

Singleton, Bridget. S Lent LC AA Co., Md., from *Thornton* Jul 1775. M.

Sipthorp, Alexander. S s at Walton & R Summer 1772 T *Justitia* Jan 1773. Bu.

Sircomb, Thomas. S 14 yrs Summer 1731 LC Knt Co., Md., from *Falcon* Apr 1732. De.

Skae, John. S Lent R 14 yrs Summer 1759. St.

Skate, Lucy. S Jun T *Tryal* Jul 1754. L.

Skatt, Timothy Featherstonehaugh. S Jul T *Tayloe* Jul 1774. L.

Skelt, John. S Feb T *Thames* Mar 1754. L.

Skelton, Eleanor. S Summer T Aug 1749 *Thames*. K.

Skelton, Richard. S Oct 1738 LC QA Co., Md. Jun 1739. So.

Skinner, Anthony. S Summer 1734 LC Knt Co., Md., Mar 1735 from *Falcon*. De.

Skinner, Thomas. S s mare & R 14 yrs Summer 1771 TB to Md. No.

Skinner, William. T Sep 1737 *Pretty Patsy*. L.

Skofield, Elizabeth. S for murder of her bastard child Lent R Nov 1724. Su.

Skull *als* Scull, William. S 14 yrs for receiving Aug T *Restoration* LC Bal Co., Md., Oct 1771. So.

Slade, Moses (1773). *See* Morgan. Wi.

Slade, Samuel. SQS Bristol Mar TB May LC Md from *Isabella* Jul 1775 & sold to Waters & Gartrall. G.

Slake, John. S Lent LC Bal Co., Md., Jul 1772. Do.

Slape, Thomas. S Oct 1738 LC QA Co., Md. Jun 1739. So.

Slate, James. S Jan-Apr T *Lichfield* May 1749. M.

Slater, Isaac. S Summer T *Barnard* Oct 1756. K.

Slater, John. S Jan-Apr T *Lichfield* May 1749. M.

Slaughter, John. PT Jun R Oct 1673 LC Md from *Charles* May 1674. M.

Slaughter, Mary. S Jul-Sep T *Ruby* Oct 1754. M.

Slee, Thomas. S Lent 1733 LC Knt Co., Md., from *Hawk* Apr 1735. So.

Sleeford, George. S Lent 1724 but escaped & no further record found. Li.

Slight, John. SW Jan LC AA Co., Md., from *Thornton* Jul 1775. M.

Slinney, Bridget. S Lent LC AA Co., Md., from *Thornton* Jul 1773. L.

Slocombe, George. S Oct 1738 1738 LC QA Co., Md. Jun 1739. So.

Slocombe, Isaac. S 14 yrs Lent LC Bal Co., Md., Jun 1773. So.

Sly, John. S Summer 1731 LC Knt Co., Md., from *Falcon* Apr 1732. So.

Slye, Robert. S Lent LC Bal Co., Md., Jul 1772. G.

Small, John. SQS for picking pockets Jul 1769 (RG). Be.

Small, Tobias of Romford, woolcomber. SQS Jan T May 1750 *Lichfield*. E.

Small, William. SQS Winchester s fowls Mar 1752. Ha.

Smallacombe, Thomasin. R 14 yrs Mar 1742 LC PG Co., Md. Co.

Smalley, John. S Lent T Dec 1737. Le.

Smallman, John. S s sheep & R Apr 1762. Sh.

Smallpass, Richard. S 14 yrs Summer T Oct 1750 *Rachael.* Sy.

Smart, John. S 1775. No.

Smart, Mary. S Jan T *Justitia* May 1745. L.

Smee, Robert. S for burglary Lent R 14 yrs Summer T Oct 1750 *Rachael.* E.

Smethurst, Thomas. SQS Jan 1729. La.

Smeton, William. SQS Apr 1728. La.

Smith, Abraham. S Bristol s oxen in Henbury Summer 1759 R 14 yrs Lent 1760 (BJ). G.

Smith, Alexander. S City 1752 (AHJ). Nl.

Smyth, Anne *als* Swift. R for Barbados Oct 1673 but LC Md from *Charles* May 1674. L.

Smith, Anne, widow. S Bristol Apr 1743 LC Knt Co., Md., from *Raven* Feb 1744. G.

Smith, Ann. S Feb-Apr T *Laura* Apr 1746. M.

Smith, Ann of Fryerning. SQS Jan T May 1749 *Lichfield.* E.

Smith, Ann. S Lent T *Thornton* May LC AA Co., Md., Jul 1774. M.

Smith, Barwell, S Oct-Dec 1754 T *Greyhound* Feb 1755. M.

Smith, Benjamin. S for life Oct 1751-Jan 1752 T *Thames* Mar 1752. M.

Smith, Benjamin. S Lent LC Bal Co., Md., Dec 1770 from *Trotman* & sold to Jonathan Plowman. Y.

Smith, Catherine. SQS Jan 1750 LC QA Co., Md., from *Catherine* Nov 1750. De.

Smith, Catherine. S 14 yrs Lent LC AA Co., Md., from *Thornton* Jul 1773. Sy.

Smyth, Charles. R for Barbados Oct 1673 but LC Md from *Charles* May 1674. L.

Smith, Charles. S Dec 1749-Jan 1750 T Mar 1750 *Tryal.* M.

Smith, Christopher of Skipton. S Summer 1736. Y.

Smith, Daniel of St. James, Colchester. S Lent T Jul 1745 *Italian Merchant.* E.

Smith, Daniel. S Lent 1772 LC Bal Co., Md., Apr 1773. Wo.

Smith, Deborah. AT Jul T Sep 1720, died on passage in *Gilbert* 1721 (NM). No.

Smith, Devereux. S & T Lent 1754. Wa.

Smith, Edward. S Summer 1732 AT Lent 1733. Wa.

Smith, Edward. S Dec 1749-Jan 1750 T Mar 1750 *Tryal.* M.

Smith, Edward. S Lent T Summer 1752. Wa.

Smith, Edward. S Summer T Oct 1756. Nt.

Smith, Edward *als* Piddon. S Jul 1757. Ha.

Smith, Edward. S Lent LC AA Co., Md., from *Thornton* May 1771. L.

Smith, Edward. S Lent LC AA Co., Md., from *Thornton* May 1771. M.

Smith, Elias. SQS Oct 1770 LC Bal Co., Md., Jun 1771. Sh.

Smith, Elizabeth. S s apron Jan T Apr 1735 *Patapsco* LC Annapolis Oct 1735. M.

Smith, Elizabeth. S Dec 1735 T Jan 1736 *Dorsetshire* LC Va Sep 1736. M.

Smith, Elizabeth. S Bristol Apr 1739. G.

Smith, Elizabeth. S Feb T Apr 1746. Sh.

Smith, Elizabeth. S Oct-Dec 1750 T *Thames* Feb 1751. M.

Smith, Elizabeth. S Summer T Sep 1753. O.

Smith *als* Hall, Elizabeth. S Apr-May T *Tryal* Jul 1754. M.

Smith, Elizabeth. S Jul-Sep T *Ruby* Oct 1754. M.

Smith, Elizabeth. S York 1755 (AHJ). Y.

Smith, Elizabeth. S 14 yrs for receiving from George Smith at Pinvin Lent 1762. Wo.

Smith, Elizabeth. S Summer 1773 but found pregnant, removed from ship on appeal of mother & pardoned Dec 1773. Sy.

Smith, Elizabeth wife of John. S s at Old Swinford Summer LC Md *William* Dec 1774 & sold to Thomas Smyth. Wo.

Smith, Elizabeth. S Lent LC AA Co., Md., from *Thornton* Jul 1775. M.

Smith, Francis. T Summer 1745 T Feb 1746. Ha.

Smith, George. S Summer T *Barnard* Oct 1756. Sy.

Smith, George. SQS Apr S Summer LC Bal Co., Md., Dec 1772. De.

Smith, George. S Lent LC Bal Co., Md., Jun 1773. So.

Smith, Hannah. S Sep-Oct T *Justitia* Dec 1774. M.

Smith, Hannah. S Dec T *Justitia* Dec 1774. M.

Smith, Henry. S Summer 1732. Li.

Smith, Henry. S Summer 1748 R 14 yrs Summer 1749. Y.

Smith, Henry of Little Hallingbury. SQS Oct 1749 T May 1750 *Lichfield*. E.

Smith, Henry. S Lent 1758. Nt.

Smith, Henry. S Lent LC AA Co., Md., from *Thornton* Jul 1773. K.

Smith, Henry. S Lent T *Thornton* May LC AA Co., Md., Jul 1774. M.

Smith, Henry. SQS Apr T *Thornton* May LC AA Co., Md., Jul 1774. M.

Smith, James of Aughton. SQS Jul 1722. La.

Smith, James. S Jan T *Thames* Feb 1751. M.

Smith, James. S 14 yrs Lent LC Bal Co., Md., Jun 1773. G.

Smith, James. S May T *Saltspring* Jul 1775. L.

Smith, James Elsender. S Durham 1756 (AHJ). Du.

Smith, Jane, *als* Singing Jenny. S Apr T *Justitia* May 1745. L.

Smith, Jane wife of Gabriel of Wakering, yeoman. SQS Jul T Aug 1749 *Thames*. E.

Smith, Jane. S Summer T Aug 1749 *Thames*. Sy.

Smith, Jane wife of G. Robinson. S City Michaelmas 1761. Nl.

Smith, Jane. S 14 yrs Apr-Jun 1739 T *Sea Nymph* to Md. M.

Smith, Jeremiah. S Summer T *Phoenix* Oct 1760. K.

Smith, John. S Oct R Dec 1728. Ca.

Smith, John. S Lent 1732 LC Knt Co., Md., from *Falcon* Mar 1733. So.

Smith, John, a boy. S s linen Apr T Dec 1735 *John* LC Md Sep 1736. M.

Smith, John. S 14 yrs Summer LC Knt Co., Md., from *Bideford* Nov 1737. So.

Smith *als* Sims, John. T Sep 1737 *Pretty Patsy*. L.

Smith, John. S for s from stable of Duke of Kingston & R 14 yrs Jun 1740. Nt.

Smith, John. S Jan T *Justitia* May 1745. L.

Smith, John. S Feb-Apr 1745 T *Justitia* May . M.

Smith, John. S May-Jul T *Mary* Sep 1746. M.

Smith, John. S Summer T Aug 1749 *Thames*. Sx.

Smith, John. S Exeter Sep 1749 (AHJ). De.

Smith, John. SQS Apr T May 1750 *Lichfield*. M.

Smith, John. S Sep 1750. Li.

Smith, John. S Summer T Oct 1750 *Rachael*. E.

Smith, John. S for highway robbery Summer 1751 R 14 yrs Lent T May 1752 *Lichfield*. Bu.

Smith, John. SQS Apr T May 1752 *Lichfield*. M.

Smith, John. S Apr T May 1752 *Lichfield*. L.

Smith, John. T Aug 1752 *Tryal*. K.

Smith, John. S Summer 1753 R 14 yrs Lent T *Tryal* Jul 1754. Ht.

Smith, John. S & T Lent 1754. Wa.

Smith, John. S Apr 1756. Li.

Smith, John. S York 1757 (AHJ). Y.

Smith, John. S with Joseph & William Smith s sheep Summer 1766 R for life Lent T May 1767 *Thornton* . Bu.

Smith, John. SQS Woodbridge for returning 3 times to Halesworth from Norwich 1767. Su.

Smith, John. S Summer LC Bal Co., Md., Dec 1772. St.

Smith, John. R Jul T *Tayloe* Jul 1773. M.

Smith, John. R Summer 1773 T *Justitia* Jan 1774. K.

Smith, John. S 14 yrs Sep-Oct T *Justitia* Dec 1774. M.

Smith, John. S Jul LC Md *William* Dec 1774 & sold to James Hutchings. Do.

Smith, John. S 14 yrs Jul T *Saltspring* Jul 1775. L.

Smith, John. T *Justitia* Feb 1776. L.

Smith, Jonas. S Sep 1750. Li.

Smith, Jonathan. S Oct T Oct 1749 *Mary*. L.

Smith, Joseph. S Lent 1738. Li.

Smith, Joseph. S Norwich Summer T Sep 1738. Nf.

Smith, Joseph. S Jan T *Plain Dealer* Jan 1746. M.

Smith, Joseph. S Jan T *Thames* Feb 1751. L.

Smith, Joseph. S & T Aug 1752 *Tryal*. L.

Smith, Joseph. S Summer T Oct 1756. Wa.

Smith, Joseph. S s sheep Summer 1766 R for life with William and Smith, John. S Lent T May 1767 *Thornton* . Bu.

Smith, Joseph. S May-Jul T *Tayloe* Jul 1773. M.

Smith, Lomas. SQS Ipswich 1758. Su.

Smith, Margaret. S Oct 1744-Jan 1745 T *Plain Dealer* Jan 1746. M.

Smith, Margaret. S Jul T *Phoenix* Oct 1760. M.

Smith, Martha. T Summer 1745 T Feb 1746. Ha.

Smith, Martha. S Oct 1772 T *Justitia* Jan 1773. L.

Smith, Mary. S s breeches Apr T Dec 1735 *John* LC Annapolis Sep 1736. M.

Smith, Mary. S Dec 1746 T Jan 1747 *George William*. L.

Smith *als* Ordery *als* Pepper, Mary. S Jan-Apr T Jun 1748 *Lichfield*. M.

Smith *als* Brown, Mary. S Jan T *Thames* Feb 1751. M.

Smith *als* Richardson, Mary. S Feb T *Tryal* Mar 1757. M.

Smith, Mary. S Apr T *Phoenix* Oct 1760. M.

Smith, Mary of Low Leyton. SQS Jul T *Maryland Packet* Oct 1761. E.

Smith, Mary. S Lent T *Dolphin* May 1763. Sy.

Smith, Mary. S Jul T *Beverly* Aug 1763. M.

Smith, Mary. S Summer LC Bal Co., Md., Dec 1770, sold to Andrew Buchanan, merchant. St.

Smith, Mary. S Sep-Oct 1772 T *Justitia* Jan 1773. M.

Smith, Mary. S Lent LC AA Co., Md., from *Thornton* Jul 1773. M.

Smith, Mary. S May-Jul T *Tayloe* Jul 1773. M.

Smith, Mary. S Lent T *Thornton* May LC AA Co., Md., Jul 1774. K.

Smith, Mary. S Sep-Oct 1773 T *Justitia* Jan 1774. M.

Smith, Mary. S May T *Saltspring* Jul 1775. L.

Smith, Mary. S Sep-Oct 1775 T *Justitia* Feb 1776. M.

Smith, Mary. T *Justitia* Feb 1776. L.

Smith, Matthew of St. Michael, Oxford, a lad. S Summer 1720. O.

Smith, Peter. S 14 yrs Summer 1770 LC Bal Co., Md., Jun 1771. Sh.

Smith, Richard. T Lent 1750. Li.

Smith, Richard. S Summer T Oct 1752. Wa.

Smith, Richard. S Apr-May T *Tryal* Jul 1754. M.

Smith, Richard (1756) - *See* Hurst. No.

Smith, Richard. S Apr T *Dolphin* May 1763. M.

Smith, Richard (1769) - *See* Frizer. Wo.

Smith, Richard. SQS Reading s crayfish Jan 1769 (RG). Be.

Smith, Richard. S Lent LC AA Co., Md., from *Hanover Planter* Jul 1773. L.

Smith, Robert. S Lent TB to Md Aug 1729. Db.

Smith *als* James, Robert, a boy. S for highway robbery Lent R 14 yrs Summer 1748 (GJ). Be.

Smith, Robert. SW Apr T *Thornton* May LC AA Co., Md., Jul 1774. M.

Smith, Samuel. S Summer 1732 AT Lent 1733. Wa.

Smith, Samuel. S Summer T Sep 1751 *Greyhound*. Sy.

Smith, Samuel. S Lent 1772 LC Bal Co., Md., Apr 1773. Wo.

Smith, Sarah (1774). *See* McCoy. M.

Smith, Sarah. S May-Jul T *Tayloe* Jul 1774. M.

Smith, Sarah. SQS Jul T Sep 1751 *Greyhound*. M.

Smith, Sarah. S Summer 1737. Li.

Smith, Sarah. S for perjury Dec 1773 T *Justitia* Jan 1774. L.

Smith, Solomon. SQS Feb T May 1751 *Tryal*. M.

Smith, Susan. S Jul T Dec 1735 *John* LC Annapolis Sep 1736. M.

Smith, Susanna. S May-Jul T Jul 1748 *Mary*. M.

Smith, Susanna. S Apr-May T *Tryal* Jul 1754. M.

Smith, Susannah. S Lent 1766 found pregnant by jury R Summer T *Justitia* Sep 1767. Bu.

Smith, Terence. S Apr T *Dolphin* Apr 1761. M.

Smith, Thomas. S 14 yrs Apr-Jun 1739 T *Sea Nymph* to Md M.

Smith, Thomas. S Jun 1739 T *Sea Nymph* to Md. L.

Smith, Thomas. T Jul 1747. Su.

Smith, Thomas. S Apr T *Lichfield* May 1749. L.

Smith, Thomas. S May-Jul T Aug 1749 *Thames*. M.

Smith, Thomas. S Apr T May 1750 *Lichfield*. L.

Smith *als* Broach, Thomas. SQS May T Sep 1751 *Greyhound*. M.

Smith, Thomas. T May 1751 *Tryal*. K.

Smith, Thomas (1753) - *See* Pullen. Be.

Smith, Thomas. SQS Warminster or New Sarum T *Randolph* Sep 1768. Wi.

Smith, Thomas. S 14 yrs Lent LC Bal Co., Md., Jun 1773. Sh.

Smith, William. S Feb T Apr 1735 *Patapsco* LC Annapolis Oct 1735. M.

Smith, William. T Apr 1735 *Patapsco* LC Annapolis Oct 1735. Ht.

Smith, William. S Jan-Apr T *Lichfield* May 1749. M.

Smith, William. S Jul T Aug 1749 *Thames*. L.

Smith, William. S Jan T Mar 1750 *Tryal*. L.

Smith, William. S May-Jul T Sep 1751 *Greyhound*. M.

Smith, William. S Jul T Sep 1751. No.

Smith, William. T Summer T Sep 1753. Wa.

Smith, William. T *Ruby* Oct 1754. L.

Smith, William. S May T *Beverly* Aug 1763. M.

Smith, William. S with Joseph & John Smith s sheep Summer 1766 R 14 yrs Lent T May 1767 *Thornton*. Bu.

Smith, William. T from Glasgow but shipwrecked, to be held in Newgate from Dec 1770 for another ship. Sco.

Smith, William. S Lent LC Bal Co., Md., Jul 1772. St.

Smith, William. S Sep-Oct 1772 T *Justitia* Jan 1773. M.

Smith, William. S Lent LC AA Co., Md., from *Hanover Planter* Jul 1773. M.

Smith, William (2). S Lent LC AA Co., Md., from *Thornton* Jul 1773. M.

Smith, William (1773). *See* Fuller. So.

Smith, William (1773). See Todd. Nl.

Smith, William. S Lent T *Thornton* May LC AA Co., Md., Jul 1774. L.

Smith, William. S Dec T *Justitia* Dec 1774. L.

Smith, William Watkins. S Lent T *Dolphin* May 1763. Ht.

Smithers, Ann. S Feb 1773 but pardoned same month. L.

Smithiman *als* Aston, Thomas. S s flax at Wolverhampton Summer 1750 LC QA Co., Md., from *Chester* Dec 1752. St.

Smyther *als* Guyver, Sarah. T Apr 1735 *Patapsco* LC Annapolis Oct 1735. K.

Snaesby, Samuel. S & T Jan 1736 *Dorsetshire* LC Va Sep 1736. L.

Snailum, Thomas. SQS Jul S Summer LC Bal Co., Md., Dec 1772. So.

Sneesby, Richard. S Lent LC AA Co., Md., from *Thornton* Jul 1773. K.

Snell, James. T 1746. Su.

Snell, Richard. S Chelmsford Jan 1763 (AHJ). E.

Snellock, James. S & T Sep 1751 *Greyhound*. M.

Snook, Henry. S s sheep Lent R 14 yrs Summer 1754 (GJ). Be.

Snook, Thomas. SQS Lent LC Bal Co., Md., Jul 1774. Do.

Snow, John. S Lent s from warehouse R Jun T Jul 1723 *Alexander* LC Md Sep 1723. Bu.

Snow, Robert of Hertford. S as accessory to murder Summer 1745 R 14 yrs Lent T Sep 1746 *Mary*. Ht.

Sockett, Andrew. S Sep T *Maryland Packet* Oct 1761. M.

Sodin, Samuel. S Lent T Apr 1737. Wa.

Sole, George. S Lent T Jul 1747. Bd.

Solis, Andrew (1740) - *See* Sallis. G.

Sollon, James. S Jan T *Plain Dealer* Jan 1746. L.

Solomon, Aaron. S Sep-Oct 1772 T *Justitia* Jan 1773. M.

Solomon, Barnard. S 14 yrs for receiving Oct 1773 T *Justitia* Jan 1774. L.

Solomon, Emanuel. S Feb-Apr T May 1751 *Tryal.* M.

Solomon, Joshua. S Lent T *Thornton* May LC AA Co., Md., Jul 1774. L.

Solomon, Robert, *als* Blind Isaac. S Dec 1750 T *Thames* Feb 1751. L.

Solomon, Wolfe *als* Benjamin, *als* Wolfe, Solomon. S Aug LC Md *William* Dec 1774 & sold to James Hutchings. Co.

Solomons, Joseph (1774). *See* Abrahams. L.

Solomons, Levy. T *Justitia* Feb 1776. L.

Solomons, Solomon. S Lent LC AA Co., Md., from *Thornton* May 1771. M.

Solowin *als* Quin, Margaret. S s gold rings Dec 1761 R for life Feb 1762. M.

Somerhays, John (1732). See Somers.

Somers als Somerhays, John. S Lent 1732 LC Knt Co., Md., from *Hawk* Apr 1735. So.

Sorrell, Daniel. S Lent LC Knt Co., Md., from *Bideford* Nov 1737. So.

Sorrell, Joseph. S & R at Rochester, Kent, Lent T *Dolphin* May 1763. E.

Soul, Thomas. S 14 yrs Lent LC Bal Co., Md., Jun 1773. G.

Souter, William. S Aberdeen s oxen R Jun 1774. Sco.

South, John. S Feb T *Thames* Mar 1752. L.

South, John. S s heifers Apr R 14 yrs Summer 1758 (GJ). Sh.

South, Samuel. SQS for gambling at cards Jan T *Dolphin* Apr 1761. Sy.

Southall, Joseph. S s at Dudley Jul T *Restoration* LC Bal Co., Md., Oct 1771. Wo.

Southam, Thomas, SW Lent LC AA Co., Md., from *Hanover Planter* Jul 1773. M.

Southerby, Mary. S Oct-Dec 1754 T *Greyhound* Feb 1755. M.

Southerne *als* Southwell, Thomas. S for leading food riot Dec 1766. Be.

Southward, Catherine. S Exeter Oct 1751 (AHJ). De.

Southwell, Ignatus. S Apr 1753. Li.

Southwell, Thomas (1766) - *See* Southerne. Be.

Southwood, John. S 14 yrs Lent 1742 LC QA Co., Md., from *Kent* Jun 1743. De.

Sowden, Benjamin. S Jul T *Tayloe* Jul 1774. L.

Sowdin, Solomon. T Dec 1746. Li.

Spackman, Charles. S Apr T May 1751 *Tryal*. L.

Spake, Ann. S for arson Summer 1757 R for life Lent 1758. Be.

Spalding, Elizabeth. S May-Jul T Aug 1749 *Thames*. M.

Sparke, John. SQS Jul 1732 LC Knt Co., Md., from *Falcon* Mar 1733. De.

Sparke, William. S s sheep Summer 1746 T Jan 1747. De.

Sparkes, Henry. S Summer T *Ruby* Oct 1754. E.

Sparkes, Mary. S 14 yrs Summer 1734 LC Knt Co., Md., Mar 1735 from *Falcon*. De.

Sparks, Samuel. S Feb T from Liverpool Sep 1746. St.

Sparkes, Samuel. S Dec 1754 T *Greyhound* Feb 1755. L.

Sparks, Sarah. S Jan-Jun T Jul 1747 *Laura*. M.

Sparribell, Isaac. SQS Warminster or New Sarum T *Randolph* Sep 1768. Wi.

Sparrow *als* Parrott, John. SW Jan T *Thornton* May LC AA Co., Md., Jul 1774. M.

Sparrow, John. S Lent LC Bal Co., Md., Jul 1774. Do.

Sparrow, Joseph. S Summer 1733 T Summer 1734. Li.

Sparrow, Joseph. T May 1752 *Lichfield*. Sy.

Sparrow, Robert *als* Alliston, Ambrose. S Lent T *Thornton* May LC AA Co., Md., Jul 1774. E.

Speed, John Jr. S s horse Summer 1724 R 14 yrs Mar 1725. So.

Spence, Thomas. S s horse Lent 1729 R 14 yrs Summer 1730. Y.

Spenceley, John. S s hood Jan T Apr 1735 *Patapsco* LC Annapolis Oct 1735. M.

Spencer, Aaron. T *Justitia* Feb 1776. L.

Spencer, Arthur. S Apr T May 1747. So.

Spencer, Edward. S Summer 1741 LC QA Co., Md., from *Philleroy* Apr 1742 & to serve Peter Symons. Mo.

Spencer, Edward. S Lent LC AA Co., Md., from *Thornton* Jul 1775. M.

Spencer, James. S Sep T Oct 1750 *Rachael*. L.

Spencer, Jane. R Apr T Nov 1747. So.

Spencer, John. SQS Jan 1750 LC QA Co., Md., from *Catherine* Nov 1750. G.

Spencer, John. S Lent 1773; order for release dated May 1773 received after his ship had sailed. Db.

Spencer, Joseph. S Lent T Apr 1737. No.

Spencer, Mary. S Jan-Apr T *Lichfield* May 1749. M.

Spencer, Mary. S Sep-Oct 1772 T *Justitia* Jan 1773. M.

Spencer, Thomas. SQS Apr 1728. La.

Spettigue, Burchett. S Summer 1718 LC from *Sophia* QA Co., Md. Mar 1719. De.

Spicer, John. SQS Warminster Jul TB Sep 1741 LC QA Co., Md from *Philleroy* Apr 1742. Wi.

Spicer, Jonathan. S Lent LC AA Co., Md., from *Hanover Planter* Jul 1773. M.

Spinks, Daniel of St. Olave, Southwark, carpenter. SQS Jan T *Thames* Feb 1751. Sy.

Spire, Richard. T Jun 1747. Ha.

Spires, William. S Sep-Oct 1772 T *Justitia* Jan 1773. M.

Spite, Hannah. SQS Pontefract Lent 1738. Y.

Spittle, Robert. T May 1751 *Tryal*. Sy.

Spivey, James. S Apr T May 1751 *Tryal*. L.

Spragg, Abraham. S 14 yrs Lent 1750 LC QA Co., Md., from *Catherine* Nov 1750. Wo.

Spratt, Sarah. S Lent 1737 LC Knt Co., Md., from *Hawk* Nov 1737. Ha.

Spratt, Sarah. S Lent LC Bal Co., Md., Jul 1772. Wi.

Sprightley, Hannah. S Sep-Dec 1746 T Jan 1747 *George William*. M.

Sproson, John. S Lent LC AA Co., Md., from *Thornton* May 1771. L.

Sprout, Charles. R 14 yrs Dec 1723. Be.

Spurling, Elizabeth. S Apr T *Lichfield* May 1749. L.

Spurling, Henry. T Jul 1747. Sy.

Spurling, Nicholas. S Apr T *Lichfield* May 1749. L.

Spurway, Daniel. S 14 yrs Lent 1742 LC QA Co., Md., from *Kent* Jun 1743. De.

Squire, William. S 14 yrs Lent LC Bal Co., Md., Jun 1773. De.

Squires, James. S Lent T *Thornton* May LC AA Co., Md., Jul 1774. Sy.

Squires, Mary. S Oct T *Maryland Packet* Oct 1761. L.

Squirrell, Elizabeth of St. Giles, Colchester. S Lent T Jul 1745 *Italian Merchant*. E.

Stabler, John. S Apr T *Phoenix* Oct 1760. M.

Stacey, John. S for breaking & entering Lent R 14 yrs Summer 1745 (GJ). Be.

Stacey, Robert. S Lent T *Thornton* May LC AA Co., Md., Jul 1774. Sx.

Stacy, Thomas. S Summer 1718 LC from *Sophia* QA Co., Md. Mar 1719. Do.

Stacey, Thomas. Died in prison Jun 1746. Be.

Stackhouse, Samuel. S for housebreaking Aug 1753 (WJ). St.

Staddon *als* Stanton, John. S 14 yrs Lent 1742 LC QA Co., Md., from *Kent* Jun 1743. De.

Staddow, John. S Jan T *Plain Dealer* Jan 1746. L.

Stains, Benjamin of Great Baddow. S Lent T Jul 1745 *Italian Merchant*. E.

Stains, William. S s sheep Lent R 14 yrs Summer 1754 TB to Va. No.

Stakes, Elizabeth. S Sep 1750 T Jan 1751. Ha.

Stamford, James. SQS Lent LC AA Co., Md., from *Thornton* Jul 1773. M.

Stammers, John. S 14 yrs Lent LC AA Co., Md., from *Thornton* Jul 1775. E.

Stamp, Roger. S Summer 1746 T Jan 1747. De.

Stamper, Robert. S Lent R Jun T 14 yrs Aug 1752 *Tryal*. Sy.

Stanbury, Ann. S Jan T *Plain Dealer* Jan 1746. L.

Stanbury, William. S Lent LC Knt Co., Md., from *Unity* Nov 1733. De.

Standlick, Mark. S Aug 1752 (BJ). De.

Stanford, Elizabeth. S Lent T *Thornton* May LC AA Co., Md., Jul 1774. M.

Stanford, William. S Lent T Jun 1748 *Lichfield*. E.

Stanley *als* Brown, John. S Jan-Jun T Jul 1747 *Laura*. M.

Stanley, Thomas. S Lent R Summer T for life Sep 1751 *Greyhound*. Sy.

Stannifer, Mary. S Sep-Dec 1746 T Jan 1747 *George William*. M.

Stanning, John. S & T Jan 1736 *Dorsetshire* LC Va Sep 1736. L.

Stanninot, William. S Apr T May 1751 *Tryal*. M.

Stanton, Adam. S Apr-Jun 1739 T *Sea Nymph* to Md. M.

Stanton, James. S Lent LC AA Co., Md., from *Thornton* Jul 1775. M.

Stanton, John (1742). *See* Staddon. De.

Stanton, John. S Apr T for life May 1750 *Lichfield*. M.

Stapler, John. S Mar T *Thames* Mar 1754. L.

Staples, Matthew. S Lent LC AA Co., Md., from *Thornton* Jul 1775. L.

Starling, Edward. S May-Jul T *Tayloe* Jul 1773. M.

State, Edward. S Jul-Sep T *Ruby* Oct 1754. M.

MORE EMIGRANTS IN BONDAGE

Statham, John. S Lent 1734. Nt.

Statum, John. S Summer T from London Sep 1754. Wa.

Stave, Sarah. T 1746. Su.

Staveley, Elizabeth. S Sep T *Phoenix* Oct 1760. L.

Stavenaugh *als* Howell, Elizabeth. S May T Jul 1745 *Italian Merchant*. L.

Stead, David. S Lent 1731 LC Knt Co., Md., from *Falcon* Apr 1732. So.

Steale, William. S Sep-Oct 1772 T *Justitia* Jan 1773; runaway. M.

Steane [Stein], Thomas, carpenter, aged 28. AT s mare Jul T Sep 1720 LC from *Gilbert* Md May 1721 (NM). No.

Stedman, William. R Summer 1773 T *Justitia* Jan 1774. Sy.

Steed, Benjamin. S Launceston May 1755 (AHJ). Co.

Steed, Samuel. S Summer T Aug 1749 *Thames*; runaway. K.

Steel, John. T Sep 1737 *Pretty Patsy*. L.

Steel, John. S Summer 1772 T *Justitia* Jan 1773; runaway. K.

Steel, Joseph. S 14 yrs LC Bal Co., Md., Jul 1772. St.

Steele, Mary. S Lent T *Thornton* May LC AA Co., Md., Jul 1774. L.

Steel, Richard. S May-Jul T Sep 1751 *Greyhound*. M.

Steenson, Hugh. S Summer 1752 T Lent 1753. Db.

Steenson, Joseph. S Apr T Sep 1751. Db.

Steer, Hugh. S 14 yrs for receiving Mar but pardoned Apr 1773. De.

Steer, Thomas. S Lent LC AA Co., Md., from *Thornton* Jul 1775. Sx.

Stenson, James *als* William. S Summer T Aug 1749 *Thames*. Sy.

Stent, Deborah, an old offender. S Apr for receiving linen T 14 yrs Aug 1718 *Eagle* LC Charles Town Mar 1719. L.

Stent, Thomas. S Lent LC AA Co., Md., from *Thornton* Jul 1775. Sy.

Stephen *als* Bowen *als* Lewis, David. S Carmarthen for sacrilege R Apr 1762. Wal.

Stevens, Edward. S Lent R 14 yrs Summer T *Phoenix* Oct 1760. Sy.

Stevens, Henry. S Jan-Jun T Jul 1747 *Laura*. M.

Stevens, Henry. S Dec 1750 T *Thames* Feb 1751. L.

Stephens, John. S Apr-Jun 1739 T *Sea Nymph* to Md. M.

Stevens, John. S Jan T Mar 1750 *Tryal*. L.

Stephens, John. S Sep T Oct 1750 *Rachael*. M.

Stevens, John. S 14 yrs Lent LC AA Co., Md., from *Thornton* Jul 1775. K.

Stevens, Joseph. S s lead Feb T Apr 1735 *Patapsco* LC Annapolis Oct 1735. L.

Stephens, Joseph. S Summer T from London Sep 1754. Wa.

Stephens, Morgan Benjamin. S Feb 1738 (RM). Ha.

Stevens, Richard. S Launceston May 1755 (AHJ). Co.

Stevens, Robert. S Lent LC Bal Co., Md., Jul 1772. So.

Stevens, Thomas. S & R Summer LC Md *William* Dec 1774 & sold to James Hutchings. Wa.

Stephens *als* Pearce, Thomas. S 14 yrs Summer 1732 LC Knt Co., Md., from *Falcon* Apr 1734. Co.

Stephens, Thomas. S for life Lent LC Bal Co., Md., Jun 1773. Wo.

Stevens, William. S Summer 1718 LC from *Sophia* QA Co., Md. Mar 1719. De.

Stevens, William. SQS & T May 1750 *Lichfield*. M.

Stevens, William. S 14 yrs Lent LC AA Co., Md., from *Thornton* Jul 1775. Sy.

Stephenson, Ann. S May-Jun T *Tayloe* Jul 1774. M.

Stevenson, Arthur. R for life Dec T *Justitia* Dec 1774. M.

Stephenson, Frances, spinster. SQS Lancaster Oct 1735. La.

Stevenson, Francis. T Sep 1737 *Pretty Patsy*. L.

MORE EMIGRANTS IN BONDAGE

Stephenson, John. S Lent T May 1749 *Lichfield*. E.

Sterling, Samuel. S Lent T Dec 1734. So.

Steward, Daniel. S May-Jul T Sep 1751 *Greyhound*. M.

Steward, George. S Summer T Sep 1751 *Greyhound*. E.

Steward, Margaret. S as pickpocket Lent 1726 R 14 yrs Lent 1729. Y.

Steward, Mary. S Lent 1724 but escaped & no further record found. Li.

Stewart, Alexander. S Sep-Dec 1746 T Jan 1747 *George William*. M.

Stewart, Alexander. T 14 yrs Aug 1747. No.

Stewart, Hugh. SQS Bristol s from snuff maker Aug 1753. G.

Stewart, James. R 14 yrs Jul T *Saltspring* Jul 1775. M.

Stewart, Jane. S Apr 1746 T Feb 1747. Nl.

Stewart, Joseph. S 14 yrs Summer 1738 LC QA Co., Md. Jun 1739. De.

Stewart, Margaret. SQS Jan LC Bal Co., Md., from *Adventure* Mar 1773. Du.

Stewart, Mary. S for shoplifting Apr 1746 T Feb 1747. Nl.

Stewart, Mary Jr. S Apr 1746 T Feb 1747. Nl.

Stewart, William *als* Smith, James. S Edinburgh s cattle R for life Mar 1767. Sco.

Stichbury, Alexander. S Apr T May 1750 *Lichfield*. M.

Stichbury, Isaac. S Apr T *Lichfield* May 1749. L.

Stiff, Abraham. S Apr T *Lichfield* May 1749. L.

Stiffney, John. S s shirt Jan T Apr 1735 *Patapsco* LC Annapolis Oct 1735. M.

Stiles, John. S Jan T Apr 1735 *Patapsco* LC Annapolis Oct 1735. M.

Stiles, William of Stamford le Hope. SQS Apr T May 1752 *Lichfield*. E.

Styles, William. S Jul T *Tayloe* Jul 1773. L.

Still, Moses. SQS Jan 1737 LC QA Co., Md., from *Amity* Apr 1738. Do.

Stimson, John. S Summer 1761 T Feb 1762. Li.

Stint, Richard. S Sep-Oct 1772 T *Justitia* Jan 1773. M.

Stock, Ann. S Lent LC Bal Co., Md., Jul 1772. So.

Stockman *als* MacGwin, Daniel. S & T 14 yrs Jan 1736 *Dorsetshire* LC Va Sep 1736. L.

Stockton, James of Tarbock. SQS Jan 1737. La.

Stokes, Charles. S Lent 1741 LC QA Co., Md., from *Philleroy* Apr 1742. He.

Stokes, John of Writtle. S Lent T Jul 1745 *Italian Merchant*. E.

Stokes, Joseph. S Lent 1741 LC QA Co., Md., from *Philleroy* Apr 1742. He.

Stokes, Richard. S Summer 1738 LC QA Co., Md. Jun 1739. So.

Stone, George. S Summer 1737 LC QA Co., Md., from *Amity* Apr 1738. De.

Stone, James. S Lent LC AA Co., Md., from *Thornton* Jul 1773. M.

Stone, Mary. S Lent 1731. Li.

Stone, Nicholas. S Lent T *Lichfield* May 1749. Sy.

Stone *als* Clefts, Philip. SQS New Sarum Jan TB to Va Apr 1742 LC PG Co., Md. Wi.

Stone, Samuel (1770). *See* Stone, John. So.

Stone, Thomas. S Summer 1718 LC from *Sophia* QA Co., Md. Mar 1719. So.

Stonehouse, William. S Jan T *Plain Dealer* Jan 1746. M.

Stonell, Richard. S s at West Wycombe & R Summer 1773 T *Justitia* Jan 1774. Bu.

Stoner, Francis. S Oct 1751-Jan 1752 T *Thames* Mar 1752. M.

Stoner, Sarah. S Jul-Sep T *Ruby* Oct 1754. M.

Stooke, Robert. T May 1746. De.

Stool, Mary. T May 1750 *Lichfield*. Sx.

Storer, Samuel. R 14 yrs Jul T *Saltspring* Jul 1775. M.

Storey, George. S City 1752 (AHJ). Nl.

Storey, Henry. S Jan T Apr 1735 *Patapsco* LC Annapolis Oct 1735. M.

Storey, James. SQS Jan LC AA Co., Md., from *Thornton* Jul 1775. M.

Storey, William. S Summer 1733 T Lent 1734. Li.

Storey, William. S Mar T May 1751. Sx.

Storey, William. S Dec T *Justitia* Dec 1774. M.

Storm, Michael. S Apr T May 1750 *Lichfield*. L.

Storman, Samuel. S (Southampton) Lent R 14 yrs Apr 1725. Ha.

Stothers, John. SQS Jan LC AA Co., Md., from *Thornton* Jul 1775. Sy.

Stow, Jane. S Apr T May 1750 *Lichfield*. L.

Stoward, Stephen Jr. S Lent R Summer 1725 T *Rappahannock* but died on passage. Li.

Stowers *als* Durgin, James. S for leading food riots Dec 1766 R 14 yrs Lent 1767. Be.

Stowman, Ann. S Dec 1753-Jan 1754 T *Thames* Mar 1754. M.

Stracey, Ann. S Dec 1746 T Jan 1747 *George William*. L.

Stradling, Edward. R Apr T Nov 1747. So.

Strahan, Robert. S May-Jul T *Tayloe* Jul 1773. M.

Strange *als* Naylor, Mary of St. Michael, Queenhithe, widow. SQS as incorrigible rogue & feloniously returning to Southwark after being passed to her settlement Apr T Aug 1752 *Tryal*. Sy.

Strange, Thomas. S Lent LC Bal Co., Md., Jul 1771. Wa.

Strangeways *als* Strangwith, John. S Summer 1737 R 14 yrs Summer 1738. Nl.

Stratton, Thomas. S May-Jun T Aug 1752 *Tryal*. M.

Strawbridge, Robert. T Apr 1742 LC PG Co., Md. Do.

Streak, Francis. S Lent T *Thornton* May LC AA Co., Md., Jul 1774. K.

Street, Edith. SQS Jul 1731 LC Knt Co., Md., from *Falcon* Apr 1732. So.

Street, Rebecca wife of John. S s gown Jan T Apr 1735 *Patapsco* LC Annapolis Oct 1735. M.

Street, William. S Lent 1750 LC QA Co., Md., from *Catherine* Nov 1750. So.

Stribley, Benjamin. S Launceston May 1754 (AHJ). Co.

Strickland, George. S for life Lent LC Bal Co., Md., Jul 1771. So.

Stringer, Elizabeth. S Apr T Dec 1735 *John* LC Annapolis Sep 1736. L.

Stringer, Peter. S Lent T *Thornton* May LC AA Co., Md., Jul 1774. M.

Stringer, Robert. T Jul 1747. O.

Stringer, Thomas. S for highway robbery Summer 1761 R 14 yrs Lent 1762 TB to Md. No.

Strong, Ann. T Jul 1747. Sy.

Strong, Jane. S Jul-Dec 1747 LC Knt Co., Md., from *St. George* Mar 1748. M.

Strong, John. S Jul T Jul 1748 *Mary*; runaway. L.

Strong, John. S May-Jul T Sep 1751 *Greyhound*. M.

Strong, John. S 14 yrs Summer 1772 LC Bal Co., Md., Apr 1773. Co.

Strong, Thomas. S Jan-Apr T *Lichfield* May 1749. M.

Strong, Thomas. S Mar T *Thames* Mar 1754. L.

Strood, Richard. S Summer 1751 R 14 yrs Lent T May 1752 *Lichfield*. K.

Strudwick, George. S 14 yrs Lent LC AA Co., Md., from *Thornton* Jul 1773. Sy.

Strutton, William. S Jul T Sep 1751 *Greyhound*. L.

Stryce, Silver. S Apr T May 1750 *Lichfield*. L.

Stuart, Charles. S Summer T Sep 1753. Le.

Stubbs, Ann. S Sep T *Barnard* Oct 1756. M.

Stubbs, Frances wife of John. S 14 yrs Sep T *Barnard* Oct 1756. M.

Stubbs, John. S Oct T *Barnard* Oct 1756. M.

Stubbs, Mary. S Summer T Aug 1749 *Thames*. Sy.

Stubbs, Thomas. S Mar 1734 T Feb 1735. Le.

MORE EMIGRANTS IN BONDAGE

Studder, John. S Jul-Dec 1747 LC Knt Co., Md., from *St. George* Mar 1748. M.

Sturgeon, Philip. S Lent 1741 (IJ). Su.

Sturges, John. T Feb 1748. Le.

Sturgis, Edward. S 1756 TB to Md. No.

Sturgis, Sarah (1773) - *See* Fanis. No.

Sturt, Thomas. S Lent R Jun T 14 yrs Aug 1752 *Tryal*. K.

Styles - *See* Stiles.

Suffolk, Richard. S Summer LC Bal Co., Md., Dec 1772; runaway. Wa.

Sugar, Edward. SQS Jul TB Aug T *Restoration* LC Bal Co., Md., Oct 1771. So.

Suggs *als* Preston, Mary. S May-Jul T *Tayloe* Jul 1774. M.

Suiton *als* Andrews, John. SQS Jul 1738 LC QA Co., Md. Jun 1739. So.

Suledge, Samuel. S Lent LC AA Co., Md., from *Thornton* May 1771. M.

Sullivan, Catherine of St. George, Southwark, widow. SQS May T *Tryal* Jul 1754. Sy.

Sullivan, Cornelius. S Sep-Oct T Oct 1749 *Mary*. M.

Sullivan, Dennis. S Lent LC AA Co., Md., from *Thornton* Jul 1773. M.

Sullivan, Herbert. SQS Sep T Oct 1750 *Rachael*. M.

Sullivan, Isabella. SQS Lent LC AA Co., Md., from *Hanover Planter* Jul 1773. M.

Sullivan, John. S Lent LC AA Co., Md., from *Thornton* May 1771. L.

Sullivan, Martin. S Sep-Oct T Oct 1749 *Mary*. M.

Sullivan, Timothy. S Apr T *Lichfield* May 1749. L.

Summers (Sommers), Sarah. SQS Jul 1738 LC QA Co., Md. Jun 1739. De.

Summers, Thomas. S Lent LC AA Co., Md., from *Thornton* Jul 1773. L.

Summerson, John. S & R Aug 1723. Nl.

Summerton, Hester. S Feb-Apr T *Laura* Apr 1746. M.

Summocks, George. S Lancaster 1754 (AHJ). La.

Sumner, Margaret (1773). See Reed. L.

Surfleet, Benjamin. S Lent T Apr 1766. Li.

Surtain, James. SQS Marlborough 1754 (AHJ). Wi.

Sutherland, Margaret. S May-Jul T Jul 1748 *Mary*. M.

Sutherland, Margaret. S Sep T *Barnard* Oct 1756. M.

Sutron, William. T Apr 1735 *Patapsco* LC Annapolis Oct 1735. K.

Sutton, George. S Oct 1735 T Jan 1736 *Dorsetshire* LC Va Sep 1736; indicted in
    1734 for robbery with brother John who was executed; mother Mary Sutton gave
    evidence. M.

Sutton, John. S Jan T Mar 1750 *Tryal*. L.

Sutton, Joseph. SW Jan LC AA Co., Md., from *Thornton* Jul 1775. M.

Sutton, Thomas. S Dec 1745 T *Plain Dealer* Jan 1746. L.

Sutur, Thomas. T Aug 1752 *Tryal*. K.

Swadkins, Joseph. S Lent T from London Apr 1755. Wa.

Swann, Christie. S May-Jul T *Tayloe* Jul 1773. M.

Swan, Elizabeth. S Dec 1749-Jan 1750 T Mar 1750 *Tryal*. M.

Swan, Mary. S Apr T *Dolphin* Apr 1761. M.

Swan, Peter. S Feb-Apr T *Laura* Apr 1746. M.

Swan, Priscilla. S Jul-Dec 1747 but died. M.

Swan, Robert. S Lent T *Dolphin* Apr 1761. E.

Swan, William. S s cloth from tenters Summer 1718 R 14 yrs Summer 1721 T
    Forward from London Oct 1723. Y.

Swannock, John. S Feb T Mar 1750 *Tryal*. M.

Swart, John. T Jun 1747. Ha.

Swawbrook *als* Beakley, Magdalen. S Feb-Apr T *Justitia* May 1745. M.

MORE EMIGRANTS IN BONDAGE

Sweeney, Joseph. S Bristol Jan 1756 (AHJ). G.

Sweetman, Edward. S Apr T May 1750 *Lichfield*. M.

Sweetman, Thomas. SQS Jul 1770 LC Bal Co., Md., Jul 1771. Co.

Swift, Elizabeth. S Oct-Dec 1754 T *Greyhound* Feb 1755. M.

Swift, Jeremiah. S Jan T Mar 1750 *Tryal*. L.

Swift *als* Whitaker, John. S s mare Lent R Jul 1723. Y.

Swigg, Rachael. S Launceston Feb 1758 (AHJ). Co.

Swindale, Robert. S Lent 1738. Li.

Swindles, John. S Summer LC Bal Co., Md., Dec 1772, sold to John McClellan. He.

Swinston, Francis. S Jan-Apr T Jun 1748 *Lichfield*. M.

Swinton, John. S Dec 1745 T *Plain Dealer* Jan 1746. L.

Swinyard, Edward. S Summer T *Barnard* Oct 1756. K.

Sykes, John. S Apr T *Justitia* May 1745. L.

Sykes, Nathaniel. SQS Lent LC AA Co., Md., from *Hanover Planter* Jul 1773. M.

Symes, John. SQS & T *Randolph* Sep 1768. Do.

Symes, Joseph. S 14 yrs Summer 1772 LC Bal Co., Md., Apr 1773. So.

Symonds, Elizabeth. S Lent 1733 T Feb 1734. Bd.

Symonds, Elizabeth. S & R Feb 1737 T Feb 1738. Bd.

Symonds, John. S Lent 1734 R 14 yrs Feb 1735 T *Amity* LC QA Co., Md., Mar 1736. So.

Symonds, John (1773). See Simmons. M.

Symonds, Vincent. S Jan-Jun T Jul 1747 *Laura*. M.

Symonds, William (1770) - *See* Hunt. He.

Symonds, William. S Aug LC Md *William* Dec 1774 & sold to James Hodges. Co.

Symons, Alexander. SQS Oct 1730 LC Knt Co., Md., from *Falcon* Apr 1732. Co.

Syvett, Joseph. R for Barbados Oct 1673 but LC Md from *Charles* May 1674. L.

Tackle, Abednego. S Lent 1750 LC QA Co., Md., from *Catherine* Nov 1750. So.

Tackle, John. S Lent 1750 LC QA Co., Md., from *Catherine* Nov 1750. So.

Taffs, John. S 1753 TB to Va. No.

Tagg, Hester. S Lent T Jun 1748 *Lichfield*. E.

Talbot, Francis. R for life Dec 1773 T *Justitia* Jan 1774. M.

Talbott, John. S Apr-Jun 1739 T *Sea Nymph* to Md. M.

Talbot, Mary. S May-Jul T *Tayloe* Jul 1773. M.

Tallant, Patrick. S & T Sep 1751 *Greyhound*. M.

Tambin?, Edward. S Lent 1737 LC Knt Co., Md., from *Hawk* Nov 1737. De.

Tame, John. S s bread & bacon at Steventon Dec 1766. Be.

Tamplin, Anthony. S Oct 1751-Jan 1752 T *Thames* Mar 1752 M.

Taplin, William. S & T Jun 1751. Ha.

Tapling, John. S Oct-Dec 1754 T *Greyhound* Feb 1755. M.

Tap, Elizabeth. S Sep T *Maryland Packet* Oct 1761. M.

Tapp, Henry. SQS Feb LC AA Co., Md., from *Thornton* Jul 1773. M.

Tappin, John. S Sep T Oct 1750 *Rachael*. L.

Tarr, Joane. SQS Oct 1732 LC Knt Co., Md., from *Falcon* Mar 1733. De.

Tarrant, John. S Apr-May T *Tryal* Jul 1754. M.

Tasker, David. T Apr 1735 *Patapsco* LC Annapolis Oct 1735. K.

Tate, Michael (1769) - *See* Pricket. O.

Tawton, Philip. S Lent 1735. De.

Taylor, Abraham. SQS Sep 1772 T *Justitia* Jan 1773. M.

Taylor, Alexander. SQS Jan T *Greyhound* Feb 1755. M.

Taylor, Ann. S Lent LC Bal Co., Md., Jul 1774. Sh.

Taylor, Christopher of St. James Garlickhithe. S s pearl ash Feb LC from Patapsco Annapolis Oct 1732. L.

Taylor, Edward. S Summer 1734 R 14 yrs Feb T Apr 1735 *Patapsco* LC Annapolis Oct 1735. Sy.

Taylor, Edward. S Lancaster 1755 (AHJ). La.

Taylor, Edward. S Summer LC Bal Co., Md., Dec 1770. Wo.

Taylor, Elias. S Lent T *Dolphin* May 1763. Ht.

Taylor, Elizabeth. S s petticoat Apr T Dec 1735 *John* LC Annapolis Sep 1736. M.

Taylor, Elizabeth. T 14 yrs Jun 1748 *Lichfield*. M.

Taylor, Elizabeth. S Sep T Oct 1750 *Rachael*. M.

Taylor, Elizabeth (1751) - *See* Wilson. Nl.

Taylor, Elizabeth *als* Wiseman. S Dec 1753-Jan 1754 T *Thames* Mar 1754. M.

Taylor, Francis. S Summer 1731 LC Knt Co., Md., from *Falcon* Apr 1732. So.

Taylor, Francis. S Apr T Jun 1748 *Lichfield*. L.

Taylor, Henry. S Sep T *Ruby* Oct 1754. L.

Taylor, Isaac. S Lent 1737. Li.

Taylor, Ishmael. S s shoes Sep 1735 T Jan 1736 *Dorsetshire* LC Va Sep 1736. M.

Taylor, James. S Jan T May 1746. Sx.

Taylor, James. S Summer 1772 T *Justitia* Jan 1773. Sy.

Taylor, James. SQS Sep 1772 T *Justitia* Jan 1773. M.

Taylor, Jane wife of John. S Lent LC Bal Co., Md., Jun 1773. Wa.

Taylor, John. S Lent 1734. Nt.

Taylor, John. S s cane Jul 1735 T Jan 1736 *Dorsetshire* LC Va Sep 1736. M.

Taylor, John, a youth. S & R 14 yrs Lent 1747 LC Knt Co., Md., from *St. George* Mar 1748. Bu.

Taylor, John. S for life T Aug 1749 *Thames*. M.

Taylor, John. R Jul T *Tayloe* Jul 1774. M.

Taylor, Judith. S Jun T Jul 1747 *Laura*. L.

Taylor, Margaret. S Oct T Oct 1749 *Mary*. L.

Taylor, Mary. S Lent 1735. Y.

Taylor, Mary. S Apr-May T *Tryal* Jul 1754. M.

Taylor, Michael Thomas. S for life S Lent LC AA Co., Md., from *Thornton* Jul 1773. E.

Taylor, Peter. S Dec 1752 (AHJ). Wo.

Taylor, Samuel. S Summer 1741 R 14 yrs Apr 1742 LC PG Co., Md. Wo.

Taylor, Samuel. S Dec 1749-Jan 1750 T Mar 1750 *Tryal*. M.

Taylor, Samuel. SQS Lent but pardoned May 1773. M.

Taylor, Sarah. S Apr-May T *Saltspring* Jul 1775. M.

Taylor, Stephen. S 14 yrs Lent 1742 LC QA Co., Md., from *Kent* Jun 1743. De.

Taylor, Susannah. S Jan T *Justitia* May 1745. L.

Taylor, Thomas. S 14 yrs s horse Summer 1733 LC Knt Co., Md., from *Falcon* Apr 1734. De.

Taylor, Thomas. S Aug T *Phoenix* Oct 1760. L.

Taylor, Thomas. S Chelmsford Jan 1763 (AHJ). E.

Taylor, Thomas. S Summer 1772 LC Bal Co., Md., Apr 1773. G.

Taylor, Thomas. R to be T for life Apr T *Tayloe* Jul 1773. E.

Taylor, Thomas. S s horse & R 14 yrs Summer LC Md *William* Dec 1774 & sold to Rodolph Hook. Sh.

MORE EMIGRANTS IN BONDAGE

Taylor, Thomas. S Lent LC AA Co., Md., from *Thornton* Jul 1775. Sy.

Taylor, William. S Summer 1718 LC from *Sophia* QA Co., Md. Mar 1719. De.

Taylor, William. SQS Jan LC QA Co., Md., from *Leopard* May 1738. De.

Taylor, William. S Jan-Apr T *Lichfield* May 1749. M.

Taylor, William. S Apr 1755. Li.

Taylor, William. SQS Oct 1770 LC AA Co., Md., from *Thornton* May 1771. Ht.

Taylor, William. S Lent LC Bal Co., Md., Jun 1773. Wa.

Taylor, William. SQS May T Jul 1773 *Tayloe* to Va. M.

Tea, Elizabeth. S & T 14 yrs Jan 1736 *Dorsetshire* LC Va Sep 1736. L.

Teague, Peter. S Summer 1731 but escaped from *Falcon*. Co.

Teasland, William. S Lent T Apr 1753. No.

Teddy, John. R Summer 1773 T *Justitia* Jan 1774. Sy.

Tedstill, Christopher. S Lent 1772 LC Bal Co., Md., Apr 1773. Wo.

Templer, James. S Oct T *Justitia* Dec 1774. L.

Tennant, Thomas. S Lent T Apr 1739. Le.

Tenant, William. S Summer 1736. Y.

Tepper, Sampson. S Wells & R for forging money order Jan 1738. De.

Terry, Elizabeth. S Oct-Dec 1750 T *Thames* Feb 1751. M.

Terry, Mary wife of James. S Apr-May T *Saltspring* Jul 1775. M.

Terry *als* Woodcock, William. S Apr 1753. Li.

Tew, William. S for forgery & R Lent LC Md from *Isabella* Jul 1775 having paid his own passage. Wa.

Thacker, John. S for killing a heifer Aug 1753 (WJ). St.

Thackerill, Edward. S Oct R Dec 1758 T for life Nov 1759 *Phoenix* . L.

Thackster, Thomas. S Lent 1738. Su.

Thane, James Wallis. R 14 yrs Jul T *Tayloe* Jul 1774. M.

Tharpe, Joseph. S Lent T *Tryal* Jul 1754. K.

Thatcher, Abraham. SQS Jan 1750 LC QA Co., Md., from *Catherine* Nov 1750. So.

Thatcher, Jane. S Mar T Sep 1747. Ha.

Theed, Richard of Woodford. S for highway robbery Summer 1745 R 14 yrs Lent T Sep 1746 *Mary*. E.

Therley, John. S Lent T Apr 1756. Wa.

Theron *als* Thorn, Isaac. S Dec 1746 T Jan 1747 *George William*. L.

Thomas, Ann. S Feb-Apr T *Laura* Apr 1746. M.

Thomas, Ann. S Jan-Apr T Jun 1748 *Lichfield*. M.

Thomas, Betty. S Bristol Jan 1758 (AHJ). G.

Thomas, Catherine. S May T *Beverly* Aug 1763. M.

Thomas, Charles. S Sep-Oct 1773 T *Justitia* Jan 1774. M.

Thomas, Charles. S Jul LC Bal Co., Md., Dec 1783 from *Swift*. M.

Thomas, Elizabeth, spinster. S Bristol Aug 1743 LC Knt Co., Md., from *Raven* Feb 1744. G.

Thomas, Francis. SQS Bristol Sep LC Bal Co., Md., Dec 1770. G.

Thomas, Griffith. S Oct T Oct 1749 *Mary*. L.

Thomas, Hannah. SQS & T Sep 1751 *Greyhound*. M.

Thomas, Henry. S May T *Mary* Sep 1746; shipwrecked & T Jan 1747 *George William*. M.

Thomas, James. SQS Jan LC Bal Co., Md., Apr 1773. So.

Thomas, James. S Lent LC Bal Co., Md., Jun 1773. He.

Thomas, John *als* Baker, Lewis. S Summer 1718 LC from *Sophia* QA Co., Md. Mar

1719. De.

Thomas, John. S 14 yrs Summer 1734 LC Knt Co., Md., from *Hawk* Apr 1735. So.

Thomas, John. S Apr T May 1750 *Lichfield*. M.

Thomas, John. S Apr T *Dolphin* May 1763. L.

Thomas, John. S Lent LC AA Co., Md., from *Thornton* Jul 1775. L.

Thomas, Margaret. S 14 yrs Summer 1770 LC Bal Co., Md., Jun 1771. Sh.

Thomas, Mary, spinster. S Bristol Aug 1741 LC QA Co., Md., from *Philleroy* Apr 1742. G.

Thomas, Richard. S Summer T *Barnard* Oct 1756. K.

Thomas, Robert. S 14 yrs LC Bal Co., Md., Jul 1772. He.

Thomas, Thomas. S Exeter Apr 1753 (AHJ). De.

Thomas, William, aged 28, brown hair. S Lent R 14 yrs Summer 1722 LC from *Jonathan* Md Jul 1724. Wa.

Thomas, William. S Lent LC from *Patapsco* Annapolis Nov 1733. No.

Thomas *als* Hopkins, William. T May 1746. De.

Thomas, William. S Jan-Apr T *Lichfield* May 1749. M.

Thomas, William of Sittingbourne. S Lent T May 1750 *Lichfield*. K.

Thomas, William. S Sep T *Barnard* Oct 1756. M.

Thomas, William. S Brecon s bullocks R Apr 1772. Wal.

Thomas, William. S Lent LC AA Co., Md., from *Thornton* Jul 1775. M.

Thompson *als* Jones *als* Jonas, Mary. S Jul T *Maryland Packet* Oct 1761. L.

Thompson *als* Forester, Ann. S City Christmas 1759 (AHJ). Nl.

Thompson, Andrew. S Summer T Aug 1749 *Thames*. K.

Thompson, Andrew. S Southwark Jan LC AA Co., Md., from *Thornton* Jul 1773. Sy.

Thompson, Ann. S & T Jan 1736 *Dorsetshire* LC Va Sep 1736. L.

Thompson, Ann wife of Francis. S Feb-Apr T *Laura* Apr 1746. M.

Thompson, Ann, spinster. S City Summer 1756 (AHJ). Nl.

Thompson, Ann. S Apr-May T *Saltspring* Jul 1775. M.

Thompson, Edward. S Lent LC AA Co., Md., from *Thornton* Jul 1775. K.

Thomson, Elizabeth. S Summer 1734 LC Knt Co., Md., Mar 1735 from *Falcon*. De.

Thompson, Elizabeth. S Sep-Oct T *Justitia* Dec 1774. M.

Thompson, George. S Apr 1771. Li.

Thompson, Grace. S May-Jul T *Tayloe* Jul 1773. M.

Thompson, Hannah. S Lent 1735. Y.

Thompson, James. T Sep 1737 *Pretty Patsy*. L.

Thompson, James. S Apr T *Lichfield* May 1749. L.

Thompson, John. S Jul-Sep T *Ruby* Oct 1754. M.

Thomson, James. S Lent LC Bal Co., Md., Jun 1773. Ha.

Thompson, John. SL Jul T *Tayloe* Jul 1773; runaway. Sy.

Thompson, John. R 14 yrs Jul T *Tayloe* Jul 1774. M.

Thompson, Joseph. S Jan-Jun T Jul 1747 *Laura*. M.

Thompson, Joseph. S Lent T *Thornton* May LC AA Co., Md., Jul 1774. M.

Thompson, Mary. S Apr-May 1754 T *Tryal* Jul 1754. M.

Thompson, Mary. S Aug T *Phoenix* Oct 1760. L.

Thompson, Samuel, *als* Crew, Simon. S Sep-Oct T Oct 1749 *Mary*. M.

Thompson, Samuel. S Summer LC Bal Co., Md., Dec 1770 from *Trotman* & sold to Abraham Ensor. Le.

Thompson, Susanna. S Dec 1747 LC Knt Co., Md., from *St. George* Mar 1748. L.

Tomson, Thomas. R & T Sep 1747. Nt.

Thompson, Thomas. SQS Jan T Mar 1773. Y.

MORE EMIGRANTS IN BONDAGE

Thompson, William. R for Barbados Dec 1671 but LC Md from *William & Mary* Mar 1672. M.

Thompson, William. SQS Apr 1729. La.

Thompson, William of Marefield. S for highway robbery Lent T 14 yrs Oct 1750 *Rachael*. Sx.

Thompson, William. S Jan-Apr T Jun 1748 *Lichfield*. M.

Thompson, William. SQS & T Jul 1773 *Tayloe* to Va. M.

Tompson, William. S Lent R 7 yrs Apr AT Summer LC Md *William* Dec 1774 & sold to James Hutchings. Wa.

Thorburn, James. S Summer T *Ruby* Oct 1754. K.

Thornbury, Mary. S Lent LC Bal Co., Md., Jun 1773. Wo.

Thorne, Jane. S May-Jul T Jul 1748 *Mary*. M.

Thorn, John. S Summer 1737 LC QA Co., Md., from *Amity* Apr 1738. De.

Thorne, John. S Apr T May 1752 *Lichfield*. L.

Thorne, Richard. S Summer 1731 LC Knt Co., Md., from *Falcon* Apr 1732. So.

Thorn, Robert. S Feb-Apr T May 1751 *Tryal*. M.

Thorne, Thomas. SQS Jan T Jul 1735 *Amity* LC QA Co., Md., Mar 1736. So.

Thorne, William. SQS Apr 1731 LC Knt Co., Md., from *Falcon* Apr 1732. So.

Thorn, William. S Lent 1737 LC Knt Co., Md., from *Hawk* Nov 1737. De.

Thornhill, Benjamin (1771). *See Thornton*. M.

Thornhill, Samuel. T Sep 1737 *Pretty Patsy*. L.

Thorningley, William. S May 1770. Li.

Thornton *als* Thornhill, Benjamin. S Lent LC AA Co., Md., from *Thornton* May 1771. M.

Thornton, John. S Jan-Apr T *Lichfield* May 1749. M.

Thornton, Susanna. S May-Jul T *Mary* Sep 1746. M.

Thornway, James. S Aug T *Restoration* LC Bal Co., Md., Oct 1771. St.

Thorovit *als* Thorowitz, Louisa, poor orphan aged 15. S & T Dec 1731 *Forward* but to be taken back & pardoned. M.

Thorowgood, George. S Lent R 14 yrs Summer T Aug 1752 *Tryal*. Sy.

Thorpe, James. S Aug T *Beverly* Aug 1763. L.

Thorpe, John. S Apr T for life May 1750 *Lichfield*. M.

Thorpe, Josiah. S s horse Summer 1750 T May 1751 *Tryal*. K.

Thrift, John. S Summer 1772 T *Justitia* Jan 1773; runaway from Robert McKittrick, Augusta Co., Va., 1775. Sy.

Throttle *als* Trottle, Robert. S Summer 1718 LC from *Sophia* QA Co., Md. Mar 1719. Do.

Thurchild, Edward. S Summer 1758 R 14 yrs Lent 1759 (WJ). Sh.

Thurman, Charles. S s shirt Feb T Apr 1735 *Patapsco* LC Annapolis Oct 1735. M.

Thursby, John. S Lent 1729. Nt.

Tibballs, Samuel. S Lent T *Thornton* May LC AA Co., Md., Jul 1774. M.

Tibbett, Elizabeth. S Feb-Apr T *Justitia* May 1745. M.

Tice, Whitehill (1739) - *See* Wadman. So.

Tickner, Peter. S Jul-Dec 1747 LC Knt Co., Md., from *St. George* Mar 1748. M.

Tidbury, Joseph. S Oct R 14 yrs Dec T *Justitia* Dec 1774. M.

Tiffen, Joseph. S May-Jun T Aug 1752 *Tryal*. M.

Tilletts, Samuel. S Bristol Jan 1750 LC QA Co., Md., from *Catherine* Nov 1750. G.

Tillie, James. S Dec 1754 T *Greyhound* Feb 1755. L.

Tilley, Jane. S Apr 1742. Wo.

Tillingham, George. T 1751. Li.

Tillson, Roger of Bury St. Edmunds. R for Barbados Aug 1671 but LC Md Feb 1672. Su.

Tilsey *als* Edwards, Mary. SQS Apr S Summer LC Bal Co., Md., Dec 1772. So.

Tilsley [Tillesley], John. S s sheep Lent R 14 yrs Summer 1758. Sh.

Timberwell, George of Lambeth. SQS Apr T Sep 1751 *Greyhound*. Sy.

Timperley, Robert. S 14 yrs Feb T *Tryal* Mar 1757. M.

Tindale, William. S City Christmas 1763 (AHJ). Nl.

Tindy, Richard. S Apr T May 1751 *Tryal*. L.

Tinsley, Ann. S Feb T *Thames* Mar 1754. L.

Tippens, Edward. S Lent 1741 LC QA Co., Md., from *Philleroy* Apr 1742. He.

Tippett, Jane. S Summer 1770 LC Bal Co., Md., Jul 1771. Co.

Tippett, Matthew. S s lead Jul 1735 T Jan 1736 *Dorsetshire* LC Va Sep 1736. M.

Tippett, Thomas. S Summer 1718 LC from *Sophia* QA Co., Md. Mar 1719. So.

Tipping [Tripping] *als* Smith, James. S Lent R 14 yrs Summer 1738. He.

Tipping, John. S Apr-Jun 1739 T *Sea Nymph* to Md. M.

Tipton, Francis. S 14 yrs Lent LC Bal Co., Md., Jun 1773. Sh.

Titmarsh, Susannah. T *Plain Dealer* Jan 1746. M.

Titmouse, Francis. T *Greyhound* Jan 1756. Ht.

Titten, Richard. S Oct 1751-Jan 1752 T *Thames* Mar 1752. M.

Toasland, William. S 1753 TB to Md. No.

Toasten *als* Fennister, Mary. S Dec 1746 T Jan 1747 *George William*. L.

Tobin, James. S Apr-May 1754 T *Tryal* Jul 1754. M.

Todd, Francis. S York 1761 (AHJ). Y.

Todd, James. T Jul 1747. Sy.

Todd *als* Smith, William. S Summer 1772 LC Bal Co., Md., from *Adventure* Mar 1773. Nl.

Togg, Elizabeth. S Lancaster 1763 (AHJ). La.

Tomkin, Gabriel. T delayed for him to confess accomplices but now to be T Feb 1722. L (Fleet).

Tomkin, Joseph. S 14 yrs Apr 1757 (RG). Be.

Tomkins, William. S Summer 1749 LC QA Co., Md., from *Catherine* Nov 1750. He.

Tomkins, William. S Jul LC Bal Co., Md., Dec 1783 from *Swift*. M.

Tomkinson, Edward. S Summer T from Bristol Sep 1751. St.

Tomlin, Elizabeth. S s clothing Jan T Apr 1735 *Patapsco* LC Annapolis Oct 1735. L.

Tomlin, John. S for obtaining money by false pretences Jul T *Tayloe* Jul 1774. L.

Tomlins, George. S Sep-Oct T *Justitia* Dec 1774. M.

Toms, Francis. S Mar 1753 (RG). Ha.

Toms, John. S Lent 1750 LC QA Co., Md., from *Catherine* Nov 1750. So.

Tonks, William. S & R 14 yrs Summer LC Md *William* Dec 1774 & sold to James Hutchings. St.

Toole, Christopher. SQS Exeter Oct 1734 LC Knt Co., Md, Mar 1735 from *Falcon*. De.

Tooley, Fool. S Sep-Dec 1746 T Jan 1747 *George William*. M.

Tooley *als* Tuley, John. S Lent R 14 yrs Summer T *Ruby* Oct 1754. Ht.

Topham, Sarah. S May-Jul T *Tayloe* Jul 1773. M.

Topping, John. S 14 yrs Jul T *Saltspring* Jul 1775; runaway. L.

Topping, William. S s handkerchief Oct 1735 T Jan 1736 *Dorsetshire* LC Va Sep 1736. M.

Tottle, Jasper. S Mar T Apr 1746. Sh.

Toulson, Henry. S Lent 1734. Db.

Toward, Thomas. S Summer 1737. Y.

Towe, James (1773). *See* Town. St.

MORE EMIGRANTS IN BONDAGE

Towers, John. S Lent 1737. Li.

Towle, James (1773). See Town. St.

Town *als* Towle *als* Towe *als* Craddock, James. S 14 yrs Lent LC Bal Co., Md., Jun 1773. St.

Townsend, Christopher. R for Barbados Sep 1672 LC Md Jun 1673. L.

Townsend, Christopher. SQS Oct 1734 LC Md from *Falcon* Mar 1735. De.

Townsend, Elizabeth. S Jul T Sep 1751 *Greyhound*. L.

Townsend, George. S Summer 1737 T Jan 1738. Wa.

Townsend, Mary. S 14 yrs Summer LC Knt Co., Md., from *Bideford* Nov 1737. So.

Townsend, Thomas. S 14 yrs Summer 1772 LC Bal Co., Md., Apr 1773. G.

Townsend, William. S s at South Cerney Lent 1768; pardon dated May 1768 arrived after ship had left. G.

Towsey, George. S City Aug 1731 AT Jul 1732. Nl.

Toyne, George. S Apr 1768. Li.

Tracey, Dorothy. S Jan-Apr T *Lichfield* May 1749. M.

Tracey, Robert. S & T Jan 1736 *Dorsetshire* LC Va Sep 1736. L.

Traffick, Jeremiah of Tenterden. S Lent T Jul 1745 *Italian Merchant*. K.

Trafford, John. S s sheep Aug 1753 R 14 yrs Lent 1754 (WJ). St.

Trahern, Mary. S for house breaking at Frampton Cotterell Mar 1771 (HJ). G.

Trainer, Patrick. S Lent LC AA Co., Md., from *Hanover Planter* Jul 1773. M.

Tranter, Mary. S Dec T *Justitia* Dec 1774. M.

Trantum, Samuel. S Oct T *Justitia* Dec 1774. L.

Trapp, Thomas. S Bristol Mar 1741 LC QA Co., Md., from *Philleroy* Apr 1742. G.

Travel, Thomas. S s from shop in Worcester Mar 1754 (WJ). Wo.

Treasy, Mary. S Lent 1737 LC Knt Co., Md., from *Hawk* Nov 1737. De.

Treble, William. S s at Trimborough Summer 1772, died on passage to Va on *Trimly* 1773. Su.

Tredeago [Tredegne], Thomas. S s yarn at Stroud Lent 1758. G.

Tree, Robert. S Lent R 14 yrs Summer T *Barnard* Oct 1756. Ht.

Tregurtha, Thomas. S Launceston Jan 1757 (AHJ). Co.

Treharn, Margaret. S Bristol s at Frampton Cotterell Mar T *Restoration* LC Bal Co., Md., Oct 1771. G.

Treise, John. S 14 yrs Summer 1731 LC Knt Co., Md., from *Falcon* Apr 1732. Co.

Trenarry, Richard. S Mar 1742 LC PG Co., Md. Co.

Tresize, Mary. S Launceston Feb 1758 (AHJ). Co.

Tretheway, James. S Launceston May 1754 (AHJ). Co.

Trevasius, Arthur. S 14 yrs Lent 1731 but escaped from *Falcon*. Co.

Trevil, John. S Mar 1764. Be.

Trevis, John. S Lent LC AA Co., Md., from *Thornton* May 1771. M.

Trewheela, Francis. S Launceston May 1763 (AHJ). Co.

Trimby, Stephen. S 14 yrs Lent LC Bal Co., Md., Jun 1773. Do.

Trimnell, Richard. S Jan T Mar 1750 *Tryal*. L.

Tripper, Mary. S Lent 1757. Db.

Tripping, James (1738) - *See* Tipping. He.

Tristram *als* Tristrum, Joseph. S Summer T *Ruby* Oct 1754. Ht.

Trollope, Thomas. S May 1775. Li.

Trossill, William. S Lent LC AA Co., Md., from *Thornton* Jul 1773. Sx.

Trotman, John. S s cloth at Bisley Summer LC Md *William* Dec 1774 & sold to Dorrey Jacob. G.

Trott, John. S Lent LC Potomac, Va., from *Martha* Dec 1724. So.

Trotter, John. S s horse Sep 1770 (HJ). He.

Trough, Walter. S Lent T from Bristol May 1754. Sh.

Troward, Edward. S Feb T *Tryal* Mar 1757. M.

Trowton, Robert. SQS &T *Greyhound* Feb 1755. M.

Truebridge, Mary. R Oct 1772 T *Justitia* Jan 1773. M.

Truelove, Richard. S s at Wokingham Lent 1764. Be.

Trueman, Alice. S Jan T *Thames* Feb 1751. L.

Trumble, Elizabeth. S Exeter Oct 1758 (AHJ). De.

Trump, Richard. S Summer 1740 R 14 yrs Feb T Apr 1741 *Speedwell* or *Mediterranean*. Sx.

Trussell, Ann. S Jun T *Maryland Packet* Oct 1761. M.

Trussin, Elizabeth wife of George. S Sep T Oct 1750 *Rachael*. M.

Trusty, Christopher. S Jul LC Bal Co., Md., Dec 1783 from *Swift*. M.

Trusty, John. S Lent T *Thornton* May LC AA Co., Md., Jul 1774. M.

Tuck, Henry. S Lent LC Bal Co., Md., Jul 1771. De.

Tuck, Joseph. S s gedling & R 14 yrs Summer 1727. Hu.

Tuck, Philip. S Lent 1772 but noted as having died before transportation. Wi.

Tucker, Edward. S Jan-Apr T *Lichfield* May 1749. M.

Tucker, Emanuel. SWK Oct 1772 T *Justitia* Jan 1773. K.

Tucker, Grace, wife of Richard of St. Giles in Fields. PT Apr R Oct 1673 AT Jun 1674 LC Md from *Charles* May 1674. M.

Tucker, Grace. R 14 yrs Mar T Apr 1742 LC PG Co., Md. Co.

Tucker, James. SW Jan LC AA Co., Md., from *Thornton* Jul 1775. M.

Tucker, John. S Lent 1744 LC Knt Co., Md., from *Susannah* Aug 1744. De.

Tucker, Peter. S Lent 1732 LC Knt Co., Md., from *Falcon* Mar 1733. De.

Tucker, Thomas. S Summer 1734 LC Knt Co., Md., Mar 1735 from *Falcon*. De.

Tucker, Thomas. S Jan T *Thames* Feb 1751. M.

Tucker, William. SQS Bristol Sep 1774 TB May LC Md from *Isabella* Jul 1775 & sold to Waters & Gartrall. G.

Tuckey, John. S Lent LC Bal Co., Md., Jun 1773. Wa.

Tuckley, Rebecca. S Summer 1736 T Jun 1737. Wa.

Tudor, Frances. S Lent LC AA Co., Md., from *Thornton* May 1771. L.

Tuffnal, James. S Jul T *Saltspring* Jul 1775. L.

Tufnell, John. SQS Jan LC AA Co., Md., from *Thornton* Jul 1775. M.

Tugwell, Elizabeth. S Dec 1773 T *Justitia* Jan 1774. M.

Tugwell, Thomas. S Jul LC Bal Co., Md., Dec 1783 from *Swift*. M.

Tunbridge, Samuel. S Dec 1749-Jan 1750 T Mar 1750 *Tryal*. M.

Tunicliff, Ann. S Jun T *Maryland Packet* Oct 1761. M.

Tuniola, Margaret. S Feb T *Neptune* Mar 1761. M.

Tunks, John. S Bristol Jan T Mar 1757 (AHJ). G.

Tunningley (Tunnely), John. S Lent LC Bal Co., Md., Dec 1770 from *Trotman* & sold to Mordecai son of John Price. Y.

Turbett, Mary. S Summer T Sep 1751 *Greyhound*. Sy.

Turk, Esau. S Lent LC Bal Co., Md., Jul 1772. G.

Turker, William. T May 1755 *Rose*. Sy.

Turnbull, John. S Lent T *Dolphin* May 1763. E.

Turnbull, William. S Jan-Apr T Jun 1748 *Lichfield*. M.

Turner, Elizabeth. S Sep-Oct 1775 T *Justitia* Feb 1776. M.

Turner, George. S for housebreaking at Acton Beauchamp Lent R 14 yrs Summer 1768; brother Samuel executed. Wo.

MORE EMIGRANTS IN BONDAGE

Turner, Henry. S Summer T Sep 1754. St.

Turner, James. S Apr-Jun 1739 T *Sea Nymph* to Md. M.

Turner, James. S Lent T Apr 1756. Wa.

Turner, John. S Jun 1718 T Feb 1719 *Worcester* LC Annapolis Jun 1719. L.

Turner, John of St. Michael, Colchester, husbandman. SQS Jul T Aug 1749 *Thames*. E.

Turner, John. S Lent R Jun T 14 yrs Aug 1752 *Tryal*. E.

Turner, Margaret. S Summer R & T for life Sep 1767. Y.

Turner, Samuel. S Summer T *Maryland Packet* Oct 1761. K.

Turner, Simon. T Sep 1737 *Pretty Patsy*. L.

Turner, Thomas. S Summer 1753 R 14 yrs Lent T *Tryal* Jul 1754. E.

Turner, William. SQS Bury St. Edmunds Jan 1723. Su.

Turner, William. S Jan T Mar 1750 *Tryal*. L.

Turner, William. S for housebreaking at Acton Beauchamp Lent R 14 yrs Summer 1768; brother Samuel executed. Wo.

Turner, William. SQS Sep 1772 T *Justitia* Jan 1773. M.

Turner *als* Borroughs, William. S & R 14 yrs Summer T *William* LC Md Dec 1774 & sold to James Hutchings. St.

Turrell, John of Great Leighs. SQS Jan T *Dolphin* May 1763. E.

Turrell, Mary. S Lent LC AA Co., Md., from *Thornton* Jul 1773. Sy.

Turtle, William Sr. R Summer 1772 T *Justitia* Jan 1773. Sy.

Tush, John. S Lent LC Knt Co., Md., from *Bideford* Nov 1737 So.

Tutin (Tutton), Daniel. S Mar TB May 1724 LC from *Robert* Annapolis Jun 1725. Nt.

Twanmey, John. S Sep-Oct 1773 T *Justitia* Jan 1774. M.

Twinpenny, Thomas. S Apr 1752 (WJ). Wa.

Twisbrooke, Richard. S Dec 1755 (AHJ). Wo.

Twiss, Elizabeth. S Jul T *Restoration* LC Bal Co., Md., Oct 1771. Sh.

Twiss *als* Twist *als* Hill, Mary wife of William. S s at Hodnet Summer 1771 T *Restoration* LC Bal Co., Md., Oct 1771. Sh.

Tye, Robert. SQS Woodbridge 1770. Su.

Tyers *als* Beard, Ann. S s plates Sep 1735 T Jan 1736 *Dorsetshire* LC Va Sep 1736. M.

Tyers, Sarah. S Jan T Mar 1750 *Tryal*. L.

Tyler, Edward. S 14 yrs Summer 1772 LC Bal Co., Md., Apr 1773, sold to Thomas Marsh. G.

Tyler, John. S Jul T Aug 1749 *Thames*. L.

Tyler, Joseph. S Oct 1751-Jan 1752 T *Thames* Mar 1752. M.

Tyler, Mary wife of George. S s in Worcester Lent 1755. Wo.

Tyler, Mary. S Lent T *Thornton* May LC AA Co., Md., Jul 1774. L.

Tyler, Thomas. S s sheep Lent R 14 yrs Summer 1753 (GJ). He.

Tyler, William. S Lent T *Thornton* May LC AA Co., Md., Jul 1774. Sx.

Tyrrell, Francis. S s sheep & R 14 yrs Lent T May 1772 TB to Md. No.

Tysoe, James. S 14 yrs Summer LC Bal Co., Md., Dec 1770. Wa.

Tythe, Mary. SQS & T Sep 1751 *Greyhound*. M.

Udall, John. S Oct-Dec 1750 T *Thames* Feb 1751; runaway. M.

Uden, William. S for life S Lent LC AA Co., Md., from *Thornton* Jul 1773. K.

Uffell, Roger. S Summer 1738 LC Knt Co., Md., *from Hawk* Apr 1739. Ha.

Uggles, Richard. S Lent R 14 yrs Summer T *Maryland Packet* Oct 1761. E.

Underhill, George. S Apr T *Justitia* May 1745. L.

Underhill, Robert Jr. S Summer 1718 LC from *Sophia* QA Co., Md. Mar 1719. De.

Underhill, William. S Summer 1718 LC from *Sophia* QA Co., Md. Mar 1719. De.

Underlin, George. SQS Bristol s shoes in Maryport St. Dec 1765 TB to Md Apr 1766. G.

Underwood, Jacob Fosbrook of Hertingfordbury or North Mimms. S Lent T Jul 1745 *Italian Merchant*. Ht.Underwood, Shadrach. SQS Bristol s silk handkerchiefs in Wine St. Mar TB to Md
   May 1763. G.

Unrich, Rosina. SQS Feb LC AA Co., Md., from *Thornton* Jul 1773. Sy.

Unthank, Daniel. S Summer LC Bal Co., Md., Dec 1770 from *Trotman* & sold to Aquila Price. Y.

Unthank, Joseph. T *Justitia* Feb 1776. L.

Upchurch, John. S Summer 1745 R 14 yrs Lent T *Mary* Sep 1746. Sy.

Upham, Robert. S 14 yrs Lent LC AA Co., Md., from *Thornton* Jul 1775. Sy.

Upton, Edward. S Aug T *Beverly* Aug 1763. L.

Upton, Elizabeth. S Dec 1754 T *Greyhound* Feb 1755. L.

Upton, George. SQS Feb T May 1752 *Lichfield*. M.

Uren als Calebna, Jane. S Lent LC Bal Co., Md., Jun 1773. Co.

Usherwood, Roger of Lancaster. SQS 1726-1728. La.

Vallum, John. S Southwark Mar T *Thornton* May LC AA Co., Md., Jul 1774. Sy.

Vanstechelen, Ann. S s spoons Jan T Apr 1735 *Patapsco* LC Annapolis Oct 1735. M.

Vanstone, Jonas. S 14 yrs Summer LC Knt Co., Md., from *Bideford* Nov 1737. So.

Vardy, Ann. S Lent 1739 but to remain in gaol because of lunacy. Nl.

Varndell, John. T Apr 1760 *Thetis* . Sx.

Varnial, Mary. S Oct 1773 T *Justitia* Jan 1774. L.

Varron, Thomas. S Sep T *Ruby* Oct 1754. L.

Vaughan, Benjamin. S s wool Jul 1754. O.

Vaughan, Edward. S Dec 1747 LC Knt Co., Md., from *St. George* Mar 1748. L.

Vaughan, John, aged 12. S for housebreaking Lent 1739 R 14 yrs Lent 1740. Wo.

Vaughan, John. T 1746. Nf.

Vaughan, John. S May-Jul T *Tayloe* Jul 1773. M.

Vaughan, Thomas. T *Greyhound* Feb 1755. L.

Vaughan, William, *als* Lord Vaughan, brother of Viscount Lisburn. R 14 yrs for returning from T Jan 1740 (IJ). M.

Vaughton, William. S shoplifting in Birmingham Summer 1760. Wa.

Veal, Jane. S Mar 1742 T Apr LC PG Co., Md. Co.

Veezey, Katherine. S Sep T Oct 1750 *Rachael*. M.

Vellum, John. S Southwark Mar LC AA Co., Md., from *Thornton* Jul 1775. Sy.

Vencombe, Henry (1771). *See* Farncombe. So.

Venice, Thomas. S for highway robbery Lent R 14 yrs Summer T Oct 1750 *Rachael*. Sx.

Vennas, Thomas. S Coventry s mowing scythe Aug 1771. Wa.

Venner, Isaac. SQS Sep T *Justitia* Dec 1774. M.

Ventris, Benjamin. S Oct T Oct 1749 *Mary*. L.

Venus, John. S s naval stores Summer T Aug 1749 *Thames*. K.

Verity, John. S Sep T *Ruby* Oct 1754. L.

Vernoll, George. S 14 yrs Lent LC Bal Co., Md., Jun 1773; runaway. Ha.

Vernon, Henry. S Lent T *Thornton* May LC AA Co., Md., Jul 1774. Sy.

MORE EMIGRANTS IN BONDAGE

Vicary, Hugh. S Lent 1744 LC Knt Co., Md., from *Susannah* Aug 1744. De.
Vice, Thomas of Newport Pagnell. S Lent T *Dolphin* May 1763. Bu.
Vickers, John. S May-Jul T *Tayloe* Jul 1773. M.
Vickers [Vickus], William. S s books in Temple Sep T Oct 1768 *Justitia*. L.
Vidgeon, Thomas. S s sheep Summer T Aug 1749 *Thames*. K.
Vile, Henry. Ordered for T Oct 1722. K.
Vincent, Charles. S Bristol for returning from transportation Sep 1753. G.
Vincent, Hezekiah. T May 1751 *Tryal*. Sy.
Vincent, Richard. S Lent 1737 LC Knt Co., Md., from *Hawk* Nov 1737. Co.
Vincent, Samuel. SQS Ipswich Apr 1722. Su.
Vincent, Samuel. S Chelmsford Jan 1762 (AHJ). E.
Vine, John. S Mar 1753 (RG). Ha.
Vinegar, Ann. S Lent T *Tryal* Jul 1754. Sy.
Viner, Jane. S Jan T Apr 1735 *Patapsco* LC Annapolis Oct 1735. M.
Viney, Thomas. S Summer 1748, found at large & S Lent T May 1749 *Lichfield*;
    runaway. K.
Virgo, Thomas. S s sheep Lent R 14 yrs Summer T *Barnard* Oct 1756. Bu.
Vivian, William. S Summer 1718 LC from *Sophia* QA Co., Md. Mar 1719. Co.
Vosper, Richard. S Lent T May 1746 from Appledore. Co.
Votiere, Peter. S Feb T Apr 1735 *Patapsco* LC Annapolis Oct 1735. L.

Wadcase, Richard. S Lent LC AA Co., Md., from *Thornton* Jul 1773. Bu.
Waddesley, John. S Dec 1754 T *Greyhound* Feb 1755. L.
Wade, Elizabeth (1726) -*See* Barker. La.
Wade, John. S Jan-Apr T *Lichfield* May 1749. M.
Wade, Sarah wife of Solomon. S Feb-Apr T *Laura* Apr 1746. M.
Wade, Sarah. S Dec 1772 T *Justitia* Jan 1773. M.
Wade, Sarah. S Lent T *Thornton* May LC AA Co., Md., Jul 1774. M.
Wadhams, Robert. S s hen at Walsall Lent 1759. St.
Wadhams, William. S Lent LC Bal Co., Md., Jul 1771. Wi.
Wadley, Elizabeth. S Lent T *Thornton* May LC AA Co., Md., Jul 1774. E.
Wagger, Thomas. S Lent T May 1749 *Lichfield*. K.
Wagstaffe, John of Manchester. SQS Apr 1730. La.
Waine, John. S Oct T Oct 1749 *Mary*. L.
Waite, Esther. S Oct 1758. Li.
Waite, Walter. S Oct 1756. Li.
Wakefield, Thomas. R Summer 1773 T *Justitia* Jan 1774. Sx.
Wakeling, Samuel. S Lent T *Thornton* May LC AA Co., Md., Jul 1774. L.
Wakely, Richard. S Exeter Jun 1762 (AHJ). De.
Walden, James. S Lent LC AA Co., Md., from *Thornton* Jul 1773. E.
Waldron, Joan (1747) - *See* Pain. De.
Wale, William, S s lead & T Feb 1747. O.
Wale, William. S Lent LC AA Co., Md., from *Hanover Planter* Jul 1773. M.
Walker, Alice. S Oct 1772 T *Justitia* Jan 1773; runaway. L.
Walker, Alice. S 14 yrs Jul T *Tayloe* Jul 1774. L.
Walker, Charles, S s horse Aug 1756 R 14 yrs Lent 1757 (GJ). Sh.
Walker, Edmund. SQS Jan LC Bal Co., Md., from *Adventure* Mar 1773. Du.
Walker, Francis. S Lent 1737. Wa.

Walker, Henry. SQS Chesterfield Oct 1737 T Jan 1738. Db

Walker, John. S Jan-Apr T Jun 1748 *Lichfield*. M.

Walker, John. S Jun T *Tryal* Jul 1754. L.

Walker, John. T *Justitia* Jan 1774. M.

Walker, Letitia. S Feb-Apr T May 1751 *Tryal*. M.

Walker, Mabell. S Jul T Dec 1735 *John* LC Annapolis Sep 1736. M.

Walker *als* Johnson, Mary. S Jan-Apr T Jun 1748 *Lichfield*. M.

Walker *als* Sparrow, Mary. S Jun T *Tryal* Jul 1754. L.

Walker, Mary. S Lent LC AA Co., Md., from *Thornton* Jul 1773. L.

Walker, Mary. S Jul LC Bal Co., Md., Dec 1783 from *Swift*. M.

Walker, Peter. S Apr T May 1752 *Lichfield*. L.

Walker, Richard. S May-Jul T Sep 1751 *Greyhound*. M.

Walker, Richard. S for ripping lead from house Sep T *Barnard* Oct 1756. M.

Walker, Richard. S Lent T *Dolphin* May 1763. K.

Walker, Thomas Jr. of Astley. SQS Apr 1719; S Oct 1728 for returning. La.

Walker, Thomas. S 14 yrs for receiving plate from a church Lent 1741 (GJ). St.

Walker, Thomas. S Lent LC AA Co., Md., from *Thornton* May 1771. M.

Walker, Thomas. SQS Sep 1772 T *Justitia* Jan 1773. M.

Walker, Thomas. SQS Jan T *Thornton* May LC AA Co., Md., Jul 1774. M.

Walker, William of Astley. SQS Apr 1719. La.

Walker, William. S Lent 1734. Li.

Walker, William. S Apr T May 1750 *Lichfield*. L.

Walklin, Thomas. S May-Jul T *Tayloe* Jul 1773. M.

Wall, Charles. S Oct 1772 T *Justitia* Jan 1773. L.

Wall, George. S Lent T *Thornton* May LC AA Co., Md., Jul 1774. M.

Wall, Hugh. S Bristol Apr 1743 LC Knt Co., Md., from *Raven* Feb 1744. G.

Wall, Mary. S Summer 1747 LC Knt Co., Md., from *St. George* Mar 1748. Sy.

Wall, Sarah. S Mar T Apr 1737. Wa.

Waller, Elizabeth. T Aug 1752 *Tryal*. Sy.

Waller, John. S Feb T for life Mar 1750 *Tryal*. L.

Wallington, Ann. S Feb T *Neptune* Mar 1761. M.

Wallis, Ann. S Summer T *Barnard* Oct 1756. Sy.

Wallis, George. SQS Apr 1728. La.

Wallis, Jane, spinster. S City Christmas 1756 (AHJ). Nl.

Wallis, John. S Summer 1773 T *Justitia* Jan 1774. Bu.

Wallis, Margaret. SQS S Lent LC AA Co., Md., from *Hanover Planter* Jul 1773. M.

Wallis, Samuel. S Jul LC Bal Co., Md., Dec 1783 from *Swift*. M.

Wallis, Thomas. S Sep T for life Oct 1750 *Rachael*. M.

Wallis, William *als* Husband. S s mare Summer 1722 R Jul T Oct 1723 *Forward* from London. Y.

Walls, Dorothy. S Summer 1772 LC Bal Co., Md., from *Adventure* Mar 1773. Du.

Walrond, Grace. S 14 yrs Summer 1731 LC Knt Co., Md., from *Falcon* Apr 1732. De.

Walsom, Thomas. R 14 yrs Jul T *Tayloe* Jul 1774; runaway in Va. 1775, knock-kneed barber aged 27. M.

Walter, Meredith. S s sheep Mar 1757 (WJ). G.

Walter *als* Wettie, Thomas. S Feb T Mar 1750 *Tryal*. M.

Walter, Thomas. T May 1751 *Tryal*. Sy.

Walters, Elizabeth. S Sep T *Ruby* Oct 1754. L.

Walters, John. R for life Jul T *Tayloe* Jul 1773. M.

Walters, Richard. S Lent LC Knt Co., Md., from *Unity* Nov 1733. Co.

Walther, Thomas. S s from bleaching yard Aug 1753 (WJ). St.

Walthew, Jane. S Oct 1751-Jan 1752 T *Thames* Mar 1752. M.

Walton, James. SQS Apr 1730. La.

Walton, Joseph. S May-Jul T *Mary* Sep 1746. M.

Walton, Mary. T Apr 1735 *Patapsco* LC Annapolis Oct 1735. Sy.

Walton, Thomas of Wortley. R for Africa or America Jul 1705. Y.

Wanless *als* Newby, Elizabeth. S Dec 1749-Jan 1750 T Mar 1750 *Tryal.* M.

Wapshot, James. SQS Apr T *Thornton* May LC AA Co., Md., Jul 1774. M.

Warburton, Edward of St. Bride's. S s silver can Apr T May 1718. L.

Warburton, William. S Summer LC Bal Co., Md., Dec 1772. So.

Warby, James. R Jul T *Tayloe* Jul 1773. M.

Ward, Ann. S s satin Feb T Apr 1735 *Patapsco* LC Annapolis Oct 1735. M.

Ward, Ann. S Jul T *Phoenix* Oct 1760. M.

Ward, Benjamin. S Lent T Sep 1753. Nt.

Ward, Christopher. S Feb-Apr T May 1751 *Tryal.* M.

Ward, Edward. SWK 5 yrs as incorrigible rogue Apr T *Dolphin* May 1763. K.

Ward, Edward. S 14 yrs Lent LC AA Co., Md., from *Thornton* Jul 1775. Ht.

Ward, Elizabeth. S Lent T *Lichfield* May 1749. Sy.

Ward *als* English, Elizabeth. S Jul T *Barnard* Oct 1756. M.

Ward, Henry. S Apr 1753 (AHJ). Li.

Ward, James. S Jan T Mar 1750 *Tryal.* L.

Ward, Job. S 14 yrs Summer 1738 LC Knt Co., Md., *from Hawk* Apr 1739. Ha.

Ward *als* Wade, John. R 14 yrs & T Dec 1747. Do.

Ward, John. S Apr T Jun 1748 *Lichfield.* L.

Ward, John. S Apr 1753. Li.

Ward, John. S Feb T *Thames* Mar 1754. M.

Ward, John. S for housebreaking at Hanley William Lent 1755, tried for returning Mar 1757. Wo.

Ward, John. S Dec 1772 T *Justitia* Jan 1773. M.

Ward, John. S May-Jul T *Tayloe* Jul 1774. M.

Ward, Katherine. S Summer T Oct 1759. Le.

Ward, Luke. S Jul-Dec 1747 but died. M.

Ward, Margaret. S Oct 1773 T *Justitia* Jan 1774. L.

Ward, Patrick. S Lent LC AA Co., Md., from *Thornton* Jul 1775. M.

Ward, Robert. S Jan-Apr T *Lichfield* May 1749. M.

Ward, Samuel. SQS Jul T *Justitia* Dec 1774. M.

Ward, Samuel. S Jul T *Saltspring* Jul 1775. M.

Ward, Thomas. S Jan T Sep 1736. Y.

Ward, Thomas. S Lent LC AA Co., Md., from *Thornton* Jul 1775. M.

Ward, Toby. S for highway robbery & R 14 yrs Feb 1738 (RM). Ha.

Ward, William. S Apr T *Dolphin* May 1763. M.

Ward, William. S Oct T *Justitia* Dec 1774. L.

Wardell, Leonard. S Lent T *Thornton* May LC AA Co., Md., Jul 1774. M.

Warden, Arthur. S Lent LC AA Co., Md., from *Thornton* Jul 1775. L.

Warden, Richard Morse. S Lent T *Dolphin* May 1763. Sy.

Warden, William. S Feb-Apr T *Laura* Apr 1746. M.

Wardens, James. S Dec 1772 T *Justitia* Jan 1773. M.

Wardley, Francis. S 14 yrs May T *Phoenix* Oct 1760. M.

Wardlow, William. S s coat Feb T Apr 1735 *Patapsco* LC Annapolis Oct 1735. M.

Ware, Ann. S 14 yrs Jul 1758 (GJ). He.

Ware, Edward. S Jan T *Tryal* Mar 1757. L.

Waring, Ann. S Jul T Jul 1748 *Mary*. L.

Wareing, Thomas of Walton le Dale, butcher. SQS Jan 1735. La.

Waring, Thomas. S Lent T Summer 1752. Wa.

Warley, John. S Lent 1755. Be.

Warmington, Thomas. S s cheese Apr 1751 (WJ). Wa.

Warn, Richard. T Aug 1752 *Tryal*. E.

Warner, John. S Lent R Jun T 14 yrs Aug 1752 *Tryal*. K.

Warner, Richard. S for life Dec 1746 T Jan 1747 *George William*. L.

Warner, William. S for killing deer in enclosed park Summer 1730 R 14 yrs Lent TB to Va Apr 1731; convicted for returning & executed in Charnwood Forest 1732. Le.

Warner, William of Bermondsey. S Summer T Oct 1750 *Rachael*. Sy.

Warre, William Jr. S Lent LC Bal Co., Md., Jun 1773. Ha.

Warren, Birtle. S Lent LC AA Co., Md., from *Thornton* Jul 1773. M.

Warren, James. S for housebreaking Lent R 14 yrs Summer 1734. G.

Warren, John of Buttsbury. SQS Jan T *Tryal* Jul 1754. E.

Warren, John. S Lent T *Thornton* May LC AA Co., Md., Jul 1774. M.

Warren, Margaret. S Summer T Jul 1747 *Laura*. Sy.

Warren, Margaret. T Jan 1748. Sy.

Warren, Margaret. S Summer 1741 LC QA Co., Md., from *Philleroy* Apr 1742. De.

Warren, Robert. S Summer 1734 LC Knt Co., Md., from *Hawk* Apr 1735. So.

Warren, Susanna of Great Oakley, chapwoman. SQS Jul T Aug 1749 *Thames*. E.

Warriker, Abraham. S Summer 1755 R 14 yrs Summer T *Barnard* Oct 1756. E.

Warrington, Mary. S Aug T *Beverly* Aug 1763. L.

Warrington, William. S Sep-Oct T *Justitia* Dec 1774. M.

Warwick, Christopher. S May-Jul T *Tayloe* Jul 1773. M.

Wase, David. S Lent 1729. Nt.

Wass, Mary. S Lent 1734. Nt.

Wass, Michael. S Oct 1757. Li.

Waterer *als* Waters, John Jr. T Apr 1735 *Patapsco* LC Annapolis Oct 1735. Sy.

Waterman, Cober (1754) - *See* Jones, Charles. Sh.

Waters, Catherine. S May-Jul T *Tayloe* Jul 1773. M.

Waters, Elizabeth. S Sep T *Barnard* Oct 1756. M.

Waters, Holden. T Apr 1735 *Patapsco* LC Annapolis Oct 1735. K.

Waters, Martha. S & T Sep 1751 *Greyhound*. L.

Waters, Richard. S Lent R 14 yrs Summer 1747 LC Knt Co., Md., from *St. George* Mar 1748. Sx.

Waters, Thomas. SQS 1753. No.

Waters, Thomas. S Feb T *Thames* Mar 1754. L.

Waters, Thomas. S Apr T *Dolphin* May 1763. L.

Waters, Thomas. S May-Jul T *Tayloe* Jul 1774. M.

Waters, William. T Sep 1737 *Pretty Patsy*. L.

Waters, William. S Lent LC AA Co., Md., from *Hanover Planter* Jul 1773. M.

Watkins, Christian. S Sep 1740 T *Harpooner* Jan 1741. L.

Watkins, Hannah. S Feb T *Tryal* Mar 1757. M.

Watkins, James. S Lent 1750 LC QA Co., Md., from *Catherine* Nov 1750. Mo.

Watkins, James. S Bristol Jan T Feb 1755 (AHJ). G.

Watkins, John. S Dec T *Justitia* Dec 1774. M.

Watkins, Marmaduke. S Apr T May 1752 *Lichfield*. L.

Watkins, Samuel. S Lent T Sep 1736 from Bristol. He.

Watkins, Samuel. S s money from his master Summer 1758 R 14 yrs Lent 1759. Wo.

Watkins, Thomas (1745) - *See* Williams. Be.

Watkins, William. SQS Bristol Mar 1755 (BJ). G.

Watkinson, Elizabeth. S for shoplifting Apr 1718 T May 1719. L.

Watmore, James. S Sep 1740 T *Harpooner* Jan 1741. L.

Watson, Ann. S Jul T Sep 1746 *Mary*. L.

Watson, Edward. S Lent R 14 yrs Summer 1759. Ch.

Watson, Elizabeth. S Apr T May 1750 *Lichfield*. M.

Watson, Francis. T *Tayloe* Jul 1773. M.

Watson, George. S Dec 1773 T *Justitia* Jan 1774. M.

Watson, Henry Drake. S Sep-Oct T *Justitia* Dec 1774. M.

Watson, James. S Lent T *Thornton* May LC AA Co., Md., Jul 1774. L.

Watson, James William. S Lent but enlisted in Army Apr 1771. M.

Watson, Jane wife of Andrew. S for stealing silk handkerchief in Court Summer 1747 T Jan 1748. Nl.

Watson, John. S Summer 1739. Su.

Watson, John. S Sep 1746. So.

Watson, John. S Sep T Nov 1746. Sh.

Watson, John. S Dec 1753-Jan 1754 T *Thames* Mar 1754. M.

Watson, John. S Jul-Sep T *Ruby* Oct 1754. M.

Watson *als* Madeira, Joshua. S Feb-Apr T *Laura* Apr 1746. M.

Watson, Mary wife of William. SQS Apr T Jun 1746. Y.

Watson, Mary. S Jan-Apr T Jun 1748 *Lichfield*. M.

Watson, Richard. S Oct 1773 T *Justitia* Jan 1774. L.

Watson, Robert. S for aiding a known felon Lent R Jul T Oct 1723 *Forward* to Va from London. Y.

Watson, Robert. S Jan-Apr T *Lichfield* May 1749. M.

Watson, Thomas. S Lent T Apr 1753. Wa.

Watson, Thomas. S Lent T *Dolphin* May 1763. Sy.

Watton, James. S Sep T *Ruby* Oct 1754. L.

Watton, John. S Lent 1750 LC QA Co., Md., from *Catherine* Nov 1750. He.

Watts, Ann (1770). *See* Hadley. Wa.

Watts, Charles. S Jan-Apr T Jun 1748 *Lichfield*. M.

Watts, Elizabeth. S Lent 1769 (AHJ). Wi.

Watts, Jane. R for Barbados Feb 1673 but LC Md from *Charles* May 1674. L.

Watts, John (1775). *See* Mead. E.

Watts, Richard. S Mar LC Md from LC QA Co., Md., from *Chester* Nov 1749. He.

Watts, Thomas. S Mar 1750, escaped from gaol but died before embarcation. He.

Watts, Thomas. S Lent LC AA Co., Md., from *Thornton* Jul 1775. L.

Watts, William. S Lent 1750 LC QA Co., Md., from *Catherine* Nov 1750. So.

Watts, William. R for life Sep T *Barnard* Oct 1756. M.

Waymark, Sarah of Beddington, spinster. SQS Apr T May 1750 *Lichfield*. Sy.

Wear, Samuel. T May 1751 *Tryal*. K.

Weaver, Mary. S Dec 1753-Jan 1754 T *Thames* Mar 1754. M.

Weaver, Thomas. S Summer T Aug 1749 *Thames*. E.

Webb, Henry. S Jan T *Justitia* May 1745. L.

Webb, James. SQS Jan S Summer 1772 LC Bal Co., Md., Apr 1773. So.

Webb, James. R Jul T *Tayloe* Jul 1773. M.

Webb, John. S Apr 1746 T Apr 1746 *Laura*. M.

Webb, John. S Dec 1746 T Jan 1747 *George William*. L.

Webb, John. SQS for highway robbery Jan 1769 (RG). Be.

Webb, John. S 14 yrs Lent LC AA Co., Md., from *Thornton* Jul 1775. Sy.

Webb, Mary. S Feb T Jul 1747. Nf.

Webb, Richard. SQS Jan 1733 LC Knt Co., Md., from *Hawk* Apr 1735. So.

Webb, Richard. S 14 yrs Summer 1738 LC QA Co., Md. Jun 1739. De.

Webb, Richard. S Sep T *Ruby* Oct 1754. L.

Webb, Sarah. S Jan T Apr 1735 *Patapsco* LC Annapolis Oct 1735. M.

Webb, Thomas. SQS Launceston Mar 1734 LC Knt Co., Md, Mar 1735 from *Falcon*. Co.

Webb, Thomas. S Summer LC Bal Co., Md., Dec 1772. Wa.

Webb, William. S s horse Lent R 14 yrs Summer 1747 T Jan LC Md from *St. George* Mar 1748. Wa.

Webb, William. S Jul-Sep T *Ruby* Oct 1754. M.

Webber, Humphrey of Pilton, husbandman. S 14 yrs Summer 1738 LC Knt Co., Md., from *Hawk* Apr 1739. De.

Webber, John. SQS Bristol Mar TB May LC Md from *Isabella* Jul 1775 & sold to Waters & Gartrall. G.

Webber, Mary. S Jan T *Thames* Feb 1751. L.

Webber, Thomas. S Summer 1733 LC Knt Co., Md., from *Falcon* Apr 1734. Do.

Webber, William. S Jan-Apr T *Lichfield* May 1749. M.

Webley, Ann. S Dec 1746 T Jan 1747 *George William*. L.

Webster, John. S Summer LC Bal Co., Md., Dec 1772. Wa.

Webster, Ursula. SQS Doncaster Summer 1738. Y.

Webster, William. T May 1752 *Lichfield*. Ht.

Weed, Samuel. SQS & LC Bal Co., Md., Jul 1771. Do.

Weeks, Sampson. S Lent TB to Va from QS 1736. De.

Weene, Elizabeth wife of John. T Apr 1742 LC PG Co., Md. Co.

Wefton, Thomas. S Summer 1770. Wa.

Welch, Henry. S Dec T *Justitia* Dec 1774. M.

Welch, James. S Dec T *Justitia* Dec 1774. L.

Welch, Joseph. S Lent R 14 yrs Summer T Oct 1750 *Rachael*. E.

Welch, Lawrence. S Jan-Apr T *Lichfield* May 1749. M.

Welch *als* Edwards, Martha. S Jun T *Maryland Packet* Oct 1761. M.

Welch, Mary. S Jul T *Beverly* Aug 1763. M.

Welch, Robert. S Jan T *Greyhound* Feb 1755. L.

Welch, Susannah. S Sep-Oct 1773 T *Justitia* Jan 1774. M.

Welham, James (1774). *See* Fenn. K.

Wellam, Robert. S Oct-Dec 1750 T *Thames* Feb 1751. M.

Wellard, Thomas. S Lent T Sep 1746 *Mary*. K.

Wellbrand *als* Welbred *als* Summers, Mary. S Dec T *Justitia* Dec 1774. M.

Weller, Sarah. S Summer 1772 LC Bal Co., Md., Apr 1773. So.

Welling, James. S Lent 1759 (BJ). He.

Welling, Richard. S & T Aug 1752 *Tryal*. L.

Wellington, George. S s mare Lent R 14 yrs Summer 1758 TB to Va. No.

Wellington, James. S s at Ross to be T for life Lent 1759. He.

Wells, Daniel. S 14 yrs Apr-Jun 1739 T *Sea Nymph* to Md. M.

Wells, Edward. SWK Jan LC AA Co., Md., from *Thornton* Jul 1775. K.

Wells, John. S 14 yrs Jan-Apr T Jun 1748 *Lichfield*. M.

Wells, Joseph. S Bristol Mar 1750 LC QA Co., Md., from *Catherine* Nov 1750. G.

Wells, Thomas. T Jan 1736 *Dorsetshire* LC Va Sep 1736. Sx.

Wells, Thomas. S for returning from T & executed Mar 1767 (RG). Be.

Wells, Thomas of Egham. SQS Oct 1772 T *Justitia* Jan 1773. Sy.

Wells, William. S Lent T *Thornton* May LC AA Co., Md., Jul 1774; runaway from Francis Christian, Va. In 1775. E.

Wells, William. S Jan T *Tryal* Mar 1757. L.

Welman, Matthew. T Jan 1736 *Dorsetshire* LC Va Sep 1736. Sy.

Welsh, John. S Jul-Dec 1747 LC Knt Co., Md., from *St. George* Mar 1748. M.

Welsh, John. S Lent LC AA Co., Md., from *Thornton* May 1771. L.

Welsh, Joseph. S Summer 1741 LC QA Co., Md., from *Philleroy* Apr 1742. De.

Welsh, Michael. S Lent LC AA Co., Md., from *Thornton* May 1771. M.

Welsh, Thomas. S Jan T *Plain Dealer* Jan 1746. M.

Welsh, Thomas. S May-Jul T Jul 1748 *Mary*. M.

Welthresher, Joseph. S Jul-Dec 1747 LC Knt Co., Md., from *St. George* Mar 1748. M.

Wensley, Thomas. S Summer 1731 LC Knt Co., Md., from *Falcon* Apr 1732. So.

Wentworth, Elizabeth. S Sep-Oct 1773 T *Justitia* Jan 1774. M.

Wentworth, James. S Jan T Mar 1750 *Tryal*. L.

West, Henry of Beckington, husbandman. R for Barbados Feb 1673 but LC Md in 1673. So.

West, Henry. S Lent LC AA Co., Md., from *Hanover Planter* Jul 1773. M.

West, James. S Lent LC AA Co., Md., from *Thornton* Jul 1775. Bu.

West, Jarvis. S s seat of chair Apr T Dec 1735 *John* LC Annapolis Sep 1736. M.

West, John. SQS Ipswich Jan 1722. Su.

West, John of Wormingford. SQS Jan T *Tryal* Jul 1754. E.

West, John. S Lent T *Thornton* May LC AA Co., Md., Jul 1774. L.

West, Joseph. S Jun T Jul 1747 *Laura*. L.

West, Joshua. S Feb T *Thames* Mar 1752. L.

West, Richard. S Apr-May T *Tryal* Jul 1754. M.

Westbury, William. SQS s barley at Bourton Jan 1758. O.

Westcar, John. S s horse Lent R 14 yrs Jun T Dec 1737. O.

Westendale, John. S s horse R 14 yrs Jun 1726 but recommended for pardon Jan 1728. Db.

Western, John Jr. S Lent 1724 but escaped & no further record found. Li.

Westfield, Richard. S Dec 1745 T *Plain Dealer* Jan 1746. L.

Westhall, Henry. S May T *Saltspring* Jul 1775. L.

Westlake, Joseph. S Summer 1718 LC from *Sophia* QA Co., Md. Mar 1719. De.

Westley, Samuel. S Lent T *Dolphin* May 1763. E.

Westley, William. S Lent 1746 T Jul 1747. O.

Weston, George. S Summer T *Ruby* Oct 1754. Sx.

Weston, John. S Lent T Jun 1748 *Lichfield*. Sy.

Weston, Mary. S Summer T *Ruby* Oct 1754. Sy.

Wetherall, Jane wife of Thomas. S Jul T *Beverly* Aug 1763. M.

Wetherell, George. S for burglary Lent 1721 R Jul T Oct 1723 *Forward* to Va from London. Y.

Wetherford, Thomas. S Apr T May 1750 *Lichfield*. L.

Whalock, James. S Sep-Oct T Oct 1749 *Mary*. M.

Wharton, Sarah of St. Benet Paul's Wharf. S s handkerchiefs Apr 1718.

Wharton, William. S 14 yrs Lent LC AA Co., Md., from *Thornton* May 1771. K.

Wheatley, Elizabeth. S Sep-Dec 1746 T Jan 1747 *George William*. M.

Wheatley, George. SQS Jul T *Justitia* Dec 1774. M.

Wheatley, John, aged 19. S for breaking gaol & picking pockets May 1721 (NM). No.

Wheatley, John. S Lent 1737. Li.

Wheeldon, Elias. S Lent 1732 TB Aug 1733. Db.

Wheeldon, John. SQS Bakewell Jul T Dec 1737. Db.

Wheeler, James (1738). *See* Eyre. Wi.

Wheeler, Jonas. S Bristol Aug 1741 LC QA Co., Md., from *Philleroy* Apr 1742. G.

Wheeler, Lawrence. S 14 yrs Lent 1742 LC QA Co., Md., from *Kent* Jun 1743. De.

Wheeler, Mary. S 14 yrs Summer & respited Oct 1773 T *Justitia* Jan 1774. Sy.

Wheeler, Ralph. S Jun-Dec 1745 T *Plain Dealer* Jan 1746. M.

Wheeler als Ayres, William. SQS Jul LC Knt Co., Md., from *Bideford* Nov 1737. So.

Wheeler, William. S Lent T *Thornton* May LC AA Co., Md., Jul 1774. M.

Wheeler, William. R Summer 1773 T *Justitia* Jan 1774. Ht.

Whelan, Christopher. T from Dublin by *Hercules*, LC Bal. Co., Md., Aug 1773, sold to James Wilson of Augusta Co., Virginia. Ir.

Whelan, Thomas. T from Dublin by *Hercules*, LC Bal. Co., Md., Aug 1773, sold to William Walters & Richard Guttrell. Ir.

Wherrett, John. S Lent LC Bal Co., Md., Jul 1774. Do.

Whetland, John. S Lent T Sep 1746 *Mary*. K.

Whetton, John. S Mar T Apr 1746. Wa.

Whiddon, Henry. T May 1746. De.

Whiffen, Joseph. SQS Jul LC Bal Co., Md., Dec 1772. Do.

Whitaker - *See* Whittaker.

Whitby, William. S Mar T Sep 1747. Ha.

Whitby, William. T Aug 1752 *Tryal*. M.

Whitcliff, Richard of Newington. SQS Apr T Sep 1751 *Greyhound*. Sy.

White, Alexander. S May-Jul T Sep 1751 *Greyhound*. M.

White, Ann. S Mar T Sep 1747. Ha.

White, Ann *als* Elener. S May-Jul T Jul 1748 *Mary*. M.

White, Benjamin. SL Jun T *Ruby* Oct 1754. Sy.

White, Edward. S Lent 1741 (IJ). Su.

White, Edward. S Lent T May 1749 *Lichfield*. E.

White *als* Wilkes, Elizabeth. S Oct 1744-Jan 1745 T *Plain Dealer* Jan 1746. M.

White, Elizabeth. S Jul-Dec 1747 LC Knt Co., Md., from *St. George* Mar 1748. M.

White, Elizabeth. S Summer T Sep 1751 *Greyhound*. Sy.

White, Elizabeth. S Apr T *Dolphin* Apr 1761. L.

White, Henry of Hanwell. S s linen Apr 1718 TB May 1719. L.

White, Henry. S Summer 1731 LC Knt Co., Md., from *Falcon* Apr 1732. So.

White, Henry. S Apr T *Justitia* May 1745. L.

White, James. S Summer 1733 T Dec 1734. So.

White, James. T Summer 1745 T Feb 1746. Ha.

White, John. S Lent 1734. Li.

White, John. S Lent 1738. Li.

White, John. S Jan T *Justitia* May 1745. L.

White, John. S Feb T Mar 1750 *Tryal*. M.

White, John. S Summer 1751 R 14 yrs Lent T May 1752 *Lichfield*. K.

White, John. S Lent LC Bal Co., Md., Jun 1773. Wi.

White, John. S Jul LC Md *William* Dec 1774 & sold to James Hutchings. Ha.

White, John. SQS Jan LC AA Co., Md., from *Thornton* Jul 1775. M.

White, John. S Jul LC Bal Co., Md., Dec 1783 from *Swift*. M.

White *als* Wate, Jonathan. R for Barbados Oct 1673 but LC Md from *Charles* May 1674. L.

White, Joseph. T Lent 1750. Li.

White, Joseph. S Summer T Sep 1751 *Greyhound.* Sy.

White, Margaret. S Lent 1734. Li.

White, Margaret. S Dec 1772 T *Justitia* Jan 1773. M.

White, Mary. SQS & T Sep 1751 *Greyhound.* M.

White, Mary. S Oct 1751-Jan 1752 T *Thames* Mar 1752. M.

White, Mary. S Jul LC Bal Co., Md., Dec 1783 from *Swift.* M.

White, Matthew. S Lent 1733. Le.

White, Richard. S as pickpocket & R 14 yrs Jun 1741. Li.

White, Richard. S s hats May 1735 T Jan 1736 *Dorsetshire* LC Va Sep 1736. M.

White, Samuel. T Aug 1752 *Tryal.* Sy.

White, Sarah. S Lent T *Dolphin* May 1763. E.

White, Thomas. S May-Jul T Aug 1749 *Thames.* M.

White, Thomas. S Summer T Sep 1751 *Greyhound.* Sx.

White, William of Tildesley cum Shakerley. SQS Jan 1727. La.

White, William. S for highway robbery Summer 1761 R 14 yrs Feb 1762 TB to Md. No.

White, William. S Oct T *Justitia* Dec 1774. L.

Whitefoot, Thomas. S Lent LC AA Co., Md., from *Hanover Planter* Jul 1773. M.

Whitehall, Daniel. S s grain Jul 1766. Sh.

Whitehart, Richard. R for Barbados Dec 1671 but LC Md from *William & Mary* Mar 1672. M.

Whitehead, Henry. S Lent LC AA Co., Md., from *Thornton* Jul 1773. L.

Whitehead, John. S Summer 1732. Li.

Whitehead, John. S Lent LC AA Co., Md., from *Thornton* Jul 1773, sold to John Proctor, Bal. Co. M.

Whitehouse, James. R 14 yrs Jul T *Tayloe* Jul 1774. M.

Whitehouse, Jeremiah. S 14 yrs Apr-Jun 1739 T *Sea Nymph* to Md. M.

Whiteman, Sarah. S Jul T *Phoenix* Oct 1760. M.

Whitemesh, John. R 14 yrs Sep T *Randolph* Sep 1768. Ha.

Whitewood, John. SWK Jan LC AA Co., Md., from *Thornton* Jul 1773. K.

Whitfield, Barthia. S Feb-Apr T *Laura* Apr 1746. M.

Whitfield, Richard. S Lent 1770 but escaped in London. Y.

Whitham, Thomas, vagrant & incorrigible rogue. SQS Jul 1719. La.

Whitland, Christopher. S Lincoln ?1760 (AHJ). Li.

Whitlock, Richard. S City 1758 (AHJ). Nl.

Whitmill, Richard. S Summer 1746 T Jul 1747. Wa.

Whitmore, Joseph. S Lent T from Bristol May 1755. St.

Whitmore, Lydia. S Oct T Oct 1749 *Mary.* L.

Whitmore, William. S Jan T Apr 1735 *Patapsco* LC Annapolis Oct 1735. M.

Whitnell, Richard. S Sep 1746 T Feb 1747. Wa.

Whittaker, Isaac of Manchester. SQS Apr 1730. La.

Whitaker, John (1723) - *See* Swift. Y.

Whitaker, John. S Jan T Mar 1750 *Tryal.* L.

Whitaker, John. S Sep T *Ruby* Oct 1754. L.

Whitaker, Thomas. S Lent 1735 T Lent 1736. Nt.

Whitton, Henry. SQS Beccles 1770. Su.

Whitworth, Alice. S Lent LC AA Co., Md., from *Thornton* Jul 1775. M.

Whitworth, Jonathan of Mosson. SQS Apr 1721. La.

Whitworth, Mary wife of Jonathan of Mosson (qv). SQS Apr 1721. La.

Whoulfrey, John. S Lent LC Bal Co., Md., Jun 1773. Ha.

Wickham, Catherine. S May-Jun T Aug 1752 *Tryal*. M.

Wicks, Joseph. S for burglary Lent R for life Summer 1753. Be.

Widgeon, Sarah. SQS Lent LC AA Co., Md., from *Hanover Planter* Jul 1773. M.

Widgeon, William. S Apr T *Justitia* May 1745. L.

Wigginton, John (1772). *See* East. M.

Wiggs, Francis. S Lent R 14 yrs Summer T Oct 1750 *Rachael*. Ht.

Wigley, Ann or Abigail. S Lent AT Jul 1761. Sh.

Wigley, Elizabeth. R 14 yrs Dec T *Justitia* Dec 1774. M.

Wigmore, Catherine. S Lent LC AA Co., Md., from *Thornton* Jul 1775. M.

Wigstead, John. S Chelmsford Jan 1760 (AHJ). E.

Wilcox, Charles. S & R Lent T May 1755. St.

Wilcox, John. S 14 yrs Lent LC AA Co., Md., from *Thornton* Jul 1773. Sy.

Willcocks, Henry. S Lent LC Bal Co., Md., Jul 1772. De.

Wilcox, Thomas. S Jan-Apr T Jun 1748 *Lichfield*. M.

Wild, John. S Lent T *Thornton* May 1774 but found at large in September 1775 & ordered to be hanged. M.

Wilder, Thomas. R for life for robbing Exeter stage coach Aug 1737 T Feb 1738. Ha.

Wildgoose, John, an old offender. SQS s beef Oct 1754. O.

Wilding, Henry. S 14 yrs Mar 1774 LC AA Co., Md., from *Thornton* Jul 1775. Bu.

Wilds, Hannah. S Dec 1772 T *Justitia* Jan 1773. M.

Wildy, Joan [John]. S s at Painswick Lent TB Mar 1738. G.

Wilford, Robert. S Sep 1751. Li.

Wilkerson, Robert. S for burglary & R 14 yrs Jun 1741. Li.

Wilkes, Edward. S for housebreaking at Mortimer Cleobury Lent 1755; wife Elizabeth Wilkes *als* Ellis acquitted. Wo.

Wilkes, Isaac. S May T *Beverly* Aug 1763. M.

Wilkes *als* Boswell *als* Griffiths, Mary. S Dec 1750 T *Thames* Feb 1751. L.

Wilkes, Thomas. SQS Jul T *Restoration* LC Bal Co., Md., Oct 1771. St.

Wilkes, William. S Lent LC Bal Co., Md., Jun 1773. G.

Wilkins, Henry. SQS s plough Jul 1769 (RG). Bu.

Wilkins, Henry. S 14 yrs for receiving Lent 1772. O.

Wilkins, James. S Chelmsford Jan 1753 (AHJ). E.

Wilkins *als* Philpott *als* Johnson *als* Awdrey, Jane. S Jan-Jun T Jul 1747 *Laura*. M.

Wilkins, John. S Lent T Summer 1764. O.

Wilkins, John. S Jul T *Saltspring* Jul 1775. L.

Wilkins, Mary. S for life Summer 1772 LC Bal Co., Md., Apr 1773. G.

Wilkins, Phebe. S Lent LC AA Co., Md., from *Thornton* Jul 1773. K.

Wilkins, Phillis. S Summer 1738 LC Knt Co., Md., *from Hawk* Apr 1739. Wi.

Wilkins, Samuel. S 14 yrs Lent LC Knt Co., Md., from *Bideford* Nov 1737. So.

Wilkins, Thomas. S Oct 1772 T *Justitia* Jan 1773. L.

Wilkinson, Elijah [Elisha]. S Summer 1770 but escaped in London. Hu.

Wilkinson, John, clerk. S 14 yrs Jul 1756 for performing illegal marriages; petition for relief from his wife Grace Wilkinson, T *Barnard* Oct 1756. M.

Wilkinson, Joshua. T Aug 1746. Ht.

Wilkinson, Mary. S Jan-Jun T Jul 1747 *Laura*. M.

Wilkinson, Mary. S Summer T from London Sep 1754. Wa.

Wilkinson, Richard. S Lent 1737 LC Knt Co., Md., from *Hawk* Nov 1737. De.

Wilkinson, Robert. SQS Apr 1729. La.

Wilkinson, Thomas. S 14 yrs Lent LC Bal Co., Md., Jul 1772. Sh.

MORE EMIGRANTS IN BONDAGE

Wilky, John. S Aug 1759 (WJ). St.

Willard, Nicholas. T May 1751 *Tryal*. Sx.

Willers, Robert. S Summer T *Maryland Packet* Oct 1761. E.

Willes, John. S Summer 1757 (AHJ). Wi.

Willett, Ann. S Lent LC AA Co., Md., from *Thornton* Jul 1773. M.

Willett, Jonas. S Lent 1736 S Jul 1736 LC QA Co., Md., from *Amity* May 1737. Do.

Willey, Elizabeth. SQS Jan LC AA Co., Md., from *Thornton* Jul 1775. M.

William, John *als* Neal, Thomas. T 1746. Nf.

Williams, Alice. S Summer T Aug 1749 *Thames*. Sy.

Williams, Charles. S Lent R 14 yrs Summer 1754 (WJ). Wo.

Williams, Cuthbert. S Lent 1734. Li.

Williams, Edward. S 14 yrs Summer 1772 LC Bal Co., Md., Jun 1773; runaway. Sh.

Williams, Elisha. T *Mary* Sep 1746. M.

Williams, Elizabeth. S Feb-Apr T *Laura* Apr 1746. M.

Williams, Elizabeth. S Sep-Dec 1746 T Jan 1747 *George William*; runaway. M.

Williams, Elizabeth. SQS Sep T Oct 1750 *Rachael*. M.

Williams, Elizabeth. S Mar T *Thames* Mar 1754. L.

Williams, Elizabeth. S Oct T *Barnard* Oct 1756. L.

Williams, Elizabeth. S Feb T *Neptune* Mar 1761. L.

Williams, Elizabeth wife of William. S Bristol Lent 1772. G.

Williams, Elizabeth. S Lent LC Bal Co., Md., Jul 1774. Sh.

Williams, Ellis. S Jul LC Bal Co., Md., Dec 1783 from *Swift*. M.

Williams, Henry of St. Ewen's. S Bristol s from shopkeeper in Corn Street May 1752. G.

Williams, Henry. S Jul LC Bal Co., Md., Dec 1783 from *Swift*. M.

Williams, James. S Summer 1741 LC QA Co., Md., from *Philleroy* Apr 1742. De.

Williams, James of Chipping Barnet. R Summer T Jul 1745 *Italian Merchant*. Ht.

Williams, James. S Oct 1751-Jan 1752 T *Thames* Mar 1752. M.

Williams, James. S Bristol Jan 1759 (AHJ). G.

Williams, James. S Summer LC Bal Co., Md., Dec 1770. Wa.

Williams, Jane. S Summer 1734 LC Knt Co., Md., Mar 1735 from *Falcon*. De.

Williams, Jane. S May-Jul T Sep 1751 *Greyhound*. M.

Williams, Jarrett. S 14 yrs Lent LC Bal Co., Md., Jun 1773. G.

Williams, Jervis. S Summer 1772 LC Bal Co., Md., Apr 1773. Mo.

Williams, John. S as pickpocket Summer 1729 AT Summer 1730. Db.

Williams, John. S Lent LC Knt Co., Md., from *Bideford* Nov 1737. So.

Williams, John. SQS Jul 1738 LC QA Co., Md. Jun 1739. De.

Williams, John. S Apr-Jun 1739 T *Sea Nymph* to Md. M.

Williams, John, *als* Watkins, Thomas. S for robbing Reading stagecoach & R 14 yrs Aug 1745 (RM). Be.

Williams, John. S Jul-Dec 1747 LC Knt Co., Md., from *St. George* Mar 1748. M.

Williams, John. S Summer 1748 R 14 yrs Lent T *Lichfield* May 1749. Sy.

Williams, John. S Jan-Apr T *Lichfield* May 1749. M.

Williams, John. S Oct T Oct 1749 *Mary*. L.

Williams, John of Rotherhithe. SQS Apr T May 1750 *Lichfield*. Sy.

Williams, John. S Lent LC Bal Co., Md., Jul 1774. Do.

Williams, John. S 14 yrs S Lent LC AA Co., Md., from *Thornton* Jul 1773. Ht.

Williams, John. S Sep T Oct 1750 *Rachael*. M.

Williams, John. S Lent R 14 yrs Summer T *Ruby* Oct 1754. Ht.

Williams, John. S Lent T Apr 1756. Wa.

Williams, John. SQS Lent LC AA Co., Md., from *Hanover Planter* Jul 1773. M.

Williams, John. S Jun 1783. M.

Williams, Jones. S Summer LC Bal Co., Md., Dec 1772. Mo.

Williams, Judith, spinster. SQS Bristol Dec 1774 TB May LC Md from *Isabella* Jul 1775 & sold to Waters & Gartrall. G.

Williams, Lewis. R 14 yrs Oct 1772 T *Justitia* Jan 1773. M.

Williams, Lewis. S Sep-Oct T *Justitia* Dec 1774. M.

Williams, Margaret. S Lent T *Tryal* Jul 1754. Sy.

Williams, Mary. S for murder of bastard child Lent R Summer 1741 LC QA Co., Md from *Philleroy* Apr 1742. He.

Williams, Mary. S Lent 1754. Nt.

Williams, Mary. S Lent LC Bal Co., Md., Jul 1772. Sh.

Williams, Mary. S May-Jul T *Tayloe* Jul 1773. M.

Williams, Mary. S Lent LC AA Co., Md., from *Thornton* Jul 1775. Sy.

Williams *als* Eady, Mary. S Jul LC Bal Co., Md., Dec 1783 from *Swift*. M.

Williams, Michael. S Lent LC Bal Co., Md., Jul 1772. De.

Williams, Philip. S Dec 1749-Jan 1750 T Mar 1750 *Tryal*. M.

Williams, Rice. S Summer 1754 (BJ). Mo.

Williams, Richard. S Sep-Oct T Oct 1749 *Mary*. M.

Williams, Richard. S Lent LC Bal Co., Md., Jun 1773. Sh.

Williams, Robert. S s chairpin of dray Jan T Apr 1735 *Patapsco* LC Annapolis Oct 1735. L.

Williams, Robert. T Sep 1737 *Pretty Patsy*. L.

Williams, Roger. S Lent LC Knt Co., Md., from *Unity* Nov 1733. De.

Williams, Sarah. S Dec 1753-Jan 1754 T *Thames* Mar 1754. M.

Williams, Susanna. S Jan T *Greyhound* Feb 1755. M.

Williams, Susanna. S Jan T *Tryal* Mar 1757. L.

Williams *als* Munday, Thomas. S Mar 1734 LC Knt Co., Md, Mar 1735 from *Falcon*. Do.

Williams, Thomas. S Jul T Jul 1748 *Mary*. L.

Williams, Thomas. T *Lichfield* May 1749. L.

Williams, Thomas. S Dec 1750 T *Thames* Feb 1751. L.

Williams, Thomas. S Dec 1754 T Jun 1755. No.

Williams, Thomas. S Oct 1772 T *Justitia* Jan 1773. L.

Williams, Thomas. S Lent LC Bal Co., Md., Jul 1772. Mo.

Williams, Thomas. S for life Summer 1772 LC Bal Co., Md., Apr 1773. G.

Williams, Thomas. SW Lent LC AA Co., Md., from *Hanover Planter* Jul 1773. M.

Williams *als* Morgan, William. S for highway robbery Summer 1738 R 14 yrs on account of his youth Lent TB Aug 1739. G.

Williams, William. S Jul-Dec 1747 LC Knt Co., Md., from *St. George* Mar 1748. M.

Williams, William. S Jan T Mar 1750 *Tryal*. L.

Williams, William. S 14 yrs Oct T *Barnard* Oct 1756. L.

Williams *als* McKenzie, William. R 14 yrs Dec 1773 T *Justitia* Jan 1774. M.

Williamson, Betty. S Bristol Jan 1758 (AHJ). G.

Williamson, Edward. S Dec 1745 T *Plain Dealer* Jan 1746. L.

Williamson, James. S Summer 1732. Li.

Williamson, James. S Jan T *Plain Dealer* Jan 1746. L.

Williamson, John. S Summer 1736. Li.

Williamson, John. S Jun 1739 T *Sea Nymph* to Md. L.

Williamson, John. S Summer T *Ruby* Oct 1754. Sy.

Williamson, Mary. S Jul 1751 T Feb 1752. Cu.

MORE EMIGRANTS IN BONDAGE

Willicomb, William. S s pestle & mortar Jan T Apr 1735 *Patapsco* LC Annapolis Oct 1735. M.

Willington, George. S Summer 1758 (AHJ). No.

Willins, Sarah. S Lent T *Tryal* Jul 1754. K.

Willis, John. S Lent 1735. No.

Willis, John. S Summer T *Barnard* Oct 1756. Bu.

Willis, Joseph. S Bristol Jan 1750 (AHJ). G.

Willis, Lydia. S Jan T *Tryal* Mar 1757. L.

Willis, Richard. SQS Oct 1772 LC Bal Co., Md., Apr 1773. So.

Willis, Sarah. S Oct 1751-Jan 1752 T *Thames* Mar 1752. M.

Wills, Hannah. S Bristol Jan 1759 (AHJ). G.

Wills, Hugh. S 14 yrs Summer 1734 LC Knt Co., Md., from *Hawk* Apr 1735. So.

Wills, Jacob. S Sep 1750 (AHJ). Li.

Wills, John. S Feb T Jul 1747. Nf.

Wills, Joseph. S Lent LC Knt Co., Md., from *Unity* Nov 1733. De.

Wills, Mary. S Lent R 14 yrs Jun 1734 LC Knt Co., Md, Mar 1735 from *Falcon*. De.

Willshire, Thomas. S 14 yrs s linen from yard Summer T Aug 1749 *Thames*. Sy.

Willson, Margaret. T Lent 1750. Li.

Wilmore, John. S for robbery Jul 1755 (GJ). G.

Wilson, Andrew. S s sheep Lent 1758. Nt.

Wilson, Andrew. SQS Jul 1772 LC Bal Co., Md., from *Adventure* Mar 1773. Nl.

Wilson, Ann of Manchester, spinster. SQS Jan 1730. La.

Wilson *als* Warren, Ann. SQS Dec 1749 T Mar 1750 *Tryal*. M.

Wilson, Ann. S Jul T Sep 1751. No.

Wilson, Ann. S Lent 1754. Nt.

Wilson, Ann. T *Tayloe* Jul 1774; runaway. L..

Wilson, Edward *als* Joseph. S Jun T *Maryland Packet* Oct 1761. M.

Wilson, Edward. S Sep-Oct 1773 T *Justitia* Jan 1774. M.

Wilson *als* Taylor, Elizabeth, wife of John Taylor. S City 1751 (AHJ). Nl.

Wilson, Elizabeth. S 14 yrs S Lent LC AA Co., Md., from *Thornton* Jul 1773. E.

Wilson, Hannah. S Apr-May T *Tryal* Jul 1754. M.

Wilson, James. S Apr s beef T May 1720 *Honor* but escaped in Vigo, Spain, executed Oct 1720. L.

Wilson, James. S City Summer 1751 (AHJ). Nl.

Wilson, James, an old convict. S s mare Lent R 14 yrs Summer T Aug 1752 *Tryal*. Bu.

Wilson, James. SQS Jul 1772 LC Bal Co., Md., from *Adventure* Mar 1773; runaway. Nl.

Wilson, James. S Lent LC AA Co., Md., from *Hanover Planter* Jul 1773. M.

Wilson, Jane (1751) - *See* Campbell (AHJ). Nl.

Wilson, Jeremiah. S Summer T *Ruby* Oct 1754. Ht.

Wilson, John. T Oct 1746. Be.

Wilson, John. S Summer T Oct 1750 *Rachael*. Sy.

Wilson, John. S Lent T Apr 1760. Nt.

Wilson, John. S Summer LC Bal Co., Md., Dec 1770 from *Trotman* & sold to Ezekiel Boisley. Y.

Wilson, John. S Summer 1770 LC Bal Co., Md., Jun 1771. De.

Wilson, John. S Lent LC AA Co., Md., from *Hanover Planter* Jul 1773. M.

Wilson, Joseph. S Summer 1739. Nf.

Wilson, Joseph. S Jan-Apr T *Lichfield* May 1749. M.

Wilson, Joseph. S Oct 1773 T *Justitia* Jan 1774. L.

Wilson, Margaret. S Apr-May T *Saltspring* Jul 1775. M.

Wilson, Margery. S Lent T from Bristol May 1755. St.

Wilson, Mary. S Sep T *Ruby* Oct 1754. L.

Wilson *als* Wilkinson, Mary. S Oct T *Barnard* Oct 1756. M.

Wilson, Mary. S Lent T Apr 1760. Nt.

Wilson *als* Wilkinson, Robert. S & T Jan 1736 *Dorsetshire* LC Va Sep 1736. L.

Wilson, Robert. S Sep 1740 T *Harpooner* Jan 1741. L.

Wilson, Robert. S Feb-Apr T *Laura* Apr 1746. M.

Wilson, Robert. S Jan-Apr T *Lichfield* May 1749. M.

Wilson, Samuel of Washington. S Summer 1772 T *Justitia* Jan 1773. Sx.

Wilson, Sarah. S York 1761 (AHJ). Y.

Wilson, Thomas. S Aug T from Liverpool Dec 1746. St.

Wilson, Thomas *als* Hart, Henry. S Jul LC Bal Co., Md., Dec 1783 from *Swift*. M.

Wilson, William. S & T Aug 1752 *Tryal*. L.

Wilson, William. S Lent R Summer 1753 (WJ). St.

Wilson, William. SQS Woodbridge 1765. Su.

Wiltshire, James. SQS Oct 1772 LC Bal Co., Md., Jun 1773. Wi.

Wiltshire, John. T Jan 1736 *Dorsetshire* LC Va Sep 1736. Sx.

Winch, Ellis. T May 1751 *Tryal*. K.

Winchurch, John of Newington. SQS Jan T *Thames* Feb 1751. Sy.

Wind, Mary. S & T Aug 1752 *Tryal*. L.

Windsor, William. S Apr T May 1750 *Lichfield*. L.

Winfield, Richard. S Apr T Dec 1735 *John* LC Annapolis Sep 1736. L.

Wingcot, Philip. SQS Apr T May 1752 *Lichfield*. M.

Wingfield, James. T 1746. Nf.

Wingrove, John. R for life Summer 1773 T *Justitia* Jan 1774. Sy.

Wingrove, John. S Lent LC AA Co., Md., from *Thornton* Jul 1775. Sy.

Winkworth, Hugh. T Jun 1747. Ha.Winnall, Elizabeth. S for robbery at Pedmore Mar R 14 yrs Apr LC Bal Co., Md Jul 1771. Wo.

Winnell, Thomas of St. Saviour, Southwark. SQS Apr T Sep 1751 *Greyhound*. Sy.

Winnington, Nathan. S s iron bars Jul 1735 T Jan 1736 *Dorsetshire* LC Va Sep 1736. M.

Winsall, Lewis. S 1756 TB to Md. No.

Winte, Hester. S Summer T Oct 1758. Li.

Winter, Catherine. S Feb T *Thames* Mar 1752. L.

Winter, James. S Apr T Jun 1748 *Lichfield*. L.

Winter, Samuel. S Lent T Jun 1748 *Lichfield*. Sy.

Winter, Samuel. S Mar T *Thames* Mar 1754. L.

Winter, Thomas. SQS Jan LC Bal Co., Md., Jul 1772. Wi.

Winter, Thomas (1782). *See* Winton. L.

Winton *als* Winter, Thomas. S Dec 1782 LC Bal Co., Md., Dec 1783 from *Swift*. L.

Wise, Ann. T *Justitia* Jan 1773. M.

Wise, Benjamin. S Lent T from Liverpool Aug 1738. St.

Wise, Stephen. S Summer 1721 T Jul 1723 *Alexander* LC Md Sep 1723. Sx.

Wise, Thomas. S May-Jul T Aug 1749 *Thames*. M.

Wiseman, James. S Jan-Apr T Jun 1748 *Lichfield*. M.

Wiseman, John of Burton, blacksmith. R for Barbados Feb 1673 but LC Md in 1673. So.

Wissen, John. T May 1752 *Lichfield*. E.

Withall, Thomas. R Summer 1773 T *Justitia* Jan 1774. Sy.

Withall, Thomas. S 14 yrs Jul T *Tayloe* Jul 1774. L.

Witham, Samuel. S for life Mar T *Thames* Mar 1754. L.

MORE EMIGRANTS IN BONDAGE

Witheridge, Joan. S Summer 1734 LC Knt Co., Md., Mar 1735 from *Falcon*. De.
Witheridge, Stephen. SQS Jan LC Bal Co., Md., Apr 1773. Cc.
Witherington, Henry. S Jan-Jun T Jul 1747 *Laura*. M.
Witherspoon, Robert. SQS Feb S Lent LC AA Co., Md., from *Thornton* Jul 1773. M.

Withey, Daniel of St Mary Lothbury. S s cane Sep 1718 T Feb 1719 *Worcester* LC
  Annapolis Jun 1719. LM.
Witt, James. S Dec 1753-Jan 1754 T *Thames* Mar 1754. M.
Wolfington, Henry. S Feb T for life Mar 1750 *Tryal*. M.
Wollacott, John. S Lent 1734 LC Knt Co., Md., Mar 1735 from *Falcon*. De.
Wonnell (Wormell), James. S Jan T Feb 1719 *Worcester* LC Annapolis Jun 1719. L.
Wood, Catherine. S Aug 1746 T Jan 1747. Sh.
Wood, James. S Dec 1749-Jan 1750 T Mar 1750 *Tryal*. M.
Wood, James. S Lent 1752. Nt.
Wood, John. S Summer 1718 LC from *Sophia* QA Co., Md. Mar 1719. De.
Wood, John. S 1752 (AHJ). Nl.
Wood, John. S Sep-Oct 1772 T *Justitia* Jan 1773; runaway. M.
Wood, John. S Dec 1782 LC Bal Co., Md., Dec 1783 from *Swift*. L.
Wood, Joseph. S s horse Lent R 14 yrs Summer 1737 but died in prison. Y.
Wood, Martha of St. Sepulchre. S Sep T Oct 1719 *Susannah & Sarah* LC Md Apr
  1720. L.
Wood, Mary. S Exeter Apr 1756 (AHJ). De.
Wood, Mary. SQS Jul T *Restoration* LC Bal Co., Md., Oct 1771. St.
Wood, Mary. S Lent LC AA Co., Md., from *Thornton* Jul 1773. M.
Wood, Michael. S Jul T *Tayloe* Jul 1773. L.
Wood, Paul. S Sep T *Ruby* Oct 1754. L.
Wood, Peter. S Summer 1757 R 14 yrs Lent T Apr 1758 *Lux* from London. Db.
Wood, Robert. T Sep 1737 *Pretty Patsy*. L.
Wood, Robert. S Dec 1749-Jan 1750 T Mar 1750 *Tryal*. M.
Wood, Robert. S Bristol Jan 1757 (AHJ). G.
Wood, Robert. SQS Oct 1772 LC Bal Co., Md., Jun 1773. St.
Wood, Samuel. S for having two wives Sep 1750 (WJ). Wa.
Wood, Solomon. S Lent LC AA Co., Md., from *Thornton* May 1771. L.
Wood, Thomas. S Apr 1757. Li.
Wood, Thomas. S Lent LC AA Co., Md., from *Thornton* May 1771. K.
Wood, Zachariah. SQS & T *Justitia* Sep 1767. Sy.
Woodason, Richard. S Summer 1738 LC Knt Co., Md., *from Hawk* Apr 1739. Ha.
Woodcock, Robert. S Dec 1750 T *Thames* Feb 1751. L.
Woodcock, Thomas. S Lent T from Bristol May 1755. St.
Woodcock, William (1753) - *See* Terry. Li.
Woodfield, Jane. S 14 yrs Lent LC AA Co., Md., from *Thornton* May 1771. Sy.
Woodfield, Maria. S Lent LC AA Co., Md., from *Thornton* May 1771. Sy.
Woodhall, Edward. S Lent LC Bal Co., Md., Jun 1773. St.
Woodham, Richard. S Apr T May 1718 Tryal LC Charles Town Aug 1718. M.
Woodhead, Charles. T *Justitia* Feb 1776. L.
Woodhouse, Christopher. S City 1760 (AHJ). Nl.
Woodhouse, James. S Lent T May 1756. Nt.
Wooding, John. S Lent R 14 yrs Summer T Aug 1749 *Thames*. Bu.
Woodland, Christopher. S Dec 1753-Jan 1754 T *Thames* Mar 1754. M.
Woods, Edward. S 14 yrs Feb T *Tryal* Mar 1757. M.

Woodward, Anthony. T Dec 1746. Li.

Woodward, Catherine. S Jul T Dec 1735 *John* LC Annapolis Sep 1736. M.

Woodward, Elizabeth. S Jul T *Maryland Packet* Oct 1761. L.

Woodward, Elizabeth. S for returning from T Apr 1742. St.

Woodward, Elizabeth. R Summer T *Barnard* Oct 1756. Ht.

Woodward, James. S Lent T *Thornton* May LC AA Co., Md., Jul 1774. M.

Woodward, John. S Summer 1738 LC QA Co., Md. Jun 1739. De.

Woodward, John. S Jan-Jun T Jul 1747 *Laura*. M.

Woodward, John. S Bristol Jan 1750 LC QA Co., Md., from *Catherine* Nov 1750. G.

Woodward, William. SQS Ipswich Jul 1724. Su.

Woodward, William of Loughton. SQS for leaving his parish of settlement Jul 1772. Bu.

Woolcott, George. S Aug T *Restoration* LC Bal Co., Md., Oct 1771. So.

Woollard, James. S Jan T *Plain Dealer* Jan 1746. L.

Woolley *als* Lawrence, Rebecca. S May-Jul T *Mary* Sep 1746. M.

Wooley, William. S Apr-May T *Saltspring* Jul 1775. M.

Woolner, William. S Oct-Dec 1754 T *Greyhound* Feb 1755. M.

Woolridge, Roger. S Apr T May 1752 *Lichfield*. L.

Woone, Grace. S Launceston Jan 1757 (AHJ). Co.

Woons, John. S 14 yrs Lent 1732 LC Knt Co., Md., from *Falcon* Mar 1733. De.

Woor, Thomas. S s grain on River Wye Lent 1757 (GJ). G.

Wootton *als* Hudson, Alice. S Sep-Oct 1775 T *Justitia* Feb 1776. M.

Wootton, Margaret. S Summer LC Bal Co., Md., Dec 1770. Wa.

Wootton, Mary. S & T 14 yrs Jan 1736 *Dorsetshire* LC Va Sep 1736. L.

Workman, Daniel. S Mar T May 1746. Wi.

Wornoll, John. T May 1751 *Tryal*. K.

Worrall, Simon. S Oct 1760. Li.

Worrell, Francis. S Feb T *Thames* Mar 1752. L.

Worrell, Francis. S 14 yrs Apr-May T *Tryal* Jul 1754. M.

Worsfold, Thomas. SQS Jan S Lent LC AA Co., Md., from *Thornton* Jul 1773. Sy.

Worth, Andrew. SQS Oct 1771 LC Bal Co., Md., Jul 1772. De.

Worth *als* Bibey, Mary. S Dec 1773 T *Justitia* Jan 1774. M.

Wotton, Michael. S Lent 1731 LC Knt Co., Md., from *Falcon* Apr 1732. De.

Wray/Wrey, Jacob. S s horse Lent R 14 yrs Summer 1757. O.

Wreathcocke, William. R & T May 1736 *Patapsco* R 14 yrs for returning Jan 1740. M.

Wright, Ann. S Dec 1747 LC Knt Co., Md., from *St. George* Mar 1748. L.

Wright, Benjamin. S & R 14 yrs Summer LC Md *William* Dec 1774 & sold to James
& Joshua Howard; runaway. St.

Wright, Charles. S Lent LC Bal Co., Md., Jul 1774. Wi.

Wright, Edward. S Oct T *Justitia* Dec 1774. L.

Wright, Elizabeth. S Aug T *Beverly* Aug 1763. L.

Wright, Frances (1676). *See* Russell. L.

Wright, George. S Apr T May 1751 *Tryal*. L.

Wright, George. S Summer T Oct 1755. Le.

Wright, George. S Sep T *Barnard* Oct 1756. M.

Wright, Henry. S Aug T *Beverly* Aug 1763. L.

Wright, James of St. Marylebone. S s silver spoons Feb LC from Patapsco Md Oct
1732. M.

Wright, James. S Oct T *Justitia* Dec 1774. L.

Wright, John. S Lent R 14 yrs Summer 1728. Nf.

Wright, John. S & T Jan 1736 *Dorsetshire* LC Va Sep 1736. L.

MORE EMIGRANTS IN BONDAGE

Wright, John. S Apr-Jun 1739 T *Sea Nymph* to Md. M.
Wright, John. S Jul-Dec 1747 LC Knt Co., Md., from *St. George* Mar 1748. M.
Wright, John. S Summer 1750 T May 1751 *Tryal*. K.
Wright, John. S Summer 1753 R 14 yrs Lent T *Tryal* Jul 1754. Sx.
Wright, John. S Summer T *Lux* Aug 1757. Db.
Wright, John. S & T Nov 1759 *Phoenix* . M.
Wright, John. S Jul T *Phoenix* Oct 1760. M.
Wright, John (1766). *See* Everett. M.
Wright, John. S & T Jan 1766 *Tryal*. M.
Wright, John. S Lent R 14 yrs Summer 1766. Wo.
Wright, John. S Oct 1766 T Jan 1767 *Tryal*. M.
Wright, John. SQS Jul T Aug 1769 *Douglas*. M.
Wright, John of St. Margaret, Westminster. SW Apr T *Thornton* May LC Md Jul 1774. M.
Wright, Jonas. R for Barbados Jul 1663. L.
Wright, Joseph, *als* Broadway, Robert. S for murder Lent 1724 R 14 yrs Lent 1725 LC from *Robert* Annapolis Jun 1725. Sh.
Wright, Joseph. S Feb T Mar 1730 *Patapsco* LC Annapolis Sep 1730. M.
Wright, Joseph. S Summer T from London Oct 1738. Wa.
Wright, Joseph. AT Summer 1755. Y.
Wright, Joseph. S s sheep Summer 1758 R 14 yrs Lent 1759 TB to Md. No.Wright,
Joseph. S Lent R 14 yrs Summer 1760 but pardoned for Army service Jul 1761. St.
Wright, Lucretia wife of John of Broxbourne. SQS Apr T Jun 1764 *Dolphin*. Ht.
Wright, Lydia. S & T Dec 1736 *Dorsetshire* . L.
Wright, Margaret of St. Olave, Southwark. R for Barbados Aug 1662. Sy.
Wright, Martha. S & T Oct 1732 *Caesar* . L.
Wright, Martha. S Summer T Lux Aug 1757. Db.
Wright, Mary. S Feb-Apr T *Laura* Apr 1746. M.
Wright, Peter. S Apr T May 1750 *Lichfield*. M.
Wright, Reuben. S Jul LC Bal Co., Md., Dec 1783 from *Swift*. M.
Wright, Richard. S s lead Lent T Jul 1745 *Italian Merchant*. Sy.
Wright, Richard of Fobbing, singleman. SQS Apr T May 1752 *Lichfield*. E.
Wright, Samuel. S Summer LC Bal Co., Md., Dec 1770 from *Trotman* & sold to Philip Chamberlain. X.
Wright, Samuel. S Lent T *Thornton* May LC AA Co., Md., Jul 1774; runaway. Sy.
Wright, Theodosia. S Summer T Oct 1758. Wa.
Wright, Thomas. S for housebreaking Sep 1750 (WJ). Wa.
Wright, Thomas. S & T Sep 1751 *Greyhound*. M.
Wright, Thomas. S & T Aug 1752 *Tryal*. L.
Wright, Thomas. S 1754 TB to Va. No.
Wright, Thomas. S May 1770. Li.
Wright, William. S Summer T Oct 1756. Wa.
Wright, William. S 14 yrs LC Bal Co., Md., Jul 1772. St.
Wright, William. SQS Jan LC AA Co., Md., from *Thornton* Jul 1775. M.
Wyatt, John. S Lent 1731 TB Aug 1733. Db.
Wyatt, John. S Lent LC AA Co., Md., from *Hanover Planter* Jul 1773. L.
Wyatt, Martha. S Summer LC Md. from *Reformation* Aug 1722. De.
Wyatt, Richard. S 14 yrs Lent 1750 LC QA Co., Md., from *Catherine* Nov 1750. Wo.
Wyatt, Thomas. S Feb T *Thames* Mar 1752. L.

Wyatt, William. S Jan T *Thames* Feb 1751. L.
Wynde, Sarah. S s at Ludlow Lent 1764. Sh.
Wynn, Benjamin. S for murder Summer 1752 R 14 yrs Mar 1753. Co.
Wynn, John. S Sep-Oct 1775 T *Justitia* Feb 1776. M.

Yardley, Edmund. S s iron Sep 1750 (WJ). Wa.
Yardley, Elizabeth. S Sep T Oct 1750 *Rachael*. M.
Yardley, Mary. S s butter Sep T Oct 1750 *Rachael*. M.
Yarmouth, Edward of Rotherhithe. SQS Apr T Sep 1751 *Greyhound*. Sy.
Yate, Margaret. SQS Apr 1728. La.
Yates, Thomas. S Summer 1732 AT Lent 1733. Wa.
Yeates, Mary. S Sep 1740 T *Harpooner* Jan 1741. L.
Yeates, William. S Dec 1754 T *Greyhound* Feb 1755. L.
Yellow Jack (1773). *See* Hawkins, John. Wa.
Yeoman *als* Newman, Richard. S Jan 1717 T 14 yrs May 1718 *Tryal* LC Charles
    Town Aug 1718. L.
Yeoman, John. T Aug 1752 *Tryal*. Ht.
York, William. SQS Exeter Oct 1733 LC Knt Co., Md., from *Falcon* Apr 1734. De.
Youman, Susanna. S Feb T *Neptune* Mar 1761. L.
Young, Edward. S Jan T *Justitia* May 1745. L.
Young, Elizabeth. S for perjury Dec 1773 T *Justitia* Jan 1774. L.
Young, Frances. S 1757 TB to Va. No.
Young, James. S Summer T Aug 1749 *Thames*. Sy.
Young, Jane. S Lent R 14 yrs Summer 1761; held back because of her young
    suckling child. Sh.
Young, John Eldridge. S Lent T *Thornton* May LC AA Co., Md., Jul 1774. Sx.
Young, John. SQS Jul 1772 LC Bal Co., Md., from *Adventure* Mar 1773. Nl.
Young, John. S & T for life Sep 1751 *Greyhound*. M.
Young, Mary. S Oct T *Barnard* Oct 1756. M.
Young, Richard. T 1751. Nf.
Young, Staines. S Lent R Summer 1761. Le.
Young, William. S s gelding Summer 1726 R 14 yrs Dec 1726. Ca.
Younger, James. R 14 yrs Dec 1773 T *Justitia* Jan 1774. M.
Younger, Sarah. SQS May T Jul 1773 *Tayloe* to Va. M.
Yowell, John. S Jan T *Plain Dealer* Jan 1746. M.

Zell, Thomas. S Jan T *Plain Dealer* Jan 1746. M.

Biographical Notes on Some Transportees to Maryland by Robert Barnes with Some Additions by the Compiler

The following brief notes have been culled from a variety of sources for which the abbreviations adopted are:

AMG: The Annapolis *Maryland Gazette.*

BA Co: Baltimore Co., Maryland.

CELR: Cecil County Land Records.

CMSP: Calendar of Maryland State Papers.

ESVR: F. Edward Wright, *Maryland Eastern Shore Vital Records.*

KE Co: Kent Co., Maryland.

KECR: Kent County Court Records.

MDAD: Maryland Administration Accounts.

MINV: Maryland Inventories Liber.

MWB: Maryland Will Book.

QALR: Queen Anne's County Land Records.

Abbott, John from Somerset, arr. 1718.

A John Abbott witnessed the will of Sarah Robinson of Dorchester Co. on 11 Feb 1728/9 (MWB 19:700). He or another John Abbott died in Talbot Co., leaving a will dated 18 Aug 1729 and proved 23 Nov 1729, naming a wife Elizabeth (MWB 19:916).

Arney, John from Somerset, arr. 1718.

John Arney, surety to [Samuel Wickes of KE Co.?] died by 15 June 1733 when his administrator John Gresham was paid from the estate of Samuel Wickes (MDAD 12:75).

Arthur, John, Mar 1734-7; Cornwall QS, 157

On 23 Dec 1748 John Arthur was a creditor of the estate of Richard Walters of KE Co. (MDAD 25:238).

Batt, George from Dorset, arr. 1731.

George Batt married Mary Courtney on 3 Jan ----- in St. Luke's Parish, Queen Anne's Co. (ESVR 2:53).

Bennett, George from Devon, arr. 1718.

George Bennett, servant man of Thomas Mountseer of Queen Anne's Co. was mentioned in the latter's will made on 1 April 1723 (MWB 18:181). On 18 Dec 1735 George Bennett witnessed a deed (QALR RTA:446). He witnessed various wills on 23 April 1739, 15 Dec 1740, and 18 July 1749 (MWB 22:110, 321, 23:455).

George Bennett (or Burnett) married Elizabeth Briley on 1 Dec 1735 (St. Luke's Parish Register: 41; *ESVR* 2:50).

Bennett, Samuel from Cornwall, arr. 1718.

On 16 Aug 1735 Samuel Bennett was listed as having been paid from the estate of James Thomas of Kent Co. (MDAD 13:249). Samuel Bennett of Kent Co. died by 25 Jul 1749, when his estate was appraised by John Gleaves and George Medford and valued at £318.12.5. No creditors or next of kin were listed. Margaret Bennett, administratrix, filed the inventory on 12 Aug 1749 (MINV 41:81). Samuel and Margaret Bennett had the following children b. in St. Paul's Parish, Kent Co (*ESVR* 2:18): William, b. Feb ---; Samuel, b. 19 Dec ---; Temperance, b. ---; and [-?-], dau., b. ----.

Another Samuel Bennett of Kent Co. died by 29 April 1751 when his estate was appraised by Pa. Whichcote and George Griffith, and valued at £296.10.7. No creditors listed. Sarah Chapman signed as next-of-kin. William Absley (surviving) Administrator, filed the inventory on 2 May 1751 (MINV 60:483).

Samuel Bennett, an Englishman who once taught school in the Province, should apply to the printer (*AMG* 15 Aug 1750).

Brewer, Edward from Somerset, arr. 1733.

On 25 June 1741 Edward Brewer was left personalty in the will of Finley Cameron, planter, of Queen Anne's Co. (MWB 22:367).

Case, James from Dorset, arr. 1732.

On 12 Oct 1743 John Davis and Arthur Emory Jr., appraised the personal estate of James Case at £7.12.10. No kin signed. William Greenwood, administrator, filed the inventory on 20 Oct 1743 (MINV 28:184) and filed an account showing an inventory of £7.12.10 (MDAD 20:294).

Chaplin, Samuel from Somerset, arr. 1731.

On 28 April 1753 Samuel Chaplin as executor filed the inventory of Barnett Holland of Kent Co. (MINV 56:99). On 14 Aug 1776 he and James Claypoole appraised the estate of James Barrow of Kent Co. (MINV 124:392).

Collins, John from Devon, arr. 1734.

John Collins married Margaret McDaniel on 12 Dec 1745 in Shrewsbury Parish, Kent Co. (Barnes, *Md. Marr. 1634-1777*).

Collins, Walter from Devon, arr. 1718.

On 6 Jan 1735 Walter Collins signed the inventory of William Owens as one of the next-of-kin (MINV 21:467). He was living on 18 May 1752 when, as Walter Collins of Queen Anne's Co., planter, aged 53, he deposed as to the nuncupative will of John Brand of the same Co. (MWB 28:341). He had married. Rebecca [-?-] by 1728, when he appeared as a surety for her in Kent Court. (KECR? N:417).

Crapp, Mary from Cornwall, arr. 1718.

On 2 April 1720 Mary Crap [*sic*] was a witness to the will of Thomas Emerson of Talbot Co. (MWB 16:24).

Cutler [not Butler], Francis; Jan 1734-7; Somerset QA, 23.

Francis Cutler married Eleanor Wooden on 30 Jan 1745 in St. Paul's Parish, BA Co. (Barnes, *Md. Marr. 1634-1777*:45).

Dingle, William from Devon, arr. 1731.

William Dingle and Ann Cook were married by one of Leeds' Marriage Licenses on 12 April 1739 in Talbot Co. On 7 Jan 1761 William Dingle, administrator, distributed the estate of William Sewell of Dorset Co. (BFD 3:68). On 27 April 1762 William Dingle and John Dingle signed the inventory of George West of Dorset Co. as next-of-kin (MINV 81:300) On 2 Dec 1768 he witnessed the will of William Bunt of Dorset Co. (MWB 36:599).

Ellis, Joseph from Devon, arr. 1731.

There were men named Joseph Ellis who died in St. Mary's and Somerset Co. On 20 June 1743 Joseph Ellis was a creditor of John Tillotson of QA Co. (MINV 19:451); Joseph Ellis married Rachel [-?-] who had (*ESVR* 2:33): Mary, b. 24 Dec 1738, baptised April 1739 in St. Luke's Parish, Queen Anne's Co.

Freestone, Walter from Somerset, arr. 1718.

On 20 March 1725 Walter Freestone of St. Paul's Parish, planter, having been duly admonished by the Vestry of the said parish, did at various times including 21 April 1726, adulterously frequent the company of Katherine Hopkins, spinster. He was ordered to receive 21 lashes (KECR JS#22:192). At August Court 1728, Freestone was charged with intended murder against Patrick Clark (KECR JS#22:260; see also JS#WK:23, 26). Freestone received a payment from the estate of John Walltham of Kent Co. on 27 June 1724 (MDAD 6:76). On 16 March 1731 he was listed as having been paid from the estate of Samuel Thomas of Queen Anne's (MDAD 11:595). He died leaving a will dated 3 Dec 1742 and proved 30 Jan 1741 leaving his entire estate, real and personal, to his wife Mary. Jackson Griffiths and Christopher Knight witnessed the will (MWB 22:460). No inventory or administration account seem to have been filed in the Prerogative Court.

Frost, William from Devon, weaver, arr. 1730.

Query if either of these William Frosts could be the William Frost who appeared in Baltimore Co. by 1749 and was dead by 1753.

Gayer, Andrew from Devon, arr. 1718.

By 1724 he was in Kent Co. Court complaining that he and his wife had been assaulted by Johnna and Mary Wilson (KECR JS#22:264). In Nov 1725 Andrew "Guyer" was indicted by that Court for felony (KECR JS#22:112).

Grantlett, John from Cornwall, arr. 1718.

On 11 Nov 1730 John Grantlett was paid from the estate of William Mackey of Kent Co. (MDAD 11:170). On 24 March 1734 he witnessed the will of Henry Monk, Sr. of Kent Co. (MWB 21:417). John Grantlett, of Kent Co., died (date unknown), when his estate was appraised by Michael Blackiston and John Ambrose, and valued at £21.6.9. Charles Smith and Charles Hynson signed as creditors. No next-of-kin shown. Administratrix (name not given) filed the inventory on 16 Feb 1742 (MINV 27:307). John Grantlett married Elizabeth [-?-] and were the parents of the following children, whose births were recorded in St. Paul's Parish, Kent Co. (*ESVR* 2:22, 23): William b. 15 Oct 1726; Mary, b. 10 March 1728; Joseph, b. —, buried 19 Nov 1734; and Joseph, b. 9 Oct 1737.

Gregory, Anthony from Devon, arr. 1718.

Anthony Gregory married Lydia Grace on 5 June 1734 in St. Peter's Parish, Talbot Co. (*ESVR* 2:73). They were the parents of (*ESVR* 2:71): Sarah, b. 22 March 1736.

In 1738 he made his mark on a petition from Talbot Co. to create a new parish (*CMSP: Black Books*, Item 374). In 1748 he served in the Talbot Militia (??P:81). Anthony Gregory of Talbot Co., planter, died leaving a will dated 28 July 1762 and proved 7 Sep 1762. His wife was to have the tract and plantation called Newbegin and Turner's Chance. He named his children John, William, dau. (unnamed), the wife of John Beung or Benny, dau. Rebecca wife of Thomas Studham, and daus. Mary, Elizabeth, Lydia, Ann, Grace, and Esther. His wife and son John were named executors. Ambrose Kinniment, Hugh Wilson, and Mabel Benny witnessed the will (MWB 31:735). Samuel Cockayne and Edmund Farrell appraised Gregory's personal estate on 24 Oct 1762 at £168.9.1. Mabel and Sarah Benny Signed as next-of-kin.

Lydia Gregory, executrix, filed the inventory on 18 Feb 1763 (MINV 79:455). Cockayne and Farrell appraised a second inventory on 13 Aug 1763, setting a value of £144.16.8 on the personal goods. James and Sarah Benny signed as next-of-kin. Ambrose and Lydia Kinnimont, or Kiddiment, the executors, and John Gregory filed the inventory on 4 Oct 1763 (MINV 82:35).

Grierson, John was for many years a minister of the non-parochial Chapel of the Savoy and was arraigned in December 1755 for officiating at the marriage on 27 June of the same year of Joseph Vernham, aged 25, bachelor, and Jane Henrietta Poitier, spinster, without licence or banns. Jane had been born on 8 June 1736, and was therefore a minor, and intended to marry against the wishes of her father. Grierson was found guilty and ordered to be transported for 14 years: he died shortly after his arrival in Maryland, "his constitution broke by the persecutions of his enemies."

Letters from his daughter Clementina Vane Grierson to friends in London survive in the records of the High Court of Admiralty. (*See* PRO: HCA 32/231/268.)

Jacob, Thomas from Cornwall, arr. 1718.

A Thomas Jacob witnessed the will of Henry Hollingsworth of Cecil Co. on 23 Feb 1721 (MWB 17:100). Thomas Jacobs [sic] was named as overseer in the will made 18 March 1728/9 of Isaac James of Cecil Co. (MWB 19:733). However, there was a Thomas Jacob in Cecil Co. before 1718 (CELR).

Lane, Robert from Dorset, arr. 1734.

On 14 Oct 1751 Robert Lane filed the inventory of Daniel Lambden of Talbot Co. (MINV 48:10). He may be the Robert Lane of Kent Co. who died by 8 Aug 1770 when Nathan Hatchison and Benjamin Recard appraised his personal property at £53.16.0. Sarah and Richard Lane signed as next-of-kin. John Page administrator, filed the inventory on 24 Aug 1770 (MINV 106:16). A second inventory was taken on 26 April 1771 and amounted to £4.19.0 Ancy Lane and Sary Lane signed as next-of-kin. John Page filed the inventory on 18 Oct 1771 (MINV 107:392). Page filed an account of the estate on 18 Oct 1771 and listed payments of £39.1.1 (MDAD 67:11). A second account, for Robert Page Lane [sic] was filed by John Page on 24 Feb 1773 (MDAD 67:453).

Lang, James from Devon, arr. 1734.

The plantation "where James Long or Lang now lives" was mentioned in the will of John Hawkins of Queen Anne's Co. on 12 Sep 1744 (MWB 24:263). On 1 April 1745 Simon Knox made his will and left the wearing apparel of his deceased wife to Margaret Lang, not yet of age, dau. of James Lang. James Lang witnessed the will (MWB 28:464).

Lean, Richard from Devon, arr. 1730.

Some time before 24 June 1754 Richard Lean made his mark on a petition signed by several debtors in Queen Anne's Co. gaol asking for better food during their confinement (*CMSP: Black Books*, item 796).

Legg, William from Dorset, arr. 1718.

There was another William Legg in Queen Anne's Co. prior to the arrival of William Legg, the convict.

Linguard, Isaac, a coachman, gave evidence to a Surrey court in 1741 which led to the conviction of Richard Coleman for the murder of a young girl named Sarah Green in Newington churchyard. Linguard drove Coleman to his place of execution but was later discovered to have perjured himself and was ordered to be transported. In attempting to board a ship to return to England he was drowned. In August 1751 two men named Welch and Jones were tried and convicted of the murder.

Mead, Methuselah from Somerset, arr. 1732.

On 16 June 1748 Methusalah Mead was a creditor of Andrew Price of Queen Anne's Co. (MDAD 25:18); see also MDAD 31:242); and on 12 Feb 1749 was a creditor of the estate of William Vickers of Talbot Co. (MDAD 27:284). On 11 April 1764 Methusalah Mead witnessed the will of Thomas Crane of Queen Anne's Co. (MWB 32:111).

O'Bryan, William from Cornwall, arr. 1718.

In 1754 a William O'Bryan appeared in a list of schoolmasters in Queen Anne's Co. He was the only one who took the necessary oath (*CMSP: Black Books*, items 807, 808).

Osgood (Hosegood), George from Somerset, arr. 1732.

As George Osgood he died in Queen Anne's Co. by 31 Oct 1757 when John Davis and Arthur Emory appraised his personal estate at £31.10.10. No kin signed. Elizabeth Osgood, administratrix, filed the inventory on 14 Feb 1758 (MINV 65:18).

Patty, Charles from Cornwall, arr. 1718.

On 12 May 1735 Charles Pattey, or Patty, was listed as a debtor in the account of John Ward of Cecil Co. (MDAD 13:186). On 25 Jan 1736 he was paid from the estate of Henry Ward, gent., of Cecil Co. (MDAD 15:321).

Pippen, John from Somerset, arr. 1718.

On 10 July 1725 he witnessed a deed in Queen Anne's Co. (QALR

IKC:29). NB: Other Pippens and Pippins appear in the Co. later on.

Sellwood, Sarah from Somerset, arr. 1718.

In Nov 1725 she was indicted by the Kent Co. Grand Jury for fornication. Later in that session she was accused of having borne a bastard child and ordered to receive 15 lashes and to pay 283 lbs. tobacco for court costs (KESR JS#22:111, 114).

Sparkes, Mary from Devon, arr. 1734.

A Mary Sparks married William Wilkinson on 6 April 1758 in St. Luke's Parish, Queen Anne's Co. (Barnes, *Md. Marr. 1634-1777*).

Stacy, Thomas from Dorset, arr. 1718.

Thomas Stacy, of St. Paul's Parish, labourer, was indicted by Kent Co. Grand Jury for stealing a side of tanned leather in Nov 1727. He was sentenced to stand in the pillory for half an hour and to receive 21 lashes (KECR JS#22:338).

Swift *alias* **Smith, Richard**, convicted in 1764 for receiving stolen candles was transported to Maryland from where he immediately embarked for Halifax, Nova Scotia and from there to Liverpool. When he re-appeared in England he was tried at the Warwickshire Assizes for having returned before the expiry of his term and his mistress took money to Coventry expecting to have to bury him. But, to the amazement of all, and because of a minor discrepancy in the account given of goods he was alleged to have stolen, he was acquitted. He kept a journal of his travels and with it a letter from his favourite mistress Eliza Olives dated Mile End, 16 February 1765: *Sorry to hear of your misfortune. Excuse me for not writing sooner but I could get no body to write for me that I could trust.* Swift had amongst his papers a Pass issued in Baltimore Co. on 25 August 1764 issued by Nuxton Gay describing him as aged about 50 and 5'6" tall, of fresh complexion but pitted with smallpox with two scars on the left side of his face, and allowing him to travel about his lawful business; and another Pass issued in Philadelphia on 29 September 1764 detailing where he was to stop on his way to New York.

Taylor, William from Devon, arr. 1718.

He might be the William Taylor who witnessed the will of Edward Scott of Kent Co. on 28 Oct 1725 (MWB 18:420).

Tippett, Thomas from Somerset, arr. 1718.

Christian Tippett, wife of Thomas Tippett, of St. Paul's Parish, labourer, was presented to the Grand Jury that on 10 Sep 1728 she stole certain goods and chattels of Richard Foulstone. (KECR JS#WK:46).

Underhill, Robert, Jr. from Devon, arr. 1718.

On 27 May 1727 Robert Underhill made a payment to the estate of Richard Bell of Cecil Co. (MDAD 8:383).

Vivian, William from Cornwall, arr. 1718.

He was delivered to the Kent Co. Court in March 1725 for fathering a bastard (KECR JS#22:144). A William Vivian witnessed the will of William Elmes of Kent Co. on 31 Jan 1731/2 (MWB 20:430).

Webb, Richard from Somerset, arr. 1732.

Richard Webb married Susannah Williams on 1 March 1746 in St. Luke's Parish, Queen Anne's Co. (Barnes, *Md. Marr. 1634-1777*).

Wilkinson, John, another established minister at the Savoy Chapel, was prosecuted less than a year after John Grierson (*q.v.*) for the same offence of officiating at a marriage performed without licence or banns. In this case the couple were George Drawwater, bachelor aged 25, and Mary Johnston, spinster aged 19, who lived in the parish of Christ Church, Surrey. The Chapel was described by the accused during the trial as "scarce fit for a stable," and the prosecution as having been conducted with "the most unrelenting malice." Wilkinson, condemned to be transported for 14 years, sailed for Virginia on the *Barnard* in October 1756.

Wills, Hugh from Somerset, arr. 1734.

Hugh Wills married Mary Richards on 25 Oct 1737 in St. Luke's Parish, Queen Anne's Co. (Barnes, *Md. Marr. 1634-1777*). On 13 Sep 1749 he was listed as a creditor of the estate of James Roberts of Queen Anne's Co. (MDAD 27:60). He may be the Hugh Willis [*sic*] who signed the inventory of William Becks of Kent Co. as a creditor on 17 Aug 1766 (MINV 90:344).

CONVICT SHIPS TO THE AMERICAN COLONIES 1671-1783

This list comprises all the ships known to have been contracted to the justices of London, Middlesex and the Home Counties to carry convicts to America. Ships contracted by the justices of other counties have been included where references to them have been discovered in county records and journals but the latter listings are incomplete. All the convict ships noted in the two previous volumes in this series have been included as well as a further number identified through additional research. The figures quoted for numbers transported, though based on official documents, are likely to be short of the true number because some returns failed to include felons from the regions.

Sailing	Name of Ship	Master	From	Destination	No. of Felons	Reference(s)
Sep 1671	Baltimore	John Dunch	London	LC Md. Feb 1672	9+	MSA records
Sep 1671	William & Mary	?	London	LC Md. Mar 1672	15+	MSA records
Nov 1671	Elizabeth?	?	London	arr. Md. Feb 1672	11+	MSA records
Dec 1673	Charles	Benoni Eaton	London	LC Md. May 1674	49	MSA records
Dec 1674	?	Benjamin Cooper	London	LC Md. Feb 1675	41+	MSA records
Dec 1716	Lewis	Roger Laming	London	Jamaica	30	T53/25/224
Jan 1717	Queen Elizabeth	?	London	Jamaica	23	T53/25/225
May 1718	Tryal	?	London	S. Carolina		Bond
May 1718	Unknown	?	London	Barbados & Antigua		Bond
Aug 1718	Eagle[1]	Robert Staples	London	S. Carolina	107	T53/27/36
Aug 1718	Sophia	John Law	Bideford	LC Md. Mar 1719		MSA CR49,080-IK A
Feb 1719	Worcester	Edwin Tomkins	London	Maryland	97	T53/27/220
May 1719	Margaret	Wm. Greenwood	London	Maryland	113	T53/27/266
Oct 1719	Susannah & Sarah	Peter Wills	London	Maryland	91	T53/27/415
May 1720	Honour[2]	Robert Russell	London	Virginia	60	T53/28/157
Aug 1720	Owners Goodwill	Thomas Apps	London	Maryland	16	T53/28/332
Oct 1720	Gilbert	Darby Lux	London	Maryland	131	T53/28/331
Apr 1721	Mary	John Friend	?	arr. Va. Jun 1721		Bond

Sailing	Name of Ship	Master	From	Destination	No. of Felons	Reference(s)
Aug 1721	Owners Goodwill	John Lux	London	Maryland	34	T53/29/147
Aug 1721	Prince Royal	Thos. Boyd	London	Virginia	117	T53/29/146
Sep 1721	Reformation	Philip Weare	Exeter	Maryland		Md. Records
Oct 1721	William & John	John Thompson	London	Maryland	29	T53/29/453
Jan 1722	Gilbert	Darby Lux	London	Maryland	143	T53/29/451
Feb 1722	Christabella	Ambrose Griffin	London	Jamaica		Bond
Jul 1722	Alexander	John Grayham	London	Nevis	109	T53/29/531
Oct 1722	Forward	Daniel Russell	London	Maryland	106	T53/30/118
Feb 1723	Jonathan³	Darby Lux	London	Maryland	36	T53/30/341
May 1723	Victory	William Wharton	London	West Indies	8	T53/30/339
Jul 1723	Alexander	John King	London	Maryland	70	T53/30/340
Oct 1723	Forward	Daniel Russell	London	Virginia	167	T53/30/453
Feb 1724	Anne⁴	Thos. Wrangham	London	Carolina	74	T53/31/77
Jul 1724	Robert	John Vickers	London	Maryland	44	T53/31/255
Oct 1724	Martha	William Read	Lyme Regis arr. Md. Dec 1724			Dorset Records
Oct 1724	Forward⁵	Daniel Russell	London	Virginia	109	T53/31/376
Dec 1724	Rappahannock Mcht.⁶	John Jones	London	Maryland	84	T53/31/376
Apr 1725	Sukey	John Ellis	London	Maryland	112	T53/32/93
Sep 1725	Forward	Daniel Russell	London	Maryland	120	T53/32/219
Nov 1725	Rappahannock Mcht.	Charles Whale	London	Virginia	79	T53/32/220
Feb 1726	Supply	John Rendell	London	Maryland	77	T53/32/385
Jun 1726	Loyal Margaret	John Wheaton	London	Maryland	75	T53/32/386
Oct 1726	Forward	Daniel Russell	London	Virginia	130	T53/33/292
Mar 1727	Rappahannock Mcht.	Charles Whale	London	Maryland	80	T53/33/296
Jun 1727	Susanna	John Vickers	London	Virginia	107	T53/33/364
Sep 1727	Forward	William Loney	London	Virginia		Bond
Dec 1727	?Oak	William Williams	London	America		Bond
May 1728	Unknown	Samuel Waller	London	New York		Bond
Jun 1728	Elizabeth	William Whithorne	London	Virginia	141	T53/34/154
Nov 1728	Forward	William Loney	London	Virginia	100	T53/34/303
Mar 1729	Patapsco Merchant	Darby Lux	London	Maryland	96	T53/34/418

Sailing	Name of Ship	Master	From	Destination	No. of Felons	Reference(s)
Nov 1729	Forward	William Loney	London	Virginia	154	T53/35/43
Mar 1730	Patapsco Merchant	Darby Lux	London	Maryland	106	T53/35/174
Sep 1730	Smith	William Loney	London	Virginia	232	T53/35/379
Nov 1730	Forward	George Buckeridge	London	Virginia		T53/35/380
Mar 1731	Patapsco Merchant	Darby Lux	London	Maryland		T53/35/496
Apr 1731	Bennett	James Reed	London	Virginia	118	T53/35/498
Sep 1731	Falcon	Matthias Marsh	Bideford	LC Md. Apr 1732		MSA CR20,516-8535
Oct 1731	Smith	William Loney	London	Virginia	109	T53/36/138
Dec 1731	Forward	George Buckeridge	London	Virginia	92	T53/36/212
May 1732	Patapsco Merchant	Darby Lux	London	Maryland	79	T53/36/306
Oct 1732	Falcon	Matthias Marsh	Bideford	LC Md. Mar 1733		MSA CR40,516-8535
Oct 1732	Caesar	William Loney	London	Virginia	141	T53/36/424
Feb 1733	Smith	George Buckeridge	London	Md. or Va.	162	T53/37/10
Apr 1733	Patapsco Merchant	Darby Lux	London	Maryland		T53/37/11
Apr 1733	Unity	Thomas Rowe	Bideford	LC Md. Nov 1733		MSA CR40,516-8535
Dec 1733	Falcon	Matthias Marsh	Bideford	LC Md. Apr 1734		MSA CR40,516-8535
Jan 1734	Caesar	William Loney	London	Virginia	139	T53/37/212
Apr 1734	Patapsco Merchant	Darby Lux	London	Maryland	64	T53/37/304
Sep 1734	Falcon	Matthias Marsh	Bideford	LC Md. Mar 1735		MSA CR40,516-8535
Sep 1734	Hawk	William Hopkins	Bideford	LC Md. Apr 1735		MSA CR40,516-8535
Dec 1734	Caesar	William Loney	London	Virginia	125	T53/37/446
Apr 1735	Patapsco Merchant	Darby Lux	London	Maryland	99	T53/38/80
Apr 1735	Squire	?	Liverpool	arr. Md. Aug 1735		Derbys. records
Dec 1735	John	John Griffin	London	Maryland	50	T53/38/255
Jan 1736	Squire	?	Liverpool	arr. Md. Apr 1736		Derbys. records
Feb 1736	Dorsetshire	William Loney	London	Virginia	170	T53/38/256
May 1736	Patapsco Merchant	Francis Lux	London	Maryland	124	T53/38/337
Sep 1736	Amity	Robert Maine	Bideford	LC Md. May 1737		MSA CR49,082-RTB
Dec 1736	Dorsetshire	William Loney	London	Virginia		T53/38/456
Apr 1737	Hawk	William Hopkins	Bideford	LC Md. Nov 1737		MSA CR42,840-8536
May 1737	Forward	John Magier	London	Virginia	67	T53/39/123

Sailing	Name of Ship	Master	From	Destination	No. of Felons	Reference(s)
Sep 1737	Pretty Patsy	Francis Lux	London	Maryland	135	T53/39/121
Sep 1737	Amity	Robert Maine	Bideford	LC Md. Apr 1738		MSA CR49,082-RTB
Oct 1737	Raven	Thomas Kenney	Bideford	LC Md. Nov 1737		MSA CR42,840-8536
Jan 1738	Leopard	Matthias Marsh	Bideford	LC Md. May 1738		MSA CR49,082-RTB
Jan 1738	Dorsetshire	John Whiting	London	Virginia		T53/39/182
Jun 1738	Forward	John Magier	London	Va. or Md.	152	T53/39/248
Sep 1738	Hawk	William Hopkins	Bideford	LC Md. Apr 1739		MSA CR42,840-8536
Oct 1738	Amity	Robert Maine	Bideford	LC Md. Mar 1739		MSA CR49,082-RTB
Oct 1738	Genoa	Darby Lux	London	Maryland		T53/39/409
Jan 1739	Dorsetshire	John Whiting	London	Virginia		T53/39/408
Apr 1739	Forward	Benj. Richardson	London	Virginia		T53/39/448
Jul 1739	Sea Nymph	Adam Muir of Md.	London	Maryland		Bond
Oct 1739	Duke of Cumberland	William Harding	London	Virginia	76	T53/40/45
Feb 1740	York	Anthony Bacon	London	Maryland	115	T53/40/170
Jun 1740	Essex	Ambrose Cock	London	Md. or Va.	117	T53/40/204
Jan 1741	Vernon	Henry Lee	London	Maryland	58	T53/40/289
Jan 1741	Harpooner	John Wilson	London	Virginia	99	T53/40/290
Apr 1741	Mediterranean	George Harriot	London	Maryland}	160	T53/40/338
Apr 1741	Speedwell	William Camplin	London	Maryland}		T53/40/337
May 1741	Miller	John Dixon	London	Maryland	9	T53/40/339
May 1741	Catherine & Eliz.	William Chapman	London	Maryland	23	T53/40/339
Aug 1741	Sally	William Napier	London	Maryland	7	T53/40/415
Sep 1741	Philleroy	Peter Symons	?Exeter	LC Md. Apr 1742		MSA CR49,082-RTB
Oct 1741	Sea Horse	John Rendell	London	Virginia	144	T53/40/414
Oct 1741	Kitty	Robert Anderson	London	Maryland	2	T54/40/416
Feb 1742	Industry	Chas. Barnard	London	Maryland	83	T53/40/484
Apr 1742	Shaw	?	Liverpool	arr. Md. Jun 1742		Derbys. records
Apr 1742	Bond	John Gardiner	London	Maryland	84	T53/40/485
Apr 1742	Samuel[7]	John Everard	London	Maryland		E134/26 Geo 2/Trin 5
Jun 1742	Bladon	Samuel Laurence	London	Maryland	56	T53/41/129
Sep 1742	Forward[8]	John Sargent	London	Maryland	76	T53/41/130

Sailing	Name of Ship	Master	From	Destination	No. of Felons	Reference(s)
Dec 1742	Kent	John Bissick	Bideford	LC Md. Jun 1743		MSA CR49,082-RTB
Feb 1743	Shaw	?	Liverpool	arr. Md. May 1743		Derbys. records
Apr 1743	Bond	Matthew Johnson	London	Maryland	1	T53/41/326
Apr 1743	Justitia[9]	Barnet Bond	London	Virginia	132	T53/41/227
May 1743	Indian Queen	Edward Maxwell	London	Maryland	32	T53/41/326
Sep 1743	Raven	John Bissick	Bideford	LC Md. Feb 1744		MSA CR42,840-8537
Oct 1743	Globe	John Bissick (sic)	Bideford	LC Md. Mar 1744		MSA CR42,840-8537
Nov 1743	George William	Lachlin Campbell	London	Virginia		T53/41/327
Feb 1744	Neptune	James Knight	London	Maryland	99	T53/41/419
Apr 1744	Susannah	William Kenny	Bideford	LC Md. Aug 1744		MSA CR42,840-8537
May 1744	Justitia	John Johnstoun	London	Virginia	105	T53/41/462
Oct 1744	Susannah	James Dobbins	London	Maryland	61	T53/42/64
May 1745	Justitia	John Johnstoun	London	Virginia		T53/41/461
Jul 1745	Italian Merchant	Alexander Reid	London	Maryland	39	T53/42/220
Aug 1745	Virginia Merchant[10]	Richard Hutchinson	London	Virginia		HCA15/44
Jan 1746	Plain Dealer[21]	James Dobbins	London	Maryland	136	T53/42/220
Apr 1746	Laura	William Gracie	London	Maryland	84	T53/42/220
Sep 1746	Mary[12]	John Johnstoun	London	Virginia	52	T53/42/335
1746	William & Anne	?	London	arr. Md. Aug 1746		NGSQ
Jan 1747	George William	James Dobbins	London	Virginia	61	T53/42/335
Jul 1747	Laura	William Gracie	London	arr. Md. Oct 1747	88	T53/42/427
Jan 1748	St. George	James Dobbins	London	LC Md. Mar 1748	103	T53/42/519
Jun 1748	Lichfield	John Johnstoun	London	Virginia	124	T53/43/101
Jul 1748	Mary	John Ramsey	London	Virginia		T53/43/136
Jan 1749	Laura	William Gracie	London	Virginia	120	T53/43/190
May 1749	Lichfield	John Johnstoun	London	Maryland	150	T53/43/273
Aug 1749	Thames	James Dobbins	London	Maryland	112	T53/43/320
Nov 1749	Mary	Leonard Gerrard	London	Virginia	58	T53/43/320
Apr 1750	Tryal	John Johnstoun	London	Maryland	134	T1/340/20, T53/45/116
May 1750	Lichfield	William Gracie	London	Maryland	138	T1/340/33, T53/43/445
Jun 1750	Catherine	Peter Marshall	Bideford	LC Md. Nov 1750		MSA CR49,082

Sailing	Name of Ship	Master	From	Destination	No. of Felons	Reference(s)
Jul 1750	?Mary	Leonard Gerrard	London	Virginia		London bonds
Oct 1750	Rachael	John Armstrong	London	Maryland	95	T1/342/35, T53/43/491
Jan 1751	Thames	James Dobbins	London	Annapolis, Md.	131	T53/44/63
May 1751	Tryal	John Johnstoun	London	Maryland		T1/346/29
Aug 1751	Happy Jennett	?	Liverpool	arr. Md. Oct 1751		Derbys. records
Sep 1751	Greyhound	William Gracie	London	Virginia	153	T1/349/1, T53/44/243
Feb 1752	Thames	James Dobbins	London	Annapolis, Md	119.	T53/44/325
May 1752	Lichfield	Leonard Gerrard	London	Maryland	138	T1/348/8, T53/44/326
Jun 1752	Bideford	John Knill	Bristol	Md.		Md. Records
Jul 1752	Nightingale[13]	John Lancey	London	Md.		T53/44/379
Aug 1752	Tryal	John Johnstoun	London	Md.	107	Md. Records
Oct 1752	Chester	John Lorain	Bristol	Md.		T1/348/26, T53/44/395
Dec 1752	Greyhound	William Gracie	London	Md.	111	T1/351/17, T53/44/445
Apr 1753	Thames	James Dobbins	London	Md.	143	T1/353/29, T53/44/475
Jul 1753	Tryal	John Johnstoun	London	Va.	108	T1/358/1, T53/45/116
Dec 1753	Whiteing	Matthew Johnson	London	Va.	116	T53/45/116
Mar 1754	Greyhound	Alexander Stewart	London	Maryland	5	T53/45/116
Apr 1754	Thames	James Dobbins	London	Annapolis, Md.	150	T53/45/116, T53/45
Jun 1754	Tryal	Isaac Johns	London	arr. Md. Sep 1754	128	
Aug 1754	Unknown	Capt. Davis	Bristol	Annapolis, Md.	69	
Aug 1754	Bideford	John Cole	Bristol	arr. Md. Dec 1754		
Oct 1754	Ruby	Edward Ogle	London	Va.	133	CO5/750
Feb 1755	Greyhound	Alexander Stewart	Bristol	arr. Md. Apr 1755	78	T53/45/117
May 1755	Rose	Thomas Slade	Md.	arr. Md. Jun 1755		T53/45/117, CO5/750
Sep 1755	Tryal	William McGachin	Md.			T1/361/39
1756	Bella[14]	?	Bristol	Md. or Va.	65	T1/361/67, T53/45/117
Jan 1756	Greyhound	Alexander Stewart	Bristol	arr. Md. Apr 1756	51	T90/153
Apr 1756	Lux	?	London	arr. Md. Jun 1756	100	CO5/750, T53/45/117
Jun 1756	Lyon	James Dyer	London	Md.		CO5/750, T1/365/98

Sailing	Name of Ship	Master	From	Destination	No. of Felons	Reference(s)
Oct 1756	Barnard	Philip Weatherall	London	Va.	114	T53/45/575
Mar 1757	Tryal	Alexander Scott	London	Md.	99	T53/46/110
Apr 1757	Lux	?	London	?Md.		Sheriffs' Cravings
May 1757	Frisby	?	Bristol	Md.		*Bristol Intelligencer*
Jun 1757	Thomas & Sarah		London	arr. Md. Jul 1757		Md records
Sep 1757	Thetis	James Edmonds	London	arr. Md. Dec 1757	175	T1/378/64, T53/46/233
Oct 1757	Betsey	William Strachan	Bristol	arr. Md. Dec 1757		CO5/750
Mar 1758	Dragon	William McGachin	London	Md.	90	T1/387/17, T53/46/234
Apr 1758	Peace	Thomas Lovering	Bideford	arr. Md. Jun 1758		CO5/750
Apr 1758	Eugene	Jonathan Tallimay	Bristol	arr. Md. Jun 1758		CO5/750
Sep 1758	Tryal	George Freebairn	London	arr. Md. Jan 1759		T1/387/29, CO5/750
Sep 1758	Lux	----- Wilcocks	London	Baltimore, Md.		Sheriffs' Cravings
Sep 1758	Betsey	Allan Boyd	Bristol	arr. Md. Nov 1758		CO5/750
Dec 1758	The Brothers	William McGachin	London	Md.	104	T1/390/156, T53/46/234
Feb 1759	?Dragon	Matthew Craymer	London	America		Mddx Bond
Apr 1759	Thetis	Thomas Spencer	London	Md.		T1/391
Apr 1759	Maryland Merchant	Thomas Gray	Bideford	arr. Md. Jun 1759		CO5/750
Oct 1759	Mary	William McGachin	London	arr. Va. Jan 1760		CO5/1448
Dec 1759	Phoenix	Dougal McDougal	London	Md.	133	T1/397/15, T53/47/56
Mar 1760	Friendship	Matthew Craymer	London	Md.	49	T1/401, T53/47/56
Apr 1760	Thetis	William McGachin	London	Md.	88	T1/401, T53/47/56
Oct 1760	Phoenix	Benjamin Dawson	London	Md.	104	T53/48/56
Mar 1761	Neptune	?	London	Md.	80	T53/48/56
Apr 1761	Atlas	Dougal McDougal	Bristol	Md.		T90/153
Apr 1761	Dolphin	Alexander Ramsay	London	Md.	40	T53/48/56
Oct 1761	Maryland Packet	Thomas Gray	London	Md.	96	T53/48/57
Oct 1761	British King	Benjamin Dawson	London	arr. Va. Jan 1762		CO5/1448
Apr 1762	Neptune	Matthew Craymer	London	Va.	40	T1/418, T53/48/56
Apr 1762	Dolphin	?	London	arr. Md. Jun 1762	85	T1/418, T53/48/56
May 1762	Sally	Nicholas Andrew	London	Md.		*Sufferings of W.G.*
Sep 1762	Betsey		Bideford	arr. Md. Nov 1762		CO5/750

Sailing	Name of Ship	Master	From	Destination	No. of Felons	Reference(s)
Nov 1762	Prince William	Dougal McDougal	London	Va.	91	T1/418, T53/48/57
Mar 1763	Neptune	Colin Somervell	London	Md.	65	T1/423, T53/48/57
May 1763	Dolphin	Matthew Craymer	London	Md.	64	T53/48/57
May 1763	Albion	John Cole	Bristol	arr. Md. Aug 1763		NGSQ, Bristol Journal
Aug 1763	Beverly	Robert Allan	London	Va.	121	T53/49/136
Sep 1763	Betsey	Nicholas Andrew	?Bristol	arr. Md. Nov 1763		
Dec 1763	Neptune	Colin Somervell	London	Md.	114	T1/423, T53/49/137
Mar 1764	Tryal	William McGachin	London	Md.	166	T1/429, T53/49/137
Apr 1764	Little Nancy	W. Temple	Bristol	arr. Va. Jun 1764	18+	CO5/1450
Apr 1764	Albion[15]	Thomas Spencer	Bristol	Md.		Bristol Journal
Jun 1764	Dolphin	Dougal McDougal	London	Va.	141	T1/429, T53/49/137
Sep 1764	Justitia	Colin Somervell	London	Va.	206	T1/429, T53/49/137
Jan 1765	Ann	Richard Dowdall	Hull	arr. Va. Mar 1765	116	CO5/1450
Jan 1765	Tryal	John Errington	London	Va.	155	T1/437, T53/49/138
Apr 1765	Ann	Christopher Reed	London	Va.		T1/437, T53/49/138
Apr 1765	Young Samuel	Thomas Spencer	Liverpool	Md.	153	CO5/1449
Apr 1765	Justitia	Joseph Kendall	London	arr. Va. Jun 1765		T1/437, T53/50/92
Sep 1765	Lady Walpole	Colin Somervell	London	Va.	129	CO5/1449
Sep 1765	Tryal	Edward Davidson	Whitehaven	arr. Va. Nov 1765	168	T1/449, T53/50/92
Jan 1766	Ann	John Errington	London	Va.	183	T1/449, T53/50/92
Apr 1766	Justitia	Christopher Reed	London	Md.	147	T1/450, T53/550/93
Oct 1766	Tryal	Colin Somervell	London	arr. Va. Nov 1766	175	T53/50/93
Jan 1767	Randolph	John Price	Bristol	Va.	194	T90/156
Apr 1767	Thornton	Christopher Reed	London	Md.		T1/460/4, T53/50/93
May 1767	Justitia	Colin Somervell	London	Md.		T1/456, T53/50/93
Sep 1767	Unknown	John Gill	London	America		Bond
Dec 1767	Neptune	James Arbuckle	London	Va.	145	T1/465
Feb 1768	Thornton	Christopher Reed	London	Md.	179	T1/465, T53/51/132
May 1768	Tryal	Dougal McDougal	London	Va.	102	
Sep 1768	Randolph	John W. Price	Bristol	arr. Md. Nov 1768		Md. Gazette

Sailing	Name of Ship	Master	From	Destination	No. of Felons	Reference(s)
Oct 1768	Justitia	Colin Somervell	London	Va.	143	T1/465, T53/51/132
1768	Rodney[16]	?	Newcastle	America		*Gents' Mag.*
1769	?Bristol	Isabella	?	arr. Md. Jul 1769		NGSQ
Feb 1769	Thornton	Christopher Reed	London	Md.	153	T1/470, T53/51/132
Apr 1769	Friendship	?	London	America		SP 44/90/134
May 1769	Tryal	Dougal McDougal	London	Md.	113	T53/51/132
Sep 1769	Douglas	Wm. Breckenridge	London	?Md.	135	T1/470, T53/51/132
Oct 1769	Hawk	Bennet Mathews	Dublin	Md.		T64/312
Dec 1769	Justitia	Colin Somervell	London	Va.	120	T1/478, T53/51/133
Apr 1770	Thornton	Dougal McDougal	London	Md.	182	T1/478, T53/51/133
May 1770	Caesar	John Slingsby	Newcastle	America but wrecked		SP 44/90/241
Jul 1770	Scarsdale	Christopher Reed	London	Va.	167	T1/478, T53/51/133
Oct 1770	Trotman	Joseph Blickenden	Bristol	LC Md. Dec 1770		MSA CR40,516 f. 29
Dec 1770	Justitia	Colin Somervell	London	Va.	126	T1/483, T53/52/46
May 1771	Thornton	Dougal McDougal	London	LC Md. Jul 1771	150	T1/483
Jul 1771	Restoration	James Thomas	Bristol	arr. Md. Oct. 1771		*NGSQ*
Jul 1771	Scarsdale	Christopher Reed	London	Va.	169	T1/483, T53/52/46
Jan 1772	Justitia[17]	Neil Gillis	London	Va.	228	T1/483, T53/52/47
Apr 1772	Thornton	John Kidd	London	Va.	172	T1/490
Jul 1772	Tayloe	Dougal McDougal	London	Va.	167	T1/490
Jul 1772	Grange Bay	Neil Somerville	London	Va.	11	T1/490
Aug 1772	Trimly[18]	James Page	London	arr. Va. Dec 1772		HCA 16/61, 30/184
Jan 1773	Justitia	Finlay Gray	London	Va.	185	Bonds
Mar 1773	Adventure	Wharton Wilson	Newcastle	LC Md. Jun 1773		MSA CR 40,516
May 1773	Thornton	John Kidd	London	LC Md. Jul 1773	161	MSA CR 40,516
May 1773	Hanover Planter	William McCulloch	London	LC Md. Jul 1773	111	MSA CR 40,516
Jul 1773	Hercules	John Norwood	Dublin	LC Md. Aug 1773		MSA CR 40,516, f.368
Jul 1773	Betsey	R. Hunter	Waterford	LC Md. Aug 1773		MSA CR 40,516, f.369
Jul 1773	Tayloe	John Ogilvy	London	Va.	161	Bonds
Oct 1773	Swift[20]	George Straker	Newcastle	Baltimore, Md.		HCA 16/43
Jan 1774	Justitia	Finlay Gray	London	Va.	170	Bonds

Date	Ship	Captain	Port	Destination	Number	Source
May 1774	Thornton	John Kidd	London	LC Md. Jul 1774	237	MSA CR 40,516
Jul 1774	Tayloe	John Ogilvy	London	Va.	95	Bonds
Jul 1774	Aston Hall	John Parker	?London	arr. Md. Sep 1774		NGSQ
Oct 1774	William	James Thomas	Bristol	arr. Md. Dec 1774		Md. Records
Jan 1775	Justitia	John Kidd	London	arr. Va. Mar 1775	141	Bonds
Apr 1775	Elizabeth	Thomas Spencer	Bristol	arr. Md. Jun 1775		Md. Records
May 1775	Thornton	Finlay Gray	London	LC Md. Jul 1775	229	MSA CR 40,516
May 1775	Isabella	James Thomas	Bristol	arr. Md. Jul 1775		Md. Records
Jul 1775	Saltspring	John Ogilvy	London	arr. Md. Jul 1775		Mddx Bond
Sep 1775	Rebecca	Capt.. Brown	London	Baltimore, Md.		PRO: E389/245
Oct 1775	Justitia	John Kidd	London	Md.	65	Bonds
Jan 1776	Jenney	?	Newcastle	arr. Va Apr 1776		Va. Gazette
Oct 1783	Swift[20]	Thomas Pamp	London	LC Md. Dec 1783		MSA CR40,516, f.383-389

NOTES

1. The *Eagle* was formerly employed in the black slave trade (PRO: C11/1094/23).

2. Fifteen felons on board the *Honour* mutinied and forced her captain to put them ashore at Vigo.

3. The *Jonathan* was also a former black slaver which caught fire and sank in Maryland in June 1724 (PRO: C11/1400/2, 2581/8).

4. The *Anne* was a black slaver between 1717 and 1720.

5. A contingent of convicts from Lincolnshire who were designated to embark on this ship escaped (PRO: C11/260/69). Many were subsequently rounded up and loaded on to another ship where most perished.

6. Captain Jones died of smallpox when his ship reached Falmouth. The convicts aboard were heavily infected with "gaol fever" and thirty-eight of them died before journey's end (PRO: C11/1223/28).

7. The *Samuel* was captured by a Spanish privateer (PRO: E134/26 Geo.2/Trin.5).

8. When she arrived at Potomac fifty-eight of the seventy-four convicts embarked in London were found to have died. Captain Sargent was indicted in 1744 for offences committed against his passengers but was discharged (PRO: HCA 1/20/5). On her homeward voyage the *Forward* was taken prize by a Spanish privateer (PRO: C11/2499/9).

9. Captain Bond was also indicted in 1744 for murder and robbery on the high seas, and was also acquitted (PRO: HCA 1/20/5).

10. The *Virginia Merchant* carrying 109 convicts was captured by the French while on passage to Virginia (PRO: HCA 15/44).

11. The *Plain Dealer* was intercepted by the French *Zephyre* and in the subsequent engagement the convicts fought valiantly before their ship was wrecked on the French coast with the loss of most on board.

12. The *Mary* appears to have been lost at sea (Papers in Middlesex Records).

13. But the ship was destroyed by arson off Lundy Island (HCA1/58, *Tyburn Chronicle*).

14. The *Bella* with 51 felons from the Oxford Circuit on board was captured by the French shortly after leaving Bristol. The ship was carried to Spain from where the felons reached Lisbon to create many disturbances. Many were ferried back to England on HMS *Wager* and in April 1761 put on board the *Atlas* at Bristol bound for Maryland.

15. The *Albion* left Bristol on 12 May 1764 but had to put back because of contrary winds. The convicts hatched a scheme to carry the vessel to Spain and got their irons off with the help of a convicted blacksmith. In quelling the ensuing riot two of the felons were wounded. The ship set sail again on 2 June 1764.

16. Bound for Maryland with a cargo of convicts, the *Rodney* was driven to Antigua and wrecked. The survivors were reduced to eating their shoes to survive. (*Gentleman's Magazine* for May 1768).

17. The crew of the *Justitia* sued for their wages on their return to London; the ship's log book is on file (PRO: HCA 15/58).

18. The crew of the *Trimly* also sued for payment of their wages; this ship's log book is also on file (PRO: HCA 16/61/188, 30/184).

19. The log book of the *Swift* accompanies the crew's suit for payment of wages (PRO: HCA 16/63).

20. This ship sailed from London to Baltimore in August 1783 with 143 convicts but they rebelled and many escaped. The ship sailed again in October 1783 and, according to Maryland records, landed 87 convicts in Baltimore on Christmas Eve. (See *Emigrants in Chains*, pp. 153-154, Genealogical Publishing Co., Inc., Baltimore, 1992).

www.ingramcontent.com/pod-product-compliance
Lightning Source LLC
Chambersburg PA
CBHW061016280326
41935CB00009B/987